BOYD'S COMMENTARY for the Sunday School 2019–2020

VOLUME ONE HUNDRED FOURTEEN

These commentaries are based on the International Uniform Sunday School Lesson Outlines, copyrighted by the Division of Christian Education, the National Council of the Churches of Christ in the U.S.A., and used by permission.

R. H. Boyd, D.D., LL.D., Founder (1896–1922)

H. A. Boyd, D.D. (1922–1959)

T. B. Boyd, Jr., D.D. (1959–1979)

T. B. Boyd III, D.D. (1979–2017)

LaDonna Boyd, MBA
President/CEO (2017–Present)

www.rhboyd.com

David Groves, D.Min., Ph.D.
Director of Publications

EDITORIAL STAFF
Tia Ferrell, M.S.
(Coordinator)
Olivia M. Cloud, M.R.E.
Landon Dickerson, M.T.S.
Amy L. Lee, B.S.
Niger A. Woodruff, M.Div.
Brittany Batson, B.A.
Freida Crawley, B.S.
Carla Davis, B.A.

Dr. Ricky Woods
Dr. Frank Houston
Dr. Chandra Bennett
Writers

Jasmine Cole, M.F.A.
Cover Design

R.H. Boyd Publishing Corporation
6717 Centennial Blvd.
Nashville, Tennessee 37209-1017

For Customer Service and Toll-Free Ordering, Call
1-877-4RH-BOYD (474-2693)
Monday–Friday
8 a.m.–5 p.m. Central Time or
Fax Toll-Free (800) 615-1815

www.rhboyd.com

@ R.H. Boyd Publishing Corporation
@rhboydco
@rhboydco
#BoydsCommentary
#rhbpc

COMMENTARY 2019–2020

A Word from the Publisher

Welcome.

For well over a century, *Boyd's Commentary for the Sunday School* has been a staple in Christian education. This year's edition carries on that tradition. Our theologians and editorial staff have invested long hours of research and study of select Old and New Testament text to enrich your personal examination of God's Word. It is our prayer you will be inspired and uplifted as you use this resource to enhance your preparation of the Gospel message.

Onward,

LaDonna Boyd, *President/CEO*

A Word from the Director

The Word of God has to be understood in order for people to reconcile and apply it to their life situations. *Boyd's Commentary for the Sunday School* has been crafted precisely for that purpose. It is the one resource that carefully exegetes and interprets the Scripture passages selected for study for the entire year of lessons. Both teachers and preachers alike will find this an informative, inspirational, and exciting tool to help them prepare purposeful lessons and sermons. Please enjoy your study.

Rev. David Groves, D.Min., Ph.D.

NOTE FROM THE EDITOR

The layout of the *2019–2020 Commentary* has been formatted for easy use in the classroom. In keeping with our rich history of publishing quality Christian literature, we have added the Unifying Principle as a feature that will enhance our commentary. Listed below is an explanation of each feature and the intended use of each.

Lesson Setting: Gives the basic time line and place for the events in the lesson.

Lesson Outline: Provides the topics used in the exposition of the lesson.

Unifying Principle: States the main idea for the lesson across age groups. This feature allows the teacher to understand exactly what each lesson is about.

Introduction: Gives the thesis and any background information that will be useful in the study of the lesson.

Exposition: Provides the exegetical study done by the writer, breaking down the text for discussion.

The Lesson Applied: Provides possible life applications of the biblical text for today's learners.

Let's Talk About It: Highlights ideas from the text in a question-and-answer format.

Home Daily Devotional Readings: Located at the end of each lesson, the topics are designed to lead into the following lesson.

Know Your Writers

Dr. Ricky Woods

Dr. Ricky A. Woods was named senior minister of First Baptist Church-West in Charlotte, NC in 1995, and has worked tirelessly not only to serve as minister to the church's members, but also to help the church serve as a community beacon of social justice. He often is asked to speak throughout the city, state, and country. He formerly served as the Samuel DeWitt Proctor Senior Mentor at United Theological Seminary in Dayton, Ohio, helping scores of ministers throughout the nation receive doctoral degrees. A graduate of North Carolina A&T State University in Greensboro with a Bachelor of Science degree in economics, Dr. Woods graduated *cum laude* with a Master of Divinity degree from the Samuel DeWitt Proctor School of Theology of Virginia Union University in Richmond, Virginia, and then earned the Doctor of Ministry degree from United Theological Seminary in Dayton. Dr. Woods also is a member of the World Baptist Alliance, serving on the World Aid Committee. He is a member of the Academy of Homiletics, which is a professional organization made up of persons who teach preaching in North America. Dr. Woods is married to the former Laura Annette Hill, and they are the proud parents of one daughter, Lauren Adelle, a student at Hampton University.

Dr. Frank Houston

Dr. Frank Warren Houston is a native of Morristown, Tennessee. He earned a bachelor's degree in English from Carson Newman University and received his Master of Divinity and Ph.D. in New Testament studies from The Southern Baptist Theological Seminary in Louisville, Kentucky.

He currently serves as senior pastor-teacher of First Baptist Church of Georgetown, Kentucky. He is a member of Who's Who of America and the American Academy of Religion.

Dr. Chandra Bennett

Dr. Chandra Bennett is a native of Conway, Arkansas. After graduating from high school with highest honors, she earned her bachelor's degree from Fisk University in Nashville, Tennessee. Shortly thereafter, she moved to Michigan where she completed her master's degree at Moody Theological Seminary-Michigan. After relocating to Nashville, she received her doctorate in education from Tennessee State University.

Dr. Bennett learned the fundamentals of publishing by serving as an editor at R.H. Boyd Publishing Corporation for more than three years. She continued to grow at LifeWay Christian Resources, where she was hired to develop a Bible study curriculum for urban churches (YOU). She then was promoted to serve as publishing team leader, overseeing teams that produced four magazines and four daily devotionals. Recently, she responded obediently to the Lord's next assignment—teaching high school English at Cane Ridge High School in Antioch, Tennessee.

A published writer of numerous articles and lessons, Dr. Bennett has been preaching and training church leaders for more than 10 years. She is passionate about raising her daughter Brooklyn to love Jesus; teaching God's Word and seeing others mature in Christ; and training Christian educators, sharpening their ability to reach people in their ministry contexts.

2019–2020 LESSON OVERVIEW

The Fall Quarter (September–November 2019) traces the account of God's faithfulness to Israel beginning with the historical narratives of Genesis, Exodus, and Numbers. The teaching matrices of the first unit focus attention on God's providential care, while lessons in the second unit invite reflection on the faithful response people offer out of gratitude for God's provision. Biblical texts in Unit II include a study of the Ten Commandments as well as Gospel stories of grateful response (see Luke 7), from the centurion whose servant Jesus healed to the woman who anointed Jesus' feet. In Unit III, the lessons shift to the early church, and texts from selected New Testament letters explore what it means to live out our faith as members of Christ's body.

The Winter Quarter (December 2019–February 2020) studies the personal and corporate expressions of worship. The first three lessons of Unit I center on King David, known as "a man after God's own heart." David is a strong example of a spiritual leader who worships God in his own life and who also takes bold measures to ensure Israel's right worship as prescribed in God's holy covenant. The fourth lesson, December 22, departs from David's story to look at worship through the eyes of Mary's Song in Luke 1. Her worshipful song of thanksgiving and praise is reminiscent of many of the Hebrew psalms attributed to David. Unit II returns to the David narrative, this time to explore worship through the building of the temple in Jerusalem. While David put all the plans in place for constructing a house for God, it was his son Solomon whom God ordained to complete the work. The closing lessons of the Winter Quarter draw their lessons from the Gospels in order to sit at the feet of Jesus and learn from His teaching on honoring God through our worship.

The Spring Quarter (March–May 2020) picks up the biblical theme of God's justice as it is expressed through the prophetic words of Amos, Habakkuk, Micah, and Malachi. Each of the prophets, in his own way, conveys God's instruction for the right use of power and God's judgment when power is misused or abused. Lessons six and seven fall on Palm Sunday and Easter, moving to New Testament texts pointing to Christ as the defender of divine justice. The remaining lessons of the quarter return to the Old Testament prophets and challenge learners to make present-day applications. How is the church of the twenty-first century called to partner with God in shaping a just world?

The Summer Quarter (June–August 2020) picks up the cycle theme of God as sovereign, liberating, and all wise. In this particular quarter, the focus is the many facets of God's wisdom as recorded in the Book of Proverbs, in Jesus' teaching as presented in the Gospels, and in the New Testament letter attributed to James. The variety and diversity of biblical genres invites exploration of both practical wisdom and spiritual wisdom.

Boyd's Commentary for the Sunday School (2019–2020)

6717 Centennial Blvd.
Nashville, TN 37209–1017

Printed in the United States of America.

PREFACE

The *2019–2020 Boyd's Commentary* has been formatted and written with you in mind. This format is to help you further your preparation and study of the Sunday school lessons.

We have presented a parallel Scripture lesson passage with the *New Revised Standard Version* alongside the *King James Version*. This allows you to have a clearer and more contemporary approach to the Scripture passages each week. This version is reliable and reputable. It will bless you as you "rightly divide the word of truth" (2 Tim. 2:15, KJV).

These lessons have a new look, but they still have the same accurate interpretation, concise Christian doctrine, and competent, skilled scholarship.

The abbreviations used throughout the commentary are as follows:

KJV — *King James Version*
NIV — *New International Version*
NKJV — *New King James Version*
NLT — *New Living Translation*
NRSV — *New Revised Standard Version*
RSV — *Revised Standard Version*
TLB — *The Living Bible*
NEB — *New English Bible*
JB — *Jerusalem Bible*
ESV — *English Standard Version*

To the pastor: Our hope is that this commentary will provide context and insight for your sermons. Also, we hope this commentary will serve as a preparatory aid for the message of God.

To the Bible teacher: This commentary also has you in mind. You can use it as a ready reference to the background of the text and difficult terms that are used in the Bible. To be sure, this commentary will provide your lesson study with the historical context that will enable you to interpret the text for your students more effectively.

This text is for anyone who wants to get a glimpse at the glory of God. This commentary seeks to highlight and lift the workings of God with His people and to make God's history with humanity ever-present.

We hope and pray God will bless you and keep you as you diligently study His mighty and majestic Word. Remain ever steadfast to our one eternal God. Keep the faith, and pray always.

CONTENTS

FIRST QUARTER

UNIT THEME: GOD IS FAITHFUL

I. September 1—**Faith and Doubt**
Topic: Spared! (Genesis 19:1, 15–26, 29) 12

II. September 8—God Answers Prayer
Topic: Heart's Desire (1 Samuel 1:9–20) 18

III. September 15—Bread from Heaven
Topic: Where's the Food? (Exodus 16:1–8, 13–15) 24

IV. September 22—God Hears Our Cry
Topic: We Don't Believe You! (Numbers 13:1–2, 17, 25–28; 14:1–2, 5–10) 30

V. September 29—God Forgives
Topic: One More Chance (Numbers 14:10–20) 36

UNIT THEME: RESPONSES TO GOD'S FAITHFULNESS

VI. October 6—Obedient Faith
Topic: Do As You're Told (Deuteronomy 4:1–8, 12–13) 42

VII. October 13—Blessed for Faithfulness
Topic: Doing Right Pays Off (1 Kings 17:8–16) 47

VIII. October 20—Faith Can Heal
Topic: Just Say the Word (Luke 7:1–10) 52

IX. October 27—Faith Saves
Topic: Extravagant Love (Luke 7:37–48) 58

UNIT THEME: FAITH LEADS TO HOLY LIVING

X. November 3—Self-Examination
Topic: Look in the Mirror (2 Corinthians 13:1–11) 64

XI. November 10—Be Examples of Faith
Topic: Let It Shine (1 Thessalonians 1:2–10) 70

XII. November 17—Live Holy Lives
Topic: Dare to Be Different! (1 Peter 1:13–25) 76

XIII. November 24—Stick to Your Faith
Topic: Believing Promises (2 Peter 1:1–15) 82

CONTENTS

SECOND QUARTER

UNIT THEME: DAVID HONORS GOD

I. December 1—David Worships God in Jerusalem
Topic: Celebrate! (1 Chronicles 15:1–3, 14–16, 25–29) 90

II. December 8—A Heart Filled with Gratitude
Topic: Showing Gratitude (1 Chronicles 16:8–12, 19–27) 96

III. December 15—Building God's House
Topic: Negotiating Obedience (1 Chronicles 17:1, 3–4, 11–14; 21:18, 21–27) 102

IV. December 22—The Lord Is With You
Topic: Graciously Accepting Praise (Luke 1:39–56) 108

V. December 29—**David's Prayer**
Topic: A Greater Plan (1 Chronicles 17:16–27) 113

UNIT THEME: DEDICATING THE TEMPLE OF GOD

VI. January 5—A Place for the Ark
Topic: A Long-Anticipated Celebration (1 Kings 8:1–13) 119

VII. January 12—Solomon's Speech
Topic: I Promise! (1 Kings 8:14–21) 125

VIII. January 19—Solomon's Dedication Prayer
Topic: A Bright Future (1 Kings 8:22–30, 52–53) 131

IX. January 26—Solomon's Blessing
Topic: Commitment to Success (1 Kings 8:54–61) 137

UNIT THEME: JESUS TEACHES ABOUT TRUE WORSHIP

X. February 2—Single-minded Obedience
Topic: Passing the Tests (Matthew 4:1–11) 143

XI. February 9—Piety That Honors God
Topic: The Pitfalls of Showing Off (Matthew 6:1–8) 149

XII. February 16—The Prayer of Jesus
Topic: Ask for What Really Matters (Matthew 6:9–15) 155

XIII. February 23—Perseverance in Prayer
Topic: Making the Request (Luke 11:5–13) 161

CONTENTS

THIRD QUARTER

UNIT THEME: GOD REQUIRES JUSTICE

I. March 1—Called to Accountability
Topic: Seeking Justice (Amos 5:18–24) 168

II. March 8—A Prayer for Justice
Topic: Ending Injustice (Habakkuk 1:1–4, 12–14) 174

III. March 15—Consequences for Injustice
Topic: Getting What They Deserve (Habakkuk 2:6–14) 180

IV. March 22—Corrupt Leaders
Topic: Doing Justice (Micah 3:1–2, 9–12; 6:6–8) 186

V. March 29—Leading Justly
Topic: Justice for All (Malachi 2:1–9; 3:5–6) 191

UNIT THEME: GOD PROMISES A JUST KINGDOM

VI. April 5—God's Just Servant
Topic: Seeking a Champion of Justice (Isaiah 42:1–9) 197

VII. April 12—Resurrection Hope
Topic: Hope for a Better Life (1 Corinthians 15:1–8, 12–14, 20–23, 42–45) 203

VIII. April 19—Injustice Will Be Punished
Topic: Justice Prevails (Esther 7:1–10) 209

IX. April 26—The Lord Loves Justice
Topic: What Goes Around Comes Around (Isaiah 61:8–11; 62:2–4) 214

UNIT THEME: CALLED TO GOD'S WORK OF JUSTICE

X. May 3—**A Vision of Restoration**
Topic: The Return of Joy (Zephaniah 3:14–20) 219

XI. May 10—Peace and Justice Reign
Topic: A New Day Is Coming! (Zechariah 8:1–8, 11–17) 224

XII. May 17—Practice Justice
Topic: Just Rewards (Jeremiah 21:8–14) 229

XIII. May 24—Repent of Injustice
Topic: Do the Right Thing (Jeremiah 22:1–10) 234

XIV. May 31—Return to Love and Justice
Topic: Measure Up! (Hosea 11:1–2, 7–10; 12:1–2, 6–14) 239

CONTENTS

FOURTH QUARTER

UNIT THEME: WISDOM IN PROVERBS

I. June 7—The Call of Wisdom
Topic: Listen Up! (Proverbs 1:1–4, 7–8, 10, 20–22, 32–33) 245

II. June 14—The Value of Wisdom
Topic: Seeking Meaning (Proverbs 2:1–11) 251

III. June 21—The Gifts of Wisdom
Topic: Wisdom's Rewards (Proverbs 8:8–14, 17–21) 257

IV. June 28—Wisdom's Feast
Topic: Invitation to Wisdom (Proverbs 9:1–6, 8–10, 13–18) 263

UNIT THEME: WISDOM IN THE GOSPELS

V. July 5—Wisdom's Vindication
Topic: Wisdom in Action (Matthew 11:7–19) 269

VI. July 12—The Boy Jesus
Topic: Wisdom That Amazes (Ecclesiastes 3:1, 7;
Luke 2:39–52) 275

VII. July 19—The Wisdom of Jesus
Topic: Wisdom That Astounds and Offends (Mark 6:1–6) 281

VIII. July 26—Wisdom: the Way, Truth, and Life
Topic: Finding One's Way (John 14:1–14) 287

UNIT THEME: FAITH AND WISDOM IN JAMES

IX. August 2—Faith and Wisdom
Topic: Ask for It (James 1:1–11) 293

X. August 9—Hearing and Doing the Word
Topic: "Talk Is Cheap" (James 1:19–27) 299

XI. August 16—Faith without Works Is Dead
Topic: "Just Do It" (James 2:14–26) 305

XII. August 23—Taming the Tongue
Topic: "Bite Your Tongue" (James 3:1–12) 311

XIII. August 30—Two Kinds of Wisdom
Topic: Wise Up! (James 3:13–18; 5:7–12) 316

**For a full bibliography of sources used, please consult the accompanying CD.*

First Quarter

September

October

November

FAITH AND DOUBT

ADULT TOPIC:
SPARED!

BACKGROUND SCRIPTURE:
GENESIS 18:16–19:29

GENESIS 19:1, 15–26, 29

King James Version

AND there came two angels to Sodom at even; and Lot sat in the gate of Sodom: and Lot seeing them rose up to meet them; and he bowed himself with his face toward the ground;

• • • • • •

15 And when the morning arose, then the angels hastened Lot, saying, Arise, take thy wife, and thy two daughters, which are here; lest thou be consumed in the iniquity of the city.

16 And while he lingered, the men laid hold upon his hand, and upon the hand of his wife, and upon the hand of his two daughters; the LORD being merciful unto him: and they brought him forth, and set him without the city.

17 And it came to pass, when they had brought them forth abroad, that he said, Escape for thy life; look not behind thee, neither stay thou in all the plain; escape to the mountain, lest thou be consumed.

18 And Lot said unto them, Oh, not so, my LORD:

19 Behold now, thy servant hath found grace in thy sight, and thou hast magnified thy mercy, which thou hast shewed unto me in saving my life; and I cannot escape to the mountain, lest some evil take me, and I die:

20 Behold now, this city is near to flee unto, and it is a little one: Oh, let me escape thither, (is it not a little one?) and my soul shall live.

New Revised Standard Version

THE two angels came to Sodom in the evening, and Lot was sitting in the gateway of Sodom. When Lot saw them, he rose to meet them, and bowed down with his face to the ground.

• • • • • •

15 When morning dawned, the angels urged Lot, saying, "Get up, take your wife and your two daughters who are here, or else you will be consumed in the punishment of the city."

16 But he lingered; so the men seized him and his wife and his two daughters by the hand, the LORD being merciful to him, and they brought him out and left him outside the city.

17 When they had brought them outside, they said, "Flee for your life; do not look back or stop anywhere in the Plain; flee to the hills, or else you will be consumed."

18 And Lot said to them, "Oh, no, my lords;

19 your servant has found favor with you, and you have shown me great kindness in saving my life; but I cannot flee to the hills, for fear the disaster will overtake me and I die.

20 Look, that city is near enough to flee to, and it is a little one. Let me escape there—is it not a little one?—and my life will be saved!"

MAIN THOUGHT: And it came to pass, when God destroyed the cities of the plain, that God remembered Abraham, and sent Lot out of the midst of the overthrow, when he overthrew the cities in the which Lot dwelt. (Genesis 19:29, KJV)

Genesis 19:1, 15–26, 29

King James Version

21 And he said unto him, See, I have accepted thee concerning this thing also, that I will not overthrow this city, for the which thou hast spoken.
22 Haste thee, escape thither; for I cannot do anything till thou be come thither. Therefore the name of the city was called Zoar.
23 The sun was risen upon the earth when Lot entered into Zoar.
24 Then the Lord rained upon Sodom and upon Gomorrah brimstone and fire from the Lord out of heaven;
25 And he overthrew those cities, and all the plain, and all the inhabitants of the cities, and that which grew upon the ground.
26 But his wife looked back from behind him, and she became a pillar of salt.

• • • • • •

29 And it came to pass, when God destroyed the cities of the plain, that God remembered Abraham, and sent Lot out of the midst of the overthrow, when he overthrew the cities in the which Lot dwelt.

New Revised Standard Version

21 He said to him, "Very well, I grant you this favor too, and will not overthrow the city of which you have spoken.
22 Hurry, escape there, for I can do nothing until you arrive there." Therefore the city was called Zoar.
23 The sun had risen on the earth when Lot came to Zoar.
24 Then the Lord rained on Sodom and Gomorrah sulfur and fire from the Lord out of heaven;
25 and he overthrew those cities, and all the Plain, and all the inhabitants of the cities, and what grew on the ground.
26 But Lot's wife, behind him, looked back, and she became a pillar of salt.

• • • • • •

29 So it was that, when God destroyed the cities of the Plain, God remembered Abraham, and sent Lot out of the midst of the overthrow, when he overthrew the cities in which Lot had settled.

LESSON SETTING

Time: 1868 B.C.
Place: Sodom (Jordan Valley)

LESSON OUTLINE

I. Lot Meets the Angels (Genesis 19:1)
II. Impending Danger (Genesis 19:15–17)
III. The Rescue (Genesis 19:18–23)
IV. The Danger of Looking Back (Genesis 19:24–26, 29)

Unifying Principle

People's lives often are affected by what others have done or are doing on their behalf. How do the actions of others affect our lives? Genesis says God preserved Lot when Sodom was destroyed because of the righteousness of his uncle Abraham.

Introduction

Born in Ur of the Chaldeans, Lot was brought by his uncle Abraham to Canaan, where they became chieftains of two large shepherd enterprises. When their two competing herds became too large, God blessed both Lot and Abraham to such an extent they were able to separate and continue to remain individually prosperous and wealthy. When the split occurred, Abraham elected to relocate in the highlands of the land of "milk and honey" while Lot chose the fertile Jordan Valley and subsequently the cities of Sodom and Gomorrah. God is preparing to destroy these cities and has plans to save Lot and his family. Often the focus is centered on the weakness of Lot's wife, who infamously became a pillar of salt. Lot's stubbornness usually is overlooked.

Exposition

I. Lot Meets the Angels (Genesis 19:1)

One evening, we find Lot sitting "in the gate" of the city of Sodom, which indicates the city was a walled fortress, not unlike most of the citadels of the period. The Hebrew term used is רַעַשׁ *shar-ar*, which actually describes a gateway that could indicate it was the entrance to the town or a guard's station used to keep watch over the city. Several scholars believe Lot's presence in the gatehouse suggested he was an official or judge of Sodom; however, the aggressive men, whom Lot would later battle, noted he came into the city as an alien and to them, a pompous one acting like a judge (see Gen. 19:9). Whatever the reason, during the evening, two men appeared before Lot.

The Hebrew uses the term דְאָלַמ *mal-ak*, meaning "angels" but also "messengers of the Lord." Interestingly, the two men who visited Lot were a part of the triumvirate of angels who had previously visited Abraham at Mamre (Gen. 18:2). As with Abraham, when Lot saw the men, he rose to meet them and then bowed down, a customary sign of respect of this period.

II. Impending Danger (Genesis 19:15–17)

After a trying night, the dangers of the previous evening had not subsided; therefore, the angels devised a plan that would save Lot and his family from the horrors of the wicked city. The description of the scene reveals a mob mentality that suggests Lot's adversaries acted as a pack of wild animals that were determined to hunt their intended prey. The passage describes the pack as both young and old (Gen. 19:3–15).

As morning (רַחַשׁ *sha-har*) finally arrived, the angels urged or pressed Lot to leave the wicked city. They implored Lot to gather his family, which consisted of his wife and two daughters, who Lot had actually offered to the mob as a substitute for the men whom they wished harm. Recall that Lot had been warned God was going to destroy the city and had pleaded with his future sons-in-law to leave the area; however, Lot's efforts were ignored because the young men thought Lot was joking. Now as the angels push Lot to leave, he becomes reluctant to find the momentum needed to grasp the seriousness of the moment. The angels plead with Lot, literally begging him to escape or else he will be caught in the conflagration that was soon to occur. The Hebrew term used is הפס *sa-fa*, meaning "to take or carry away, be swept away," or ultimately, "destroyed." Lot has to be pressed to get up or to spring into action, for doom is approaching.

What is Lot thinking and why is he exhibiting this sense of lethargy? Was he tired from the previous night of despair? While we are not provided with a description of Lot's energy conundrum, we are given an idea he was hesitant because he did not have time to plan for an escape that would allow him to save his wealth and personal belongings.

III. The Rescue (Genesis 19:18–23)

Continuing in his obstinance, Lot rejects the advice of the angels. It would appear Lot attempts to shift the angels' instructions by cajoling their sensibilities. Notice the adulation: "your servant has found favor in your sight" and "you have magnified your lovingkindness" or concern by "saving my life." Lot somehow believes if he escapes to the mountains, the impending disaster will overtake him, and he will surely die. It seems as if he has at least finally understood the seriousness of the situation and realized the importance of the angels' concern and God's intervention. The cities of Sodom and Gomorrah will be destroyed, and the surrounding regions will suffer collateral damage.

The Scriptures do not reveal exactly when Lot realizes his circumstances, but when he does, we have an idea of it; however, Lot continues to challenge God's plan. Lot intones he now senses a problem with fleeing to the mountains because they are too far away, and the disaster of God's wrath would overtake him in his flight.

Incredibly, Lot does not consider he is in God's care and he and his family are protected wherever they are. The Hebrew term הָעָר *ra-kah-ha* is translated "disaster" but strongly means "evil" or "misfortune." Lot senses the presence of evil; however, it also was possible to consider the harm to have been of God, or otherwise, he is not being forthright in his argument with the angels. Recall the aforementioned accolades that would have been enough blustery rhetoric to convince a conceited man; but God sent to Lot angels or messengers (not men) who should not have been easily persuaded. Nonetheless, in an act that resembles God's trust in Abraham's judgment and heart, Lot was able to convince the angels to consider his perspective.

Notice that Lot begs to be allowed to go to a small town (the size of which he emphasized) to seek shelter from the forthcoming destruction. Continuing his conniving dialogue, Lot believes that in also this village, his life could be saved the same as if he goes to the mountains. The town Lot chose was called Zoar, which means "little town." Why Lot would have chosen to go to Zoar is incredulous because he was taken prisoner during a war that also saw Sodom and Gomorrah taken by Chedorlaomer and his allies. Lot was spared by the intervention of the Lord and Abraham, who rescued his nephew from certain death. As Lot reached Zoar, the signal for God to explode the cities in utter annihilation had begun.

IV. The Danger of Looking Back (Genesis 19:24–26, 29)

The account paints a picture of the method used by God to enact His destruction on the cities in the region, with Sodom and Gomorrah being prominently mentioned. God rained (רטמ *men-ther*) on them a lethal mixture of brimstone (תִירְפָג *go-freet*), or sulfur, and fire. Sulfur was a well-known mineral of the region and in biblical imagery served as a sign of divine destruction. Because of its combustible tendencies, sulfur was unstable and ignited rapidly; and due to its poisonous fumes, it became toxic when inhaled. Sulfur, or brimstone, also was used as a fumigant or cleansing agent.

The walled fortifications of these cities were designed to stop men from invading their grounds but were no match for the "poured out" elements that rained down from heaven. Everything (buildings, livestock, crops, and more) were consumed in the conflagration of God's wrath, including those wicked humans that could not be salvaged. Recall, sulfur or brimstone was used as a fumigant; here, we witness God "fumigating" the scourge of the immoral and unrighteous.

Again, notice the path of destruction was not limited to Sodom and Gomorrah, but included all of the cities and villages of the Jordan Valley except for one, the hamlet of Zoar. In contemporary society, we are acquainted with sanctuary cities in which people of different persuasions are protected from prejudicial mistreatment. In this situation, God allowed Zoar to become a sanctuary city for Lot and his family. However, God's provisions could not save a prominent member of the family because of her disregard for God's instructions and a mistimed lack of faith.

Ironically, we have witnessed the image of Lot, who vacillated and wavered in his desire to leave Sodom. The angels had an exasperating few days convincing Lot to escape and then wrestling with him as to the destination of his refuge. All eyes are focused on Lot as the rogue of this account in which he, although portrayed as righteous and worthy of being saved, is rebelling against God (if not with his actions, in his attitude and spirit). Previously, the other members of the family seem to be resigned to their fate and in compliance with the directions of the angels; however, a breakdown in discipline occurs. Lot's wife (אִשָּׁה *e-shah*) decided to take one last glimpse of her home, her belongings, and her city. If she could not let go of her thoughts of her present possessions, she surely could not have related to the knowledge God would provide new possessions, just as He was providing an opportunity for a new life. Whatever her weakness, Lot's family had been warned during their escape not to look back (verse 17). This may seem insignificant but becomes an important aspect in the set of instructions given by the angels. Nonetheless, in utter disregard to those instructions, Lot's wife was turned into a pillar (נְצִיב *net-sieve*) or column of salt (מֶלַח *me-lah*)!

Although this account is centered on the persons of Lot and his family, in the background of this rescue, God is remembering His servant Abraham. Lot is portrayed as a righteous man, worthy of God's salvation; however, the relationship between God and Abraham is furthermore extraordinary because Lot's rescue by extension is collateral in the bond between Abraham and his God. As aforementioned, Abraham had previously rescued Lot from the kings of the valley, but God had been with Abraham. On this occasion, Lot is saved by God, as a gesture or show of favor toward Abraham, whose covenant with God is obviously magnificent. In a summary of the final scene of destruction and devastation, God overthrew these cities where Lot now formerly lived!

The Lesson Applied

This account is a sad exposé of those people under God's protection who create their own rules. While ignoring the simplest of commands, people of Sodom and Gomorrah created a way of life that displeased God. The displeasure included the disobedience of Lot's wife, who looked ɔack, and the end result is she is turned nto the salt pillar. When humans drink too nuch salt water, their organs shut down. Ɔue to the destructive nature and potential ɔf salt, it also is used as a connotation of nan turning away from God. Jesus spoke ıbout our being the salt of the earth or a "season" to bring the lost to Him. He also ɔresented salt as a preservative to condition he earth. Lot's wife, however, as herself a ɔillar of salt, could do neither! Rather than ın agent that brings spice or flavor, or an nstrument that serves as one who believes n God's promises, she forever will be a ymbol of someone who perished because he failed to obey God.

Let's Talk About It

1. **What lessons can we learn from the lives of Lot and his wife as we await the return of Jesus Christ?**

Lot seems to have been lazy, wanting to take an easy way out of his situation. Although he was culturally agrarian, he had accumulated the customs and behaviors of the city. Because of this, Lot may have desired to move into another city rather than face life in the rugged mountains. As Christians we too occasionally become indifferent in our quest to please God and actually cling to the trappings and things of the world and our own little lives. As the people of God, we can trust God will place us along the paths of righteousness. It may sometimes seem boring, especially if we measure our life of discipleship as a believer and follower of Jesus Christ against those commonplace things the rest of the world is doing or thinking each and every day. When we behave in such a manner, the question becomes: Are we putting ourselves in a position to miss God's blessings simply because we are spiritually lazy? Do not miss the blessings God has especially for you. Do not turn back and take your eyes off of God. He is leading you to a more beautiful and blessed life of righteousness in His sight. That is the way you should want to go. That is the way Christ would have you to go.

The other lesson we learn from Lot is that it doesn't pay to ignore God's will or to disobey Him. Lot's wife took God's word for granted and refused to consider the magnitude of God's command. Her glance backward was more than a reaction to the calamity behind her; it was outright disobedience and defiance to God's command. Rebellion against God has consequences for all of us. Her becoming a pillar of salt was the direct result of failing to appreciate and honor the salvation she had been given. Let us not throw the Lord's grace back in His face through flagrant acts of disobedience and disregard for God's wise advice.

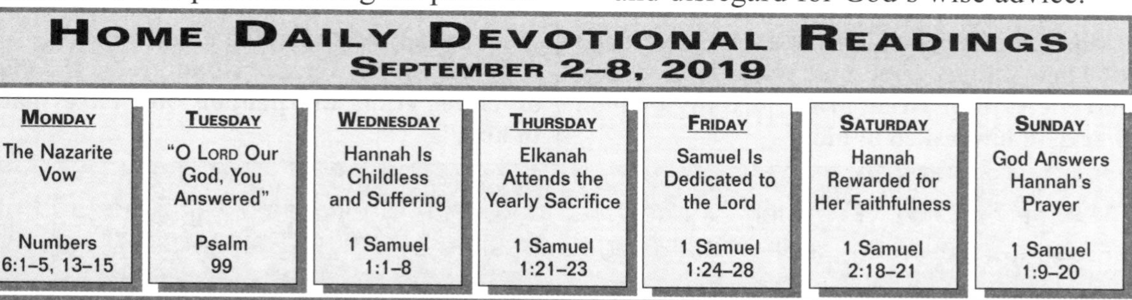

Home Daily Devotional Readings
September 2–8, 2019

Monday	Tuesday	Wednesday	Thursday	Friday	Saturday	Sunday
The Nazarite Vow	"O Lord Our God, You Answered"	Hannah Is Childless and Suffering	Elkanah Attends the Yearly Sacrifice	Samuel Is Dedicated to the Lord	Hannah Rewarded for Her Faithfulness	God Answers Hannah's Prayer
Numbers 6:1–5, 13–15	Psalm 99	1 Samuel 1:1–8	1 Samuel 1:21–23	1 Samuel 1:24–28	1 Samuel 2:18–21	1 Samuel 1:9–20

GOD ANSWERS PRAYER

ADULT TOPIC:
HEART'S DESIRE

BACKGROUND SCRIPTURE:
1 SAMUEL 1:1–2:10

1 SAMUEL 1:9–20

King James Version

SO Hannah rose up after they had eaten in Shiloh, and after they had drunk. Now Eli the priest sat upon a seat by a post of the temple of the LORD.
10 And she was in bitterness of soul, and prayed unto the LORD, and wept sore.
11 And she vowed a vow, and said, O LORD of hosts, if thou wilt indeed look on the affliction of thine handmaid, and remember me, and not forget thine handmaid, but wilt give unto thine handmaid a man child, then I will give him unto the LORD all the days of his life, and there shall no razor come upon his head.

12 And it came to pass, as she continued praying before the LORD, that Eli marked her mouth.
13 Now Hannah, she spake in her heart; only her lips moved, but her voice was not heard: therefore Eli thought she had been drunken.
14 And Eli said unto her, How long wilt thou be drunken? put away thy wine from thee.

15 And Hannah answered and said, No, my lord, I am a woman of a sorrowful spirit: I have drunk neither wine nor strong drink, but have poured out my soul before the LORD.
16 Count not thine handmaid for a daughter of Belial: for out of the abundance of my complaint and grief have I spoken hitherto.
17 Then Eli answered and said, Go in peace: and the God of Israel grant thee thy petition that thou hast asked of him.

New Revised Standard Version

AFTER they had eaten and drunk at Shiloh, Hannah rose and presented herself before the LORD. Now Eli the priest was sitting on the seat beside the doorpost of the temple of the LORD.
10 She was deeply distressed and prayed to the LORD, and wept bitterly.
11 She made this vow: "O LORD of hosts, if only you will look on the misery of your servant, and remember me, and not forget your servant, but will give to your servant a male child, then I will set him before you as a nazirite until the day of his death. He shall drink neither wine nor intoxicants, and no razor shall touch his head."
12 As she continued praying before the LORD, Eli observed her mouth.

13 Hannah was praying silently; only her lips moved, but her voice was not heard; therefore Eli thought she was drunk.
14 So Eli said to her, "How long will you make a drunken spectacle of yourself? Put away your wine."
15 But Hannah answered, "No, my lord, I am a woman deeply troubled; I have drunk neither wine nor strong drink, but I have been pouring out my soul before the LORD.
16 Do not regard your servant as a worthless woman, for I have been speaking out of my great anxiety and vexation all this time."
17 Then Eli answered, "Go in peace; the God of Israel grant the petition you have made to him."

MAIN THOUGHT: Then Eli answered and said, Go in peace: and the God of Israel grant thee thy petition that thou hast asked of him. (1 Samuel 1:17, KJV)

1 Samuel 1:9–20

King James Version	*New Revised Standard Version*
18 And she said, Let thine handmaid find grace in thy sight. So the woman went her way, and did eat, and her countenance was no more sad.	**18 And she said, "Let your servant find favor in your sight." Then the woman went to her quarters, ate and drank with her husband, and her countenance was sad no longer.**
19 And they rose up in the morning early, and worshipped before the LORD, and returned, and came to their house to Ramah: and Elkanah knew Hannah his wife; and the LORD remembered her.	**19 They rose early in the morning and worshiped before the LORD; then they went back to their house at Ramah. Elkanah knew his wife Hannah, and the LORD remembered her.**
20 Wherefore it came to pass, when the time was come about after Hannah had conceived, that she bare a son, and called his name Samuel, saying, Because I have asked him of the LORD.	**20 In due time Hannah conceived and bore a son. She named him Samuel, for she said, "I have asked him of the LORD."**

LESSON SETTING

Time: 1127 B.C.
Place: Ramah and Shiloh

LESSON OUTLINE

I. Hannah's Depression (1 Samuel 1:9–11)
II. Hannah's Prayer (1 Samuel 1:12–18)
III. Hannah's Prayer is Answered (1 Samuel 1:19–20)

Unifying Principle

People often feel no one hears them when they express their deepest desires. Is anyone really listening? Hannah, who had no children, asked God for a son, promising to dedicate him to God's service; and soon she conceived and gave birth.

Introduction

Elkanah has two wives, which is not uncommon in this agrarian society; their names are Hannah and Peninnah. The problem is Peninnah is quite fertile and has produced several children, whereas Hannah is infertile and childless. The anguish of not being able to produce children, especially a son, is almost destructive to Hannah. Living in a land filled with pagan influences and attractions, Hannah turns to Yahweh, whom she firmly believes will hear her plight. This account is not simply about God blessing Hannah with a son, but about the strength of her faith, even in a state of depression.

Exposition

I. Hannah's Depression (1 Samuel 1:9–11)

Elkanah had brightened Hannah's mood by expressing his love and devotion for her, which he indicates is of far greater value than ten sons (verse 8). After arriving in Shiloh, Hannah, who had been encouraged not to be sad, is convinced she should eat her meal, which was probably dinner. In Hebrew, the term קום *qu-fav-mem* is used, which means "to rise, or to get up."

The verb in the sentence structure indicates Hannah rose after she ate. Samuel's insertion of Hannah's eating and drinking reveals a change in her demeanor, her confidence, and subsequently, her faith. The author does not indicate what she ate or drank; however, her food probably consisted of bread, a staple of their diet, and meat from the double portion that was available from Elkanah's sacrifice. The drink, although not identified, was probably wine because Hannah would later be accused of being drunk.

After Hannah rose in the morning, she went to the tabernacle, which by this time, resembled a permanent building more than the previous tent. Several items suggest this: One is that Hannah finds Eli, the priest, sitting in the doorframe (הָזוּזְמ *mea-zu-zah*) or "between the door posts," on a chair (אֵסִּכ *ke-sea*), "seat," or "seat of honor." The term used here is *temple*; however, the words *tabernacle* and *temple* are used interchangeably. There would be only one temple, which would be located in Jerusalem. The house of the Lord (see the same phrase in 3:15) is called "the temple of the Lord" in verse 9. The Ark of the Covenant was no longer kept in a tent as it had been during the years the Israelites wandered in the wilderness. It was now kept in a building with a doorpost (verse 9) and at least two doors (3:15). The large temple in Jerusalem, however, was not yet in existence. It was not built until the reign of Solomon (1 Kings 6).

The author places such importance on Hannah's meal due to her state of depression, which resulted from taunting by Peninnah, and her usual custom of going on partial hunger strikes during their yearly sojourn to Shiloh. As with other situations whereby men had children with a second wife or concubine, tension existed in the relationship. Recall the hostility between Sarai (later Sarah) and Hagar and Leah and Rachel, which created serious issues for the families. Because children, especially males, were so valued, jealously invaded these arrangements, as the women often resorted to hateful taunting about the other's barrenness.

Hannah wept bitterly but prayed to the Lord. Again, depending on how one views the sentence structure, we could translate this verse as Hannah being bitter in her soul or inner sanctum, the word (Heb., רַמ *mar*), means "bitter." As she considered her situation, she found that for yet another year she was barren and could not produce a child. Succumbing to the emotional pressure, Hannah began to weep bitterly in her prayer to Yahweh. Interestingly, the word is derived from the account of the children of Israel who during the Exodus arrived at the waters of Marah but could not drink because the water was bitter; therefore, it was named *Marah* (Exod. 15:23).

II. Hannah's Prayer (1 Samuel 1:12–18)

Hannah was at the tabernacle praying to the Lord. Eli was sitting in the doorway and happened to observe Hannah's fervent appeal. Hannah may have been praying in the proximity of the Ark of the Lord; however, Eli seemed to be drawn to the actions of her mouth (הֶפ *peh*). Many people pray silently with their eyes closed; in this scene, Hannah was moving her lips but was not speaking. However, she had an emotional conversation with the Lord, speaking (רבד *de-bear*) from her heart.

The Hebrew term used is בֵל (*lev*), which is initially translated as "heart" but is better understood as one's "inner self," capturing the anguish of her pain. Therefore, a more accurate rendering would be that as Hannah prayed to the Lord, she was speaking in and from her inner self. Eli, who could be accused of eavesdropping, could not hear her prayer. He assumed Hannah was drunk (רוֹכִּשׁ *she-kor*) from too much wine. Apparently, drunkenness was not uncommon, even at the tabernacle and by women. Incredibly enough, Eli's belief that Hannah was intoxicated may have stemmed from the idea she was a victim of too much participation in the festival.

Mistaking Hannah's condition, Eli was not amused and retorted by asking her, "How long will you behave like someone who is drunk and exhibit this detrimental behavior?" Eli demanded Hannah put away her wine (ייַן *ya-in*), or literally "stop drinking." While the original Hebrew of "making yourself drunk" and "putting away your wine from you" is too wooden and clumsy, the image is clear: Eli is disappointed with Hannah, especially being a woman, in this seemingly derogatory state.

A rather mild-mannered Hannah responded to Eli saying, "No, my lord," assigning the proper respect and title to his office. She confessed she was suffering from an oppressed (הֶשָׁק *ka-shay*) spirit that had severely strained her countenance. Hannah explained she was not drunk from wine, but her demeanor was as such because she was "pouring out" (ךפשׁ *sha-phak*) herself before the Lord. Notice the wordplay of the pouring out of her soul as compared to the pouring out of wine! Hannah, overcome by years of torment, let it go in the presence (הֶנָפ *pa-neh*), in the face, of Yahweh. Hannah was not ashamed of her actions before Eli nor before the Lord. Her prayer emanated from the wellspring of her soul or inner being.

III. Hannah's Prayer is Answered (1 Samuel 1:19–20)

Do not assume that when Elkanah and Hannah returned home and had sexual relations, it was unusual for this to occur. Their sex life was more than likely routine, yet they were not able to become pregnant. It is probable Hannah and Peninnah were around the same age, which made it all the more painful when Peninnah taunted Hannah about her inability to conceive. This couple was not beyond child-producing years; notice they had tried, and Peninnah was successful but Hannah was not. Therefore, there is no reason to think she was like Sarah or Elizabeth, who were beyond childbearing years.

Elkanah and Hannah had worshiped the Lord in Bethel before they left, which means they had participated in the remainder of the festival. Notice that Peninnah is not mentioned again. Obviously, Hannah is the focus of the account; and it is probable that for the first time, Elkanah and Hannah were able to spend quality time together at the feast, which had never occurred. Hannah's mood had changed, and her depression had disappeared, which created a situation through which her presence was pleasurable. Hannah's previous moods could have created a situation in which no one wanted to be in her presence, spoiling the overall atmosphere of the occasion; but God had heard her prayer. The important point that cannot be overlooked is that Hannah's faith allowed her to become blessed, even in her seemingly simple but important request. Hannah was sincere in her belief God was with her, and therefore, her demeanor was drastically changed!

The couple's previous attempts had been futile; but in what must be seen as the grace or favor of God, the Lord heard the prayers of Hannah and graciously delivered on her request. The situation was special in that the Lord did not forget Hannah but remembered more than just her prayers—He counted her humility and sincerity. Since God remembered Hannah, it will seem fitting that Hannah would remember her promise to the Lord.

Interestingly, the NASB states Elkanah had relations with Hannah, his wife. The Hebrew term used is עדי *ya-da*, which means "to know, notice, or to learn." This does not make literal sense as to the understanding of what is being stated. Why would the account say Elkanah "knew" Hannah, when it is obvious, in contemporary understanding, he already had been acquainted with Hannah, who was his wife? Hebrew frequently uses the euphemism "to know" to refer to sexual intercourse. The words *Elkanah knew Hannah* are biblical English, not contemporary English. Translators of other languages need to be sure the meaning is clear and should also avoid using an expression that could be considered too explicit or vulgar for use in the Bible. Some readers of English find the expression "had intercourse" (*Today's English Version, Revised English Bible*) too explicit and offensive. Something such as "had relations with" (*New American Bible*) may be more acceptable. Most languages have euphemistic expressions to describe sexual relations without being too explicit—some use "slept with" or a more unusual idiom that can be understood clearly by all readers.

In the proper time (הָפוּקְת *te-qu-phah*), cycle or course of her time, Hannah conceived and gave birth. The original Hebrew reads "at the turn of the day," meaning at the end of her pregnancy. Remember, the Lord "heard" or accepted the prayers of Hannah; and when the family returned to their home in Ramah, God continued to remember (רכז *za-kar*), name her prayer, and bless her (and her family) with a son, who is named Samuel (לֵאוּמְשׁ *Shem-uel*). Although Samuel's name means "name of God," it also is closely associated with Hannah's asking the Lord for this child.

When the family returned to Shiloh for the festival the next year, Hannah would return with a son who was promised in the tabernacle. God's blessing for Hannah will have greater implications and blessings for the nation, as Hannah's request and God's gift will extend beyond this immediate family.

The Lesson Applied

God intervenes in the lives of infertile couples, allowing them to conceive children who would become heroes of the faith. Several examples are Sarah and Isaac, the childless wife of Manoah, and Elizabeth and Zechariah. The plague of Baalism haunted God's people, and ideas of female fertility were based in the worship of these false gods of fertility. Pagan belief systems were predictable; if a woman was infertile, she was not favored by whichever pagan fertility god was in vogue. Living in this cultural context, those loyal to Yahweh had to believe He would not overlook their needs. Infertility in these believing women would be conquered, and God would raise the children of these blessings to be His servants.

Let's Talk About It

1. **This text posits the power of prayer as a viable resource when all other measures have failed. Why does Hannah turn to the vehicle of prayer?**

   Hannah realized the God's power to evoke change in her circumstances through prayer. She prayed for divine intervention to alter her course in life. She understood barrenness and the implications that came with it. However, she also believed God was not hampered by human impediments and decided to appeal to Him. Her request for a child was granted. Because of her plea to God, Hannah's song of joy became the model for Mary's song of divine selection, the Magnificat (see and compare 1 Samuel 2:1-11 with Luke 1:46-55).

   The Scriptures are replete with instances where the suffering cast their hope and faith upon God to overturn their obstacles. Hezekiah and others, found themselves in similar circumstances and turned to God in light of their situation and, likewise, found divine favor and experienced holy intervention. For example, Hezekiah was told that his life was about to end, but he appealed to God and was granted fifteen more years to live (2 Kings 20:1-7).

   Also, the prophet Elisha came face-to-face with the vast army of Syria, but God revealed to him legions of angels that enveloped the Syrian military and gave the prophet protection (2 Kings 6:8-18).

   In the New Testament parables of the Persistent Widow and the Pharisee and Publican, Jesus insisted that people should always pray and not faint (Luke 18:1-9 and 10-14). Jesus confirmed that persistence in prayer pays off. The persistent widow received favor from the unjust judge because she refused to walk away unfulfilled. Also, Jesus affirmed the tax collector's recognition of God's ability to forgive sin despite the fact that the Hebrew people regarded him as a despicable traitor.

   The importance of prayer is further confirmed in John 17, in the only prolonged prayer uttered by Jesus. Additionally, prayer is shown to be the primary in seeking His guidance, as Jesus admonished His disciples to seek first the Kingdom of God and His righteousness with the promise that God will also supply one's other needs (Matthew 6:33).

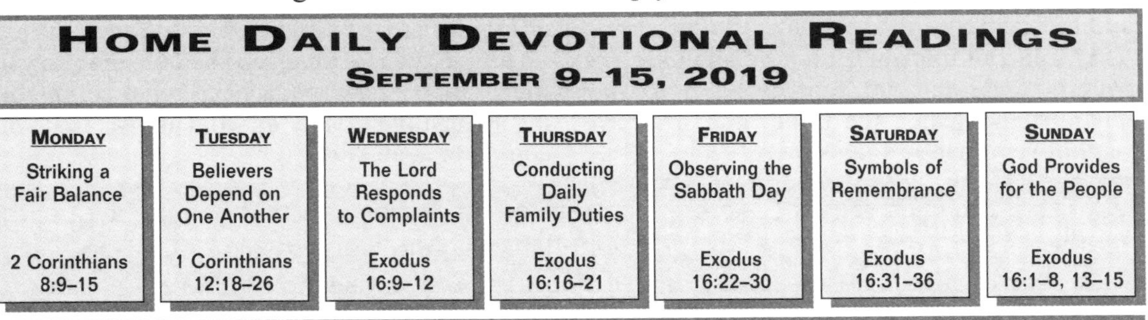

Home Daily Devotional Readings
September 9–15, 2019

Monday	Tuesday	Wednesday	Thursday	Friday	Saturday	Sunday
Striking a Fair Balance	Believers Depend on One Another	The Lord Responds to Complaints	Conducting Daily Family Duties	Observing the Sabbath Day	Symbols of Remembrance	God Provides for the People
2 Corinthians 8:9–15	1 Corinthians 12:18–26	Exodus 16:9–12	Exodus 16:16–21	Exodus 16:22–30	Exodus 16:31–36	Exodus 16:1–8, 13–15

Bread from Heaven

Adult Topic: Where's the Food?

Background Scripture: Exodus 16

Exodus 16:1–8, 13–15

King James Version

AND they took their journey from Elim, and all the congregation of the children of Israel came unto the wilderness of Sin, which is between Elim and Sinai, on the fifteenth day of the second month after their departing out of the land of Egypt.

2 And the whole congregation of the children of Israel murmured against Moses and Aaron in the wilderness:

3 And the children of Israel said unto them, Would to God we had died by the hand of the Lord in the land of Egypt, when we sat by the flesh pots, and when we did eat bread to the full; for ye have brought us forth into this wilderness, to kill this whole assembly with hunger.

4 Then said the Lord unto Moses, Behold, I will rain bread from heaven for you; and the people shall go out and gather a certain rate every day, that I may prove them, whether they will walk in my law, or no.

5 And it shall come to pass, that on the sixth day they shall prepare that which they bring in; and it shall be twice as much as they gather daily.

6 And Moses and Aaron said unto all the children of Israel, At even, then ye shall know that the Lord hath brought you out from the land of Egypt:

7 And in the morning, then ye shall see the glory of the Lord; for that he heareth your murmurings against the Lord: and what are we, that ye murmur against us?

New Revised Standard Version

THE whole congregation of the Israelites set out from Elim; and Israel came to the wilderness of Sin, which is between Elim and Sinai, on the fifteenth day of the second month after they had departed from the land of Egypt.

2 The whole congregation of the Israelites complained against Moses and Aaron in the wilderness.

3 The Israelites said to them, "If only we had died by the hand of the Lord in the land of Egypt, when we sat by the fleshpots and ate our fill of bread; for you have brought us out into this wilderness to kill this whole assembly with hunger."

4 Then the Lord said to Moses, "I am going to rain bread from heaven for you, and each day the people shall go out and gather enough for that day. In that way I will test them, whether they will follow my instruction or not.

5 On the sixth day, when they prepare what they bring in, it will be twice as much as they gather on other days."

6 So Moses and Aaron said to all the Israelites, "In the evening you shall know that it was the Lord who brought you out of the land of Egypt,

7 and in the morning you shall see the glory of the Lord, because he has heard your complaining against the Lord. For what are we, that you complain against us?"

MAIN THOUGHT: And when the children of Israel saw it, they said one to another, It is manna: for they wist not what it was. And Moses said unto them, This is the bread which the Lord hath given you to eat. (Exodus 16:15, KJV)

EXODUS 16:1–8, 13–15

King James Version	*New Revised Standard Version*
8 And Moses said, This shall be, when the LORD shall give you in the evening flesh to eat, and in the morning bread to the full; for that the LORD heareth your murmurings which ye murmur against him: and what are we? your murmurings are not against us, but against the LORD.	**8 And Moses said, "When the LORD gives you meat to eat in the evening and your fill of bread in the morning, because the LORD has heard the complaining that you utter against him—what are we? Your complaining is not against us but against the LORD."**
• • • • • •	• • • • • •
13 And it came to pass, that at even the quails came up, and covered the camp: and in the morning the dew lay round about the host.	**13 In the evening quails came up and covered the camp; and in the morning there was a layer of dew around the camp.**
14 And when the dew that lay was gone up, behold, upon the face of the wilderness there lay a small round thing, as small as the hoar frost on the ground.	**14 When the layer of dew lifted, there on the surface of the wilderness was a fine flaky substance, as fine as frost on the ground.**
15 And when the children of Israel saw it, they said one to another, It is manna: for they wist not what it was. And Moses said unto them, This is the bread which the LORD hath given you to eat.	**15 When the Israelites saw it, they said to one another, "What is it?" For they did not know what it was. Moses said to them, "It is the bread that the Lord has given you to eat.**

LESSON SETTING

Time: 1462 B.C.
Place: The Wilderness of Sin (between Elim and Sinai)

LESSON OUTLINE

I. The Lord Provides Manna (Exodus 16:1–7)
II. The Lord Provides Meat (Exodus 16:8–15)

UNIFYING PRINCIPLE

People often are unhappy with what they have in life. How can people truly be satisfied? Despite the complaining of the Israelites as they wandered in the wilderness, God provided meat and bread for them.

INTRODUCTION

Israel has been led out of Egypt and into the oasis of Elim. It seems as if rejoicing and good times are in place for the nation. God, however, instructs them to move again, for Elim is not their final destination. Their journey takes them to an area called the Wilderness of Sin, which is a desert, the opposite of Elim. Here, they lack food; but rather than relying on the God who had freed them, they bitterly complain and grumble in rebellion against Him. This is an account of God's love and mercy, despite the actions of the Israelites.

EXPOSITION

I. THE LORD PROVIDES MANNA (EXODUS 16:1–7)

The recently delivered Israelites have broken camp at Elim and are setting out to their new destination. Before they left Egypt, the Lord had commanded Moses and Aaron to change their calendar. While they suffered under Egyptian captivity, Israel also was subject to Egyptian chronology. At their release, God provided a new beginning. One of the items that accompanied this new beginning was the initiation of a new calendar. God commanded Moses to consider the month of their release the "beginning of months for you;" it was "the first month of the year for you" (Exod. 12:2). The new month would be known as Abib (later Nisan), which corresponded to the present months of March through April. This was the spring of the year and was compatible for travel from Egypt and thus, Elim.

Moses had led the entire (לֹכ *kol*, meaning "all" or "whole") congregation (הָדֵע *e-dah*, "community") of Israel and arrived in the wilderness (רָבְדִמ *mid-bar*), or desert of Sin, which is approximately 120 miles from Goshen, where most of Israel lived during the captivity. Elim, which was considered an oasis consisting of seventy palm trees and twelve springs, was thought to be located a few miles from the wilderness. Since their arrival was on the fifteenth day of the second month, they came to the desert during the second new month of Ziv, which corresponds to our months of April through May.

The wilderness of Sin was another large area probably along the west coast of the Sinai Peninsula. In this case, Sin has no relation to the English word *sin.* It is simply the name of a place and possibly has some connection with the word *Sinai.* The title "Wilderness of Sin" also may be expressed as "the wilderness named Sin" or "the Sin Wilderness."

In a reference to the creation sequence, the people are to work for six days, and on the sixth day, they will be given further instructions. On this day, they will gather twice as much as they gathered and prepared on each of the first five days. Enough was supplied each day for only that one day, except on Friday, when twice as much was to be gathered to provide enough for that day and the Sabbath. They were told they must follow these instructions and gather during these six days because "on the seventh day, the Sabbath, there will be none" (Exod. 16:26). At this juncture, it seems as if the vocal minority has disappeared because there are not any other complaints; however, Moses will face them again, which reveals the Lord already knows of their dissatisfaction.

II. The Lord Provides Meat (Exodus 16:8–15)

Continuing in his exaltation of the Lord, Moses exclaims the promise of God is guaranteed, stating *this will happen*, which was added to the phrase by translators for emphasis and is not part of the original Hebrew. The idea is the glory and splendor of the Lord will reach its zenith when the people are furnished food from heaven. Notice God has planned their sequence of meals: meat in the evenings (twilight) and bread in the mornings.

Again, Moses further stresses the Lord has heard their grumblings, as if to state that if they were trying to keep their complaints secret, they had not been successful—the Lord knows the heart and mind of His people. Additionally, Moses restates the incessant gripes were directed against the Lord and the poison piled upon Moses and Aaron would not have any effect on the mission of God and His quest to direct Israel into what would later be the "land of promise."

Grumblings seems to be a resounding theme that is re-stated again and again, as if the repetition is needed to underscore the people's disbelief, their rebellion, and sadly, their ungratefulness toward the Lord who had brought them out of Egyptian captivity. Moses changes his approach by having Aaron encourage the congregation that was assembled before them to come near (ברק *qa-rab*), or "to step up to," or "to get or come closer" to the Lord. The image is they would hear from the Lord *Himself* rather than from Moses and Aaron, since their messages seemed to be viewed as second-handed appeals to convince them their position in this wilderness was an improvement over their existence in Egypt. Moreover, by repeating that the Lord is painfully aware of their misgivings, it appears Moses is virtually taunting the skeptics, as they had created chaos and confusion in the minds of an already shaky group of people. If the nation was to get closer to the Lord, they would have to do more than simply approach Him physically; they would have to get closer to Him spiritually.

While Aaron was speaking to the people, a miraculous event occurred: Something directed their attention to an area of the desert where there was made manifest the appearance of the Lord. Notice that the glory of the Lord (Yahweh) appeared in the direction of the wilderness, the place to where He had guided them; and it was from this direction that the nation witnessed His glory. In a scene that is reminiscent of John's later vision—"we beheld or saw His glory," in speaking of Jesus (John 1:14)—God's glory was on full display, appearing in or on a cloud (וָנָע *a-nan*) or group of clouds. The phrase *appeared in the cloud* literally means "was seen" or "became visible." It is possible to restate the verse as: "And suddenly, they saw the dazzling light of Yahweh shining from a cloud." "The cloud" has the definite article attached, which suggests this cloud has been mentioned before, such as "the pillar of cloud" in 13:21. Most scholars, however, relate this cloud to the one in connection with the tabernacle mentioned in 40:34, which comes from the Priestly tradition ("P"), according to the Documentary Hypothesis. This theorum assigns sections of the Pentateuch to various authors who are identified by the letters JEDP. This "P" cloud represents the glory or presence of Yahweh, while the "J" cloud in 13:21 (from the Yahwist tradition) was a guiding cloud. Since this "P" cloud has not yet before been mentioned, 16:10 in T*oday's English Version* has "a cloud" (also in the *Jerusalem Bible*). Translators are advised to follow this interpretation. In this appearance, verse 7 indicates they saw the glory of the Lord (Exod. 16:7).

Moses then received confirmation from the Lord that He had definitely heard the grumblings of an ungracious people, whom Yahweh has affectionately led from Elim into this land. Continuing to reveal the pattern of His love, Yahweh has Moses tell the nation the next phase of their sustenance will be the gift of meat. They previously had been granted an offering of bread and now, the complement of meat will secure the requirement of their diet. God has given directions to the people: They shall eat the meat at twilight (evening) and eat the bread (manna) in the morning.

God finishes this set of guidelines with a flourish by reiterating that, because of these gifts, the people of Israel will *know* "I am the Lord, your God." This statement is significant in that the people should realize only a loving and provisional God could provide food in such an arid and unforgiving land. Second, the people must embrace He is their God who has brought them from Egyptian bondage into a new life of security and freedom. Since it was Yahweh who had been their rescuer, it will be Yahweh who will be their protector. They should know God had been with them thus far; however, it would seem many of the people simply did not care.

Next, we see the promise of the Lord in action as He supplies the meat, which for the first time is identified as quail (שְׂלָו *se-lav*). This small, short-winged, and bullet-headed bird is easily caught when exhausted from flight and is considered a delicacy. Interestingly, on a later occasion, God used quail to bring a plague on the people (Num. 11:31–34). The amount of birds furnished was such that they covered or were all around the camp (מַחֲנֶה *ma-cha-neh*)—the amount was large enough to describe the size of an encampment of an army! In the morning, the dew (טַל *tal*) or light rain fell upon the land; however, when the heat of the sun appeared, the moisture evaporated, and there existed a fine (דַּק *daq*), thin, and delicate substance laying on the ground. The description here resembles the frosting layered on certain breakfast cereals, such as Kellogg's Frosted Flakes®. Without the insertion of the Lord, these phenomena never could have occurred in such a parched landscape.

When the sons of Israel saw it, they hesitated, astonished, and asked, "What is it?" They never had witnessed anything like this and had no idea what the substance was. Moses and Aaron stepped up and exclaimed, "It is the bread from the Lord." Their leaders were not afraid of this unknown substance because it was a provision from the Lord, who had delivered meat to eat with the fine bread. The emphasis here is the Lord has given you these items for food. There should have been great rejoicing, but many did not follow Moses's instructions for gathering. Later, the people will grumble again, this time for the lack of water.

The Lesson Applied

This is an account of an ungrateful people who would not trust the God who had delivered them from Egyptian slavery and, as part of His plan, led them to this place in the wilderness. You would think they would have been determined to follow the Lord and trust Him in everything He had planned for their future. However, rebel leaders (who were probably jealous of Moses's leadership), caused an insurrection among the people, who were obviously easily swayed. Nonetheless, God heard Moses's plea and provided food for the people. What cannot be missed is that God *already knew* they would need food and would provide for them. The issue here was the lack of trust and faith that was on full display from an ungrateful people.

Let's Talk About It

1. **Jesus Christ teaches us to pray to God and ask Him for our daily needs. Do you have a story of God providing you with all the daily provisions in your life?**

2. **Why is it important to remember how God has provided for us in the past? How does remembrance of what God has done help us face the future?**

3. **The children of Israel asked God for bread, but God gave them something they did not recognize. When you remember God's provision in your own life, can you recall when and how God answered your prayer with something you at first may not have recognized as good?**

Manna, a Hebrew word that is best understood as "bread from heaven," sustained the Israelites during the entire time they spent wandering through the Wilderness of Sin. The bread's unique nature was emphasized by its very name, *man hu*, literally meaning "what is it?" However, the word *man* is not a Hebrew word. In Arabic and Aramaic, *man* means "who," but the context suggests "what." It also is possible to translate *manna* as "What is this?" or "What is this stuff?" The importance here was God was the One who provided the manna, which only affords us as Christians a deeper understanding of the phrase taught to us in Jesus's prayer. Jesus instructs His disciples to ask God to "give us this day, our daily bread" (Matt. 6:11).The daily provision of manna is also an occasion for instruction concerning the Sabbath, or seventh day of the week, as a day of solemn rest. Already established in Genesis 2:2–3, the Sabbath is explicitly found in the natural order, and thus occurs here, even before its mention in the Ten Commandments, also called the Decalogue, found in Exodus 20:8–11. A different description is found in Numbers 11:7–9, giving rise to the early legend that the taste of manna varied according to the eater's preference.

As a community of faith and body of believers called Christians, we can rest assured God will provide us with all the bread and nourishment we need for life. God is the sovereign ruler and governor over all of creation. He will take care of us. When Jesus teaches the disciples to pray daily for bread, Jesus is teaching them and us to rely on God alone for each day's supply of necessities without any anxieties to stockpile or hoard things for later because God always will provide us with just enough.

Home Daily Devotional Readings

September 16–22, 2019

Monday	Tuesday	Wednesday	Thursday	Friday	Saturday	Sunday
Praise the Lord!	Spying Out the Land	Reporting Mixed Reviews	Moses Resists God's Proposal	God Decides Who Will Enter Canaan	Moses Intercedes for God's People	Don't Doubt; Trust God's Promises
Psalm 106:1–12, 48	Numbers 13:17–24	Numbers 13:30–33	Exodus 32:7–14	Deuteronomy 1:34–40	Numbers 14:13–20	Numbers 13:1–2, 17, 25–28; 14:1–2, 5–10

GOD HEARS OUR CRY

ADULT TOPIC:
WE DON'T BELIEVE YOU!

BACKGROUND SCRIPTURE:
NUMBERS 13:1–14:10

NUMBERS 13:1–2, 17, 25–28; 14:1–2, 5–10

King James Version

AND the LORD spake unto Moses, saying,

2 Send thou men, that they may search the land of Canaan, which I give unto the children of Israel: of every tribe of their fathers shall ye send a man, every one a ruler among them.

• • • • • •

17 And Moses sent them to spy out the land of Canaan, and said unto them, Get you up this way southward, and go up into the mountain:

• • • • • •

25 And they returned from searching of the land after forty days.

26 And they went and came to Moses, and to Aaron, and to all the congregation of the children of Israel, unto the wilderness of Paran, to Kadesh; and brought back word unto them, and unto all the congregation, and shewed them the fruit of the land.

27 And they told him, and said, We came unto the land whither thou sentest us, and surely it floweth with milk and honey; and this is the fruit of it.

28 Nevertheless the people be strong that dwell in the land, and the cities are walled, and very great: and moreover we saw the children of Anak there.

• • • 14:1–2, 5–10 • • •

1 And all the congregation lifted up their voice, and cried; and the people wept that night.

2 And all the children of Israel murmured against Moses and against Aaron: and the whole congregation said unto them, Would God that we had died in the land of Egypt! or would God we had died in this wilderness!

New Revised Standard Version

THE LORD said to Moses,

2 "Send men to spy out the land of Canaan, which I am giving to the Israelites; from each of their ancestral tribes you shall send a man, every one a leader among them."

• • • • • •

17 Moses sent them to spy out the land of Canaan, and said to them, "Go up there into the Negeb, and go up into the hill country,

25 At the end of forty days they returned from spying out the land.

26 And they came to Moses and Aaron and to all the congregation of the Israelites in the wilderness of Paran, at Kadesh; they brought back word to them and to all the congregation, and showed them the fruit of the land.

27 And they told him, "We came to the land to which you sent us; it flows with milk and honey, and this is its fruit.

28 Yet the people who live in the land are strong, and the towns are fortified and very large; and besides, we saw the descendants of Anak there.

• • • 14:1–2, 5–10 • • •

1 Then all the congregation raised a loud cry, and the people wept that night.

2 And all the Israelites complained against Moses and Aaron; the whole congregation said to them, "Would that we had died in the land of Egypt! Or would that we had died in this wilderness!

MAIN THOUGHT: If the LORD delight in us, then he will bring us into this land, and give it us; a land which floweth with milk and honey. (Numbers 14:8, KJV)

NUMBERS 13:1–2, 17, 25–28; 14:1–2, 5–10

King James Version	*New Revised Standard Version*
••••••	••••••
5 Then Moses and Aaron fell on their faces before all the assembly of the congregation of the children of Israel.	**5 Then Moses and Aaron fell on their faces before all the assembly of the congregation of the Israelites.**
6 And Joshua the son of Nun, and Caleb the son of Jephunneh, which were of them that searched the land, rent their clothes:	**6 And Joshua son of Nun and Caleb son of Jephunneh, who were among those who had spied out the land, tore their clothes**
7 And they spake unto all the company of the children of Israel, saying, The land, which we passed through to search it, is an exceeding good land.	**7 and said to all the congregation of the Israelites, "The land that we went through as spies is an exceedingly good land.**
8 If the LORD delight in us, then he will bring us into this land, and give it us; a land which floweth with milk and honey.	**8 If the LORD is pleased with us, he will bring us into this land and give it to us, a land that flows with milk and honey.**
9 Only rebel not ye against the LORD, neither fear ye the people of the land; for they are bread for us: their defence is departed from them, and the LORD is with us: fear them not.	**9 Only, do not rebel against the LORD; and do not fear the people of the land, for they are no more than bread for us; their protection is removed from them, and the LORD is with us; do not fear them."**
10 But all the congregation bade stone them with stones. And the glory of the LORD appeared in the tabernacle of the congregation before all the children of Israel.	**10 But the whole congregation threatened to stone them. Then the glory of the LORD appeared at the tent of meeting to all the Israelites.**

LESSON SETTING

Time: 1461 B.C.
Place: Kadesh-barnea, (Wilderness of Zin)

LESSON OUTLINE

I. Spies in the Land (Numbers 13:1–2; 17)
II. The Report of the Spies (Numbers 13:25–28)
III. The People Rebel (Numbers 14:1–2, 5–10)

UNIFYING PRINCIPLE

When life puts obstacles in our paths, we are tempted to abandon the promises the future holds. Why don't we believe the promises made to us? Caleb and Joshua believed God would lead Israel to possess the Promised Land and tried to persuade the people to trust God's faithfulness.

INTRODUCTION

Israel is approaching the borders of Canaan, the Promised Land, which God has given as a gift to the people of Israel. As the people gather to develop a plan of occupation, the need to scout the land becomes evident. Israel needed to know the strength of the inhabitants of the land and whether they could overcome the prowess and strength of the population. Since the taking of the land would become a military operation, they needed to know if the occupants of Canaan had a standing army or militia. Moses and Aaron sent twelve spies into the land, and ten came back with a negative report that the land could not be taken. However, the remaining two infiltrators returned with a positive assessment that affirmed the land could be seized. The following is an account as to how this unfolded.

Exposition

I. Spies in the Land (Numbers 13:1–2; 17)

While Israel was camped at Kadesh-barnea, the Lord spoke to Moses and issued a set of instructions in preparation for the occupation of Canaan. Moses was instructed to send a group of chosen men that would serve as infiltrators to spy (רות *tur*) or reconnoiter the land (ץֶרֶא *erets*) or region. The commands they were given were related to the promise that God was to provide, give (ןתנ *nathan*), or present the land to Israel as a gift. It appears from Deuteronomy 1:22–23 that the sending of the spies to search out the land was suggested by the people and approved by Moses; and here, it is permitted by the Lord. God had commanded them to go and take possession of the land, and the motion to send the spies was an expression of their unbelief.

The men chosen for the task were to select from each of their fathers' twelve ancestral (אָב *ab*) tribes (הֶטַּמ *mat-te*) that were ruled or led (אִישָׁנ *nasi*) by their sheikhs. Verses 4–15 list the names of each man and his respective tribe. Recall that the names of the tribes reflect the names of Jacob's sons, with the exception of Manassah and Ephraim. These tribes are Leah's sons, Reuben, Simeon, Levi, Judah, Issachar, and Zebulun; Rachel's sons, Joseph and Benjamin; Rachel's maid Bilhah's sons, Dan, Naphtali, and Zilpah; and Leah's maid's sons, Gad and Asher. Manassah and Ephraim were the sons of Joseph who were adopted by Jacob (Gen. 48:5), and they replaced Joseph and Levi as part of the original twelve—Levi's preisthood gave birth to the priesthood of Moses and Aaron, who were designated as Levites or Levitical priests whose sole duty was to serve Israel.

It was this group that Moses sent to spy on the hill country of the Negev and thus, the land of Canaan. Circa 930 B.C., these twelve tribes would later form the nation of Israel that will be unified under the kings Saul, David, and Solomon but later divided under Jeroboam, who became the king of the Northern Kingdom (Israel), and Rehoboam, king of the Southern Kingdom (Judah).

II. The Report of the Spies (Numbers 13:25–28)

The spies sent by Moses reconnoitered the land for forty days, and at the end of the appointed time, they returned with a report. It is interesting the spies were in the country for forty (עַבְרַא *ar-ba*) days, as this number is significant in biblical lore—the days ascribed to the rain in Noah's account, the years of David's reign, and obviously, the number of years that Israel remained in the wilderness.

When the spies appeared before Moses and Aaron with their report, they brought back samples of the agricultural richness of the land. Israel was camped in the region of Paran, at Kadesh, located in the Wilderness of Zin. Israel obviously had migrated northwest to this region, which also is known as Kadesh-barnea. This is part of the hill country region of Canaan known as the Negev. The spies returned with clusters of grapes, pomegranates, and figs that revealed the prowess of the land to produce quality fruit (יְרִפּ *peri*) or produce. The imagery of the richness of these crops is evident, as when the men came to Eshcol (meaning "cluster"), they cut down a branch from a single cluster of grapes and had to carry it on a pole between two men, revealing the considerable size of the fruit (Num. 13:23–24). Eschol had a reputation as a region that specialized in the quality and size of its grapes. Intrigued by large and bountiful examples, the people definitely were impressed.

III. The People Rebel (Numbers 14:1–2, 5–10)

The people of Israel found themselves extremely disappointed, suffering a terrible letdown over the report from the group of men who had been sent into the region that was promised them. Upon receiving and understanding the details, the congregation lifted its body and in unison or one voice (לוֹק, *kol*) cried out in anguish and disappointment. Theirs was such a degree of distress that they wept (הכב *bakah*) or cried throughout the night (הָלְיָל *lay-il*). It seems as if the people were crushed they had followed Moses and Aaron this incredible distance and had undergone some perceived hardships only to now be faced with the specter that maybe they should simply turn around and return to Egypt.

Their reaction was to do that which they had shown themselves capable of doing in other trials—they grumbled against Moses, Aaron, and ostensibly, against the Lord. In an act of somewhat ludicrous comparison, the question was posed, "Should we have died in Egypt or in this wilderness?" Incredibly, their mind-set was upon dying, and now they were casting about the idea that perishing in one location was superior to the other. An interesting set of comments reveal the mind-set of these frustrated people as they shouted against Yahweh by asking why the Lord had brought them into this land to be "killed by the sword," indicating their being overrun in warfare or plundering, their wives and children being captured and sold as slaves, or better yet, spoils (זַב *baz*), warfare plunder, or booty.

The cowered people grumbled against the Lord, their memories seemingly foggy, as if they were suffering from a tragic streak of spiritual amnesia. Recall the many statements issued by Yahweh to constantly remind Israel that it was the Lord who had brought them out of Egypt became painfully necessary.

In front of and before all the people, Moses and Aaron knew what to do—they fell on their faces, not in adulation or submission to Israel, but in supplication to the Lord. The brothers knew only the Lord would be able to deliver the promises He had set forth; He had not brought Israel this far to abandon it to its own devices and fate. Totally committed, Moses and Aaron understood both the mission and the gift that was being granted to Israel. These leaders of Israel obviously had spent much time in prayer with the Lord and, therefore, had a greater understanding of that which was needed to accomplish the assignment. Regretfully, many of the rebel leaders of the camp missed the opportunity to be some of God's emissaries due to their walking by sight and not by faith. Moses and Aaron, however, remained steadfast in their approach and their commitment to Yahweh. Their prostrate position unto the Lord signified total obedience to Him and His will.

Two of the men who were sent as spies had a different evaluation of the situation. These two men are identified as Joshua, son of Nun, and Caleb, son of Jephunneh. Joshua, who was originally named Hoshea (Num. 13:8), from the tribe of Ephraim, exhibited an unwavering sense of faith and trust in the promises of the Lord and will later become Moses's most trusted lieutenant and disciple. Joshua also will become one of Israel's greatest heroes of the faith. Caleb, from the tribe of Judah, was supportive of Joshua and the positive report that the land could be taken; and he later would be allowed to enter the land as a reward for his faithfulness. When they were rebuffed by the other men who had accompanied them on the mission, they became severely depressed and as a sign, tore their clothes. The tearing of clothes is a ritual gesture of grief or an act of uncontrollable rage. Recall that Reuben tore his clothes when he returned to the pit and found Joseph was missing (Gen. 37:2); King Hezekiah tore his clothes when he received a threatening letter from the Assyrian monarch (Isa. 37:1); and Caiaphas tore his robe as Jesus revealed He is the Son of God (Matt. 26:65). Joshua and Caleb, in an expression of rage (but also, a lament that the other men and subsequently, the people could be so discouraging), tore away (ערק *qara*) or ripped their garments (דֶגֶב *be-ged*) or clothing.

Providing a positive report, Joshua and Caleb extolled the virtues of the land, pronouncing it was a "very, very" good land. These men had a mind-set that depended upon the Lord, stating that if the Lord was pleased with them, then He would give Israel the land (again, using the metaphor) flowing with milk and honey. The key to this assessment is that these men were grounded in their belief that only the Lord could provide the victory and the seizure of the land, and that total faithfulness in Him was now warranted, not a wavering of their confidence and allegiance. Joshua and Caleb literally beg Israel not to cower under the situation but to be strengthened by the knowledge that the Lord would deliver the land.

However, the people must show courage and not rebel (דרמ *ma-rad*) or revolt against Yahweh in their quest. Additionally, they were encouraged not to exhibit a sense of fear (ארי *ya-re*) or to be afraid of what they would face because the Lord would be with them. The Hebrew word צֵל (*tsel*), meaning "protection" or "shadow," provides a more direct understanding of God's complete commitment to encompassing their needs and movements in the time of battle, if only He is willing (חפץ *cha-pets*), delights, or takes pleasure in the attitudes of the people.

Sadly, the response of the people was to kill Joshua and Caleb by "covering them with stones" (מגר *ragam*) or stoning them, which was the preferred method of public execution. This is incredulous! In contemporary verbiage, a question could be interjected: "Are you kidding me?"

The Lesson Applied

The account of Israel's plight was revealed not so much as an indicator of its military power but as an assessment of its lack of faith in the Lord. Previous examinations of its grumblings and lack of trust have been explored; however, by now, when faced with a new challenge, the people should have been looking to the Lord to deliver them from the issue. Unfortunately, the negative report of the ten spies outweighed the positive report from Joshua and Caleb. It is interesting to note the people did not call for the stoning of the ten but wanted to kill Joshua and Caleb because they dared to believe the Lord would deliver the land into their hands.

Let's Talk About It

1. **What relationship might fear and faith have in your life? How are your fears grounded in unbelief? Where may you be denying God's goodness and doubting His promises?**
2. **What are the consequences of fear and unbelief in your life of faith? How should the goodness of God and God's promises affect how you view your life's circumstances?**
3. **What promises from the Word of God can we put our whole trust in as we live out our Christian faith? What blessings does God offer all those who trust and obey Him?**

What do we do when life presents us with difficult challenges and changes that seem to be insurmountable problems in a society that has "gone wild" and turned its back on God? What is the proper approach by which Christians can navigate a world filled with evil and sin? The perpetrators of school shootings, church shootings and burnings, and the hate-filled rhetoric and acts of division from those in lofty political offices have one common denominator—a severe disconnection with the church and ostensibly, the Lord. These menaces to society are not Christian, nor do they belong to the Church. True Christians must fight these evils with the weapons supplied by heaven, not those acquired through online sources. The weapons of faith, hope, and love are the things designed to give us an advantage in defending ourselves and others in the conflicts of this present age. Faith, hope, and love do not inflict harm. Rather, they defend the weak and innocent. The way of faith, the truth of hope, and life of love that we have in Jesus Christ protects the vulnerable least of these among us in our various communities. This means the church must do all it can to provide a secure place for worship. It cannot allow fear to prevent our faith from trusting God. But it can no longer pretend that we live in a society that does not honors God.

Home Daily Devotional Readings
September 23–29, 2019

Monday	Tuesday	Wednesday	Thursday	Friday	Saturday	Sunday
Bless the Lord Who Forgives	Jesus Forgives Our Sins	God's Forgiveness Doesn't Allay Suffering	God's Forgiveness May Involve Harsh Judgments	Children Suffer for Adults' Sins	People Rebelled and Were Defeated	The Lord Says, "I Do Forgive"
Psalm 103:1–14	Acts 10:34–43	Numbers 14:21–25	Numbers 14:26–30	Numbers 14:31–35	Numbers 14:39–45	Numbers 14:10–20

GOD FORGIVES

ADULT TOPIC:
ONE MORE CHANCE

BACKGROUND SCRIPTURE:
NUMBERS 14:10–23

NUMBERS 14:10–20

King James Version

BUT all the congregation bade stone them with stones. And the glory of the LORD appeared in the tabernacle of the congregation before all the children of Israel.

11 And the LORD said unto Moses, How long will this people provoke me? and how long will it be ere they believe me, for all the signs which I have shewed among them?

12 I will smite them with the pestilence, and disinherit them, and will make of thee a greater nation and mightier than they.

13 And Moses said unto the LORD, Then the Egyptians shall hear it, (for thou broughtest up this people in thy might from among them;)

14 And they will tell it to the inhabitants of this land: for they have heard that thou LORD art among this people, that thou LORD art seen face to face, and that thy cloud standeth over them, and that thou goest before them, by day time in a pillar of a cloud, and in a pillar of fire by night.

15 Now if thou shalt kill all this people as one man, then the nations which have heard the fame of thee will speak, saying,

16 Because the LORD was not able to bring this people into the land which he sware unto them, therefore he hath slain them in the wilderness.

17 And now, I beseech thee, let the power of my Lord be great, according as thou hast spoken, saying,

18 The LORD is longsuffering, and of great mercy, forgiving iniquity and transgression, and by no means clearing the guilty, visiting the

New Revised Standard Version

BUT the whole congregation threatened to stone them. Then the glory of the LORD appeared at the tent of meeting to all the Israelites.

11 And the LORD said to Moses, "How long will this people despise me? And how long will they refuse to believe in me, in spite of all the signs that I have done among them?

12 I will strike them with pestilence and disinherit them, and I will make of you a nation greater and mightier than they."

13 But Moses said to the LORD, "Then the Egyptians will hear of it, for in your might you brought up this people from among them,

14 and they will tell the inhabitants of this land. They have heard that you, O LORD, are in the midst of this people; for you, O LORD, are seen face to face, and your cloud stands over them and you go in front of them, in a pillar of cloud by day and in a pillar of fire by night.

15 Now if you kill this people all at one time, then the nations who have heard about you will say,

16 'It is because the LORD was not able to bring this people into the land he swore to give them that he has slaughtered them in the wilderness.'

17 And now, therefore, let the power of the LORD be great in the way that you promised when you spoke, saying,

18 'The LORD is slow to anger, and abounding in steadfast love, forgiving iniquity and transgression, but by no means clearing the guilty,

MAIN THOUGHT: Pardon, I beseech thee, the iniquity of this people according unto the greatness of thy mercy, and as thou hast forgiven this people, from Egypt even until now. (Numbers 14:19, KJV)

King James Version	*New Revised Standard Version*
iniquity of the fathers upon the children unto the third and fourth generation.	**visiting the iniquity of the parents upon the children to the third and the fourth generation.'**
19 Pardon, I beseech thee, the iniquity of this people according unto the greatness of thy mercy, and as thou hast forgiven this people, from Egypt even until now.	**19 Forgive the iniquity of this people according to the greatness of your steadfast love, just as you have pardoned this people, from Egypt even until now."**
20 And the LORD said, I have pardoned according to thy word.	**20 Then the LORD said, "I do forgive, just as you have asked.**

LESSON SETTING

Time: 1461 B.C.
Place: Kadesh-barnea (Wilderness of Zin)

LESSON OUTLINE

I. **Israel Rejects God (Numbers 14:10–11)**
II. **God Decides to Punish Israel (Numbers 14:12)**
III. **Moses' Plea for Israel (Numbers 14:13–16)**
IV. **God's Punishment Revealed (Numbers 14:17–20)**

UNIFYING PRINCIPLE

Everyone wrongs others, even those who love us and those whom we love. When we mess up, is forgiveness possible? According to Numbers, God forgave the rebellious people of Israel and promised to lead their descendants forward to the Promised Land.

INTRODUCTION

This is an account of a sincere servant who believed in the Lord's mission and refused an opportunity for the Lord to elevate him personally to a position of greatness. This servant had a devoted and personal relationship with Yahweh that allowed him to voice his opinion on the current subject and beg God to change His mind, sparing the people of Israel from an unmitigated disaster. This man remembered he once wanted to refuse to be involved in the mission of God, then through the journey realized Yahweh is the God of All. His pleading with God to change His mind may remind us of Abraham asking God to spare Sodom and Gomorrah; however, this servant happens to be Moses.

EXPOSITION

I. ISRAEL REJECTS GOD (NUMBERS 14:10–11)

God is frustrated with His people. He appears in the meeting place before the people where He speaks only to Moses. As incredulous as it may sound, Yahweh is angry and disappointed. It seems as if all He had done for the people is not appreciated. The people He loves choose not to follow His will. They also don't indicate by their actions that they want to serve as His chosen people.

In this account, God is "venting" to Moses, who has remained a true and faithful servant. Moses has several issues, but his faithfulness and love for God is not one of them. Moses's anger will later prove to be his undoing, and he will try God's patience one time too many. However, at this point, Moses is on the receiving end of God's exasperation.

God's question of how long the people will spurn (נאץ *naats*) Him has severe implications. The Hebrew term means "to treat disrespectfully," indicating the people refused to follow the Lord because they did not revere Him. How this is possible is unfathomable. Nonetheless, the people do not fear Yahweh (which is not to be thought of as being afraid of Him). They do not admire or love God, which indicates a lack of worship. This may be due to the influence of idolatry or past grumblings. Some scholars translate this term as the people's provoking God. However, that would present an image that portrays the people as issuing a challenge to God. The accuracy of the term indicates simply that the people have rejected God and the commandments that accompany His will.

The second part of God's question to Moses was centered around the people's belief and trust in Yahweh. Because of their disobedience and apathy, Israel had chosen to believe in themselves and trust their own judgment. Their lack of belief had altered their sensibilities to such a degree they contemplated going on their own. In their continued lack of good judgment, it became easier to be swept up in the popular idol worship of their times, which did not require a total commitment. Their worship of idol gods could be accomplished according to the whims and schedules of misguided people.

Because God had reminded the nation of His past provision, Yahweh now tells Moses those blessings and provisions had been granted only through the mercies of heaven. God reminded Moses He had always been with them. The Hebrew term קֶרֶב *qereb* is translated as "in the midst of, but in the passion of this moment" is better understood in that God had been in their "inner or inward parts" understanding their most poignant wants and needs. This emotional nature of the Lord reflects upon His knowing every thought and movement in the physical and spiritual nature of Israel. God wanted His people to love Him as their God.

II. God Decides to Punish Israel (Numbers 14:12)

God said that He will smite the Israelites, the Hebrew term (הכנ, *nakah)* meaning to strike them with a preempted assault from which they could never recover. The Hebrew term (דֶּבֶר) deber means "pestilence," but has a more tragic prediction that later will be acknowledged by the entire world—the bubonic plague. This plague, although not described in Hebraic medical terms, ripped apart Europe during the period known as the Dark Ages. Spread by the fleas from infected small animals, especially rats, the illness attacked the people who lived in close proximity. Known as "Black Death," the disease caused the deaths of approximately forty to sixty percent of the population.

This account has moved from Israel having been the nation of promise to their now being faced with a people of missed opportunity. God now planned to dispose

(ירש *yarash*) of Israel, His chosen people, because of their rejection of His love and principles. The aforementioned term is interesting because it reveals a reverse meaning: "to take possession of," which represents taking the land in the seizing of Canaan but also that God would "take possession of" the hearts and minds of the people. Unfortunately, God chose the opposite. He will give His people their freedom to go alone and their choices will not be covered by His security and majesty. He will discipline Israel.

For some it may seem as if God is a vindictive and cantankerous deity who is simply petulant. He is not. God is a loving Lord. God offers His protection and blessings. He was not going to break the covenant sealed through Abraham because of the ungrateful Israelites. As an example, God loved Abraham and listened to his suggestions when God was planning to destroy Sodom and Gomorrah. Recall that Abraham asked if righteous men were found that God would spare the cities. God promised if the prescribed number of virtuous men could be found, the cities would be saved. Unfortunately, the cities were destroyed, but the passages reveal the nature of the relationship between God and Abraham. Likewise, the covenant would not be in danger because of the unrepentant Israelites.

God promises Moses his descendants will become greater, mightier, and more numerous than the group he led. This is an interesting proposition, because Moses could have easily become arrogant and developed a "me first" attitude. However, Moses was sincere and had a heart for God and a heart "like" God's.

III. Moses' Plea for Israel (Numbers 14:13–16)

Moses's answer to the Lord was precious, in that he deferred his opportunity to advance his personal standing in the eyes of the people, both his friends and his enemies. Moses could have flaunted the probability of becoming the progenitor or father of the nation. He could have smirked at his enemies while getting revenge against those who had challenged and rejected his leadership.

Moses, who obviously knew Egyptian culture, responded by saying that when the Egyptians hear of Moses's elevation to the presumed "Father of the Nation," the word of the Spirit of the Lord will be compromised. Moses shared that Israel was saved because of the strength (כֹּחַ *koach*) or might of the Lord and the Israelites could not have delivered themselves from slavery. Moses said, "It was You who brought us out" of the land of bondage and misfortune. It was only the power of the Lord that led (הלע *alah*) the ascension of the people to a higher place in their history. Additionally, it is interesting to note the pronunciation of this term, *a-lah*, is close to the term *Allah*, the Arabic word meaning God! For Moses, Yahweh is the leader of the nation and the world. As with Abraham, Moses was sincere in his love for the people, and it showed in his response to the Lord. Moses realized nothing would have been accomplished in this journey without the Lord's direction.

Moses shared the Egyptians will spread gossip about God's vacillation and refer to Him as an untruthful God who does not keep His promises. Notice that Moses was concerned about the stories that could be told to the inhabitants of this land, the Canaanites and ostensibly to the Israelites as well. Moses was not concerned with what might be thought in Egypt. They are not returning to Egypt, but this reveals Egypt had contact with both the people of Canaan and, remarkably, with the fence-sitters of Israel who remained connected to the country that had enslaved them.

Extolling the nature and power of the Lord, Moses exclaimed the enemies know that God dwells (בשׁי *yashab*) or lives in the midst of the people. Moses acknowledges that Yahweh's appearance (וַיִּן *ayin*) is seen "eye to eye," meaning that all of the people see Him. This is not to say God is seen in His majestic form; however, He is witnessed in a theophanic image, mostly in the cloud(s) (וָנָע *anan*) of fire (שֵׁא *esh*) by both day and night (הָלְיָל *layil*). As God leads the people in this pillar (דומַע *ammud*) or column, He retains both order and hope because all will benefit from the goodness and provision of the Lord. Moses realized Israel's best will be granted because of the leadership of Yahweh and, therefore, does not want God to abdicate His relationship to Israel.

Moreover, if God decided to shun Israel, the people (both Israel and the Canaanites) will ridicule the fame and knowledge of the Lord, who is known by the Egyptians firsthand. God's enemies will delight in spreading the rumor that the God Israel followed from Egypt is a sadistic deity who fooled the people into the wilderness, lowering their status, albeit to that of a second-class citizenship, only to delight in their destruction. Moses surmised the "word on the streets" would be the Lord destroyed (תומ *muth*) Israel by slaughtering (טחשׁ *shachat*) the people because He did not have the power to deliver them the land He had promised. This is not to be confused with God's deliverance of the people to the land; additional rumors could be that Pharaoh freed these former slaves on his own accord for numerous reasons, thus reducing God's influence in the Exodus. The importance for Moses was to refute the idea that Yahweh could not deliver the land of Canaan to Israel because the Canaanites were stronger than Israel and their pagan gods, greater and more powerful than Yahweh!

IV. God's Punishment Revealed (Numbers 14:17–20)

So now, Moses prayed his all-powerful and all-knowing God will be understanding in the judgment of this situation, saying the great power of the Lord is revealed in the vision that is in place (yet is possibly being jeopardized if God changes His mind and rejects Israel). Moses recognized several great attributes of Yahweh: God is slow to anger and is filled with love and kindness for His people. In Moses' praise, he also recognized God as a God of forgiveness and redemption. However, Israel deserved to be punished (עֲשָׂפ *avon*) because it was guilty of its misdeeds. The people must now face the anger (ףאַ *aph*) of the Lord. Israel's crimes were numerous, but their greatest transgression (עֲשָׂפ *pesha*) was a lack of trust and ultimate rejection of God's leadership.

In his prayer, Moses realized he must mitigate the damages because God may choose to forgive but then serve punishment upon the latter generations of the families, such as their grandchildren (םִישֵׁלְשׁ *sheloshim*) and their children after them. Yes, God had the power to forgive (סלח *salach*) or pardon Israel for their actions; however, this power resides only in the wisdom and love of the Lord.

Moses pleaded that God would forgive the issues and guilt of the people according to the greatness and the majesty of His will. Additionally, Moses was reminiscent about times when God had forgiven Israel while in Egypt and during their travels to this land. Moses' attitude was remarkable in that his devotion to the people is cemented in his relationship to the Lord. Moses reveals that trusting and depending on Yahweh is the prudent thing to do. So, the Lord forgave and pardoned the offenders of Israel, subscribing to the recommendations and faith of Moses. Notice Moses does not describe any virtues Israel possessed that would justify God's pardons, but he appeals to God's nature and His plan for them.

The Lesson Applied

Israel tests the patience of God as its people continue to disregard God's commands and reject His sovereignty. They complain and disrespect Moses's leadership, and God has finally had enough. The mere fact this occurred on the part of the Israelites is a stark reality and a lesson that must not be lost to our contemporary generation. As humanity continues to reject the church (in all denominations and faiths), we are breaking God's heart but also placing ourselves in a position to incur His punishment, which will continue to plague our descendants and families. Although Moses asked God to spare Israel from punishment, the punishment was tempered and not completely removed. Believers who are committed to the Lord must be sincere in following His direction.

Let's Talk About It

1. God makes promises to us. What promise did God make to the Israelites? What promises has God made to you?

2. The Israelites complained about the divine leading they received. As believers and followers of Jesus Christ how do we defeat a spirit of grumbling?

The Israelite people had the promises of God in their sight and still showed contempt to the God who brought them out of slavery and supplied their needs throughout their journey. Christians are not immune to being armchair quarterbacks who question decisions from leadership, not motivated out of sincerity or concern, but from a position of jealously and envy. This destroys morale. Sadly, the ones who gripe the most usually do not have any solutions.

Home Daily Devotional Readings
September 30–October 6, 2019

Monday	Tuesday	Wednesday	Thursday	Friday	Saturday	Sunday
Praise God's Works	Mediator of the New Covenant	God Made a Covenant with Us	Remember That You Were There	Make No Heavenly or Earthly Idols	God Will Not Abandon You	Commit to Covenant Obedience
Psalm 111	Hebrews 8:1–12	Deuteronomy 5:1–7	Deuteronomy 4:9–11	Deuteronomy 4:14–24	Deuteronomy 4:25–31	Deuteronomy 4:1–8, 12–13

OBEDIENT FAITH

ADULT TOPIC:
DO AS YOU'RE TOLD

BACKGROUND SCRIPTURE:
DEUTERONOMY 4:1–14; 5:1–21

DEUTERONOMY 4:1–8, 12–13

King James Version

NOW therefore hearken, O Israel, unto the statutes and unto the judgments, which I teach you, for to do them, that ye may live, and go in and possess the land which the LORD God of your fathers giveth you.

2 Ye shall not add unto the word which I command you, neither shall ye diminish ought from it, that ye may keep the commandments of the LORD your God which I command you.

3 Your eyes have seen what the LORD did because of Baalpeor: for all the men that followed Baalpeor, the LORD thy God hath destroyed them from among you.

4 But ye that did cleave unto the LORD your God are alive every one of you this day.

5 Behold, I have taught you statutes and judgments, even as the LORD my God commanded me, that ye should do so in the land whither ye go to possess it.

6 Keep therefore and do them; for this is your wisdom and your understanding in the sight of the nations, which shall hear all these statutes, and say, Surely this great nation is a wise and understanding people.

7 For what nation is there so great, who hath God so nigh unto them, as the LORD our God is in all things that we call upon him for?

8 And what nation is there so great, that hath statutes and judgments so righteous as all this law, which I set before you this day?

• • • • • •

12 And the LORD spake unto you out of the midst of the fire: ye heard the voice of the

New Revised Standard Version

SO now, Israel, give heed to the statutes and ordinances that I am teaching you to observe, so that you may live to enter and occupy the land that the LORD, the God of your ancestors, is giving you.

2 You must neither add anything to what I command you nor take away anything from it, but keep the commandments of the LORD your God with which I am charging you.

3 You have seen for yourselves what the LORD did with regard to the Baal of Peor—how the LORD your God destroyed from among you everyone who followed the Baal of Peor,

4 while those of you who held fast to the LORD your God are all alive today.

5 See, just as the LORD my God has charged me, I now teach you statutes and ordinances for you to observe in the land that you are about to enter and occupy.

6 You must observe them diligently, for this will show your wisdom and discernment to the peoples, who, when they hear all these statutes, will say, "Surely this great nation is a wise and discerning people!"

7 For what other great nation has a god so near to it as the LORD our God is whenever we call to him?

8 And what other great nation has statutes and ordinances as just as this entire law that I am setting before you today?

• • • • • •

12 Then the LORD spoke to you out of the fire. You heard the sound of words but saw no

MAIN THOUGHT: Ye shall not add unto the word which I command you, neither shall ye diminish ought from it, that ye may keep the commandments of the LORD your God which I command you. (Deuteronomy 4:2, KJV)

DEUTERONOMY 4:1–8, 12–13

King James Version	*New Revised Standard Version*
words, but saw no similitude; only ye heard a voice.	**form; there was only a voice.**
13 And he declared unto you his covenant, which he commanded you to perform, even ten commandments; and he wrote them upon two tables of stone.	**13 He declared to you his covenant, which he charged you to observe, that is, the ten commandments; and he wrote them on two stone tablets.**

LESSON SETTING

Time: 1461 B.C.
Place: Kadesh-barnea (Wilderness of Zin)

LESSON OUTLINE

I. Israel is to Obey God's Law (Deuteronomy 4:1–4)
II. Israel Has Been Taught the Law (Deuteronomy 4:5–8)
III. Remembering the Presence of God (Deuteronomy 4:10–13)

UNIFYING PRINCIPLE

People desire and appreciate faithfulness in all of their relationships. How are we to respond to the faithfulness of others? Deuteronomy 4 and 5 set forth obedience as God's expectation of Israel in response to God's faithful deliverance.

INTRODUCTION

In this account, we find Moses reminding Israel about the events at the mountain of Sinai (Horeb), where God issued the Ten Commandments, also known as the Decalogue. Exodus 20 is retold in Deuteronomy 4 and 5 to encourage the present generation to follow the laws of the covenant. Although the present group Moses addresses was not at the original giving of the Commandments, Moses revealed God would be in their presence, recounting how God manifested Himself among them, allowing the people to actually feel His presence and hear His voice.

EXPOSITION

I. ISRAEL IS TO OBEY GOD'S LAW (DEUTERONOMY 4:1–4)

Moses begins this section with a clarion call for Israel to listen or "give heed" to the statutes (חֹק *choq*), rules, but also terms and conditions of the judgments (מִשְׁפָּט *mishpat*), decisions, or regulations God is teaching. These instructions are to be followed explicitly, and the people are expected to serve as examples of God's leadership. Many of these regulations are needed for battle, the taking of the land and the aftermath of the fight that will produce casualties and collateral damage. Notice how Moses tells the people they will take possession of the land. Moses's encouragement positions him as both a coach and cheerleader for the Lord as the land is being given to Israel. At this point, Moses presses the need for each person to execute the Commandments or—as James will later describe—prove themselves by being doers of the word (James 1:22). James relates that those who oppose this mind-set are delusional and must maintain their allegiance to the Lord. For Moses, the rules of godly living will have to be known and understood as Israel lives out God's vision, realizing it is the Lord who will give them the victory.

II. Israel Has Been Taught the Law (Deuteronomy 4:5–8)

Moses reminds Israel he has been faithful to the Lord and has educated them in the laws of God. He taught (דמל *lamad*) them in a series of both faith and life applications, and their skills will become honed by the exercising of their trust in following Yahweh.

One purpose of the Law was to give the Israelites a full life as they obeyed God (vv. 1–4). In verses 5–8, another purpose of the Law is revealed: to make Israel morally and spiritually unique among all the nations and, thereby, draw other nations to the Lord. In contrast with all other nations, Israel was not to be distinguished by its natural resources, wealth, or military might but by its moral skill and close relationship to God, both of which would come from obeying its moral constitution. The imagery here is centered not on the instructor Moses, but on the instructions given to the people, because a lack of confidence continues to emerge in the faithlessness of Israel. Israel is implored to keep these Commandments and start the practice now, in preparation for their entrance into Canaan, where God knows their faith and obedience will be challenged.

Therefore, Israel must keep God's Commandments for their guidance and protection. Although "keep them" reflects the Hebrew term דמל *shomer*, "to keep or observe," the idea is Israel is to honor the Law by observation, through "watching out" for their brothers and sisters in a manner of accountability and support. However, the greatest aspect of this imagery is that the Law, given by Yahweh, was to be held in such high esteem that Israel would actually *guard* these laws in reverence of the Lord. Additionally, Moses repeated they are to live them by doing (השׂע asah), in both the letter of the law and in the spirit in which they were given.

Reaching out to Israel's best, Moses encourages them to seek the wisdom (הָמְכָח (*chokmah*) and also the skills they inherently possess because they are God's chosen people. Israel has the ability to show its understanding (הָנִיב *binah*), discernment, and insight into the direction the Lord has for them. Moses shares with them their understanding is essential because Israel is to be an example for all nations to follow, a perfect example of living within the realm of a loving God. The reaction of the other nations will be to respect Israel as a nation filled with wise men (מָכָח *chakam*) who are skillful and experienced in the Law of the Lord. Additionally, Israel also would be the envy of all other nations because of the Law.

III. Remembering the Presence of God (Deuteronomy 4:10–13)

Verse 10 begins with the word *remember,* which is not part of the original text; however, translators added the term for emphasis and clarity. Moses simply said to Israel, "The day you stood before the Lord," which was understood to mean it was important the message not be lost or forgotten. The essence of this verse relates to the account of Exodus 19, at which time the revelation and the Law were given by the Lord at Mount Sinai, also known as Horeb.

Israel had arrived at the desert of Sinai in the third month, which is estimated to have been during the months of May–June, after their departure from Egypt. As Israel camped at the base of the mountain, Moses ascended the peak to confer with the Lord. Yahweh gave Moses a message to deliver to the newly-freed nation, in that they were to be reminded who had brought them from Egyptian slavery and how God had cared for them during the most trying of circumstances. Now, Israel was to keep the terms of the covenant God provided and adhere to the stipulations that would guide their future.

The covenant, in the form of a suzerain treaty, was a common agreement amongst kings or rulers of nations that stood between themselves and their vassals or the common people. The treaty contained provisions that were designed to be a benefit to all parties, as they explained the roles of both the monarchs and the people. However, each one of these agreements had a proviso that could be viewed as sinister, as it contained clauses for punishment for any of the offending party that reneged on their part of the covenant. These treaties usually favored the rulers because they had the power (which the people lacked) to enforce or punish the offending servants. Yahweh had the power to enforce the provisions of the covenant, which will be evident in the dispersal of His wrath, but He chose instead to love Israel and to allow the people to follow the agreement out of their love for Him.

Moses was instructed to assemble (להק *qahal*) or summon the people so they would themselves hear His words and respect (ארי *yare*) Yahweh. The concept of "fearing" the Lord was based on their devotion to Him and not necessarily their fear of Him; nonetheless, being afraid to disobey God served as a powerful motivator!

Continuing the message of the past events, Moses reminded Israel that "you came near and stood at the foot of the mountain." The position of the people at the foot of the mountain is important, not simply because of their physical whereabouts but because it served to remind the people they were there as a personal witness to what God said. Being a witness to an event is more powerful than simply hearing a second-handed account of what may have happened; problems can arise because people often add to or do not tell the entire story. However, Israel was there to hear the Lord; they were summoned and approached (ברק *qarab*) or "stepped up" to witness the epic event of hearing the voice of God.

The people must have been in awe at the spectacle of a burning mountain whose fire reached to the very heart of the heavens! Moses had experienced this mountain of fire when he received his call to return to Egypt and tell the Pharaoh to "let My people go." Modern images of massive fires in the hills of California may serve to provide contemporary Christians an understanding of the power and devastation of such wildfires that, in many cases, cannot be controlled. The present image was a frightening scene of darkness (לֶפָּרֶע *araphel*) that provoked emotions of deep gloom and dark clouds that encompassed the entire smoke-filled area.

Then Israel witnessed a scene that is rare in the pantheon of people who have encountered the presence of God. As the theophany occurred—a visual manifestation of God to humans—He spoke to them from a cloud or pillar of fire, which served as a shield to shadow His awesomeness and protect the people from the power of His majesty (which otherwise would have been lethal). They could not see the form or image of God; however, they heard His voice. As an eyewitness to such an event, Israel surely realized that it was in the presence of an all-powerful God!

The Lesson Applied

Moses' reminder of the day God issued the Ten Commandments (Decalogue) was not new. The account found in Deuteronomy 4:13 was restated in Deuteronomy 5. The Commandments of Exodus 20 represent an eclipsed period of approximately forty years, and Moses' comments were that God made the covenant at Horeb (Sinai). The agreement was not only to the people of that day but extended to the people of the present and future generations and descendants of the nation (Deut. 5:2–3). These laws and Commandments were honored by God, but sadly, eventually would be rejected and dishonored by Israel, whom God would continue to love and eventually redeem in the person of Jesus Christ.

Let's Talk About It

1. What have you seen God do in your life and the lives of others that helps you continue to trust and obey Him?

2. How is obeying God important to living a meaningful life?

God has established rules for humankind that are designed for optimal living. His laws are not designed to prevent us from enjoyment in life. Instead, when we live within the parameters of obedience to Him, we can have the assurance of a meaningful life.

3. What are some of the blessings you have received from being obedient to God?

God loves His people and continues to work in the lives of believers and followers of Jesus Christ. In preparation for the surrendering of ourselves to Him into a life of eternal bliss, God's love is graciously given to us. Over time, mostly due to the actions of humans, God, in His infinite mercy, will amend His commandments in order to maintain a relationship with humanity. Under the old covenant, people sacrificed animals to symbolize the bond between God and His people. Because of the sacrifice made by Jesus, animal sacrifices are no long needed for worship and forgiveness. He is our once-and-for-all sacrifice..

Home Daily Devotional Readings
October 7–13, 2019

Monday	Tuesday	Wednesday	Thursday	Friday	Saturday	Sunday
Keep God's Commandments	On the Mountain with Jesus	Prophetic Examples of Faithfulness	Paul in Faithfulness Restores Life	God-sent Raven Feeds Elijah	Elijah Restores Life to Widow's Son	Widow's Faithfulness Rewarded
Proverbs 3:1–10	Matthew 17:1–7	Luke 4:24–30	Acts 20:7–12	1 Kings 17:1–7	1 Kings 17:17–24	1 Kings 17:8–16

BLESSED FOR FAITHFULNESS

ADULT TOPIC:
DOING RIGHT PAYS OFF

BACKGROUND SCRIPTURE:
1 KINGS 17:1–24

1 KINGS 17:8–16

King James Version

AND the word of the LORD came unto him, saying,

9 Arise, get thee to Zarephath, which belongeth to Zidon, and dwell there: behold, I have commanded a widow woman there to sustain thee.

10 So he arose and went to Zarephath. And when he came to the gate of the city, behold, the widow woman was there gathering of sticks: and he called to her, and said, Fetch me, I pray thee, a little water in a vessel, that I may drink.

11 And as she was going to fetch it, he called to her, and said, Bring me, I pray thee, a morsel of bread in thine hand.

12 And she said, As the LORD thy God liveth, I have not a cake, but an handful of meal in a barrel, and a little oil in a cruse: and, behold, I am gathering two sticks, that I may go in and dress it for me and my son, that we may eat it, and die.

13 And Elijah said unto her, Fear not; go and do as thou hast said: but make me thereof a little cake first, and bring it unto me, and after make for thee and for thy son.

14 For thus saith the LORD God of Israel, The barrel of meal shall not waste, neither shall the cruse of oil fail, until the day that the LORD sendeth rain upon the earth.

15 And she went and did according to the saying of Elijah: and she, and he, and her house, did eat many days.

16 And the barrel of meal wasted not, neither did the cruse of oil fail, according to the word of the LORD, which he spake by Elijah.

New Revised Standard Version

THEN the word of the LORD came to him, saying,

9 "Go now to Zarephath, which belongs to Sidon, and live there; for I have commanded a widow there to feed you."

10 So he set out and went to Zarephath. When he came to the gate of the town, a widow was there gathering sticks; he called to her and said, "Bring me a little water in a vessel, so that I may drink."

11 As she was going to bring it, he called to her and said, "Bring me a morsel of bread in your hand."

12 But she said, "As the LORD your God lives, I have nothing baked, only a handful of meal in a jar, and a little oil in a jug; I am now gathering a couple of sticks, so that I may go home and prepare it for myself and my son, that we may eat it, and die."

13 Elijah said to her, "Do not be afraid; go and do as you have said; but first make me a little cake of it and bring it to me, and afterwards make something for yourself and your son.

14 For thus says the LORD the God of Israel: The jar of meal will not be emptied and the jug of oil will not fail until the day that the LORD sends rain on the earth."

15 She went and did as Elijah said, so that she as well as he and her household ate for many days.

16 The jar of meal was not emptied, neither did the jug of oil fail, according to the word of the LORD that he spoke by Elijah.

MAIN THOUGHT: And the barrel of meal wasted not, neither did the cruse of oil fail, according to the word of the LORD, which he spake by Elijah. (1 Kings 17:16, KJV)

LESSON SETTING

Time: 884 B.C.
Place: Zarephath (Phoenicia)

LESSON OUTLINE

I. Elijah Is Directed to Go to Zarephath (1 Kings 17:8–10)
II. Elijah Asks the Impossible (1 Kings 17:11–12)
III. The Blessings of the Lord Revealed (1 Kings 17:13–16)

Unifying Principle

When people are denied the necessities of life, they may give up hope. What is the reward for faithful obedience in times of hardship? The widow of Zarephath faithfully ministered to God's prophet, and she was miraculously provided for throughout the time of famine.

Introduction

On occasion, God places us in positions we do not want to handle. In this episode, the Lord instructs Elijah to leave the brook that once sustained him but has now dried up. He must go to Zarephath of Sidon, where a widow will give him food. Zarephath is located in Phoenicia, the heart of Baalism. Here, Yahweh will defeat Baal in his own territory, and God's people will fare better under Yahweh than under Baal. Elijah will encounter a widow and her son who need God's help and receive assistance from the Lord. Because Yahweh lives—and Baal does not—Elijah possesses power Ahab, Jezebel, and their prophets do not.

Exposition

I. Elijah is Directed to Go to Zarephath (1 Kings 17:8–10)

The prophet Elijah, at God's command, is not provided with the full extent of this mission—he must move on blind faith in the Lord—inasmuch as the sentence actually reads he was directed to go toward Zarephath, which is of Sidon, and look there for a widow (הָנָמְלאַ *almanah*) who will sustain (לוכ *kul*) or provide for him. The *New Revised Standard Version* is implicit in the immediacy of the command, saying, "Go now to Zarephath," which does not reveal how long Elijah is expected to remain in Zarephath but suggests his stay is long enough to experience the widow and the lesson of God's provisions. *The New Jerusalem Bible* renders the expression "to give you [Elijah] food."

Zarephath actually is located in Phoenicia and Sidon, another city that seems to hold more importance as the city-state power of the region and explains the phrase that refers to Zarephath as belonging to or "of Sidon." An ancient Phoenician city-state, Sidon is located at modern Ṣaidā, approximately twenty-two miles north of Tyre and an equal distance south of Beirut, Lebanon. Like other Phoenician cities, the people of Sidon were dependent on sea trade for their livelihood.

Sidon is called the firstborn of Canaan at Genesis 10:15 (see 1 Chron. 1:13; KJV "Zidon"); in the Old Testament, Phoenicians in general are commonly referred to as "Sidonians." Both Jesus and Paul visited Sidon (Mark 7:31; Acts 27:3), and Jesus compares Gentile Sidon favorably to Jewish cities of Galilee that had not responded to his preaching (Matt. 11:21–22). Jesus would later recall the famine was caused by this drought when He spoke of Elijah. Additionally, Jesus would provide the time line as to the extent of the famine saying, "There were many widows in Israel in the days of Elijah, when the sky was shut up for three years and six months, when a great famine came over all the land; and yet Elijah was sent to none of them, but only to Zarephath, in the land of Sidon, to a woman who was a widow" (Luke 4:25–26).

II. Elijah Asks the Impossible (1 Kings 17:11–12)

The woman obviously agreed and went to get the water, which meant either there was a well or she had brought some water in some kind of vessel for her use during her task of gathering wood. As she was going to "fetch" (לקח *laqach*) or go get it, Elijah now asks the woman what seems to be an improbable request. The NASB rendering could be confused as alluding to the fact she already had a piece of bread in her hand while working. However, the phrase "please bring me a piece of bread in your hand" does not mean literally she already was holding a piece of bread while gathering wood. It simply means Elijah requested she give him a piece of her bread that possibly was part of a lunch she had packed. He asked her to get it "in [her] hand" (יָד *yad*), and he did not ask if he could go and get it himself. The amount of bread is described as a morsel (פַּת *path*), possibly amounting to mere crumbs. This piece of bread obviously is quite small and reflects the status of the woman's poverty. Some theologians argue one should not say "a slice of bread," since this piece would have been broken off by hand.

Elijah was rebuffed because the woman exclaimed she did not have any bread. She had water or access to water, which may have indicated the woman was going to get Elijah water from a well (or an animal trough) that actually belonged to the town. If this is accurate, the widow did not have any bread and also did not own or possess any source of water! The wooden statement is she only had enough flour (קֶמַח *qemach*), which probably was barley because wheat was a more expensive grain, for that which would have filled the palm (כַּף *kaph*) or hollow of her hand, again demonstrating her dire state of poverty. The NKJV translates that she has flour in a bin and oil in a jar, which describes what she had at home.

Her statement "as the Lord your God lives" (חַי *chay*), or is alive and living, is more accurately understood as "in the life of Yahweh." The woman immediately exclaims she does not have any bread (מָעוֹג *magog*), or that which later will be asked for in the form of a cake. (Pronunciation of the term *magog* should not be confused as the enemies of God or the Messiah found in Rev. 20:8.) Additionally, the woman has a small amount of oil (ןמֶּשׁ *shemen*); the expression *ha she-men* indicates the type of oil described is olive oil, and examples of this are found in 1 Kings 17:12, 14, 16. However, the term for *olive* (זַיִת *zayith*) does not appear in verse 12. (See Exod. 30:24.) The widow describes she has the oil in a jar (צַפַּחַת *tsappachath*) or jug, not to be confused with the earlier use of כְּלִי *keli*, meaning "vessel" or "cup."

Notice the widow has gathered only two (שְׁנַיִם *shettayim*) sticks, or "a couple," as the NKJV translates. Nevertheless, the image of her picking up only a "few" sticks (such as the NASB and NIV translate), or an indeterminate number, provides a glimpse into the woman's lack of strength or frailty, as she is already in the stages of starvation. Verse 12 introduces the mention of (but not the physical appearance of) her son (ןב *ben*); and the language does not use the term *yeled*, meaning a young "child." The sticks obviously are for firewood that she may cook one last meal, which she and her son will eat (לכא *akal*) and then die (תום *muth*). The expression "that we may eat, and die" does not refer to Elijah.

III. The Blessings of the Lord Revealed (1 Kings 17:13–16)

At this juncture, the scene seems to move to the home of the widow, as Elijah now displays the confidence and faith he has in the Lord, comforting her fear (ירא *yare*) and telling her "not to be afraid" of what she perceives as the end of her life. In asking the woman to give what she does not have, Elijah requests she prepare the meager meal, in the form of a bread-cake, and give it to him first; then afterward, make one for herself and her son. The term *bread-cake* possibly is used to describe a loaf of bread. The Hebrew noun rendered "cake" (also in 1 Kings19:6) refers to a flat, round loaf baked on a hot stone or hot coals. We should avoid giving the impression of a light, sweet dessert-type cake since this loaf contained no sugar. Recall, the woman stated she had just enough ingredients for one meal, which would be for herself and her son only! The prophet is asking for the impossible and furthermore, taking advantage of an impoverished widow and her equally destitute son.

Notice the son seems incapable of caring for his mother or himself. Although nothing is known about the condition of the son, obviously he is without a source of income and may be physically or mentally destitute. Nevertheless, he is, along with his starving mother, preparing to die.

This action may seem selfish on the part of Elijah. This family is living in extreme poverty and does not seem to have any way out of their status. They have given up all hope of living and have decided to meet their fate, which is death by starvation. Their plight will soon be miraculously resolved!

Elijah's answer to the plight of the widow and her family is to stress the blessings and benevolence of the Lord, who is poised to save the family and Elijah from starvation. He reveals to her the bowl of flour will not "come to an end" (הלכ *kalah*), or be finished or exhausted, nor shall the amount of the jar of oil decrease (רסח *chaser*) or become empty until the drought ends, which will be the day the Lord sends relief in the form of rain upon the land. The phrase "the jug of oil will not run dry" is found in the language of the NIV and NAB (*New American Bible*), which stresses the control God exhibits over nature. The subsequent phrase "until the day that the Lord sends rain upon the earth" finds the emphasis of the text on the expression "until the day," which should not be interpreted that the flour and oil would cease to exist on the very day the rains started. Rather, the intent is to assure the woman there would be sufficient flour and oil until the time when the earth would produce these things again.

The text leaves implicit the significance of the rain, as compared with the *New Living Translation* which is rendered "until the time when the Lord sends rain and the crops grow again." "Upon the earth" is literally "upon the face of the earth."All that was prophesied through the word of Elijah became fact in that both the household and Elijah were supplied food for many days, which (for the widow and her son) would turn out to be years to come, until the Lord brought relief from the drought that was caused by the lack of rain.

The Lesson Applied

When we look around to limited resources and think, "Why should I give to this, or why should I support that?" we become the reason we have limited resources. Elijah encountered a woman who was anxious about the lack in her life and initially displayed her fear and misunderstanding of the situation through her reluctance to share the portions of her meal. People who believe their lives are in jeopardy often will resort to a "me first" attitude that some may refer to as a survival instinct or skill. This account should not be viewed simply as a "feel good" narrative describing Jehovah-jireh (Gen. 22:14)—the Lord who provides—but a lesson that teaches us "you cannot beat God giving." It also conveys trust in God displayed through tenacious faith.

Let's Talk About It

1. How does God meet your needs?

2. How do the people in your life know you are a child of God? How is your faith in God evident to others?

3. What step of faith do you feel you need to take at this particular moment in your life? What direction do you need to walk in faith?

When a moment of severe weather approaches our communities, we easily can witness the shelves of our local grocery stores being stripped bare of daily food provisions under the guise of "stocking up," which in truth, can serve as a mask for the concepts of fear, hoarding, and greed. Additionally, many gas stations are guilty of price gouging gasoline, food items, and water during moments of severe weather and disastrous situations—situations in which the need of the people most adversely affected may be dominated by the amount of the supply.

As Christians, we serve a God who has a surplus of resources that are never in short supply. When we are asked to be givers, we should follow His instructions to the letter because we can be the cause of obstructed blessings for ourselves. We never should withhold anything God requires of us, so our jars never shall be exhausted.

Home Daily Devotional Readings

October 14–20, 2019

Monday	Tuesday	Wednesday	Thursday	Friday	Saturday	Sunday
The Prayer of Faith Is Powerful	Your Faith Has Made You Well	Believers Are Blessed	Bartimaeus Healed by Faith	Faith Is Expressed Through Actions	Jesus Raises Widow's Son	Jesus Heralds the Centurion's Healing Faith
James 5:13–18	Mark 5:25–34	Galatians 3:6–9	Mark 10:46–52	Luke 6:46–49	Luke 7:11–17	Luke 7:1–10

FAITH CAN HEAL

ADULT TOPIC:
JUST SAY THE WORD

BACKGROUND SCRIPTURE:
LUKE 7:1–10

LUKE 7:1–10

King James Version

NOW when he had ended all his sayings in the audience of the people, he entered into Capernaum.

2 And a certain centurion's servant, who was dear unto him, was sick, and ready to die.

3 And when he heard of Jesus, he sent unto him the elders of the Jews, beseeching him that he would come and heal his servant.

4 And when they came to Jesus, they besought him instantly, saying, That he was worthy for whom he should do this:

5 For he loveth our nation, and he hath built us a synagogue.

6 Then Jesus went with them. And when he was now not far from the house, the centurion sent friends to him, saying unto him, Lord, trouble not thyself: for I am not worthy that thou shouldest enter under my roof:

7 Wherefore neither thought I myself worthy to come unto thee: but say in a word, and my servant shall be healed.

8 For I also am a man set under authority, having under me soldiers, and I say unto one, Go, and he goeth; and to another, Come, and he cometh; and to my servant, Do this, and he doeth it.

9 When Jesus heard these things, he marvelled at him, and turned him about, and said unto the people that followed him, I say unto you, I have not found so great faith, no, not in Israel.

10 And they that were sent, returning to the house, found the servant whole that had been sick.

New Revised Standard Version

AFTER Jesus had finished all his sayings in the hearing of the people, he entered Capernaum.

2 A centurion there had a slave whom he valued highly, and who was ill and close to death.

3 When he heard about Jesus, he sent some Jewish elders to him, asking him to come and heal his slave.

4 When they came to Jesus, they appealed to him earnestly, saying, "He is worthy of having you do this for him,

5 for he loves our people, and it is he who built our synagogue for us."

6 And Jesus went with them, but when he was not far from the house, the centurion sent friends to say to him, "Lord, do not trouble yourself, for I am not worthy to have you come under my roof;

7 therefore I did not presume to come to you. But only speak the word, and let my servant be healed.

8 For I also am a man set under authority, with soldiers under me; and I say to one, 'Go,' and he goes, and to another, 'Come,' and he comes, and to my slave, 'Do this,' and the slave does it."

9 When Jesus heard this he was amazed at him, and turning to the crowd that followed him, he said, "I tell you, not even in Israel have I found such faith."

10 When those who had been sent returned to the house, they found the slave in good health.

MAIN THOUGHT: Wherefore neither thought I myself worthy to come unto thee: but say in a word, and my servant shall be healed. (Luke 7:7, KJV)

LESSON SETTING

Time: A.D. 27
Place: Capernaum

LESSON OUTLINE

I. **The Centurion's Servant is Ill (Luke 7:1–5)**
II. **Jesus Heals the Centurion's Servant (Luke 7:6–10)**

Unifying Principle

People often have faith in another person based on the good reputation of that person. But how does one authentically demonstrate trust in someone else? The centurion in Luke demonstrated his trust in Jesus' ability to heal by telling Him just to speak a word.

Introduction

The account presented in this section reveals a man who placed his faith in the power of Jesus. Having never witnessed a miracle of Jesus personally, the faith of the centurion amazes even Jesus. As a pagan Gentile, the centurion did not have a cultural background that would have permitted him to believe mere faith could possibly heal his servant, who also just happened to be a valued member of the household.

The backstory has several interesting subplots, such as the Jewish elders currying favor with both the centurion and Jesus; the unspoken role and influence of the centurion's servant; and the healing of the servant itself. It is evident, however, the centurion allowed his faith in Jesus Christ to override any inhibitions he initially may have had in approaching Jesus with a request to heal the sick servant. Nonetheless, the bold and faithful action of the centurion allowed Jesus to contrast the faith of the Jews to that of this sincere Gentile.

Exposition

I. The Centurion's Servant is Ill (Luke 7:1–5)

Luke chronicles the movement of Jesus, who had completed the mission of preaching and teaching several great discourses, one being the Sermon on the Plain. This series of messages accomplished part of His mission to the Gentiles. His voice was firmly placed in the ears of the people, as was the case after which He exclaimed that the words of Isaiah 61:1 had been fulfilled upon their hearing (Luke 4:18–21). With the completion of this series of messages, Jesus departs for and enters Capernaum, His unofficial base of operations and His adopted hometown.

Living in Capernaum was a centurion, a captain of one hundred men, who is not the typical commander. Recall the entire region was under the military occupation and control of the Roman Empire. The people, both Jews and Gentiles, were considered subhuman, constantly being degraded and denied the privileges of living in a free society. Anyone connected with the Roman army was to be avoided and considered dangerous. However, this commander is facing a situation that will reveal the goodness of his humanity and compassion.

As part of his circle, he has a slave who is identified as someone important. Luke does not identify the slave as a woman or a man, which could determine the value of the servant. This scenario is not uncommon, and it is more than likely the centurion had more than one slave; however, this particular slave was highlighted. For reasons not documented, this servant was deemed precious in the sight of the centurion. It is noteworthy to observe how different the treatment of slaves ranged in diverse households. Some slaves might be treated harshly, as their status could be that of indentured servants working off a debt for their freedom; whereas, other slaves actually might be treated as co-laborers, working alongside their owners. Nevertheless, any form of slavery was an abhorrent position that was unhealthy to the lives of the slaves and their so-called owners. Although the arrangement of the centurion's operation is not discussed, he was worried about the servant who was extremely sick.

The Greek term used to describe the servant's state is κακῶς *kakos*, meaning he is "badly," cruelly sick to the extent he is on the verge of death. The centurion is worried because of the value of the slave. The focus of this account, however, is not on the significance of the servant but on the heart of the centurion.

The centurion has the best military and civilian physicians at his disposal, and it is probable these medical men were summoned to treat the slave. However, despite all their efforts, it became obvious their treatments were not effective in the healing of the servant. The centurion is informed by someone, possibly another servant in his household, about a person who could heal the servant. This would not be the first occurrence when a person of the faith, who just happened to be a slave or someone's servant, introduced his master to the saving power of the Lord. Recall the account of Naaman, the leprous "commander of the army of the king of Syria" (see 2 Kings 5), who was informed by an Israelite slave girl that his leprosy could be cured by the prophet Elisha in Samaria by immersing himself seven times in the Jordan River. Although he felt slighted, Naaman heeded his servant's pleas and complied with the prophet's directive, and his leprosy vanished. The commander praised the God of Israel, and Jesus recalled the incident as an example of God's care for a Gentile (Luke 4:27). In this case, it is important for the centurion to get help for his slave.

Upon hearing the healing stories of Jesus, he sought out some of the Jewish elders (πρεσβύτερος, *presbuteros*)—this word is from where the term *presbyter* or *presbyterian* originates—to locate Jesus and have Him come, as the original language reads, "to save his slave." The condition of the servant is highlighted because the Greek term used is διασῴζω *diasozo*, meaning "to rescue, save, or to safely bring through a danger." The servant obviously was dying, and all attempts to restore him had failed; however, the message the centurion received was Jesus could rebuff the specter of death hovering over the servant and thoroughly deliver the slave from death. Whatever the message given to the centurion, his desperation to have the servant healed made him seek out the man known as Jesus.

II. Jesus Heals the Centurion's Servant (Luke 7:6–10)

As Jesus and the elders began to walk toward the centurion's house, Jesus noticed some of the centurion's friends were coming to meet the group. The encounter took place far away (μακράν *makran*), but not too distant (ἀπέχω *apecho*), from where the servant was ill. The friends knew they were looking for Jesus and probably had faith He would save their sick friend. However, they were sent with a message that could be misconstrued as possibly having prohibited the healing the servant was in desperate need of (the healing only Jesus could provide). They were commanded to say to Jesus, "Lord, do not trouble (σκύλλω *skullo*) Yourself or bother to come to the house." The Greek σκύλλω οὐ actually can be translated as "trouble yourself not" to come to the house.

With this message, the centurion is offering respect because there was an implicit agreement Jewish people would defile themselves by entering the house of an infidel. Jesus, however, did not share in this thought process. Instead, He would be deemed guilty of consorting with so-called unsavory characters, such as He did when eating with Matthew and allowing a certain woman to anoint Him. Not to equate the centurion with Jesus, but the heart of the man is becoming clearer; he obviously is a man of compassion, and his treatment of his servants seems to be genuine. Luke refers to the ones he sent out to meet Jesus as friends, although they probably were fellow servants who would have been given the task of searching out Jesus, not the nobles of the house. Recall that Jesus will tell His disciples, "I no longer call you slaves (servants), for the slave does not know what his master is doing; but I have called you friends, for all things I have heard from My Father, I have made known to you" (John 15:15). These servants understood the gravity of their fellow servant's illness and wished Jesus to come to their friend.

At some point in the narrative, the centurion appears and takes over the conversation with Jesus. Luke does not provide any information to make anyone believe the centurion knew Jesus, but it is obvious he knew who Jesus was! The army veteran tells Jesus he does not consider himself worthy to have Jesus enter his home or to come to Jesus; however, as a sign of his faith, he states all Jesus has to do is simply say the word, and his servant will be healed (ἰάομαι *iaomai*) or cured.

This verse becomes an interesting component in the account because it provides several answers to previous questions. First, the sex of the servant will continue to be masked; however, the original Greek term παῖς *pais* is translated as a "child" but does not identify boy or girl. Although the English translation of verse 7 refers to the word *servant*, that term is actually *doulos*, not *pais*. Therefore, the servant this centurion loves is a child, but we do not know the age of the child and must take into account the age of maturity in this culture—twelve or thirteen years old is not the same as we accept in this present society.

The centurion defined his position to Jesus, not so much as in detailing the scope of his military duties but in an abbreviated tense as to who he was, by exclaiming he was a man of great authority. The term used here to describe his position is ὑπό *hupo*, meaning "under, by, or, under obligation to command troops and maintain civilian order." Additionally, this means he is placed under authority from Rome to command in the manner of his superiors, thus clarifying the phrase "under authority." Therefore, the centurion has the power to act (ἐξουσία exousia) in the name of Rome, saying that "when I say to this one, 'Go!' And he goes." He is not shy in the description of his rank (however sincere his proclamations); nevertheless, his person pales in comparison to Jesus. While the centurion has the authority and power to command people, Jesus has the power, authority, and dominion over all cosmic elements and life itself. This centurion may never have faced defeat on the battlefield in subjugating civilian resistance, but he realizes if his servant is to be healed, he has to place his faith in the hands of Jesus.

Jesus was astonished at the sincerity of the centurion and the genuine concern for his servant. However, the central message of verse 9 is a focus on the faith displayed by the centurion. As Jesus listened to the man's statement, He (Jesus) turns (στρέφω *strepho*) not only His direction but also His attention to the crowd (ὄχλος *ochlos*) or multitude that had been following (ἀκολουθέω *akoloutheo*) Him. Jesus' statement to the crowd was that in all of Israel, He could not find (εὑρίσκω *heurisko*), or had not found, a man of such faith. In both his statements and his actions, the centurion's faith (πίστις *pistis*) revealed he completely trusted Jesus and Jesus' ability to heal the sick servant in his household. The narrative never moves to reveal any command or suggestion that Jesus must actually and physically go to the centurion's house. The belief in Jesus was so thorough in the assessment that He was in complete command of the situation even at a distance.

This is another teaching moment for those who witnessed this miraculous event. Jesus describes His statement as one of great faith in that this Gentile's faith was a welcome contrast to the unbelief of the Jews. The lesson was not lost, as the crowd would witness such an event and hence realize their faith or lack thereof. Jesus was stating it is difficult to find people with such a high degree of faith who would believe if Jesus simply would speak the word, the need would be fulfilled and occur at His command! Although the centurion had not said it, he believed Jesus would alleviate the situation by whatever methods He chose.

Notice Jesus never physically goes to the centurion's house. Jesus never verbally recites some "magical chant." Moreover, Jesus never actually sees nor touches the sick servant. Yet, the overriding belief, at this point in the biblical narrative, before any news of the servant having been healed, is that the servant will in truth be healed!

The account reaches its conclusion by the witness of the power of faith the centurion had in Jesus as he and his group of servants now prepare to return (ὑποστρέφω *hupostrepho*), or "turned back" to the house, without any evidence of Jesus fulfilling his request. On the way, the centurion and the rest of the household servants are met by other members of the household bearing great news that the healing has taken place! Previously, the concern was a near-death servant; however, a miracle has occurred, and the servant-child has been healed or has been found to be healthy (ὑγιαίνω *hugiaino*). The pinnacle of the centurion's faith was realized when he and all of the servants who had been in the company of Jesus arrived at the house and found the servant to be in good health (NASB); they found the servant well (ESV), or found the servant well who had been sick (NKJV).

The Lesson Applied

The centurions found throughout the New Testament offer a positive perspective on how a Roman military officer is able to become closely aligned to the movement of Jesus Christ and a believer of the faith. As an example, Luke mentions two centurions by name: Cornelius, the first Gentile convert (Acts 10:1, 22, 30, 44) and Julius, the officer charged to secure Paul's arrival at Rome (27:1, 3, 43). Another who supervised the crucifixion of Jesus and the other two men confessed, after Christ had died, that He truly was the "Son of God" (Matt. 27:54; Luke 23:47). Though the names of other centurions are not given, they are treated favorably as believers in Jesus Christ. However the challenge is always to become a follower of Jesus and not just merely a believer in Jesus Christ.

Let's Talk About It

1. **Jesus Christ shows us the only thing He is assessing is whether or not we have real true faith in Him. Where and when are you tempted to think God will bless you only because of your good works?**
2. **The centurion showed a level of faith that amazed Jesus. What might you need to think, say, or do to have Jesus Christ amazed at your level of faith?**
3. **Sometimes people may not go to your church or be a part of your particular faith community but still have a sincere love for God. The centurion was neither a Jew, a member of the Jewish community, or a disciple of Jesus Christ. His faith in Jesus was unusual. Who have you experienced outside of your community who had an usual faith in God?**

All persons are originally created by God and have an inner desire to return to Him, regardless of their position in life. The kindness of the centurion may have been initially questioned because a servant was consider to be the property of another person; however, "centurion" was only his work and not who he was as a person. The unnamed centurion truly was sincere about the sickness of his child-servant and sought Jesus' intervention. Additionally, the other servants revealed their compassion for their debilitated comrade. All of humanity is better served when we are able to look upon each other with the love of the Lord, cementing our concern and care for each other as people and not mere objects or things. What acts of kindness, especially toward those unlike us, have we displayed recently? Seek to love God and live at peace with all persons.

Home Daily Devotional Readings

October 21–27, 2019

Monday	Tuesday	Wednesday	Thursday	Friday	Saturday	Sunday
God's Salvation for All People	Your Sins Are Forgiven	Salvation Requires Enduring Witness	All Who Call Will Be Saved	Treat Each Other Like Jesus Does	Leaders Reject God's Messenger	Her Many Sins Have Been Forgiven
Isaiah 52:7–10	Luke 5:20–26	Mark 13:9–13	Romans 10:5–13	John 13:12–20	Luke 7:24–30	Luke 7:37–48

FAITH SAVES

ADULT TOPIC:
EXTRAVAGANT LOVE

BACKGROUND SCRIPTURE:
LUKE 7:36–50

LUKE 7:37–48

King James Version

AND, behold, a woman in the city, which was a sinner, when she knew that Jesus sat at meat in the Pharisee's house, brought an alabaster box of ointment,

38 And stood at his feet behind him weeping, and began to wash his feet with tears, and did wipe them with the hairs of her head, and kissed his feet, and anointed them with the ointment.

39 Now when the Pharisee which had bidden him saw it, he spake within himself, saying, This man, if he were a prophet, would have known who and what manner of woman this is that toucheth him: for she is a sinner.

40 And Jesus answering said unto him, Simon, I have somewhat to say unto thee. And he saith, Master, say on.

41 There was a certain creditor which had two debtors: the one owed five hundred pence, and the other fifty.

42 And when they had nothing to pay, he frankly forgave them both. Tell me therefore, which of them will love him most?

43 Simon answered and said, I suppose that he, to whom he forgave most. And he said unto him, Thou hast rightly judged.

44 And he turned to the woman, and said unto Simon, Seest thou this woman? I entered into thine house, thou gavest me no water for my feet: but she hath washed my feet with tears, and wiped them with the hairs of her head.

New Revised Standard Version

AND a woman in the city, who was a sinner, having learned that he was eating in the Pharisee's house, brought an alabaster jar of ointment.

38 She stood behind him at his feet, weeping, and began to bathe his feet with her tears and to dry them with her hair. Then she continued kissing his feet and anointing them with the ointment.

39 Now when the Pharisee who had invited him saw it, he said to himself, "If this man were a prophet, he would have known who and what kind of woman this is who is touching him—that she is a sinner."

40 Jesus spoke up and said to him, "Simon, I have something to say to you." "Teacher," he replied, "speak."

41 "A certain creditor had two debtors; one owed five hundred denarii, and the other fifty.

42 When they could not pay, he canceled the debts for both of them. Now which of them will love him more?"

43 Simon answered, "I suppose the one for whom he canceled the greater debt." And Jesus said to him, "You have judged rightly."

44 Then turning toward the woman, he said to Simon, "Do you see this woman? I entered your house; you gave me no water for my feet, but she has bathed my feet with her tears and dried them with her hair.

MAIN THOUGHT: And stood at his feet behind him weeping, and began to wash his feet with tears, and did wipe them with the hairs of her head, and kissed his feet, and anointed them with the ointment. (Luke 7:38, KJV)

Luke 7:37–48

King James Version	*New Revised Standard Version*
45 Thou gavest me no kiss: but this woman since the time I came in hath not ceased to kiss my feet.	**45 You gave me no kiss, but from the time I came in she has not stopped kissing my feet.**
46 My head with oil thou didst not anoint: but this woman hath anointed my feet with ointment.	**46 You did not anoint my head with oil, but she has anointed my feet with ointment.**
47 Wherefore I say unto thee, Her sins, which are many, are forgiven; for she loved much: but to whom little is forgiven, the same loveth little.	**47 Therefore, I tell you, her sins, which were many, have been forgiven; hence she has shown great love. But the one to whom little is forgiven, loves little."**
48 And he said unto her, Thy sins are forgiven.	**48 Then he said to her, "Your sins are forgiven."**

LESSON SETTING

Time: A.D. 27
Place: Capernaum

LESSON OUTLINE

I. A Woman Invades Jesus' Dinner (Luke 7:37–38)
II. The Host of the Dinner Reacts (Luke 7:39)
III. The Parable of Two Debtors (Luke 7:40–43)
IV. Jesus Forgives the Woman (Luke 7:44–48)

Unifying Principle

People often respond to forgiveness with loving acts. What can we do to show gratitude to those who forgive us? In Luke, the sinful woman showed her gratitude to Jesus by washing His feet with her tears and anointing Him with expensive oil.

Introduction

The account of Jesus visiting the home of a Pharisee named Simon is interesting. Jesus was an invited a dinner guest but did not receive the basic cultural hospitality of the period. Somehow, an unnamed woman enters Simon's house and treats Jesus as royalty. She sees in Jesus a Savior who is the answer to her issues. Jesus rebukes Simon's treatment of the woman by relating a parable that is an example of forgiveness.

Exposition

I. A Woman Invades Jesus' Dinner (Luke 7:37–38)

Jesus encountered a group of disciples who were aligned with John the Baptist. These men wanted to know if Jesus was the "Expected One" about whom John had spoken. Jesus must have convinced them because they went back to their group satisfied. Jesus had spoken highly of John, saying there was no greater man than John (Luke 7:28), acknowledging his role and his dedication to righteousness and the Kingdom. However, all of the people who were in the periphery were not pleased. Several Pharisees (Φαρισαῖος *Pharisaios*) and lawyers (νομικός *nomikos*)—not scribes (γραμματεύς *gramma-*

teus) who often are associated with the Pharisees—who had not been baptized by John, rejected the purpose of both John and Jesus. One of these men invited Jesus to dinner, and Jesus accepted.

Upon entering the home of the Pharisee, Jesus took His place and reclined in the normal eating position of the culture. Somehow, a woman who was a resident of the city learned Jesus was in the home of this particular Pharisee, whom Luke identifies as Simon. The way the woman was able to gain entry into the residence is not mentioned; nevertheless, she is able to maneuver herself into the dining area. The woman was not invited, and she had a shady reputation among the populace seeing as she was referred to as a sinner (ἁμαρτωλός *hamartolos*). Our contemporary understanding of her label may seem insignificant, for "all have fallen short of the glory of God"; but in their derisive scorn for the woman, she was to be avoided. The unnamed woman also was considered to be unclean and may have been a prostitute in the city.

The woman had sought Jesus and brought an alabaster container filled with an expensive oil. Mark identifies this costly ointment as pure nard (spikenard) that was valued at three hundred denarii, the annual wages of a day laborer. In the Matthean account, the oil is not identified; but the Greek term in verse 37 is μύρον *my-ron*, translated as "ointment, perfume, or perfumed oil."

Although the way this woman gained access into the house has been questioned, what happens next is incredible. She approached Jesus. For Luke, it is important to describe her position; she was standing (ἵστημι *histemi*) or stood behind (ὀπίσω *opiso*) Him. Jesus may not have seen her initially but sensed her presence, as with the woman who had an issue with hemorrhaging (issue of blood), who He had felt touching the hem of His garment.

The woman in today's account was in such an emotional state she was wracked with agony. She began crying and, although she was behind Jesus, maneuvered herself in such a manner that her tears fell on His feet. Luke describes the state of the woman as that "she was crying so hard that she wet His feet." However, the Greek term used, βρέχω *brecho*, goes beyond the meaning of "wet"; it also means "to send rain," revealing just how hard she was crying. As she tried to compose herself, she began to dry or wipe the amount of moisture she had "cried" onto His feet. Then she began to anoint and massage the feet of Jesus with the perfume she brought.

Luke does not describe the reaction of Jesus; nonetheless, the setting suggests He was impressed by her sincerity.

II. The Host of the Dinner Reacts (Luke 7:39)

The reaction of the Pharisee could be inferred as astonishing, yet predictable. His respect for Jesus waned as he witnessed His allowing this woman to touch Him! As a result, the Pharisee's disdain over this occurrence certainly puts in question the motive of his dinner invitation. Luke uses the term καλέω *kaleo*, which can be translated as "invite"; however, with the sinister aftermath and reaction to Jesus' handling of the situation (the Pharisee's also knowing Jesus had dined with Matthew, a known tax collector), the term could mean the man essentially summoned or called Jesus to dinner in order to investigate His motives and movement.

The general complaint focused on the actions of the woman and Jesus' response to her actions. Those who were offended, such as the Pharisee, had their own prejudicial reasons steeped in an air of superiority. Jesus would not have been offended by the presence or actions of the woman because He had women who were also disciples. Simon could not have been offended by the use of the perfume because it would not have been something that belonged to or was sought after by men. The reaction of the Pharisee was simply to castigate the woman and rebuke Jesus.

In his arrogant disapproval, the Pharisee said to himself that if this Man were a prophet, He should not have behaved as He did. The Pharisee obviously had heard about Jesus being a great man of wisdom and understanding; however, Jesus' reputation had come from the people and not the aristocracy such as the circle of this Pharisee. Luke reports the man questioned Jesus' status as a prophet (προφήτης *prophetes*) but ironically does not refer to Jesus as *rabbi* (ῥαββί *rhabbi*), my "master, teacher, or master teacher"! Continuing with his thoughts, the Pharisee distanced himself from the woman by assuming Jesus should have known what kind (ποταπός *potapos*) of woman she was, a woman of some sort of ill-repute. The term used also suggests she was an alien or foreigner from another country.

III. The Parable of Two Debtors (Luke 7:40–43)

Recall that the Pharisee had said these things to himself; however, Jesus read the inner thoughts of this man and reacted to him by saying, "Simon, I have something to say to you," revealing his name. Now, at this point, Simon incredibly calls Jesus "teacher" (ῥαββί *rhabbi*), asking Him to reveal what is on His mind. Jesus begins with a parable about a moneylender or someone in our society who could be identified as a loan shark, who provided money to two men. Both were in debt to the hustler. However, the amount of money owed the moneylender was different, as one owed five hundred denarii and the other, only fifty. Recall that the denarius (δηνάριον *denarion*) is a silver Roman coin that has been estimated as the debt of one hundred denarii owed by one servant to another in Jesus' parable on forgiveness in Matthew 18:28, and it was worth less than fifteen dollars. The obvious difference between these amounts may seem to indicate the situation of the man who owed less was not as serious as the one who owed much.

Unfortunately, in this situation, each man, due to his individual circumstances, was not in a position to pay his debts to the moneylender. The loan shark, in a moment of compassion, decides to forgive the debts of both men, showing equal favor to each. Remember that since the beginning of human interaction, moneylenders are in the business of making money from the high percentage of interest charged to victims who cannot afford to borrow from reputable agencies. As with check-cashing establishments and other legal predatory lenders, the prey of these practices is most often one who already lacks the earning power of the culture. When these two borrowers could not pay what was owed yet were offered forgiveness of their loans, they were probably shocked! Jesus then inserts the "hook," asking the Pharisee which one of these two men loved or appreciated the lender more?

Simon, in a moment of self-assurance, answered that the person who was in the deepest amount of debt, or the one who owed much more, surely appreciated the lender more. This debtor was in for five hundred denarii and appeared to warrant greater forgiveness than the one who owed only fifty. The ESV reads, "he canceled the larger debt," while the NIV mentions the one who had the bigger debt was identically forgiven.

IV. Jesus Forgives the Woman (Luke 7:44–48)

Jesus then turned toward the woman and asked Simon, "Do you see this woman?" Simon either conveniently had forgotten the customs of hospitality or considered Jesus unworthy, because water was not offered by Simon nor his servants, and His feet were not washed. The woman who had been deemed unworthy by Simon had used her tears for water and her hair to dry Jesus's feet. Simon would have had plenty of water and towels, but it was painfully obvious the woman had a greater sense of love for Jesus, which Simon lacked.

At this point, Simon, probably was perplexed because this part of the lesson did not have anything to do with the parable of the men and the moneylenders. He may have been thinking, *Just where is Jesus going with this?*

Continuing, Jesus reminds Simon he "did not afford Me the traditional greeting with a kiss" to the cheek; whereas, the woman had continued to kiss Jesus' feet since He had arrived. This scenario is better understood as "since she had arrived," she had not ceased kissing His feet. Notice that Simon's treatment of Jesus differed vastly from the woman's. In contrast, Simon saw himself as pure and righteous and, therefore, did not need to treat Jesus in a special manner. In effect, he did not seem to think Jesus could do anything for him. Perhaps, the more noticeable item is that she went beyond the foot-washing and anointed Jesus with her perfumed oil, which Simon also omitted in his display of hospitality.

Jesus skillfully moves to the apex of the parable of the debtors with a comparison of the woman who has many sins (which had never been in question) with the man who was in debt for the most amount of money yet had his debt erased equally to the man with the smaller debt. Stating that because she loved much, or was filled with great love, the heart of the woman was just, and she would be afforded mercy and compassion.

The key to understanding this principle is Jesus' statement that "he who is forgiven or has been forgiven much has the mind-set to love much." Jesus knew the heart of the woman, and although she was besieged by problems, she was in a position to be redeemed!

In the parable, both debtors are sinners, and both have considerable debts. One denarius was equivalent to one day's wage for a common working man. Quite simply, it would take fifty working days to eliminate the one man's debt and 5ive hundred the other! What Jesus was saying was that according to conventional, outward morality, the woman was a "five hundred percent sinner," and Simon a "fifty percent sinner." Outwardly, she was ten times as sinful. Consequently, the "high-class" moralist had the same problem as the "low-class" prostitute. Jesus taught that while it is easier to forgive a smaller debt, the grace of God allows forgiveness of a larger liability for anyone who is dedicated to the faith.

The Lesson Applied

This account in Luke is not to be confused with Jesus' visit to the home of Simon the leper found in the Gospels of Matthew (26:6–7) and Mark (14:3). The Simon presented in this Lukan scenario is identified as Simon the Pharisee. Additionally, the unnamed woman is identified as a sinful woman, whereas during Jesus' visit to Bethany in the last week of His life, Mary is identified as the one who took a pound of costly perfume of pure nard and anointed the feet of Jesus and wiped them with her hair (John 12:3).

Regardless of the need to keep the accounts separate, the imagery in Luke's version of events remains clear: Jesus is able to elevate the most troubled denizens of society to a fullness of life based on love and forgiveness.

Let's Talk About It

1. **With whom do you identify more: Simon the Pharisee or the sinful woman? Have there been certain times in your life when you identified more with Simon the Pharisee or the sinful woman?**
2. **The sinful woman was so thankful for Jesus that she wiped Jesus' feet with her hair. How do you thank Jesus for the forgiveness of your sin debt?**
3. **How do you respond to the forgiveness of God through Christ?**

On occasion, we find ourselves in need of assistance, and someone steps up to help us. Those who are sensible and respectful are generally grateful toward the ones who assist us, and our expressions of gratitude may take on many forms. The most basic of methods we can use to convey appreciativeness is found in the simple yet heartfelt words, "Thank you." If we are able to understand the foundation of this expression toward each other, why are we not able to convey these same thoughts to Jesus, who provides every reason for our thanksgiving as the source of our blessings? In many situations, we exhibit our gratitude in degrees, based on the extent of kindness shown toward us. We fall short of God's compassion when we attempt to use any type of measuring stick in our thankfulness toward Him.

Home Daily Devotional Readings
October 28 – November 3, 2019

Monday	Tuesday	Wednesday	Thursday	Friday	Saturday	Sunday
Weigh the Evidence Carefully	Building Up Your Faith Community	Preparing for the Lord's Supper	Honor Your Elders	Test the Spirits	Give Generously to Enrich Your Life	Examine Yourselves in Your Faith Living
Deuteronomy 19:15–20	1 Thessalonians 5:12–22	1 Corinthians 11:26–29	1 Timothy 5:17–22	1 John 4:1–8	2 Corinthians 9:10–15	2 Corinthians 13:1–11

SELF-EXAMINATION

ADULT TOPIC:
LOOK IN THE MIRROR

BACKGROUND SCRIPTURE:
2 CORINTHIANS 13:1–11

2 CORINTHIANS 13:1–11

King James Version

THIS is the third time I am coming to you. In the mouth of two or three witnesses shall every word be established.

2 I told you before, and foretell you, as if I were present, the second time; and being absent now I write to them which heretofore have sinned, and to all other, that, if I come again, I will not spare:

3 Since ye seek a proof of Christ speaking in me, which to you-ward is not weak, but is mighty in you.

4 For though he was crucified through weakness, yet he liveth by the power of God. For we also are weak in him, but we shall live with him by the power of God toward you.

5 Examine yourselves, whether ye be in the faith; prove your own selves. Know ye not your own selves, how that Jesus Christ is in you, except ye be reprobates?

6 But I trust that ye shall know that we are not reprobates.

7 Now I pray to God that ye do no evil; not that we should appear approved, but that ye should do that which is honest, though we be as reprobates.

8 For we can do nothing against the truth, but for the truth.

9 For we are glad, when we are weak, and ye are strong: and this also we wish, even your perfection.

New Revised Standard Version

THIS is the third time I am coming to you. "Any charge must be sustained by the evidence of two or three witnesses."

2 I warned those who sinned previously and all the others, and I warn them now while absent, as I did when present on my second visit, that if I come again, I will not be lenient—

3 since you desire proof that Christ is speaking in me. He is not weak in dealing with you, but is powerful in you.

4 For he was crucified in weakness, but lives by the power of God. For we are weak in him, but in dealing with you we will live with him by the power of God.

5 Examine yourselves to see whether you are living in the faith. Test yourselves. Do you not realize that Jesus Christ is in you?—unless, indeed, you fail to meet the test!

6 I hope you will find out that we have not failed.

7 But we pray to God that you may not do anything wrong—not that we may appear to have met the test, but that you may do what is right, though we may seem to have failed.

8 For we cannot do anything against the truth, but only for the truth.

9 For we rejoice when we are weak and you are strong. This is what we pray for, that you may become perfect.

MAIN THOUGHT: Examine yourselves, whether ye be in the faith; prove your own selves. Know ye not your own selves, how that Jesus Christ is in you, except ye be reprobates? (2 Corinthians 13:5, KJV)

2 Corinthians 13:1–11

King James Version	*New Revised Standard Version*
10 Therefore I write these things being absent, lest being present I should use sharpness, according to the power which the Lord hath given me to edification, and not to destruction.	**10 So I write these things while I am away from you, so that when I come, I may not have to be severe in using the authority that the Lord has given me for building up and not for tearing down.**
11 Finally, brethren, farewell. Be perfect, be of good comfort, be of one mind, live in peace; and the God of love and peace shall be with you.	**11 Finally, brothers and sisters, farewell. Put things in order, listen to my appeal, agree with one another, live in peace; and the God of love and peace will be with you.**

LESSON SETTING

Time: circa A.D. 56
Place: Macedonia

LESSON OUTLINE

I. Paul Must Go to the Church at Corinth (2 Corinthians 13:1–4)
II. The Corinthians' Self-Test (2 Corinthians 13:5–6)
III. Reasons to Address the Church at Corinth (2 Corinthians 13:7–10)
IV. Conclusion and Benediction (2 Corinthians 13:11–13)

Unifying Principle

People often set goals to achieve personal growth. What can we do to gauge our personal development? Following previous difficulties, Paul now forcefully reminds the Corinthians to examine themselves in comparison to God's standards for faithful living.

Introduction

Paul is saddened by the events and actions of the church at Corinth. Demeaned, his authority as the leader of the church has been questioned by rumor, disrespect, and jealously. Paul is writing his second letter to address the issues of the church, while planning to travel there from Macedonia. The tenor of this letter pales in comparison to his first letter because of the sorrowfulness of its contents. Scholars note a third follow-up letter existed and was delivered by Titus; however, it is missing. Regardless of Corinth's issues, Paul remains certain the mission of Jesus Christ will not fail.

Exposition

I. Paul Must Go to the Church at Corinth (2 Corinthians 13:1–4)

Paul is planning a strategic return to the church at Corinth. Several versions state that Paul says *if* I come again, as though to indicate there may have been some hesitancy in his plans; however, the Greek renders the conjunction as *when* I come to Corinth again. Paul reminds the Corinthians this is the third occasion he will be coming to them, and the visit seems not to be one of pleasantries.

The members have been inconsistent in their actions and dedication to the faith. The church is dealing with issues of falling away from the faith, failure to provide funds for the relief of the poor in Jerusalem, and the challenge of Paul's authenticity and leadership of the church.

Noting these issues desperately need to be resolved, Paul indicates there will be some sort of trial or hearing on the problems that have plagued the church. His instructions are that every fact and accusation presented at this hearing must be heard and established by the word of two or three witnesses.

Paul reminds the people that when he was there, or when he last came to Corinth on his second visit, he had previously forewarned them: "I have already said" the church must follow the tenets of the faith. Although his message is being delivered in a letter, his absence does not dilute the importance of the message. Paul directs his warning to those who had separated themselves from church discipline and direction, addressing those who had sinned before or had sinned in the past; however, Paul also includes the remaining group of offenders.

Once more issuing a warning, Paul wants it known the guilty parties will not be spared. Many versions include "will not spare anyone" to make the reading more understandable. With the usage of this seemingly harsh language, Paul appears to be revealing his former persecutor traits; however, he will not place any of the offenders under a death sentence. He loves the members of the Corinthian church, but his dedication to the mission of Jesus is quite serious.

Invoking the centrality of the cross, Paul emphasizes the church must continue to follow its basis for existence. Jesus was crucified not because He lacked anything or was a weak man, but because He took on the form of a human to endure this particular execution as a one-time sacrifice for the separation of humanity. Nevertheless, Jesus was resurrected and maintains the symbol of power that is the basis of the faith. For Paul, Jesus is not a dead god but the Lord of the living who cares for His people because of the innate inadequacy of humankind to obtain eternal life and to maintain a healthy relationship with Him. Yet, Jesus lives in them because of the power and will of God. Paul realizes and presses the fact that humanity alone does not possess the ability to walk with Jesus; nonetheless, Paul encourages the members not to allow their shortcomings to be an obstacle.

II. The Corinthians' Self-Test (2 Corinthians 13:5–6)

We are reminded Paul is in a constant state of self-reflection, and his writings support his confidence and dedication to the faith. An example of his self-assurance can be found when he speaks of being in Jesus Christ, "I have found reason for boasting (καύχησις *kauchesis*), or exuding a proud sense of confidence, in all things pertaining to God" (Rom. 15:17). Additionally, the salutation in several of his letters usually contains a self-description in which Paul refers to himself as a bond servant (δοῦλος *doulous*) or slave of Christ Jesus (Rom. 1:1), which further cements his devotion and dedication to the faith.

Now, Paul is challenging the Corinthians to a similar level of personal scrutiny, commanding they test themselves. Using the Greek term πειράζω *peirazo*, which is translated as "to make proof of," is better rendered as "to prove yourselves" or at least "to make an attempt to show yourselves worthy" to the subject of the faith. It is important these members recognize their positions in both the church and in Jesus. Paul's wording "yourselves" is purposefully and definitively emphatic; it is "yourselves, not I, whom you should examine." The stress and focus on this opening phrase is about self-examination, self-evaluation, or better yet, self-approval!

Continuing to encourage the members, Paul reminds them they have the spirit and compassion of Jesus Christ within them, in their lives and the scope of all of their activities. They must have a sense of blessed assurance Jesus is actually theirs! This indicates the believer has total access to Jesus in all conditions and circumstances; yet one has to believe in this concept, which is foreign to worshipers of idolatry. Paul is not merely proposing some off-handed idea, but easily could be referring to the beginning (when God made humans in His image) and the provision of Jesus as Savior, reclaiming and redeeming humankind for eternity. The Corinthians must know exactly what Jesus personally means to them and acknowledge He is their Lord and Master.

III. Reasons to Address the Church at Corinth (2 Corinthians 13:7–10)

Paul does not want those who oppose him to be guilty of any wrongdoing; he says "we pray" (εὔχομαι *euchomai*) to God that "you" have not committed any form of evil (κακός *kakos*), not so much toward Paul but against the church and by extension, against God. Paul further prays that "we, ourselves" may seem to be approved or faultless; however, it is not his intention to be misunderstood. Paul understands his weaknesses and wants these members to know they are subject to the same standards of the Lord; therefore, the encouragement is to do what is right (ποιέω *poieo*) and commit to the practice of righteous living. Additionally, Paul notes it may seem "we are not approved," but this is not an indictment against his leadership. The purpose of his prayer, which is framed both negatively and positively, is that "we don't pray like this in order to justify ourselves, but to get you to do what is right, even if we appear to be failures." Another possible model showing more clearly the continuation of the testing theme can be as follows: "We are not trying to make ourselves look good, but we pray you will do what is right, even if people think we have failed the test."

From his Damascus Road experience, Paul knew he was being held and confirmed by the power of God. This was a personal insertion and did not include the Corinthians because the truth (ἀλήθεια *aletheia*) was Jesus; and Paul could only follow the guidance of his Lord and Master. Paul was on a mission, and he could not "kick against the goads" (Acts 26:14); he was mandated to follow the call and will of Jesus.

Nonetheless, Paul states "we" (which includes the Corinthians), must rejoice (χαίρω *chairo*) when "we, as believers" are weak. In a human perspective, this statement is nonsensical; how does one be glad in a state of weakness? If we look at athletes who depend on their strength, prowess, and ability to win games, weakness is a negative aspect. If we, as humans, exhibit weakness, someone inevitably will attempt to take advantage of our vulnerability; therefore, we must be conditioned to never display signs of weakness. However, we are steeped in the glory of a Savior who makes human thoughts obsolete. In what appears to be an oxymoronic statement, weakness being turned into strength can come only from God. Paul is not ashamed of his dependency on Christ; to the contrary, he is proud and prays the Corinthians will accept this belief system and be made complete. Paul uses the Greek term καταρτισις *katartisis*, which goes further by defining those who are preparing and being equipped; a better rendering of the Greek account might read that Paul prayed for their Christian maturity.

Paul writes that when the Corinthian church receives the contents of his letter, the members are to heed its instruction. Paul acknowledges, even in absentia, that all of the issues that have been previously presented can be resolved and when he arrives to meet with the church members, he prays his visit will be pleasant, with no need for severities (ἀποτόμως *apotomos*) or abrupt actions. Again, reasserting his authority given by Jesus, he reassures the members his purpose for coming to the church and the city is to restore the fissures in the foundation of the church and its faith. His mission and power, granted by the Lord, is to be used for "building up" (οἰκοδομή *oikodome*), not for καθαίρεσις *kathairesis*, the "pulling down or destroying" of the members.

IV. Conclusion and Benediction (2 Corinthians 13:11–13)

Paul closes his letter by saying, "Finally, brothers and sisters, rejoice, be comforted and made complete," and encourages them to remain in what is contemporarily known as "one accord." The use of the adverb "finally" (λοιπός *loipos*) can mean the situation has reached a conclusion; but it also means to rest assured all will be well when Paul arrives. In the remaining time frame, the Corinthians are to live in peace (εἰρήνη *eirene*) and contentment because they are filled with the love of God, from God; and if they can accomplish this, Paul asserts God's love and peace will securely be with them.

Most all of the English Bible translations conclude Paul's letter at verse 14; however, the original Greek manuscript contains the concluding benediction of "the grace of the Lord Jesus" in verse 13, omitting a need for a fourteenth verse. In the original, verses 11 and 12 run consecutively, becoming one verse. In verse 12, Paul encourages friendship by asking the members to greet (ἀσπάζομαι *aspazomai*) or welcome one another with a holy kiss. Remember that when visiting one's home in this culture, the custom was to greet the guests with a kiss, as well as water for the feet and hair; therefore, this is not beyond their normal understanding and beliefs.

Additionally, when Paul says "all the saints greet you," it should not be taken as the inhabitants of Corinth. The Christians who send greetings are in Paul's company or in the place where Paul is staying when he is writing this letter. It therefore may be more in line with Paul's intention to translate as "all the people of God who are here." Since the persons giving the greetings are not present in Corinth and therefore cannot greet the Corinthians directly, some translations insert the word "send," as in *Today's English Version*.

The Lesson Applied

When Paul speaks of "passing the test," he is not comparing this to some type of examination one can pass (or fail) and does not have to deal with again. This test is a constant force within the lives of Christian believers because the subject matter may seem flexible and subjective. One believer may feel he is living a wholesome lifestyle, whereas, according to another believer's standards, the aforementioned lifestyle may be severely lacking. Christian believers of the faith should realize we face "the test" daily and our ability to pass this assessment is based on our relationship with Jesus and the belief we can be secure in Him.

Let's Talk About It

1. **We know God has a plan, purpose, and calling for everyone. However, not all people are called to pastoral leadership. How do you know if you are called to pastoral leadership? What criteria do you use to test the authority of a spiritual leader?**

2. **Jesus Christ lives in the hearts of all believers. However, we are not called merely to believe in Him. We are called to follow Him. What are some ways you test yourself to see if you truly have faith to follow Jesus?**

3. **Recall a moment of weakness in your life of faith. How were you given the strength to endure?**

Paul had to address the jealousy directed toward the leadership of the church. Jealousy is an issue that has plagued even the healthiest of congregations because someone or some group of people is determined to resist the leadership of the pastor, or in this particular case, the Apostle Paul. The individuals who resist, however, have not been called to the position of pastor, and their fight is not against the spiritual leadership of the community of faith, but against the Lord. The Apostle Paul was appointed to his position by the Lord; he was not self-appointed or merely hired by a committee.

If one were to borrow from the lyrics of Michael Jackson's "Man in the Mirror," in which life's reflections begin with the man or woman in the mirror needing to "change his ways," no message could be clearer. If we want to make the church and the world a better place, we must take a look at ourselves in the mirror, test ourselves, and make the necessary change! Christians believe we possess all the essential tools to do just that, through Jesus Christ.

Home Daily Devotional Readings
November 4–10, 2019

Monday	Tuesday	Wednesday	Thursday	Friday	Saturday	Sunday
Suffering Leads to Endurance, Character, Hope	Reconciliation Through Jesus Christ	Be Ready for Christ's Coming	Live Christ's Mind and Character Daily	Under Persecution Proclaim Jesus the Christ	Facing Temptation, Stay Loyal to Christ	Examples of Faith to All Believers
Romans 5:1–5	Romans 5:6–11	Matthew 24:36–44	Philippians 2:5–11	Acts 17:1–9	2 Thessalonians 2:1–12	1 Thessalonians 2:1–10

BE EXAMPLES OF FAITH

ADULT TOPIC:
LET IT SHINE

BACKGROUND SCRIPTURE:
1 THESSALONIANS 1:2–10

1 THESSALONIANS 1:2–10

King James Version

WE give thanks to God always for you all, making mention of you in our prayers;

3 Remembering without ceasing your work of faith, and labour of love, and patience of hope in our Lord Jesus Christ, in the sight of God and our Father;

4 Knowing, brethren beloved, your election of God.

5 For our gospel came not unto you in word only, but also in power, and in the Holy Ghost, and in much assurance; as ye know what manner of men we were among you for your sake.

6 And ye became followers of us, and of the Lord, having received the word in much affliction, with joy of the Holy Ghost.

7 So that ye were ensamples to all that believe in Macedonia and Achaia.

8 For from you sounded out the word of the Lord not only in Macedonia and Achaia, but also in every place your faith to God-ward is spread abroad; so that we need not to speak any thing.

9 For they themselves shew of us what manner of entering in we had unto you, and how ye turned to God from idols to serve the living and true God;

10 And to wait for his Son from heaven, whom he raised from the dead, even Jesus, which delivered us from the wrath to come.

New Revised Standard Version

WE always give thanks to God for all of you and mention you in our prayers, constantly

3 remembering before our God and Father your work of faith and labor of love and steadfastness of hope in our Lord Jesus Christ.

4 For we know, brothers and sisters beloved by God, that he has chosen you,

5 because our message of the gospel came to you not in word only, but also in power and in the Holy Spirit and with full conviction; just as you know what kind of persons we proved to be among you for your sake.

6 And you became imitators of us and of the Lord, for in spite of persecution you received the word with joy inspired by the Holy Spirit,

7 so that you became an example to all the believers in Macedonia and in Achaia.

8 For the word of the Lord has sounded forth from you not only in Macedonia and Achaia, but in every place your faith in God has become known, so that we have no need to speak about it.

9 For the people of those regions report about us what kind of welcome we had among you, and how you turned to God from idols, to serve a living and true God,

10 and to wait for his Son from heaven, whom he raised from the dead—Jesus, who rescues us from the wrath that is coming.

MAIN THOUGHT: So that ye were ensamples to all that believe in Macedonia and Achaia. For from you sounded out the word of the Lord not only in Macedonia and Achaia, but also in every place your faith to God-ward is spread abroad; so that we need not to speak any thing. (1 Thessalonians 1:7–8, KJV)

LESSON SETTING

Time: circa A.D. 51
Place: Corinth-Thessalonica

LESSON OUTLINE

I. **Paul Commends the Thessalonians (1 Thessalonians 1:2–5)**
II. **Imitators of the Apostles and the Lord (1 Thessalonians 1:6–8)**
III. **Rejecting Idols and Waiting for Jesus (1 Thessalonians 1:9–10)**

UNIFYING PRINCIPLE

People often look for positive examples to emulate. How can we be positive examples for others? Exhibiting strong faith and committing loving acts even in the midst of trials and persecution, the Thessalonians were praised because they were positive examples.

INTRODUCTION

Paul commends the Thessalonians for their faithfulness, steadfastness, and adherence to the standards and conduct of the Christian faith. The church in this city has to battle the influences of idolatry and the scorn of the Jewish community, who has rejected the mission and purpose of Jesus Christ. Although the church is largely Gentile, Paul is impressed with the overall example of the Christian lifestyle the Thessalonians have produced, noting their reputation has spread from the north of Macedonia to the south of Achaia, which encompasses the Grecian countryside. Timothy will serve as a go-between and ambassador while Paul is not in the city. Paul composes the two Thessalonian letters during his second missionary journey from the Greek city of Corinth.

EXPOSITION

I. PAUL COMMENDS THE THESSALONIANS (1 THESSALONIANS 1:2–5)

Paul is writing to the church at Thessalonica, stating he and his companions (probably Silvanus and Timothy) are exuberantly praying for the health and life of the church and its members. Their sincere prayers reflect a deep conviction and devotion to the Lord, as they acknowledge they give thanks and are appreciative to God for the members. Notice the transliteration of the Greek term here closely resembles the word *Eucharist*, which is a Christian ceremony commemorating the Lord's Supper or Communion.

Paul mentions that his prayers are continual. The communication between the church and Paul must have been strong because it would allow him to be specific in his lifting up members of the church in prayer. Paul is not merely paying "lip service." Paul's prayer routine reflects Jesus's encouragement that men should always pray and never lose heart (Luke 18:1). Paul is not a fake apostle; he prays for the Ephesians in much the same manner, encouraging them not to "cease giving thanks for you, making mention of you in my prayers" (Eph. 5:16). The apostle uses this discipline as a foundation of his relationship with the Lord, praying or speaking to Him constantly.

Paul addressed his fellow Christians as *brothers*. Using the Greek term ἀδελφός *adelphoi* (plural) fifteen times in this one brief epistle and seven times in

2 Thessalonians, Paul did not claim superiority over them, but recognized the equality of all the redeemed in the sight of their heavenly Father, as he taught elsewhere (1 Cor. 12:14–27) and as the Lord taught (Matt. 23:9). Paul had come a long way from being a proud Pharisee to the place where he could consider Gentiles his equals before God. He reminded his readers they were beloved by God. Even Paul's incidental statements are filled with the warm realization of God's presence and love.

Knowing (μνημονεύω *mnemoneuo*), or constantly bearing them in mind, Paul compliments the Thessalonians by stating they remembered their work that obviously had been guided by love and consistency. Their specific work (ἔργον *ergon*) or action in the faith is not described; however, what is important is that it reflects the ideal Christian behavior of Jesus Christ. Moreover, their lifestyles promulgated a consistent steadfastness (ὑπομονή *hupomone*) derived through their labor (κόπος *kopos*) of love, knowing their hope was rooted and grounded in Jesus Christ, who serves as a witness for the Thessalonians and stands in the presence of (ἔμπροσθεν *emprosthen*), or in the face of, God the Father (πατήρ *pater*).

The words *before our God and Father* are related to the rest of the sentence probably because they are linked with "hope," which produces endurance "in the sight of Him who is our God and Father." Most modern translations restructure the verse to bring together "we remember" and "before our God and Father," although these phrases are widely separated in the Greek. This brings out more clearly the parallel between verses 2 and 3, which emphasizes, "Every time we pray, we think of you and thank God, our Father, for you all." Paul reassures his brothers they are genuinely loved by God because of His divine selection.

Paul reminds the church the Gospel (εὐαγγέλιον *euaggelion*) did not come to the faithful simply in word only. This does not diminish the power of the Scriptures or the writings, but provides an imagery of the living word of the Lord. *The Word* versus the term *word* (λόγος *logos*) are not to be compared because the capitalized version represents Jesus, and the language of the New Testament Scriptures is simply about Jesus.

The word of the Gospel in this case is about the lifestyle of the Gospel, supported by the power and will of the Holy Spirit. The church will be the medium whereby the Gospel is spread; and there are certainly instances about which we are reminded the Gospel could have been impeded, such as when Paul refused the personal support of the Corinthian church, but decided to endure the many obstacles he faced, so there would not be any hindrance to the Gospel of Jesus Christ (1 Cor. 9:12).

This imagery insists believers must be fully convicted (πληροφορία *plerophoria*), with full assurance or certainty, in a time period when the expression "bought in" is used. Moreover, Christians must be totally "sold out" or "souled" out to the premise and promise of the Gospel of Jesus Christ. Paul offers his Christian lifestyle and devotion to the Lord by reminding the Thessalonians they know what type of people they have proven to be. Proving oneself is difficult when living a life filled with subjective definitions and a set of values that is constantly vacillating. Paul uses the term οἷος *hoios*, meaning "what sort of or what kind of manner"; the word *people* or *men* is added to clarify the thought but is not part of the original. "What kind of men" salutes the reputation of Paul and his companions, which is such that they are on full display. Paul relates they have proven themselves, meaning they became to the Thessalonians what they claimed to be.

II. Imitators of the Apostles and the Lord (1 Thessalonians 1:6–8)

Paul shifts his attention from his group to the Thessalonians. Paul compliments the church for being committed in a society where idolatry continues to plague the region. In his adulation of the faithful, Paul observes one of the reasons for their success is they have chosen to adhere to the practice of the faith by becoming imitators of the apostles, Silvanus and Timothy, and the Lord. The concept of Paul's referring to the Thessalonian faithful as imitators must not be seen as a negative connotation, such as would an imitation leather coat or a faux fur, a fur coat imitation that is not authentic or is cheaply made. To the contrary, the Thessalonians are to be applauded; in Paul's perspective, these Christians' proclivity to imitating the apostles can be compared to the relationship between a teacher and his student.

Paul commends the Thessalonians for their dedication and commitment to the faith, in spite of the tribulations and afflictions they faced. While their problems are not documented here, Paul nonetheless recognized they faced these challenges with a high degree of joy based in the Holy Spirit.

Paul is delighted in the comportment of the Thessalonians and, as a response to their behavior, notes they have become examples of the faith themselves. The Thessalonians' devotion to the faith will leave a lasting impression on fellow believers (πιστεύω *pisteuo*) who trust their devotion to the Lord. The aura of the Thessalonians is not limited to the northern regions of Macedonia, where Thessalonica is located, but also spreads to the southern area of Achaia. In this, Paul is saying their faith has encompassed the entire peninsula of Greece!

Continuing to encourage the members, Paul notes the word of the Lord, both in speech and deed, has been sounded forth (ἐξηχέω *execheo*) from this church, being heard in the aforementioned regions and emanating beyond the city, radiating everywhere their faith toward (πρός *pros*) the name of God has traveled. For Paul, the message of the Lord is so indelible in the Thessalonians that he does not have to say anything (λαλέω *laleo*); he does not have to speak for them. Paul is satisfied with their commitment to the Lord.

III. Rejecting Idols and Waiting for Jesus (1 Thessalonians 1:9–10)

The actions of the Thessalonians served as evidence of their conversion and subsequent commitment to the Lord. The current feeling and respect of the church members has spread among the community and into the outlying regions, creating an aura that shines light on both the church and the Gospel of Jesus. Paul is more than pleased the witness of the Thessalonian church is infectious to such a degree any non-members could possibly be in a state of curiosity, which would prayerfully lead to conversion and acceptance into the faith.

The joy experienced by Paul and his companions became well-known, even in the reception of them when the group last came to the city. Paul uses the term εἴσοδος *eisodos*, which provides a better rendering to mean the acceptance of the church, or an endearing mind-set between the participants. Paul is impressed his visit was without controversy and was an affirmation to the bonding power of Jesus. Remember, the members of the church at Thessalonica were largely composed of converts from pagan religions and not from Judaism.

Paul will later in the letter show his concern for their sufferings, especially at the hands of their fellow countrymen, plus the obstacles that were put in place to impede their quest to become "soldiers of the cross" (see 1 Thess. 2:13–18). Paul further commends the Thessalonians for their acceptance and embrace of God; while resisting social scrutiny, they had rejected the popular idols (εἴδωλον *eidolon*) and false gods that dominated the populace and the region. An example of the widespread idolatry is seen in the address Paul gave to the intellectuals of Athens. In the midst of the Areopagus, Paul noticed objects of their worship and an altar "TO AN UNKNOWN GOD." He had to proclaim to these men just who the God of the universe is; these men were close to knowing God, and if they would only seek Him, they would be able to find Him (Acts 17:22–27).

Impressed with their resiliency, Paul further commends the Thessalonians' choice in accepting a living and true God; however, the sentence structure of the original is more impactive, which reads "they turned to a living God that is true!"

Paul now encourages the Thessalonians to wait for Jesus, God's Son, to return from heaven (οὐρανός *ouranos*). Paul introduces here, at the end of the first section, a theme he will discuss in greater detail in 4:13–5:11 and which will be one of the two main subjects of his Second Letter to the Thessalonians. Paul always is anxious the Thessalonian Christians maintain a balance between the present and future dimensions of Christian experience. The link between the two is Jesus, whose name is in an emphatic position at the climax of a long sentence that actually began in verse 9. Paul may have had in mind the plural aspect of "heavens" through which Jesus Christ passed when He ascended from the earth (Acts 1:9–11), rather than the seat of His heavenly rule at the right hand of the Father in singular "heaven" (Rev. 4:2–11). If so, he said the Thessalonians were looking for Jesus's coming through the clouds, literally, "out of the heavens."

But it was not the clouds, or the signs of His coming, or even His deliverance that interested these believers; it was the person of Jesus, the Son of the living God. He was the object of their hope and the focus of their attention. Declaring God raised Jesus from the human state of death, however, Paul praises the realization that it will be Jesus who is responsible for rescuing (ῥύομαι *rhuomai*) and delivering the faithful from the wrath (ὀργή *orge*) to come, which is better rendered that Jesus will rescue us from the coming wrath!

"The coming wrath" has been expressed in many examples, such as the "Day of the Lord," when Old Testament prophets warned about a future Day of the Lord that would bring doom as well as deliverance. Another example is from Joel, who called it a "great and terrible" day, which none would be able to endure (Joel 2:11). Amos also depicted it as a day of darkness and gloom, a day of unexpected disaster (Amos 5:18–20). The New Testament distinguishes between Jesus' first coming—His incarnation—and the second coming, or Christ's return. On that day, judgment will occur of the living and the dead, and to the faithful who are eagerly awaiting His return, Jesus will grant eternal life.

The Lesson Applied

The Thessalonian church serves as an example of a group of dedicated believers who demonstrated the power to resist the forces of afflictions and pressures to conform to what was considered the normal worship standards of the region. In our contemporary society, churches face many similar pressures to conform to the whims of people who have rejected the church, its members, and the authenticity of the faith. When the church feels we have to compete with other venues to survive, we have lost our hope in Jesus. Competition only exists between the church and outside sources if these idioms are as attractive to Christians as is the church.

Let's Talk About It

1. Paul's letter gives new believers guidance on holy living, hope for the future, and encouragement through suffering. What are some examples of the things God used to get your attention and expose you to the message of the Gospel as a new believer?

Many Christians admire and look to fellow believers who have overcome great obstacles in their lives. In the body of believers, even the most faithful and the strongest of Christians need the support and encouragement of one other, and personal witness can be an enduring help. A preaching professor once shared with his class of eager students about his disdain for what is referred to as "Ecclesiastical Nudity," in which personal examples are used as illustrations in the delivery of a sermon. It was the professor's theory it actually diminished the message and eroded the respect of the preacher. Some components of his theory might be factual; however, personal illustrations of Jesus Christ in the life of a believer become a powerful witness in that, "if He can deliver me, He can deliver you."

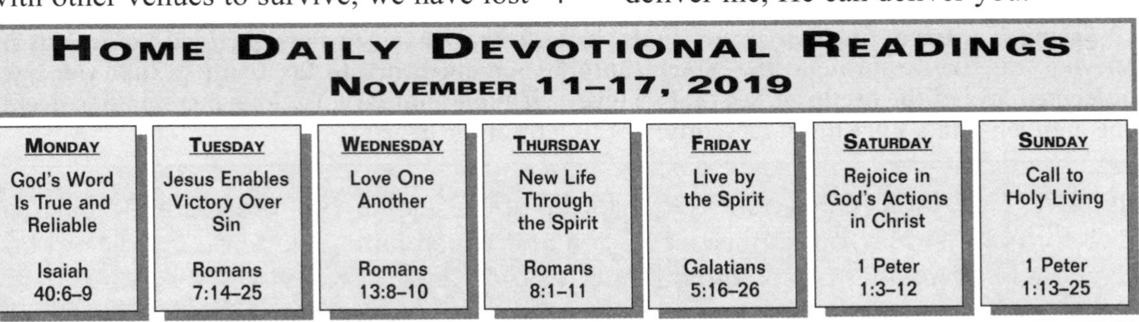

Home Daily Devotional Readings

November 11–17, 2019

Monday	Tuesday	Wednesday	Thursday	Friday	Saturday	Sunday
God's Word Is True and Reliable	Jesus Enables Victory Over Sin	Love One Another	New Life Through the Spirit	Live by the Spirit	Rejoice in God's Actions in Christ	Call to Holy Living
Isaiah 40:6–9	Romans 7:14–25	Romans 13:8–10	Romans 8:1–11	Galatians 5:16–26	1 Peter 1:3–12	1 Peter 1:13–25

LIVE HOLY LIVES

ADULT TOPIC:
DARE TO BE DIFFERENT!

BACKGROUND SCRIPTURE:
GALATIANS 5:22–23; 1 PETER 1

1 PETER 1:13–25

King James Version

WHEREFORE gird up the loins of your mind, be sober, and hope to the end for the grace that is to be brought unto you at the revelation of Jesus Christ;
14 As obedient children, not fashioning yourselves according to the former lusts in your ignorance:
15 But as he which hath called you is holy, so be ye holy in all manner of conversation;
16 Because it is written, Be ye holy; for I am holy.
17 And if ye call on the Father, who without respect of persons judgeth according to every man's work, pass the time of your sojourning here in fear:
18 Forasmuch as ye know that ye were not redeemed with corruptible things, as silver and gold, from your vain conversation received by tradition from your fathers;
19 But with the precious blood of Christ, as of a lamb without blemish and without spot:
20 Who verily was foreordained before the foundation of the world, but was manifest in these last times for you,
21 Who by him do believe in God, that raised him up from the dead, and gave him glory; that your faith and hope might be in God.

22 Seeing ye have purified your souls in obeying the truth through the Spirit unto unfeigned love of the brethren, see that ye love one another with a pure heart fervently:

New Revised Standard Version

THEREFORE prepare your minds for action; discipline yourselves; set all your hope on the grace that Jesus Christ will bring you when he is revealed.
14 Like obedient children, do not be conformed to the desires that you formerly had in ignorance.
15 Instead, as he who called you is holy, be holy yourselves in all your conduct;
16 for it is written, "You shall be holy, for I am holy."
17 If you invoke as Father the one who judges all people impartially according to their deeds, live in reverent fear during the time of your exile.
18 You know that you were ransomed from the futile ways inherited from your ancestors, not with perishable things like silver or gold,

19 but with the precious blood of Christ, like that of a lamb without defect or blemish.
20 He was destined before the foundation of the world, but was revealed at the end of the ages for your sake.
21 Through him you have come to trust in God, who raised him from the dead and gave him glory, so that your faith and hope are set on God.
22 Now that you have purified your souls by your obedience to the truth so that you have genuine mutual love, love one another deeply from the heart.

MAIN THOUGHT: As obedient children, not fashioning yourselves according to the former lusts in your ignorance: But as he which hath called you is holy, so be ye holy in all manner of conversation. (1 Peter 1:14–15, KJV)

1 Peter 1:13–25

King James Version	*New Revised Standard Version*
23 Being born again, not of corruptible seed, but of incorruptible, by the word of God, which liveth and abideth for ever.	**23 You have been born anew, not of perishable but of imperishable seed, through the living and enduring word of God.**
24 For all flesh is as grass, and all the glory of man as the flower of grass. The grass withereth, and the flower thereof falleth away:	**24 For "All flesh is like grass and all its glory like the flower of grass. The grass withers, and the flower falls,**
25 But the word of the Lord endureth for ever. And this is the word which by the gospel is preached unto you.	**25 but the word of the Lord endures forever." That word is the good news that was announced to you.**

LESSON SETTING

Time: circa A.D. 63
Place: Rome

LESSON OUTLINE

I. Grace: Sobriety in Holiness (1 Peter 13:13–16)
II. Grace: Sobriety in Fear (1 Peter 13:17–19)
III. Grace: Sobriety in Love (1 Peter 13:20–25)

Unifying Principle

People admire those who live according to what they say. How can we put our beliefs into action? First Peter teaches believers we must live holy lives and do good, loving deeds for others, thus demonstrating we trust in God and have been born anew.

Introduction

Peter writes this first of two letters to Christian "aliens," who are referred to as "sojourners," scattered throughout the world. The members of his dispersed congregation are largely Gentile, and they are suffering tribulations living as Christians in pagan societies. Silvanus (Silas) may have served as Peter's secretary in the composition of this letter, which was portrayed to have been written from "Babylon" (5:13) to elude trouble with the authorities, while the actual place of writing was Rome. Peter commends his people for their sincerity and dedication to the faith and expands several reasons for remaining in the bond. Using the concept of grace as his thesis, Peter employs the imagery of sobriety in Christian living.

Exposition

I. Grace: Sobriety in Holiness (1 Peter 13:13–16)

Peter begins this section of his first letter by encouraging his readers to prepare their minds for action. The goal of this section is to teach that the grace of the Lord brings security in the lives of the believers. They are encouraged to prepare their minds for action; however, Peter uses the Greek term (ἀναζώννυμι *anazonnumi*, which prominently means "to gird up," the terminology of which only occurs in 1 Peter 1:13, where it is applied to the mind being held in constant preparation. It is taken from the custom of the eastern nations who, when they had occasion to exert themselves (as in journeying, running, and such), used to bind up their long-flowing garments by a girdle or belt about their hips. The original reads "gird up your loins" (ὀσφῦς *osphus*), but the imagery is rendered as "gird up the loins of your mind." The phrase "minds for action" (NASB) is not in the original; moreover, other versions read, "Gird up the loins of your mind" (NKJV) and "with the minds that are alert" (NIV). The idea is that the believers constantly should be ready to battle the forces of evil, both mentally and in the spirit.

Peter is speaking of a deliberate mind-set by which believers possess an aggressive attitude toward Christianity. Peter commands Christians use this aggression to display a sober (νήφω *nepho*) attribute and lifestyle that originates in the mind (διάνοια *dianoia*) and thoughts of the believer. This will create a positive disposition and temperament among fellow believers of the faith. Additionally, the motif of being sober is found in the extension (not part of the original); "to be sober in spirit" (NASB) is to convey the depth of this mind-set and the alignment with the gift of the Holy Spirit.

Peter continues by instructing his readers to place their hope completely in the grace they will receive at the revelation (ἀποκάλυψις *apokalupsis*) of Jesus Christ. The idea of attaching their hope to the grace provides the image of a bonding with this gift of God. Other translations may read "set your hope on the grace" (ESV) and "rest your hope on the grace" (NKJV); nevertheless, these believers must secure themselves to celestial promises that can be realized only through Jesus Christ.

Peter creates a comparison between obedient and disobedient children in a metaphorical manner. Although he does not highlight the negative children, this aspect remains present. The original is rendered "as an obedient (ὑπακοή *hupakoe*) child (τέκνον *teknon*)," which must not be confused or taken literally. Peter is speaking of adult Christians who must behave in a certain manner or face the consequences of their actions. Recall that Paul warned the wrath of God would come upon the children's disobedience (Eph. 5:6) because they allowed themselves to conform to the preaching of "empty words" by empty-headed charlatans.

Additionally, Peter is warning the readers not to become arrogant in the false belief that further guidance in the Lord is not necessary. Recall that Paul remonstrated with the members of the Roman church not to be conformed to the things of this world but to be transformed by the renewing of your mind (Rom. 12:2). Peter insists his readers resist any and all attractions that would allow the trappings of society to shape their lifestyle into that which would be contrary to the image of Christ.

The description intended here resembles a reverse account of the potter's wheel; Peter warns not to conform (συσχηματίζω *suschematizo*), assimilate, or become molded into an image of something or someone that is unworthy to be in the fellowship. The sense of conformity that is Peter's warning here is not specific; however, in its generalities, Peter understands the nature of carnal cravings and desires.

As if to draw upon the lessons of the last Commandment, that "you shall not covet" (Exod. 20:17), Peter speaks of the former lusts (ἐπιθυμία *epithumia*) that are rooted in ignorance. While the term *ignorance* (ἄγνοια ganoia) may seem harsh and offensive, especially in contemporary society where no one is comfortable with being called ignorant or illiterate, Peter is not attempting to marginalize his readers. His application of the term is understood that at one time, believers lacked knowledge of the Lord, prior to their conversion to Christianity. Some scholars take this as proof the letter is written primarily for Gentiles, since they are described as ignorant in many parts of the New Testament (compare Acts 17:30). Furthermore, "ignorance" here refers primarily to a lack of knowledge of God and would not be an appropriate description of Jews. However, others maintain both Gentiles and Jews are included. Therefore, a rendering closer to the original sentence structure may read "in the ignorance of your former cravings."

II. Grace: Sobriety in Fear (1 Peter 13:17–19)

Peter begins his thought by inserting the conditional conjunction *if* and creating a situation in which the believer has the choice or freedom to either accept or reject God. First, the condition stipulates the believer acknowledge or address God as Father, emulating Jesus's prayer of "our Father, who is in Heaven," and the supreme being who judges or evaluates the labor of each individual Christian. God loves all Christians by the merit of their individual lives, and His review is impartial (ἀπροσωπολήμπτως *aprosopolemptos*), or impartially granted, without respect to persons.

Because of their personal connection to the Lord, the Christian readers of this missive are to conduct their lives in the fear of His assessments. Peter uses the term φόβος *phobos*, meaning "fear" or "panic," to indicate the seriousness of Christian conduct in the eyes of the Lord. This usage is not to be confused with the meaning of the Hebrew term in Joshua 24:14, "Now therefore, fear (*yare'*) the Lord," which promotes the idea of respect or reverence for the Lord. Peter is deliberate in conveying a sense of terror in our incurring the wrath of God for our misdeeds and missteps.

Our contemporary word *phobia* is derived from the Greek term; and Peter promotes the seriousness of displeasing the Lord during the period we stay on (παροικία *paroika*) or occupy the earth. This term is better rendered as the time we sojourn in a foreign country, providing credence to the concept that "this world is not [our] home."

Peter draws the imagery based on the Old Testament rules of redemption where a close relative was under obligation to redeem an impoverished family member who had sold himself into slavery (Lev. 25:47–49), or to regain possession of family land that had been sold (vv. 25–26, 33). The person who rescues the relative is known as the redeemer, who has the monetary capital necessary to pay the price of the said redemption. The New Testament model of redemption closely resembles that of the Old and was understood as a price paid for the purchase of freeing a slave or the release of prisoners. Peter notes his fellow Christians are redeemed; however, the cost of this process was not based on pecuniary items, such as silver, gold, or anything that could be bartered or used in exchange for goods. The payment could not have been accomplished by the aforementioned tangible items, which were valued by their fathers in the culture of the period. These traits are considered futile (μάταιος *mataios*) and quite useless when compared to the actual cost of human redemption. Peter refers to silver and gold as perishable (Φθαρτός *phthartos*) or corruptible items that eventually disintegrate and lose their value. The people of the period simply had inherited (πατροπαράδοτος *patroparadotos*) these traditional aspects of society. Again, referring to Old Testament imagery, the cost of this ransom was the precious blood shed from a lamb that was unblemished (ἄμωμος *amomos*) and spotless (ἄσπιλος *aspilos*). In combining these terms in this phrase, the lamb had to be unstained and above reproach. Only the blood of One who could sufficiently cover this situation would satisfy God; the price that was paid for the redemption (λυτρόω *lutroo*) or ransom was the blood of Jesus that allowed believers to be released from the captivity of sin, not the practiced methods that were known to men.

III. Grace: Sobriety in Love (1 Peter 13:20–25)

Expiation for the sins of the people was the object of the entire system of sacrificial worship. One may believe God began to plan the need for Jesus to be given to the world during the turbulent periods of the Assyrian invasion or the Babylonian exile; however, humanity was in trouble prior to these times, during which an overly large segment of humanity rejected God. The need for redemption and reconciliation began with the mistakes of Adam and Eve and their banishment from Eden.

New Testament references to expiation are focused on the atonement accomplished through Christ's crucifixion. Paul refers to Christ as "an expiation or propitiation (ἱλασμός *hilasmos*), by his blood" (Rom. 3:25); and similarly, Christ is called "the expiation for our sins" (1 John 2:2; 4:10). Jesus did not simply "show up" during the period of the New Testament but has been with the Father from the beginning of time. In the Prologue of John, he explains "in the beginning was the Word [Jesus]," and He was with God (John 1:1–2). Now, Peter is expounding this imagery to explain Jesus was foreknown (προγινώσκω *proginosko*), as documented in the fourth Gospel; prior to our knowledge of Him, He was known by all elements of heaven, such as the angels, and ordained to be the Savior by God the Father, from the beginning, the foundation (καταβολή *katabole*) or creation of the world (κόσμος *cosmos*).

Peter notes Jesus appeared in these "last" times or days for the sake or redemption of you (us) who are believers in God and of the faith. Remember, Peter, like most of the disciples, believed Jesus would return during his lifetime, and his letter provides encouragement to the believers to remain committed to the faith. Peter acknowledges God, His Father, raised Jesus from the dead and gave Him glory, which also can be thought of as His raising Him with "all power," versus the limited power He had with the limitations placed on His human form. Nevertheless, our faith and hope are placed in God.

Peter concludes this section by reminding his readers their dedication and obedience (ὑπακοή *hupakoe*) to the truth of the faith has purified (ἁγνίζω *hagnizo*) the souls of the believers. This result occurred because of their noted submission and their desire to follow Jesus and become one of His disciples. Another rendering of the use of this term, *hagnizo*, is that Peter, borrowing from Jewish imagery, intones that their souls have been cleansed from defilement. The fruit of their obedience results in a genuine or sincere love for their brothers and sisters that emanates from the heart. The life changes his readers are experiencing will endure because their "new birth" occurred through the living word of God.

The Lesson Applied

Christians understand the power of holy living but struggle with consistency because of the pressures society places on them to conform to its styles and norms. Christian living is not based on the strength of the believer; however, it is realized by the demonstrated power we receive from our obedience to the truths of the faith, which are infused by the grace of God. The aforementioned referral to the Nicodemus query of being "born again" is a well-known story and is cherished by Christians. In the case of this lesson, we are encouraged to connect our "second birth" to our ability to embrace a holy lifestyle and enjoy the fruits of this labor, knowing that because of our relationship, our choice will not be in vain.

Let's Talk About It

1. **What is your personal motivation for preparing your mind for action, disciplining yourself, and setting all your hope on the grace Jesus Christ will bring you when He is revealed?**

2. **Holy living is a mark of faithful discipleship. The hope of heaven is assured to us through Jesus Christ. Holy living is for the living of a faithful life. Why do you want to live a holy life in the here and now on the earth?**

On many occasions our consistency is challenged in the doing of good deeds and loving of others, especially those who can be offensive and viewed as derisive. The Lord, however, pushes us to become better humans than society would define us to be. It is a painful and most difficult struggle to follow Jesus' command to "pray for [our] enemies" when it is much easier to pray exclusively for family and friends. Nonetheless, this command is not based on the desires of culture but is realized in lives that are driven by the laws of heaven and the Lord. Additionally, we are not directed to do good deeds or pursue godly living just for the sake of appearances but instead, for use in the service and commitment of discipleship, which proves to "lift up Jesus, that He will draw all men unto Him."

Home Daily Devotional Readings
November 18–24, 2019

Monday	Tuesday	Wednesday	Thursday	Friday	Saturday	Sunday
The Spirit and the Bride Say Come	Our Dwelling Place	One Day Like One Thousand Years	The Coming Day of the Lord	This Is My Son; Listen to Him!	Solid Reasons for Hope	Always Keep the Faith
Revelation 22:14–17	Psalm 90	2 Peter 3:8–10	2 Peter 3:11–15, 17–18	Luke 9:28–36	2 Peter 1:16–21	2 Peter 1:1–15

LESSON XIII NOVEMBER 24, 2019

STICK TO YOUR FAITH

ADULT TOPIC:
BELIEVING PROMISES

BACKGROUND SCRIPTURE:
2 PETER 1

2 PETER 1:1–15

King James Version

SIMON Peter, a servant and an apostle of Jesus Christ, to them that have obtained like precious faith with us through the righteousness of God and our Saviour Jesus Christ:

2 Grace and peace be multiplied unto you through the knowledge of God, and of Jesus our Lord,

3 According as his divine power hath given unto us all things that pertain unto life and godliness, through the knowledge of him that hath called us to glory and virtue:

4 Whereby are given unto us exceeding great and precious promises: that by these ye might be partakers of the divine nature, having escaped the corruption that is in the world through lust.

5 And beside this, giving all diligence, add to your faith virtue; and to virtue knowledge;

6 And to knowledge temperance; and to temperance patience; and to patience godliness;

7 And to godliness brotherly kindness; and to brotherly kindness charity.

8 For if these things be in you, and abound, they make you that ye shall neither be barren nor unfruitful in the knowledge of our Lord Jesus Christ.

9 But he that lacketh these things is blind, and cannot see afar off, and hath forgotten that he was purged from his old sins.

New Revised Standard Version

SIMEON Peter, a servant and apostle of Jesus Christ, To those who have received a faith as precious as ours through the righteousness of our God and Savior Jesus Christ

2 May grace and peace be yours in abundance in the knowledge of God and of Jesus our Lord.

3 His divine power has given us everything needed for life and godliness, through the knowledge of him who called us by his own glory and goodness.

4 Thus he has given us, through these things, his precious and very great promises, so that through them you may escape from the corruption that is in the world because of lust, and may become participants of the divine nature.

5 For this very reason, you must make every effort to support your faith with goodness, and goodness with knowledge,

6 and knowledge with self-control, and self-control with endurance, and endurance with godliness,

7 and godliness with mutual affection, and mutual affection with love.

8 For if these things are yours and are increasing among you, they keep you from being ineffective and unfruitful in the knowledge of our Lord Jesus Christ.

9 For anyone who lacks these things is short-sighted and blind, and is forgetful of the cleansing of past sins.

MAIN THOUGHT: Whereby are given unto us exceeding great and precious promises: that by these ye might be partakers of the divine nature, having escaped the corruption that is in the world through lust. (2 Peter 1:4, KJV)

2 Peter 1:1–15

King James Version	*New Revised Standard Version*
10 Wherefore the rather, brethren, give diligence to make your calling and election sure: for if ye do these things, ye shall never fall:	10 Therefore, brothers and sisters, be all the more eager to confirm your call and election, for if you do this, you will never stumble.
11 For so an entrance shall be ministered unto you abundantly into the everlasting kingdom of our Lord and Saviour Jesus Christ.	11 For in this way, entry into the eternal kingdom of our Lord and Savior Jesus Christ will be richly provided for you.
12 Wherefore I will not be negligent to put you always in remembrance of these things, though ye know them, and be established in the present truth.	12 Therefore I intend to keep on reminding you of these things, though you know them already and are established in the truth that has come to you.
13 Yea, I think it meet, as long as I am in this tabernacle, to stir you up by putting you in remembrance;	13 I think it right, as long as I am in this body, to refresh your memory,
14 Knowing that shortly I must put off this my tabernacle, even as our Lord Jesus Christ hath shewed me.	14 since I know that my death will come soon, as indeed our Lord Jesus Christ has made clear to me.
15 Moreover I will endeavour that ye may be able after my decease to have these things always in remembrance.	15 And I will make every effort so that after my departure you may be able at any time to recall these things.

LESSON SETTING

Time: circa A.D. 66
Place: Rome

LESSON OUTLINE

I. **Our Collective Faith (2 Peter 1:1–3)**
II. **The Gift of Faith (2 Peter 1:4–9)**
III. **Being Diligent in the Faith (2 Peter 1:10–15)**

Unifying Principle

People can be harmed by the corruption that is in the world. How can we guard our heads and hearts against the negative influences of corruption? Second Peter stresses the importance of supporting one's faith with goodness, knowledge, self-control, endurance, godliness, mutual affection, and love.

Introduction

The direction of the message Peter advances in this letter is one that focuses on the relationship between the goodness of the Lord and the manner in which believers are blessed so they can live in an ethical manner. For Peter, faith and morality become an important aspect derived from the grace of God. Peter realizes he is near the end of his life and his commitment to the Gospel and his audience will continue after his death, not just in the memory of who he was, but in the remembrance of whom he served.

Exposition

I. Our Collective Faith (2 Peter 1:1–3)

Peter begins his salutation with the acknowledgement he is a servant, who is bonded or fused together with Christ. By this period in the movement of Christianity, especially to the Gentile nations, this self-identification has become common. Examples are found in the Letter of James, "a bond-servant of God" (James 1:1), and in Paul's letters, "Paul and Timothy, bond-servants of Christ Jesus" (Phil. 1:1).

In many legal scenarios, especially where people or companies are charged with handling monies, those individuals often are "bonded," secured, and insured against possible fiduciary losses. If there is any malfeasance or misfeasance, the insurance company assumes the problems. In this manner, Peter and Paul are bonded or secured in the Lord; and as part of the opening verse, they further convey the faith of the Lord is one of equal sharing through One Lord, Jesus Christ.

Peter acknowledges all have received the same kind of faith, using the Greek term ἰσότιμος *isotimos*, which means the faith is held in equal honor and has been given equally in value. The concept of being a servant in the Lord does not have any negative overtones of slavery. To be bonded with Jesus is to share in the responsibilities of apostleship while receiving the power to accomplish the goals of the faith.

Peter notes the letter is to those who have embraced the faith through grace and peace, which Peter hopes will be multiplied (πληθύνω *plethuno*) or increased in the lives of the believers and is transmitted or transferred through faith and through the knowledge of God. Peter uses the Greek term ἐπίγνωσις *epignosos*, which is better understood as "recognition," indicating one who is filled with the fervor of the faith recognizes and acknowledges it came from having a personal relationship with God and Jesus Christ, knowing about their Father-Son connection, and exercising the belief that is worthy of being a disciple.

The prayer of multiplication for grace and peace is needed in a time at which chaos is the law of the land. Remember, Peter is writing this letter from Rome to Christians, wherever they may reside. Rome is a dangerous city for Christians, and in many other countries, the evil specter of idolatry and false doctrines continues to threaten the lives of the faithful. The prayer for the increase of grace and peace is found in a knowledge and relationship with God and Jesus.

As an example of the needed knowledge of the believer, Jesus has given (δωρέομαι *doreomai*) or bestowed upon the members all that is needed to navigate their lives, both in the basic needs of survival and also the growth of the church. The gift of the Lord further sets the believer in a position to present himself as a stalwart of redemption. In a world that has seemingly "gone mad," the Christian movement is offered to the world through genuine salvation, by which the faithful may live a life of godliness (εὐσέβεια *eusebeia*) or piety.

The early church fathers, such as Ignatius of Antioch and Origen of Alexandra, developed in their understanding of the holiness of the Lord. With what they considered the true knowledge of Jesus, they forged their lives in pursuit of an ascetic and penitent form of living. Peter acknowledges the faithful are able to embrace this degree of righteousness because we were called by God, while we were yet powerless to save ourselves, and were selected by the dazzling aura of His glory and excellence (ἀρετή *arete*). Additionally, this term defines the moral goodness and virtue that can emanate only from Jesus. The readers are encouraged to display the value of one who serves as a disciple of Christ.

II. The Gift of Faith (2 Peter 1:4–9)

Again, the Lord has granted or given to us His precious (τίμιος *timios*) or valued promises, which are priceless in the eyes of the faithful. Jesus promised many items that would be available to the followers who remained committed to the words of the Lord. Examples of these promises are that His disciples could meet a resurrected Jesus in Galilee or, as in the extension to the repentant criminal who was crucified along with Jesus, who Jesus would remember when He got to "his Kingdom." Peter could relate, as well as remember, these magnificent assurances that would seem fantastic in the minds of the unbeliever or infidel; however, Christians embrace the promise of never being left outside of the security of Jesus and the promise of being with Him in paradise.

The letter, therefore, explains the faithful are able to become partakers (κοινωνός *koinonos*) or partners in His divine nature. Peter possibly is developing a theology that places us in the revelation of Jesus' attributes; however, it is probably safer to say we are a reflection of His divine nature. Peter notes we are escaped slaves, in that we were able to flee from (ἀποφεύγω *apopheugo*) the trappings that corrupt (φθορά *phthora*) and degrade the beauty of this world. Moreover, we as humans contribute to this debasement and defilement by chasing after, lusting (ἐπιθυμία *epithumia*), or craving the trinkets and lifestyles of society. Our selfish desires are fueled by insecurities regarding our position or standing with the Lord; however, believers must realize following Jesus is the solution for avoiding a contaminated lifestyle.

Peter offers this solution: The believer should constantly apply (παρεισφέρω *pareisphero*) that which is his part of the contemporary linguistic climate, and he must "bring to the table" or "bring it" in the form of diligence (σπουδή *spoude*) or eagerness, while hastening to prove himself worthy of being a disciple. We should reflect an abundance of moral excellence (ἀρετή *arete*), goodness, and virtue, which seems to be lacking in the current realm of our communities. The audience of this letter is positioned to supply (ἐπιχορηγέω *epichoregeo*) or provide this to the world because of their knowledge of the Lord.

Saving grace, which is God's gift to humanity, is a germinal grace in the lives of Christians. Out of this foundational grace, all other forms of grace spring, blossom, and spring forth. We can declare that "if love is the greatest thing, faith is the first thing or result found in Christian character." Faith is the first living cell, as it were, from which the stalk and fruit of the Christian life spring. Hence the Apostle Peter enjoins we add to our faith virtue, knowledge, self-control, patience, godliness, brotherly kindness, and love.

Peter continues his list of attributes or cells of faith (which have germinated from the stalk of love that is based upon "walking with Jesus") with self-control (ἐγκράτεια *egkrateia*), which reflects a mastery of our lives, and perseverance (ὑπομονή hupomone), which is the act of being patient when faced with difficult challenges, while waiting on the intervention of the Lord. Within the attributes of godliness and brotherly kindness, we return to the core of the seed, which is love. Although the phrases "your self-control" and "your brotherly kindness" are translated in the NASB, in the original language, the article ὁ *ho*, meaning "the," emphasizes the brotherly love of the saints.

Peter reasons that if the faithful embrace the aforementioned qualities and the fruits of these traits are blessed to increase, we become approved in the eyes of the Lord. Acquiring these attributes is not a negative aspect; they will not devalue our lives or ruin our reputation. The phrase "render you neither useless" (ἀργός *argos*) may be better understood as, while you strive to follow the Lord, you never will be considered worthless in a world that places a value system on things not of heaven. Practicing Christians are never stagnant, but are constantly refreshed by the grace of God.

Peter notes Christians will not be unfruitful (ἄκαρπος *akarpos*) in the knowledge of the Lord because our labors will assist in the growth of the faith. As in the imagery of Jesus' commentary of the two trees, "every good tree bears good fruit (καρπός *karpos*), but the bad tree bears bad fruit"; therefore, "a good tree cannot produce bad fruit, nor can a bad tree produce good fruit" (Matt. 7:17-18). If we remain faithful to the Lord, we cannot be rendered (καθίστημι *kathistemi*) impotent because when we were called into His sphere, we were appointed, and our paths were set in order to make our lives prolific and joyous.

III. Being Diligent in the Faith (2 Peter 1:10–15)

So, therefore, brothers and sisters of the faith, Peter encourages all of the membership to be zealous and purposefully committed in their diligence (σπουδάζω *spoudazo*) toward living the tenets of the faith. Additionally, they are to make certain (ποιέω *poieo*) they realize it was the Lord who called them, being confident, certain (βέβαιος *bebaios*), and secure in the knowledge of the calling. Remember the selection (ἐκλογή *ekloge*)—the divine selection—and the choice of the believer is also an election of the Christian who decides to move beyond a mundane and baseless life with no hope into a lifestyle that has a goal of the Kingdom. Peter notes Christians must do their best to practice the traits of a Christian lifestyle and do what is necessary to maintain the consistency of the faith, which will provide a modicum that will keep us from stumbling (πταίω *patio*).

For in this manner, the entrance (εἴσοδος *eisodos*) into the Kingdom (βασιλεία *basileia*), which is eternal (αἰώνιος, aionios), immortal, and everlasting, is the realm of our Lord and Savior Jesus Christ. Again, as with the criminal who asked Jesus to remember him when Jesus came into His Kingdom, the promise to the audience of this letter (and all believers throughout history) will be honored. The power to enter the realm of the Lord is not based on our abilities; Peter notes our needs will be abundantly (πλουσίως *plousios*) supplied or provided to the faithful. It will occur only in the manner prescribed by the words of Jesus, as He exclaims one must "enter through the narrow (στενός *stenos*) gate; for the gate is wide and the way is broad that leads to destruction, and there are many who enter through it. For the gate is small [or constricted (θλίβω *thlibo*)], and the way is narrow that leads to life, and [unfortunately,] there are few who will find it" (Matt. 7:13–14). However, the gifts of God will allow unrestricted access.

Peter provides a voice to the spirit of the message. He reminds his readers he is ready (μέλλω mello) to encourage their Christian lifestyles Using the term ὑπομιμνήσκω *hupomimnesko*, Peter conveys the idea we must remember what the Lord has provided, even though many may believe repeating these tenets is not necessary.

The Lesson Applied

In this part of his second letter, Peter demonstrates his love for the faithful who, although scattered throughout the known world, have a need to continue in their love for the Lord through the eschewing of a riotous set of standards and conformity to the plaudits of the world. Peter encourages his readers to live in a visible manner that will reflect the gifts of the Lord and the relationship they share with Jesus. We struggle against forces that seek to impede our progress and even possibly destroy our ethical lifestyles; however, our commitment is strengthened by the love of the Lord. When we strive toward living a sober and deliberate life in the faith, He never fails to bless us with the power needed to maintain a spiritual life.

Let's Talk About It

1. **How do you benefit from the promises of God?**
2. **What did Peter urge his readers to add to their faith? Which of these character qualities do you find most difficult to practice? Which ones do you consider the most important to add to your faith life?**

Believers make their lives meaningful by being blessings to others, helping them to achieve a godliness that makes a difference in the world. There are an inordinate number of stories in which people have been encouraged to stumble by the actions of others that may consider themselves Christians. An example is a Christian drinking with a fellow member who is an alcoholic. Rather than encouraging a life of godliness, the Christian encourages the addiction because the weak person assumes if the Christian is drinking, it must be acceptable. Being a blessing to promote godliness also means being a role model to those who are in need.

Home Daily Devotional Readings
November 25–December 1, 2019

Monday	Tuesday	Wednesday	Thursday	Friday	Saturday	Sunday
Duties of the Levitical Priesthood	David Delivers Ark to Obed-edom	Leader to Bring Ark to Jerusalem	Ark Placed in Tent in Jerusalem	Regular Worship Services Resumed	Engaging in Spiritual Worship	Rejoice in God's Faithfulness
Deuteronomy 18:1–5	1 Chronicles 13:5–8, 13–14	1 Chronicles 15:4–13	1 Chronicles 16:1–6	1 Chronicles 16:37–43	Romans 12:1–8	1 Chronicles 15:1–3, 14–16, 25–29

So, Why Teach?

Teaching is a key element in acquiring information, developing knowledge, and calling for conformity to it; therefore, it is not surprising that the Bible has much to say about teaching. The supreme command to teach central to the Great Commission issued by Jesus, which is recorded in each of the four Gospel accounts: "Go ye therefore and teach them to observe, to do, to keep, to carry out, my word."

Therefore, if your gift is teaching, then you are to teach and to do it well. In this context, teaching refers to the God-given ability to explain God's Word. The teacher has the supernatural ability to clearly instruct and communicate knowledge, specifically the doctrines of the faith and truths of the Bible (1 Corinthians 12:27–29). Christian teaching is given to the Church to enlighten the pathway to divine grace. It comes from God to the Church, to its overseer and to others to instruct, inform, indoctrinate, nurture, and educate.

Teaching is a requirement for pastors and church workers: "Now the overseer is to be... able to teach," according to 1 Timothy 3:2 and 2 Timothy 2:24. Ephesians 4:16 says that God gave gifts, and among those gifts is that of the teaching pastor. The Bible instructs the pastor to teach sound doctrine based on the written Word of God: "Command and teach these things," Paul tells Timothy (1 Timothy 4:11). Those who are taught by the pastor are then to continue the process of disseminating information: "And the things you have heard me say in the presence of many witnesses entrust to reliable people who will also be qualified to teach others" (2 Timothy 2:2).

Note here that the Gospel is "entrusted" to us, and that teachers of the Gospel must be "qualified." Part of the qualification is to be "reliable." Being reliable does not mean simply to show up, and it certainly does not mean to show up with an empty head. Its root means "to pass it along, to pass the information along, hand it to the next person." Thus, we must transfer, disseminate, and distribute the Gospel by showing them the way to God and pointing out His truth, which inputs into them the life of God.

Teaching, like preaching, was an integral part of an apostle's work (Matthew 28:19; Ephesians 4:1). Paul knew that he was a teacher of the Gospel according to God's will: "And of this gospel I was appointed a herald and an apostle and a teacher" (2 Timothy 2:11).

Jesus, of course, was the greatest Teacher, and He often is referred to as "Rabbi" or "Teacher" (e.g., Luke 13:10; John 1:38; 3:2). In fact, He was and is The Teacher of teachers. But, what did He teach? He taught God's truth. In His initial sermon, He taught "The Spirit of the Lord is upon me because He has anointed me..." (Luke 4:16–20).

What was His method of teaching? Our Lord used illustrations (Luke 7:31–32), object lessons (Matthew 6:28), current events (Luke 13:4–5), and many stories (Matthew 13; Mark 4:2). He utilized lecture (Matthew 24), dialogue (John 3), rhetorical questions (Luke 18:8), and proverbs (Luke 7:45).

He gave "homework" and followed up on it (Matthew 9:13; 12:7). He used hyperbole (Matthew 5:29), metaphor (John 9:5), and provocative language (Luke 13:32). Jesus used them all because He, always the Teacher, had the best interests of His students at heart. The subject of His teaching was always the absolute and unchanging truth of God.

What was the purpose of His teaching? Jesus said that the logical end of effective teaching is that the pupil becomes like the teacher: "The student is not above the teacher, but everyone who is fully trained will be like their teacher" (Luke 6:40). He said this in the context of a warning to disciples to be careful whom they choose as their teacher, because if "the blind lead the blind... they [will] both fall into a pit" (verse 39). Let's keep them out of the pit! Let's teach the way of God, let us open blind eyes, let us mend broken hearts, let us energize old, worn-out souls, let us revitalize dead hopes, buried ambitions, and hopeless souls. Let us free them to explore the availability of God. We can do so by teaching that He came to bridge the gap between God and humanity and gave His life on the cross for our sin.

What shall we do then? We must teach what Jesus taught, study to show ourselves approved, and rightly divide the word of Truth. The test for any teaching is whether or not it aligns with the teaching of Jesus and His apostles. It must align with what He said, with what He did, and with what He commanded. So, teach it!

SECOND QUARTER

December

January

February

DAVID WORSHIPS GOD IN JERUSALEM

ADULT TOPIC:
CELEBRATE!

BACKGROUND SCRIPTURE:
1 CHRONICLES 15

1 CHRONICLES 15:1–3, 14–16, 25–29

King James Version

AND David made him houses in the city of David, and prepared a place for the ark of God, and pitched for it a tent.

2 Then David said, None ought to carry the ark of God but the Levites: for them hath the LORD chosen to carry the ark of God, and to minister unto him for ever.

3 And David gathered all Israel together to Jerusalem, to bring up the ark of the LORD unto his place, which he had prepared for it.

• • • • •

14 So the priests and the Levites sanctified themselves to bring up the ark of the LORD God of Israel.

15 And the children of the Levites bare the ark of God upon their shoulders with the staves thereon, as Moses commanded according to the word of the LORD.

16 And David spake to the chief of the Levites to appoint their brethren to be the singers with instruments of musick, psalteries and harps and cymbals, sounding, by lifting up the voice with joy.

• • • • •

25 So David, and the elders of Israel, and the captains over thousands, went to bring up the ark of the covenant of the LORD out of the house of Obededom with joy.

26 And it came to pass, when God helped the Levites that bare the ark of the covenant of the LORD, that they offered seven bullocks and seven rams.

New Revised Standard Version

DAVID built houses for himself in the city of David, and he prepared a place for the ark of God and pitched a tent for it.

2 Then David commanded that no one but the Levites were to carry the ark of God, for the LORD had chosen them to carry the ark of the Lord and to minister to him forever.

3 David assembled all Israel in Jerusalem to bring up the ark of the LORD to its place, which he had prepared for it.

• • • • •

14 So the priests and the Levites sanctified themselves to bring up the ark of the LORD, the God of Israel.

15 And the Levites carried the ark of God on their shoulders with the poles, as Moses had commanded according to the word of the LORD.

16 David also commanded the chiefs of the Levites to appoint their kindred as the singers to play on musical instruments, on harps and lyres and cymbals, to raise loud sounds of joy.

• • • • •

25 So David and the elders of Israel, and the commanders of the thousands, went to bring up the ark of the covenant of the LORD from the house of Obed-edom with rejoicing.

26 And because God helped the Levites who were carrying the ark of the covenant of the LORD, they sacrificed seven bulls and seven rams.

MAIN THOUGHT: Thus all Israel brought up the ark of the covenant of the LORD with shouting, and with sound of the cornet, and with trumpets, and with cymbals, making a noise with psalteries and harps. (1 Chronicles 15:28, KJV)

1 Chronicles 15:1–3, 14–16, 25–29

King James Version

27 And David was clothed with a robe of fine linen, and all the Levites that bare the ark, and the singers, and Chenaniah the master of the song with the singers: David also had upon him an ephod of linen.

28 Thus all Israel brought up the ark of the covenant of the Lord with shouting, and with sound of the cornet, and with trumpets, and with cymbals, making a noise with psalteries and harps.

29 And it came to pass, as the ark of the covenant of the Lord came to the city of David, that Michal, the daughter of Saul looking out at a window saw king David dancing and playing: and she despised him in her heart.

New Revised Standard Version

27 David was clothed with a robe of fine linen, as also were all the Levites who were carrying the ark, and the singers, and Chenaniah the leader of the music of the singers; and David wore a linen ephod.

28 So all Israel brought up the ark of the covenant of the Lord with shouting, to the sound of the horn, trumpets, and cymbals, and made loud music on harps and lyres.

29 As the ark of the covenant of the Lord came to the city of David, Michal daughter of Saul looked out of the window, and saw King David leaping and dancing; and she despised him in her heart.

LESSON SETTING

Time: circa 985 B.C.
Place: Jerusalem

LESSON OUTLINE

I. Preparing a Place for the Ark of the Covenant (1 Chronicles 15:1–3)

II. Preparations of the Priests to Carry the Ark (1 Chronicles 15:14–16)

III. Presentation of Worship to the Lord (1 Chronicles 15:25–29)

Unifying Principle

Whether it be for school, work, or worship, people are incredibly joyful and excited whenever they move into a new building. The excitement for the new building and its possibilities are infectious. What is the appropriate way for people of faith to celebrate such an exhilarating occasion? David commanded the priests to invite all the musicians and all the people of Israel to join in shouting, singing, and dancing as they rejoiced in what God had done for them.

Introduction

This passage properly belongs to the section of the 1 Chronicles that includes 15:1–16:3. It also has parallels in 1 Chronicles 13:1–13 and 2 Samuel 6:1–23. Most Old Testament scholars concur the parallel passages in 2 Samuel 6 and 1 Chronicles 13 and 15 represent documents from two different sources. Since this is true, most of the primary details are quite similar. One notes, however, there are some variations in perspective and emphases in the accounts. Familiarity with all of the accounts will enhance one's knowledge of them, as well as some of the theological aspects of the accounts.

The Ark of the Covenant was to be kept in the Holy of Holies of the tabernacle, since it symbolized the throne and presence of God (Pss. 80:1; 99:1). However, the Ark had been absent from the divine sanctuary at Shiloh for more than seventy–five years. First Samuel 4 indicates the Philistines captured the Ark when Eli was a judge but returned it to the Israelites following the Lord's judgment on the Philistines. After the Israelites regained possession, the Ark was sent to Beth Shemesh and then was taken to Kiriath Jearim, where it was guarded in the house of Abinadab (1 Sam. 5:1–7:1).

Zadok and Ahimelech (2 Sam. 8:17) both served as high priests during David's reign. It is possible one served at the sanctuary in Shiloh and then moved to Gibeon (2 Chron. 1:1–6). Simultaneously, the other possibly ministered at court in Jerusalem. David pitched a tent for the Ark in the City of David, but the furnishings in the tabernacle weren't moved to Jerusalem until after Solomon had finished construction of the temple (1 Kings 8:1–4; 2 Chron. 5:1–5).

Several factors likely influenced David's decision to move the Ark to Jerusalem. First, David's personal desire to build a permanent sanctuary for the Lord certainly motivated his decision (Ps. 135:1–5). To be sure, pragmatic political reasons also moved David to locate the Ark in Jerusalem. Then, centralization of worship in the capital city would unite the various tribes and families of Israel via the different worship experiences there. Furthermore, such a move would provide a sense of protection and security from nearby, often pagan, nations. Since the Ark's presence indicated the presence of the Lord Himself, the Ark also would provide an unmistakable expression of honor for Yahweh.

Exposition

I. Preparing a Place for the Ark of the Covenant (1 Chronicles 15:1–3)

The passage under consideration is David's second attempt to relocate the Ark to Jerusalem. First Chronicles 13 records a previous, unsuccessful attempt. For twenty years after the Philistines had returned it to Israel, the Ark had been stored in the home of Abinadab, a resident of Kirjath-jearim. His son, Eleazar, served as a priest of Israel (1 Sam. 7:1–2). Two other sons of Abinadab, Uzzah and Ahio, led the cart when the Ark was being transported from Kirjath-jearim to Jerusalem (2 Sam. 6:3–4). As the processional reached the threshing floor of Chidon (either a place or the name of the owner) the oxen pulling the cart stumbled, apparently tilting the Ark. Uzzah reached out and took hold of the Ark (reached out his hand and steadied the Ark of God, NLT). That was a forbidden act, according to God's directive to Moses in Numbers 20. The result was the Lords's anger burned against Uzzah, and God struck him down for putting his hand on the Ark. So Uzzah died there before God (1 Chron. 13:10, NIV). David's reaction to the incident was anger, so much so the site was named Perez Uzzah, meaning "Breach of Uzzah."

David had another reaction to the display of God's anger at Chidon (or Nacon, in 2 Sam. 6:6). According to 1 Chronicles 13:9, David was afraid of God that day and wondered, "How can I ever bring the Ark of God to me?" He aborted the attempt to take the Ark to Jerusalem at that time. Instead, he stored it at the house of Obed-Edom, a Philistine from Gath, who was loyal to King David and Israel. During the three-month period the Ark was in Obed-Edom's house, the Lord blessed him.

After constructing several buildings for himself, David then placed priority on getting the Ark to a special place in Jerusalem. To be sure, he was now motivated by the report he had received about the prosperity of Obed-Edom's household for keeping the Ark. Now King David was told, "The LORD has blessed the household of Obed-Edom and everything he has, because of the ark of God."

So David brought the Ark of God from the house of Obed-Edom to the City of David with rejoicing (2 Sam. 6:12). David then sent the Levites, the only ones qualified to carry the Ark, on the ten-mile trip to the house of Obed-Edom. They brought the Ark to Jerusalem by carrying it on their shoulders and keeping with the Mosaic mandate. The previous attempt to deliver the Ark to Jerusalem on a cart pulled by oxen actually was a practice from pagan Philistine culture. When the Ark arrived, David had prepared a special site and a tent for it. The event involved the entire community of Israel (v. 3).

II. Preparations of the Priests to Carry the Ark (1 Chronicles 15:14–16)

One of the highly commendable characteristics about David is he learned from his past mistakes. The second attempt to locate the Ark in Jerusalem was successful mainly because David corrected some inappropriate procedures from the first attempt. He began the successful attempt by consulting with the high priests, Zadok and Abiathar. Included in that consultation were six Levites. David instructed them to consecrate themselves for the task of relocating the Ark from Obed-Edom's home to Jerusalem. David clearly understood the first attempt failed because the Levites had not carried the Ark, nor had he and the religious leaders inquired of the Lord prior to their actions (1 Chron. 15:13). David did not want to repeat that error.

In keeping with the wise insights of David, the priests and Levites consecrated—set apart—themselves for the task of moving the Ark. They were to follow the requirement to carry the Ark on their shoulders, using the poles through the hooks on the Ark (Exod. 25:14). This was a task only Levites were to fulfill (Num. 7:9). These measures were in complete compliance with the instructions of Moses (v. 15).

The preparations of the priests and Levites had a significant liturgical component. The Levites chosen were tasked with recruiting other Levites to form a Levitical choir. The choir was to be accompanied by musicians—particularly those who played harps, lyres, and cymbals. There is significance to the instruments included in the list. Clyde T. Francisco indicates, "This is the usual combination in ancient Hebrew worship, a contrast of percussion and stringed instruments. The harps and lyres were similar, but the former tended to have more strings. The lyre was the more common instrument for playing solo, and was the one played by David. There were normally more lyres in an orchestra than harps."

III. Presentation of Worship to the Lord (1 Chronicles 15:25–29)

Worship, in a variety of expressions, is the main theme of this part of the lesson. The processional of David, the elders of Israel, the military, and the religious leaders are characterized as one of "joy" or "celebration." Verse 26 indicates another form of worship being the sacrifice of seven bulls and rams (Num. 23:1; Job 42:8) in recognition of the Lord's help in the successful transition of the Ark from Gath to Jerusalem. The participants' clothing in the processional also contributed to the liturgical character of the historic event. David, the Levites, and all the singers wore robes of fine linen. Additionally, David wore a linen ephod, a short skirt- or apron-like garment that priests normally wore over their robe. David wore the ephod on the outside of his robe to keep the robe in place.

The processional is described as a festive and loud event with shouts from the people and the sounds of various musical instruments. The author also mentions the use of the "ram's horn," or shofar. The shofar is mentioned more frequently in the Bible than any other musical instrument. It particularly served to call the people of Israel together and was used at special religious events. It also was used to rally Israel during times of war. The trumpet, a straight metal instrument about two feet long and a favorite instrument of Levites, also was included along with various stringed instruments and cymbals.

The text concludes with the subtle yet significant mention of another form of liturgy—dance. As the processional entered the city of Jerusalem, Michal, David's wife and the younger daughter of King Saul, watched from a window and saw David dancing. Rhythmic movement was prominent in Hebrew culture. Dancing followed military victories (Exod. 15:20–21; Judg. 11:34; 1 Sam. 18:6; 30:16). The psalmist encouraged dancing as a form of worship (Pss. 149:3; 150:4). Festive times also usually included dancing (Luke 15:25; Matt. 14:6).

The Lesson Applied

This lesson provides several valuable lessons for contemporary Christians. David and his people displayed significant knowledge of and insight into their past. They were well aware of the things the Lord required concerning the Ark of the Covenant as conveyed by Moses. That knowledge was not limited to the priests and Levites; but rather, all members of the covenant community had that knowledge. It is true, however, in subsequent years, they acquiesced to the desires of King David. Nonetheless, they were knowledgeable of what God expected and were quick to repent, along with David, when confronted with actions that displeased God. Contemporary believers must never lose sight of the foundations and essentials of their faith. Furthermore, they should never lose sight of those things that distinguish them from other religions or unbelievers. Additionally, they should have an understanding of why such practices are important to the faith

The lesson also serves as a reminder there is inclusiveness among the people of God that should not be ignored or minimized. To be sure, some among God's people have unique roles and responsibilities. There are those whom the Lord has providentially placed in positions of leadership. That was true of Israel and is equally true of the Church as the people of God through Jesus Christ. At the time of First Samuel, however, each person in the body of the faithful is of equal worth. Just as Israel's people all shared in the relocation of the Ark—spiritual leaders, military, political leaders, and regular citizens—God's people now all must share in those events and experiences that shape His people.

Let's Talk About It

1. **What are some events in your life or in the life of your church fellowship that called for a response of comprehensive and extensive praise to God?**
2. **How was that praise expressed?**
3. **What are some errors from your past that provided insights for an appropriate or correct response to the Lord?**
4. **As a godly king, David provided both political leadership and spiritual guidance to the people of Israel. What persons, if any, in the public sector today provide spiritual guidance for you and why?**

The significance of worship in a variety of forms is another insight from this lesson. There was no singular form of worship for Israel. Singing, loud shouts, dance, instruments, expressions of joy, and other methods were offered by David and Israel. The defining characteristic was they all were offered by sincere people for the glory of God.

We must not look for the same experiences and manifestations in all. Such demands within the church lead only to perfunctory and meaningless worship experiences. Such worship is designed for the pleasure and approval of other human beings and not God. Each person's religious conduct will bear the plain impress of his or her character and disposition. This may be applied to experiences of conversion, to the beginnings of the Christian life, and also to the forms in which individuals stand related to public worship and Christian work. If we venture to make molds for the necessary Christian life, we must take care they are large and general, with no fine lines of requisite peculiarities. Christ gives new life and sends each person forth to express it according to his or her own genius and character.

We may not, even in thought, exempt anyone from its gracious influence. We may not be anxious to have the natural dispositions of human beings changed. Humanity does not need to be made other than they we are. God receives us in the same manner. We need not want to make the channel of the river bend and turn in any other and, as we think, more graceful forms. Our anxiety should concern the purity of the waters flowing down from the fountain-head, which fill the stream. Preservation of the characteristic disposition is quite consistent with all Christian culture and brings out the best in us.

Home Daily Devotional Readings
December 2–8, 2019

Monday	Tuesday	Wednesday	Thursday	Friday	Saturday	Sunday
All Nations Invited to Worship God	Response to God's Generosity	God's Saving Deeds	God's Gracious Compassion	God's Forever Covenant	God's Forever Steadfast Love	God's Wondrous Deeds for all People
Isaiah 45:20–25	Deuteronomy 26:1–11	Psalm 105:1–15	Psalm 106:40–48	1 Chronicles 16:14–18	1 Chronicles 16:28–36	1 Chronicles 16:8–13, 19–27

A HEART FILLED WITH GRATITUDE

ADULT TOPIC:
SHOWING GRATITUDE

BACKGROUND SCRIPTURE:
1 CHRONICLES 16:7–36

1 CHRONICLES 16:8–12, 19–27

King James Version

GIVE thanks unto the LORD, call upon his name, make known his deeds among the people.

9 Sing unto him, sing psalms unto him, talk ye of all his wondrous works.

10 Glory ye in his holy name: let the heart of them rejoice that seek the LORD.

11 Seek the LORD and his strength, seek his face continually.

12 Remember his marvellous works that he hath done, his wonders, and the judgments of his mouth;

•••••

19 When ye were but few, even a few, and strangers in it.

20 And when they went from nation to nation, and from one kingdom to another people;

21 He suffered no man to do them wrong: yea, he reproved kings for their sakes,

22 Saying, Touch not mine anointed, and do my prophets no harm.

23 Sing unto the LORD, all the earth; shew forth from day to day his salvation.

24 Declare his glory among the heathen; his marvellous works among all nations.

25 For great is the LORD, and greatly to be praised: he also is to be feared above all gods.

26 For all the gods of the people are idols: but the LORD made the heavens.

27 Glory and honour are in his presence; strength and gladness are in his place.

New Revised Standard Version

O GIVE thanks to the LORD, call on his name, make known his deeds among the peoples.

9 Sing to him, sing praises to him, tell of all his wonderful works.

10 Glory in his holy name; let the hearts of those who seek the LORD rejoice.

11 Seek the LORD and his strength, seek his presence continually.

12 Remember the wonderful works he has done, his miracles, and the judgments he uttered,

•••••

19 When they were few in number, of little account, and strangers in the land,

20 wandering from nation to nation, from one kingdom to another people,

21 he allowed no one to oppress them; he rebuked kings on their account,

22 saying, "Do not touch my anointed ones; do my prophets no harm."

23 Sing to the LORD, all the earth. Tell of his salvation from day to day.

24 Declare his glory among the nations, his marvelous works among all the peoples.

25 For great is the LORD, and greatly to be praised; he is to be revered above all gods.

26 For all the gods of the peoples are idols, but the LORD made the heavens.

27 Honor and majesty are before him; strength and joy are in his place.

MAIN THOUGHT: Give thanks unto the LORD, call upon his name, make known his deeds among the people. (1 Chronicles 16:8, KJV)

LESSON SETTING

Time: circa 985 B.C.
Place: Jerusalem

LESSON OUTLINE

I. A Call to Worship God With Thanksgiving (1 Chronicles 16:8–12)
II. A Call to Worship God As King (1 Chronicles 16:19–27)

UNIFYING PRINCIPLE

People easily can become discouraged when looking at the turbulent conditions in their lives and the tumultuous conditions around the world. How can we, as people of faith, find the courage to face the difficult, problematic challenges and changes in our own lives as well as the lives of the faithful around the world? David's people sang a psalm of thanksgiving and a psalm of worship to God for all the great things God had done for them and for the greatness of God's being during the times of victory celebration and seemingly devastating defeat.

INTRODUCTION

This lesson emerges from the time in Israel's history associated with the return of the Ark of the Covenant to Jerusalem. The people brought the Ark and set it inside the tent David pitched and then presented burnt offerings and fellowship offerings before God. After David had finished sacrificing the burnt offerings and fellowship offerings, he blessed the people in the name of the Lord. He appointed some of the Levites to minister before the ark of the Lord, to make petition, to give thanks, and to praise the Lord, the God of Israel. That day David first committed to Asaph and his associates this psalm of thanks to the Lord (1 Chron. 16:1–2,4,7). David previously had appointed Levites to lead and oversee worship associated with transporting the Ark from Gath to Jerusalem (1 Chron. 15:16). Those appointments were temporary and associated only with that move.

The present passage is concerned with the permanent appointments David makes after the Ark of the Covenant is in its location in the tent he had provided in Jerusalem. He selected fewer persons for the responsibilities in Jerusalem. Their responsibilities were limited to providing music and protection before the Ark of the Covenant. The first section of this passage focuses on the music, for which Asaph was given oversight. Essentially, the musicians and singers had a three-fold focus for their music. They were to "invoke" God by calling attention to the needs of the worshipers. Then, they were to give thanks to God for what He previously had done for them. Finally, they were to provide praise to God simply for who He was.

The psalm or song in 1 Chronicles 16 actually is a compilation of several other songs from the psalter. First Chronicles 16:8–22 derives from Psalm 105:1–15. Thus the Chronicler brings to a close his complicated account of the installation of the Ark in Jerusalem, the first step toward the goal of building a temple.

The second passage for this lesson belongs to the wider context that includes 1 Chronicles 16:23–33 and has its parallel in Psalm 96:1–13. Attention will be given to both the Chronicler and the psalmist in the discussion following.

Exposition

I. A Call to Worship God with Thanksgiving (1 Chronicles 16:8–12)

This passage is primarily a call to worship for Israel, the ultimate goal of which is thanksgiving. Simultaneously, there is a characterization of what that thanksgiving should look like and the variety of ways to worship God. Thanksgiving is the major motif here, yet it flows from the mighty acts of God on Israel's behalf and is connected to the character (the name) of God.

This passage expresses Israel's relationship with and dependence on the Lord, for they are to make known among the nations what He has done. This declaration calls for a witness to pagan nations about the deeds Yahweh has performed on the behalf of Israel.

Verse 9 highlights singing as a form of worship and praise as well as a medium of declaring the things God has done. The thanksgiving and worship to be offered must be theocentric—that is, centered on God. The worshipers are to "glory," "exult," "revel" in or honor the Lord's name. Those who seek Him are to rejoice.

The confessional aspect of authentic worship also is evident in this passage. The summons to look to the Lord and His strength and to seek His face continually (v. 11) are an admission of the insufficiency of human resources. Humans are dependent on the Lord's strength. They must pray. They incessantly need fellowship with God, which is essentially what it means to "seek His face." The passage reiterates the responsibility to speak of the wondrous things God has done (v. 12). Yet, perhaps as an emphasis on the importance of the Lord's requirements of His people, the verse concludes with a call to remember the judgments he has pronounced.

One encounters a nearly verbatim expression of this passage in Psalm 105:1–5. Additional expressions from 1 Chronicles 16 are found in Psalm 105:6–15, which has three major movements. The first section calls the people of Israel to worship and praise their covenant God, whose name is Yahweh.

Then follows a series of reasons why the people should praise God. This section traces the Lord's providential relationship with Israel—His call and dealings with the Patriarchs, their deliverance from Egypt, the ministry of Moses, and the giving of the land of Canaan. It also includes His blessings on Israel among the nations and His blessings on them in the wilderness.

The psalm concludes with a rationale for the Lord's blessings on Israel and a brief statement of their responsibility to worship Him. All this happened so they would follow His decrees and obey His instructions. Praise the Lord (Ps. 105:45, NLT)!

II. A Call to Worship God As King (1 Chronicles 16:19–27)

First Chronicles 16:19–27 has its parallel in the book of Psalms. Verses 19–22 of the lesson text in 1 Chronicles 16 are found in Psalm 105:1–15. Verses 23–22 are contained in Psalm 96:1b–13a. First Chronicles 16 compresses and modifies Psalm 96 and combines other passages from the Psalter. This then constituted the prayer of thanksgiving David provided to Asaph and the choir and musicians to use in the worship at the relocation of the Ark of the Covenant in Jerusalem. Both passages from the book of 1 Chronicles in their book of Psalms origins were formulated specifically for the Ark ceremony. Most Old Testament scholars concur the passages were employed at other worship experiences in the history of Israel. That is especially true of those in which a recounting of God's special activities for Israel provided the inspiration for the praise and worship.

Several Old Testament exegetes point to the post-exilic period in Israel as an occasion during which these passages were particularly appropriate. Those returning to their homeland after the Exile were faced with dark, dismal, and discouraging days. The challenges of rebuilding Jerusalem and the temple seemed nearly insurmountable. The spiritual leaders—including the priests, Levites, and prophets—garner motivation for the returning pilgrims from the passages under discussion. As Yahweh had worked in Israel's past, as confirmed by abundant evidence, He would work in their current circumstances.

Old Testament interpreter John I. Durham identifies Psalm 96 as a testimony to the royalty of God: "This exuberant hymn of Yahweh's kingship proclaims him sovereign over all peoples in all the earth as the inevitable conclusion of what he is. He has acted and continues to. He gets things done. The idol gods do not and are thus of no consequence. His kingship, which is nothing new, is a universal one. This universality—a fact because of who God is—is the special basis of the poet's new song."

All this equally applies to the portion of the psalm that is reflected in 1 Chronicles 16. Clyde T. Francisco asserts of 1 Chronicles 16: "The emphases of the psalm are upon God's rule of the whole earth, his care of his people when they were in alien lands, and the eventual recognition of Yahweh's lordship by all people. The climactic verse calls upon God to gather and 'save us' from among the nations."

First Chronicles 16:19–20 contains a series of synonymous statements highlighting the relative insignificance of Israel compared to other nations of the world. The reminiscence of Israel's past designates them "few in number, indeed very few." It also calls Israel "strangers," or "aliens." The term in contemporary times connotes "tourists" and indicates those who had no permanent dwelling place at the time. Like nomads, Israel roamed from nation to nation, from kingdom to kingdom (Ps. 105:12–13). Thus, Israel was insignificant in the eyes of all nations, kingdoms, and tribes on the earth.

In shocking contrast to that perspective, however, the psalmist testifies of Yahweh's approach to Israel: "He didn't let anyone push them around, He stood up for them against bully-kings" (v. 16, MSG). Yahweh then identified Israel as His own people and expressed His protection of them with words of warning to all the nations of the world, "Don't you dare touch my anointed ones, don't lay a hand on my prophets" (v. 22, MSG).

The basis for 1 Chronicles 16:23–25 is Psalm 96:1–4, which is an exhortation to "Sing to the LORD a new song.... praise his name" (NIV). Although there is some variation between the two passages in wording and the order in which certain ideas occur, there are some common themes between them. An emphasis on singing appears in the passage under discussion and in the parallel in Psalm 96. First Chronicles urges inclusive singing of all creation—that is, all persons—to the Lord. Furthermore, the worshipers are to declare the Lord's salvation or deliverance perpetually. The *New Living Translation* adds some clarity to the assignment of the singers: "Let the whole earth sing to the LORD! Each day proclaim the Good News that He saves."

The parallel to 1 Chronicles 16:23 in Psalm 96:1 calls for singing to the Lord a "new song" from all the earth. "New" here can mean an unheard song. It can mean "new" in terms of time or in terms of expression. The expression "new song" appears four other times in Psalms, in addition to its occurrence in Psalm 96 (Pss. 40:3; 98:1; 144:9; 149:1). It also appears in Isaiah 42:10 and Revelation 5:9 and 14:3. Fresh experiences of God's blessings, truths from His Word, renewal of one's relationship with Him following a time of crisis, or new opportunities for service can occasion a "new song." Joy over the relocation of the Ark of the Covenant in Jerusalem and its meaning provided the historical context for Israel's new song.

Psalm 96 also promotes inclusivity—Jews and Gentiles alike—in its summons to sing to the Lord. This is evident in a call to all the earth (v. 1); declaring God's glory among the nations (v. 3a); and His marvelous deeds among all peoples (v. 3). The inclusive emphasis also extends to verses 7, 9, 11, and 13 in Psalm 96.

The uniqueness of God, both in His character and in His actions, is another common theme in 1 Chronicles 16 and the parallel in Psalm 96. The greatness of God, His worthiness of praise, and His worthiness of reverential fear from all persons are indicated in 1 Chronicles 16:25. To whatever extent idol gods are to be revered by their devotees, Yahweh is to be revered exponentially much more. The MSG accurately expresses the intention of the psalmist in saying of Yahweh, "No god or goddess comes close in honor."

The theme of the absolute superiority of Yahweh over any and all other deities continues in 1 Chronicles 16:26 and Psalm 96:5. The Chronicler declares: "For all the gods of the nations are idols, but the Lord made the heavens." This verse appears verbatim in 1 Chronicles 16:5. The idols of the other nations are "feeble nothings." They are completely powerless to accomplish anything. In striking contrast, Yahweh "made the heavens" (Ps. 96:5). The implication is Yahweh, and no one else, is Creator of the cosmos.

First Chronicles 16:27 is a doxological declaration—an expression of glorification or praise to God that essentially sums up all that has gone before in the passage. The doxology speaks of the Lord and His presence in the Ark of the Covenant. The declaration is that splendor and majesty are before Him. "Strength and joy in His dwelling place" testifies to the glory and power of God in His Person. It simultaneously testifies to the glory and power of God in His presence in the Ark of the Covenant.

The Lesson Applied

The late great composer Thomas A. Dorsey told how the tragedy of losing his wife and infant son inspired the gospel staple "Precious Lord, Take My Hand." The song was his acknowledgement of his weakness and God's faithfulness.

As it was for God's people in Israel, singing is a significant component of Christian worship. This lesson is a reminder Israel's music emerged from the people's experiences with God. Real-life events gave rise to the lyrics, to the accompaniment, and to the emotion of their music. The primary purpose of their music was to exalt the Lord. There were many other byproducts of their music, but all of them were secondary to focusing on the character and acts of God in Israel's history. The worshipers experienced needed reminders of God's faithfulness to them and His purposes and plans for them. They underwent spiritual, emotional, psychological, and relational renewal as they sang. They deepened their intellectual and theological understanding of the Lord. And there likely were countless other byproducts of their music. But responsibility number one was to testify to the singular greatness of God.

Music that legitimately offers praise and worship to God always must interrogate itself. It always must ask certain questions of itself through those who sing, play, write, and even conduct music. "Why are we singing?" "For whom and about whom do we sing?" "What is the message of our music?" "To what extent does our music glorify God?" "To what extent does our music edify people in their relationship with and knowledge of God?" These are some foundational questions worthy of ongoing consideration.

Let's Talk About It

1. **What are some things for which you personally are grateful?**
2. **What are some things for which the congregation you belong to should be thankful?**
3. **What are some of God's characteristics that readily come to mind that should be material for worship music?**

Those who provide musical worship and praise also must consider seriously the sources of inspiration for their music. The nature of God, significant events in Israel's relationship with Him, milestones on the journey and faith, and even places provided inspiration for the Israelites' music. Contemporary Christians must ever do the same—look to authentic sources of inspiration for their music ministry. Christian theology provides the lyrics to a musical track to our life of faith. As the hearts of the faithful open to the goodness of God through praise and worship, divine truths will be revealed and rooted in the spirit of those seeking to love God and neighbor. Christian theology is the encouragement and strength to live with hope in Christ through the Spirit.

Home Daily Devotional Readings

December 9–15, 2019

Monday	Tuesday	Wednesday	Thursday	Friday	Saturday	Sunday
David Cannot Build the Temple	Solomon to Build the Temple	Ornan's Land Is Site of Temple	God Needs No House	God's Makes a House for David	The Lord Regards the Lowly	Two Houses Firmly Settled
1 Chronicles 22:6–13	1 Chronicles 28:2–10	1 Chronicles 21:28–22:1	2 Samuel 7:1–11	1 Chronicles 17:7–10	Psalm 138	1 Chronicles 17:1, 3–4, 11–14; 21:18, 21–27

BUILDING GOD'S HOUSE

ADULT TOPIC:
NEGOTIATING OBEDIENCE

BACKGROUND SCRIPTURE:
1 CHRONICLES 17:1–15; 21:18–30

1 CHRONICLES 17:1, 3–4, 11–14; 21:18, 21–27

King James Version

NOW it came to pass, as David sat in his house, that David said to Nathan the prophet, Lo, I dwell in an house of cedars, but the ark of the covenant of the LORD remaineth under curtains.

• • • • •

3 And it came to pass the same night, that the word of God came to Nathan, saying,

4 Go and tell David my servant, Thus saith the LORD, Thou shalt not build me an house to dwell in:

• • • • •

11 And it shall come to pass, when thy days be expired that thou must go to be with thy fathers, that I will raise up thy seed after thee, which shall be of thy sons; and I will establish his kingdom.

12 He shall build me an house, and I will stablish his throne for ever.

13 I will be his father, and he shall be my son: and I will not take my mercy away from him, as I took it from him that was before thee:

14 But I will settle him in mine house and in my kingdom for ever: and his throne shall be established for evermore.

• • • 21:18, 21–27 • • •

18 Then the angel of the LORD commanded Gad to say to David, that David should go up, and set up an altar unto the LORD in the threshingfloor of Ornan the Jebusite.

New Revised Standard Version

NOW when David settled in his house, David said to the prophet Nathan, "I am living in a house of cedar, but the ark of the covenant of the LORD is under a tent."

• • • • •

3 But that same night the word of the LORD came to Nathan, saying:

4 Go and tell my servant David: Thus says the LORD: You shall not build me a house to live in.

• • • • •

11 When your days are fulfilled to go to be with your ancestors, I will raise up your offspring after you, one of your own sons, and I will establish his kingdom.

12 He shall build a house for me, and I will establish his throne forever.

13 I will be a father to him, and he shall be a son to me. I will not take my steadfast love from him, as I took it from him who was before you,

14 but I will confirm him in my house and in my kingdom forever, and his throne shall be established forever.

• • • 21:18, 21–27 • • •

18 Then the angel of the LORD commanded Gad to tell David that he should go up and erect an altar to the LORD on the threshing floor of Ornan the Jebusite.

MAIN THOUGHT: And it shall come to pass, when thy days be expired that thou must go to be with thy fathers, that I will raise up thy seed after thee, which shall be of thy sons; and I will establish his kingdom. He shall build me an house, and I will stablish his throne for ever. (1 Chronicles 17:11–12, KJV)

1 Chronicles 17:1, 3–4, 11–14; 21:18, 21–27

King James Version

• • • • •

21 And as David came to Ornan, Ornan looked and saw David, and went out of the threshingfloor, and bowed himself to David with his face to the ground.
22 Then David said to Ornan, Grant me the place of this threshingfloor, that I may build an altar therein unto the Lord: thou shalt grant it me for the full price: that the plague may be stayed from the people.
23 And Ornan said unto David, Take it to thee, and let my lord the king do that which is good in his eyes: lo, I give thee the oxen also for burnt offerings, and the threshing instruments for wood, and the wheat for the meat offering; I give it all.
24 And king David said to Ornan, Nay; but I will verily buy it for the full price: for I will not take that which is thine for the Lord, nor offer burnt offerings without cost.
25 So David gave to Ornan for the place six hundred shekels of gold by weight.
26 And David built there an altar unto the Lord, and offered burnt offerings and peace offerings, and called upon the Lord; and he answered him from heaven by fire upon the altar of burnt offering.
27 And the Lord commanded the angel; and he put up his sword again into the sheath thereof.

New Revised Standard Version

• • • • •

21 As David came to Ornan, Ornan looked and saw David; he went out from the threshing floor, and did obeisance to David with his face to the ground.
22 David said to Ornan, "Give me the site of the threshing floor that I may build on it an altar to the Lord—give it to me at its full price—so that the plague may be averted from the people."
23 Then Ornan said to David, "Take it; and let my lord the king do what seems good to him; see, I present the oxen for burnt offerings, and the threshing sledges for the wood, and the wheat for a grain offering. I give it all."
24 But King David said to Ornan, "No; I will buy them for the full price. I will not take for the Lord what is yours, nor offer burnt offerings that cost me nothing."
25 So David paid Ornan six hundred shekels of gold by weight for the site.
26 David built there an altar to the Lord and presented burnt offerings and offerings of well–being. He called upon the Lord, and he answered him with fire from heaven on the altar of burnt offering.
27 Then the Lord commanded the angel, and he put his sword back into its sheath.

LESSON SETTING

Time: circa 985 B.C.
Place: Jerusalem

LESSON OUTLINE

I. **David Desires to Build the Lord a House (1 Chronicles 17:1, 3–4)**

II. **David's Offspring to Build the Lord a House (1 Chronicles 17:11–14)**

III. **David Builds an Altar to the Lord (1 Chronicles 21:21–27)**

Unifying Principle

People are not always able to accomplish what they desire to do for others. Is it possible to see a positive result even when our desires are not accomplished? Although God did not agree for David to build a temple, God promised his son would.

Introduction

Augustine, the bishop of Hippo in North Africa in the late fourth and early fifth centuries, prayed one prayer to the effect that God would take Augustine's will and make it God's will. The clear knowledge of that which is the Lord's will and the incorporation of it into one's own life—including the surrender of one's personal will to that of God—constitutes an indispensable aspect of one's relationship with God. Given Jesus' unforgettable words, "My Father, if it is possible, may this cup be taken from me. Yet not as I will, but as you will" (Matt. 26:39), few believers are capable of overlooking the supremacy of God's will.

However, out of sincere zeal and love for God, one unintentionally might assume one's personal desires are synonymous with those of God. This is the crux of this lesson. David erroneously assumed his desire to build the Lord a house, the temple, was also what the Lord wanted from him.

David would come to know not only is God's will a priority, God's timing is also. God's perfect will and His perfect timing involve specific purposes and specific persons, circumstances, and events for their fulfillment. God's absolute sovereignty superintends that fulfilment.

As with previous lessons, this one in 1 Chronicles 17 also has a corresponding parallel in 2 Samuel 7. Insights from there will be helpful in the narrative preserved and presented by the Chronicler.

Exposition

I. David Desires to Build the Lord a House (1 Chronicles 17:1, 3–4)

David's desire to build the Lord a house, a permanent place in which the Ark of the Covenant could be placed, surfaced from both personal sincerity and pragmatism. The king himself was residing in a permanent structure, "a palace of cedar." The Ark, on the other hand, was housed in a temporary and much more perishable tent. David reasons from the lesser to the greater. He, a mere man, has a beautiful and luxurious building. "But the Ark of God is out there in a tent" (NLT). The Chronicler straightforwardly mentions this concern was expressed after David occupied his royal palace. In fact, David expressed both interest in and intention to build the Lord's house during the king's exilic years. Psalm 132:1–5 indicates this: "Lord, remember David and all that he suffered. He made a solemn promise to the Lord. He vowed to the Mighty One of Israel, 'I will not go home; I will not let myself rest. I will not let my eyes sleep nor close my eyelids in slumber until I find a place to build a house for the Lord, a sanctuary for the Mighty One of Israel' " (NLT).

Samuel provides the insight that historical circumstances assisted in providing the opportunity for David to consider more definitely the matter of the temple. He indicates the consideration of the temple arose after David was settled in his palace. He adds, however, "and the Lord had given him rest from all his enemies around him" (2 Sam. 7:1). This was apparently a temporary respite from war, for the following chapter enumerates several additional military conquests achieved by David. Nonetheless, apart from the preoccupation with the surrounding warring enemies, David was free to concentrate on other matters, such as the Lord's house.

As noble and sincere as David's desire was, he actually stood in need of a voice of clarity and correction. That came from his consultation with the prophet and his spiritual advisor, Nathan. His presence in this passage is the first for the prophet Nathan, whose name means "gift." During David's years in exile, Gad was prophet-advisor to David (1 Sam. 22:5). Gad continued to direct David in spiritual matters after the king's coronation and beyond (2 Sam. 24:1). He and Nathan worked jointly in maintaining official records (1 Chron. 29:25, 29) and in overseeing worship (2 Chron. 29:25). During the reign of David, Nathan apparently had the more prominent role as spiritual guide to David and to Solomon as well. It was Nathan who confronted David about his sins of adultery and murder (2 Sam. 11–12). And he also helped ensure Solomon was crowned king (1 Kings 1:11).

When David shared his concerns about the Lord's house with the prophet Nathan, the prophet encouraged him, "Whatever you have in mind, do it, for God is with you" (1 Chron. 17:2). Was Nathan assuring David he was on the right path in his desires? Or was Nathan directing David to pursue his desires in order to discern the Lord's will? The balance of this part of the lesson strongly suggests the latter.

That night, the prophet Nathan receives explicit insights from the Lord for David concerning the construction of a permanent building for the Ark. The Lord affirms David is "my servant." That is a significant expression, stating David's relationship with the Lord and his position in the Lord's plans. As the Lord's servant, David is to comply with what the Lord wants. The balance of Nathan's message for David is that though a house will be built, David will not be the one to do so.

A noteworthy elaboration of the message to Nathan for David is in 2 Samuel 7. The Lord indicates He never questioned the tribes of Israel or any of their leaders as to why they had not built Him a house of cedar. The Lord then reminded David that as He had with the people of Israel in earlier days, He also had been with David, removing all his enemies. The Lord has chosen David for the primary purpose of being a ruler or caring leader over His people. Certain promises accompanied that.

God would place David's name among those of the greatest men on earth. The Lord would protect and prosper the people of Israel and David's reign. As to a house, however, the Lord would provide that Himself. The term "house" comes to have varied meaning in 2 Samuel and 1 Chronicles 17. On the one hand, it does refer to a permanent dwelling place for the Ark of the Covenant. On another hand, it also refers to the house and kingdom of David (2 Sam. 7:16). That is a statement about the perpetuity of Davidic rule expressing itself in the Messianic Age in time and eternity. The word "house" refers to the Lord's house—both a building and the people—in whom He would dwell.

II. David's Offspring to Build the Lord a House (1 Chronicles 17:11–14)

God's purposes, plans, and timing are impeccable. Long before David expressed a personal desire to construct the temple, or even had conceived the idea in his mind, the Lord had a plan for it. That the Lord did not allow David to build the temple is not so much a rejection of David as it is an affirmation of God's sovereign selection of Solomon to do so.

The revelation to David that he would not be allowed to build the temple undoubtedly came as a disappointment to the king. Perhaps of equal concern to him was the future of his lineage and kingdom. David had become Israel's second king after the Lord selected him to succeed the rejected Saul. God's rejection of Saul resulted from his continued and ever increasingly egregious disobedience to the Lord. David's reign, then and now, is designated by historians and biblical scholars alike as Israel's "Golden Age." God had made unique promises to David and Israel about the continuity of that kingdom. No wonder, then, that David would be concerned.

One of the darker hours in David's life was his sinful relationship with Bathsheba. After his marriage to her, David and she had four sons together (1 Chron. 3:1–5). Solomon, one of those sons, was to be his successor. David could go to his grave in peace knowing that and with the promise of God that He would establish Solomon's kingdom (1 Chron. 17:11). Solomon would have the privilege and responsibility to build the temple. More importantly, the Lord would establish Solomon's throne forever. This promise is the one Samuel made to David and speaks not just of the historic reigns of the two men. Rather, it speaks of the Davidic reign through the Messiah (Matt. 12:42; Ps. 89:34–37; Luke 1:32–33, 69; Acts 2:29–36; 13:22–23).

III. David Builds an Altar to the Lord (1 Chronicles 21:21–27)

Disobedience to the Lord always requires conviction, repentance, and making amends for one's errant ways according to the Lord's requirements. The opening verse of this lesson simply indicates to us the Lord's angel (messenger) commanded the prophet Gad to instruct David to erect an altar on the threshing floor of Araunah (or Ornah), the Jebusite. David had just recently purchased the site from Araunah, a member of one of the tribes possessing Jerusalem before David's defeat of them. The altar and the worship there were required by the Lord for David to be reconciled to the Lord for a prideful act.

At the instigation of Satan, David insisted on conducting a census of his fighting forces. Apparently the act was a prideful reliance on "strength in numbers" rather than reliance on God. Joab, the commander of David's forces, objected to the census and feared the spiritual repercussions that would result from it. David overruled him, and the census was done. The Lord expressed his displeasure and announced options for punishment through the prophet Gad. David and Israel could experience three months of famine, three months of pursuit and being overtaken by their enemies, or three days of plague at the hand of the Lord's angel ravaging all of Israel. David opted for the last of these. Seventy thousand people lost their lives. The angel of the Lord stood poised to bring more devastation. At that point, David and the elders expressed sorrow for the census David had ordered. David was then directed to build the altar, which he did after purchasing the site from Araunah.

David indicated the construction of the altar was an act of penance to stop further destruction among the people. He offered to pay the full value of the site. Araunah offered the property to David for free and offered to donate materials for the altar as well as the animals for the sacrifice. His plan was to, "Let my lord the king do whatever pleases him." However, David knew the hazards of doing that! So he insisted on paying market value for the site.

After paying about fifteen pounds of gold for the property, David built the altar on the same site at which Abraham placed Isaac on the altar (Gen. 22) and where Solomon would build the temple (1 Chron. 22:1; 2 Chron. 3:1). David presented burnt offerings and fellowship offerings to the Lord and prayed. The Lord indicated His acceptance of David's actions by sending fire from heaven (Lev. 9:24). At God's command, the angel sheathed his sword, indicating the end of the plague.

The Lesson Applied

Based on his long-term desire to build a permanent place for the Ark of the Covenant, David definitely did not expect the kind of counsel he received from Nathan. However, the fact he did consult with Nathan was quite commendable. And the God-given instruction David received from the prophet was essential. Out of the consultation, David discovered what his actual role was. And he also discovered what the Lord's plan was. It is impossible to do God's will apart from knowledge of what that will is. Seeking the wisdom of other believers, especially the Lord's called and equipped spokespersons, can mean the difference in that which the Lord approves and one's own well-intentioned but incorrect journey.

Let's Talk About It

1. **What are some ways you serve the Lord that have special meaning to you?**
2. **What are some resources to which you turn to assist you in knowing you are correctly pursuing God's will for you?**
3. **Reflect on times in your faith journey that you have been out of step with the Lord's will for your life.**

Paul laments that Israel's burning desire to please God is not based in knowledge or is misdirected. Further examination of the context in Romans reveals the error is a pursuit of righteousness based on personal standards of righteousness and a rejection of the Lord's standards of righteousness. The core issue is what constitutes authentic pursuit and practice of God's will. Are we seeking and/or doing that which we determine to be what the Lord wants from us and requires of us? Or are we seeking and/or doing that which the Lord actually wants from us? Sincere people sometimes pursue wrong things in their attempts to serve God or fulfill God's sovereign will.

Home Daily Devotional Readings

December 16–22, 2019

Monday	Tuesday	Wednesday	Thursday	Friday	Saturday	Sunday
John the Baptist Born to Elizabeth	Zechariah Blesses God for John's Ministry	Young Woman's Pregnancy Is Sign of Immanuel	Virgin Conception Announced to Mary	Mary Accepts Miracle of Pregnancy	Joseph Obediently Honors Mary's Role	Blessed Mothers of the Faithful
Luke 1:57–66	Luke 1:67–79	Isaiah 7:10–17	Luke 1:26–33	Luke 1:34–38	Matthew 1:18–25	Luke 1:39–56

THE LORD IS WITH YOU

ADULT TOPIC: GRACIOUSLY ACCEPTING PRAISE

BACKGROUND SCRIPTURE: LUKE 1:39–56

LUKE 1:39–56

King James Version

AND Mary arose in those days, and went into the hill country with haste, into a city of Juda;
40 And entered into the house of Zacharias, and saluted Elisabeth.
41 And it came to pass, that, when Elisabeth heard the salutation of Mary, the babe leaped in her womb; and Elisabeth was filled with the Holy Ghost:
42 And she spake out with a loud voice, and said, Blessed art thou among women, and blessed is the fruit of thy womb.
43 And whence is this to me, that the mother of my Lord should come to me?
44 For, lo, as soon as the voice of thy salutation sounded in mine ears, the babe leaped in my womb for joy.
45 And blessed is she that believed: for there shall be a performance of those things which were told her from the Lord.
46 And Mary said, My soul doth magnify the Lord,
47 And my spirit hath rejoiced in God my Saviour.
48 For he hath regarded the low estate of his handmaiden: for, behold, from henceforth all generations shall call me blessed.
49 For he that is mighty hath done to me great things; and holy is his name.
50 And his mercy is on them that fear him from generation to generation.
51 He hath shewed strength with his arm; he hath scattered the proud in the imagination of their hearts.
52 He hath put down the mighty from their seats, and exalted them of low degree.

New Revised Standard Version

IN those days Mary set out and went with haste to a Judean town in the hill country,
40 where she entered the house of Zechariah and greeted Elizabeth.
41 When Elizabeth heard Mary's greeting, the child leaped in her womb. And Elizabeth was filled with the Holy Spirit
42 and exclaimed with a loud cry, "Blessed are you among women, and blessed is the fruit of your womb.
43 And why has this happened to me, that the mother of my Lord comes to me?
44 For as soon as I heard the sound of your greeting, the child in my womb leaped for joy.
45 And blessed is she who believed that there would be a fulfillment of what was spoken to her by the Lord."
46 And Mary said, "My soul magnifies the Lord,
47 and my spirit rejoices in God my Savior,
48 for he has looked with favor on the lowliness of his servant. Surely, from now on all generations will call me blessed;
49 for the Mighty One has done great things for me, and holy is his name.
50 His mercy is for those who fear him from generation to generation.
51 He has shown strength with his arm; he has scattered the proud in the thoughts of their hearts.
52 He has brought down the powerful from their thrones, and lifted up the lowly;

MAIN THOUGHT: And Mary said, My soul doth magnify the Lord, And my spirit hath rejoiced in God my Saviour. (Luke 1:46–47, KJV)

LUKE 1:39–56

King James Version	*New Revised Standard Version*
53 He hath filled the hungry with good things; and the rich he hath sent empty away.	**53 he has filled the hungry with good things, and sent the rich away empty.**
54 He hath helped his servant Israel, in remembrance of his mercy;	**54 He has helped his servant Israel, in remembrance of his mercy,**
55 As he spake to our fathers, to Abraham, and to his seed for ever.	**55 according to the promise he made to our ancestors, to Abraham and to his descendants forever."**
56 And Mary abode with her about three months, and returned to her own house.	**56 And Mary remained with her about three months and then returned to her home.**

LESSON SETTING

Time: 4 B.C. (?)
Place: Nazareth and Jerusalem

LESSON OUTLINE

I. Mary Visits Elizabeth (Luke 1:39–45)
II. Mary's Song: Praise to God for Personal Blessings (Luke 1:46–49)

UNIFYING PRINCIPLE

People often wonder if they truly deserve the praise others give them. How can we be gracious about the honors we receive? When Elizabeth called her *blessed*, Mary humbly praised God, confessing all that had happened to her was in fulfillment of God's great plan of redemption.

INTRODUCTION

Today's lesson passage, the Lukan nativity narrative, embraces the larger scriptural context that is Luke 1:5–2:52 and includes the birth and childhood narratives of John the Baptizer and Jesus. The more narrow context for the passage is Luke 1:5–2:20 and includes the annunciation to Zechariah (1:5–25), the annunciation to Mary (1:26–38), Mary's visit to Elizabeth (1:39–56), the birth of John (1:57–80) and the birth of Jesus (2:1–20). Most of the material in these pericopes (self-contained units of Scripture) is unique to Luke, likely having emerged from an original source of his own.

New Testament scholars from many years ago identified several special interests and emphases the author of the Gospel of Luke includes. Many of these are reflected in the nativity narratives. As he does elsewhere, Luke gives much space in the nativity narratives to the roles of Elizabeth and Mary. The Holy Spirit, angels, worship (as evidenced by three special songs in the birth and infancy narratives), God's ongoing work in salvation history, and the place of common people, such as shepherds, in the mighty acts of God also are prominent in these narratives and the rest of the third Gospel.

One also notices the theme of reversal in the Gospel of Luke. The theme of reversal is expressed in the advanced age of the parents of John the Baptizer, as well as the lifelong infertility of Elizabeth. As in several Old Testament narratives (Hannah, Abraham and Sarah, Jacob and Rachel, for example), God performs a miracle to permit the conception and birth of John. And He performs the ultimate nature miracle in the conception of Jesus to a virgin.

The theme of reversal continues to be emphasized in the song Mary offers in praise of the Lord being with her as the mother of the Savior. All of the various themes and emphases in the nativity narratives especially testify to the truth that only an all-powerful God could perform the things that occurred. And they were and are all part of His plan to redeem all creation through Jesus Christ.

Exposition

I. Mary Visits Elizabeth (Luke 1:39–45)

Today's lesson text is directly connected to events that had occurred six months earlier and involved a priest named Zechariah (Zecharias) and his wife Elizabeth. Luke provides this synopsis of them in 1:5–7, highlighting their age and infertility. Gabriel, "strong man of God" (Dan. 8:15–27; 9:20–27; Luke 1:8–20), a special angel of God, visited Zechariah in the temple as he performed his priestly duties and informed him that despite Elizabeth's infertility and their old age, God would bless them with a son, whom they would name John, meaning "gift." He would have a special place in God's plan of salvation and in the life and ministry of Jesus, the coming Messiah.

In the sixth month of Elizabeth's pregnancy, God's angel appeared in northern Israel in the village of Nazareth in Galilee to teenaged girl (about age twelve to fourteen, in keeping with the culture) named Mary. His message to her was: "Do not be afraid, Mary, you have found favor with God. You will be with child and give birth to a son, and you are to give him the name Jesus. He will be great and will be called the Son of the Most High. The Lord God will give him the throne of his father David, and he will reign over the house of Jacob forever; his kingdom will never end" (Luke 1:30–33).

Mary was thoroughly bewildered by such a message. Though she legally and publicly was pledged to be married to Joseph the carpenter, she was a virgin who had not had sex with him or any other man. The angel assured her his prophesy would occur, due to the will of God and the work of the Holy Spirit. God's power also had worked wondrously in the life of her relative, Elizabeth, who would give birth to John in three months. How so for all this? "For nothing is impossible with God." Mary acquiesced to Gabriel's message: "I am the Lord's servant. May it be to me as you have said."

The angel left, and Mary packed some things and made the eighty- to one hundred-mile long trip south, through the mountains of Judea, to the home of Zechariah and Elizabeth. After Mary had greeted Elizabeth, two noteworthy things immediately occurred. The text indicates the fetus in Elizabeth's womb leaped for joy. Some would dismiss this action as anything out of the ordinary, preferring to designate it as normal activity of a developing *in vitro* child. Luke intends to convey much more than this.

It seems he means that before Elizabeth could return Mary's greeting, the child within her leapt. Beyond that, the meaning Luke has is more than an ordinary, prenatal movement. The original term Luke uses for *leap* indicates skipping or leaping, as a young sheep does in the field. In application to people, the term indicates an expression of being overcome with emotion. It implies leaping with joy or delight. But John's movement was far more than emotional. It was also spiritual. Luke probably also intends to convey the truth that in keeping with Gabriel's prophecy that John would be filled with the Spirit even from birth (1:15b), the joyous movement of John was that of the one who would be a prophet. Even in his mother's womb, he recognized Jesus, who just recently had been conceived by the power of the Holy Spirit.

The second noteworthy thing that occurred after Mary's greeting to Elizabeth was the expression of prophetic insight from Elizabeth. First of all, she recognized and expressed the unique blessing of God on the life of Mary. With a loud, exuberant voice, she exclaimed a benediction, a blessing on Mary and her child, Jesus: "Blessed are you among women, and blessed is the child you shall bear" (v. 42, NIV). The blessing here is to be coupled with that in verse 45, "Blessed is she who has believed that what the Lord has said to her will be accomplished!"

Elizabeth's statements are prompted by the reality that she was filled with the Holy Spirit (v. 41). Mary's blessedness—commendable or congratulatory status, the meaning of the original term *makarios*—is due to her unique faith in a unique situation. She is exceptionally blessed among other women because of that.

Elizabeth also expresses amazement and a further prophetic insight in verse 43. She queries, "But why is this granted to me?" That is actually a way of asking how this experience could happen to someone so unworthy. Her final prophetic insight in the episode is the recognition of Mary's yet-to-be-born son. The amazement is that the mother of her Lord should visit and share the news with her. Just as Mary had, Elizabeth also had accepted Gabriel's message about Jesus.

II. Mary's Song: Praise to God For Personal Blessings (Luke 1:46–49)

Mary's song of praise in Luke 1:46–56 is known as the Magnificat. Its full title is *Magnificat anima mea Dominum* which means, "my soul magnifies the Lord." The title is from the first words of Mary's song in Jerome's Latin translation of the Scriptures, The Vulgate. The opening words have the sense of "my soul 'enlarges,' or my soul 'makes great' the Lord." The intention of the song is not to suggest the greatness, the glory of God, can somehow be expanded by anything mere mortals do or say. Rather, one's perception in response to relationship with and praise of God can be expanded. All that can occur as the result of new understanding or insights about God, the experience of meditation or worship, or as in the case of Mary, some unique personal encounter with Him and His power. No doubt, everything she had experienced in this unique encounter, from the appearance and opening words of Gabriel, to the visit with Elizabeth, as well as Mary's private thoughts, fed into her Magnificat.

Her song embraces the entirety of Mary's being. All that is part of her existence is involved in her praise. In verse 46 she speaks of her "soul." It is from the Greek word *psychē/psuchē,* which gives the English word *mind.* In the New Testament, it is the equivalent of the Hebrew *nephesh.* And both words mean "living being." They refer to the totality of one's personhood. In verse 47, Mary says her "spirit" rejoices in God, the Savior. Here, *spirit* is *pnuema* ("air," "wind," "breath," "spirit") and indicates one's innermost being. Although the words are denotatively distinct, they are used here synonymously to indicate that with all she is, Mary praises God. She praises Him with personal abandon, holding back nothing of herself.

There are two distinct parts of Mary's song. In verses 48–50 she highlights that which God has done for her personally. In the balance of the song, she focuses on the mighty acts of God on the behalf of His people. The celebration of her personal blessings begins with a confessional statement: "For He has regarded the lowly state of His maidservant" (v. 48). The Lord had been mindful of her and her humble circumstances and yet chose her to be the mother of Jesus. Mary had no claim to fame. By the world's standards, there was nothing outstanding about her. She describes herself as a servant or slave. The term, *doulē,* for *slave* here indicates one who works in general servitude for another. In the balance of verse 48, she expresses joyful amazement at the unique place among humanity God has provided, not because of who she is, but because of God's providence to her amid her lowliness. She will be called "blessed" because of the once-for-all act of God in the Christ-event and her role in it.

The Lesson Applied

Recognition the Lord is with a person requires a response of faith from that person. There is certainly a sense in which faith is trust or confidence in the Lord and in that which the Lord declares and promises. Mary's faith demonstrates that. Yet her faith demonstrated more. She also was willing to entrust herself, unconditionally, to that which God promised to her through the angel Gabriel.

Let's Talk About It

1. **What are some life–changing encounters with God to which you can point?**
2. **How have those encounters shaped you as a person and as a believer?**
3. **What lessons would you share with others about your experiences with God?**

Mary's words to Gabriel became her life motto: "I am the Lord's servant. May it be to me as you have said." That is essentially what being a dedicated disciple, a faithful follower of Jesus is—a servant who is ever submissive and responsive to what the Lord says.

Home Daily Devotional Readings

December 22–29, 2019

Monday	Tuesday	Wednesday	Thursday	Friday	Saturday	Sunday
God's Forever Covenant with David	The Lord Will Build David's House	No God Like Our God	No People Like Our People	David Selects Materials for the Temple	David Orients Builders about Temple Construction	David's Prayer of Praise and Thanksgiving
Psalm 89:19–37	2 Samuel 7:11–17	2 Samuel 7:18–22	2 Samuel 7:23–29	1 Chronicles 22:2–5	1 Chronicles 22:14–19	1 Chronicles 17:16–27

DAVID'S PRAYER

ADULT TOPIC:
A GREATER PLAN

BACKGROUND SCRIPTURE:
1 CHRONICLES 17:16–27

1 CHRONICLES 17:16–27

King James Version

AND David the king came and sat before the LORD, and said, Who am I, O LORD God, and what is mine house, that thou hast brought me hitherto?

17 And yet this was a small thing in thine eyes, O God; for thou hast also spoken of thy servant's house for a great while to come, and hast regarded me according to the estate of a man of high degree, O LORD God.

18 What can David speak more to thee for the honour of thy servant? for thou knowest thy servant.

19 O LORD, for thy servant's sake, and according to thine own heart, hast thou done all this greatness, in making known all these great things.

20 O LORD, there is none like thee, neither is there any God beside thee, according to all that we have heard with our ears.

21 And what one nation in the earth is like thy people Israel, whom God went to redeem to be his own people, to make thee a name of greatness and terribleness, by driving out nations from before thy people whom thou hast redeemed out of Egypt?

22 For thy people Israel didst thou make thine own people for ever; and thou, LORD, becamest their God.

23 Therefore now, LORD, let the thing that thou hast spoken concerning thy servant and concerning his house be established for ever, and do as thou hast said.

New Revised Standard Version

THEN King David went in and sat before the LORD, and said, "Who am I, O LORD God, and what is my house, that you have brought me thus far?

17 And even this was a small thing in your sight, O God; you have also spoken of your servant's house for a great while to come. You regard me as someone of high rank, O LORD God!

18 And what more can David say to you for honoring your servant? You know your servant.

19 For your servant's sake, O LORD, and according to your own heart, you have done all these great deeds, making known all these great things.

20 There is no one like you, O LORD, and there is no God besides you, according to all that we have heard with our ears.

21 Who is like your people Israel, one nation on the earth whom God went to redeem to be his people, making for yourself a name for great and terrible things, in driving out nations before your people whom you redeemed from Egypt?

22 And you made your people Israel to be your people forever; and you, O LORD, became their God.

23 "And now, O LORD, as for the word that you have spoken concerning your servant and concerning his house, let it be established forever, and do as you have promised.

MAIN THOUGHT: O LORD, there is none like thee, neither is there any God beside thee, according to all that we have heard with our ears. (1 Chronicles 17:20, KJV)

1 Chronicles 17:16–27

King James Version	*New Revised Standard Version*
24 Let it even be established, that thy name may be magnified for ever, saying, The Lord of hosts is the God of Israel, even a God to Israel: and let the house of David thy servant be established before thee.	**24 Thus your name will be established and magnified forever in the saying, 'The Lord of hosts, the God of Israel, is Israel's God'; and the house of your servant David will be established in your presence.**
25 For thou, O my God, hast told thy servant that thou wilt build him an house: therefore thy servant hath found in his heart to pray before thee.	**25 For you, my God, have revealed to your servant that you will build a house for him; therefore your servant has found it possible to pray before you.**
26 And now, Lord, thou art God, and hast promised this goodness unto thy servant:	**26 And now, O Lord, you are God, and you have promised this good thing to your servant;**
27 Now therefore let it please thee to bless the house of thy servant, that it may be before thee for ever: for thou blessest, O Lord, and it shall be blessed for ever.	**27 therefore may it please you to bless the house of your servant, that it may continue forever before you. For you, O Lord, have blessed and are blessed forever."**

LESSON SETTING

Time: circa 985 B.C. (?)
Place: Jerusalem

LESSON OUTLINE

I. David's Prayer: Gratitude for Personal Blessings (1 Chronicles 17:16–19)
II. David's Prayer: Praise for Blessings to Israel (1 Chronicles 17:20–22)
III. David's Prayer: Petitions to God for Him and Israel (1 Chronicles 17:23–29)

Unifying Principle

When a person receives a great promise, he or she may feel honored. How does one respond when one has been so honored? When God promised to make him the head of a great dynasty, King David prayed a prayer of gratitude, praise, and petition.

Introduction

Prayers are prompted by a variety of circumstances. Sometimes one offers prayers to God out of a sense of one's need. Such prayers primarily will be petitions or requests. That is, they will be prayers in which a person seeks God's provision for a perceived need. Intercessory prayers, those offered on the behalf of others, belong to this category of prayers.

Sometimes one offers prayers in response to blessings the Lord has already provided. The mature, sensitive recipient of such blessings will offer God prayers of thanksgiving.

At other times, God's people will express their praise, celebratory worship, or worship in general, in prayers. Such prayers have as their primary but not exclusive goal the glorification of God. They usually focus on the character or attributes of God. But they also might be prompted by His provisions.

Life-altering experiences with the message of God often can lead to prayers. And as with other prayers, prayers that emerge from the impact of the Lord's Word can include gratitude, praise, and petition. Such is the character of the prayers in this lesson. They are inclusive of the types of prayer noted due to the effect of God's message through the prophet Nathan on King David.

David had sought to build a house for the Lord—a permanent place in which to locate the Ark of the Covenant. In a consultation with Nathan, he essentially advised David to follow his heart. The Lord, however, had other plans, and directed Nathan to advise David differently. Nathan does that in an oracle, a special message from God to David consisting of two parts.

In the first part of the oracle, the Lord, in a rhetorical question, corrects David's assumption that he would be the one to build the temple. David also is to understand the Lord's presence has been with Israel in all their travels and He at no point had required a permanent house in His honor.

The second part of the oracle of Nathan to David revolved around the Lord's ongoing activity supporting David, who was indeed destined for a lofty place among the influential leaders among people. That success would flow from three streams. First, the Lord would provide a land in which Israel would live peacefully and securely. Secondly, David could be assured through the Lord's promise that at David's death, he would be succeeded by his own descendants into perpetuity. Finally, the Lord would direct the successive kings by disciplining them when they disobeyed.

The Chronicler concludes the record of the oracle to David: "According to all these words and according to all this vision, so Nathan spoke to David" (1 Chron. 17:15, NKJV). David then sits down to offer his prayer to the Lord.

Exposition

I. David's Prayer: Gratitude for Personal Blessings (1 Chronicles 17:16–19)

Dr. Ben F. Philbeck's profile of David's overall prayer proves helpful: "The prayer resembles a hymn of praise in that while it deals with subjects related to man and his needs, its ultimate goal is the glorification of the Lord. David began his prayer by praising God for his many gracious acts in David's own life. It was not because of any good inherent in David but because of the graciousness of God's own heart that he took an insignificant shepherd and made him king." (*The Broadman Bible Commentary, Volume 3, 1 Samuel—Nehemiah*).

In the singular instance in the Old Testament of someone sitting down to pray (v. 16; 2 Sam. 17:18), David took that position before he began his prayer. Typically one who prayed would be prostrate. Neither the Chronicler nor the author of 2 Samuel offers insight about this. Yet it's reasonable to understand David's sitting position is an expression of humility. That can be supported by the title by which he refers to himself. Throughout the prayer, he calls himself "your servant" at least ten times in addressing the Lord. A servant typically would stand to receive directions from the master. David possibly adds another image to a sitting prayer posture. That is a child sitting before a parent, specifically the father, to receive instruction.

David also expresses authentic humility in God's blessings to him and his family. He expresses unworthiness of such graciousness (v. 16). He had risen from the humble beginnings of a shepherd to the role of king of Israel. David is equally amazed the Lord had spoken of the extension of David's kingdom and blessings into the future. He points to the uniqueness of God's blessings to him in this matter by rhetorically asking the Lord, "Is this your usual way of dealing with man, O Sovereign Lord?" (2 Sam. 7:19). Moreover, David is overwhelmed at the manner in which the Lord has spoken about David's status among other prominent people, especially governmental leaders (1 Chron. 17:8–15). He expresses that surprise in verse 17, "You have looked on me as though I were the most exalted of men, O LORD God."

As many other believers do at times, David found himself at a loss for words to express adequately what he desired to express (v. 18). And more amazement accompanies his perspective, since the Lord has thorough knowledge of him, "You know what your servant is really like" (v. 18, NLT).

In the final verse of this thanksgiving for his personal blessings, David expresses keen theological insight into why God's graciousness comes to people. The actions of God and the promises He made through Nathan had occurred for the benefit of David, the servant of God. Furthermore, the blessings and promises had been given to David because they all were part of God's will, His plans and intentions for David, his kingdom and its future, and for redemptive plans in and beyond time.

II. David's Prayer: Praise for Blessings to Israel (1 Chronicles 17:20–22)

This section of David's prayer is fittingly summed up in the following lines by Dr. Philbeck: "Likewise, the very existence of Israel reflects glory on Israel's God. The Lord reversed the customary order of affairs in which the nations of the world choose the god whom they serve. Instead, the Lord had called Israel into being and had repeatedly exerted himself in history on her behalf." All David has to articulate about Israel (and throughout the prayer) is inextricably linked with the uniqueness of God. And all Israel is a witness to His uniqueness: "O LORD, there is none like You, nor is there any God besides You, according to all that we have heard with our ears" (v. 20, NKJV). The uniqueness of God was a fundamental tenet in Israel's theology and finds expression in multiple passages in the Old Testament (Exod. 15:11; 18:11; Deut. 3:24; Pss. 86:8; 89:6; Isa. 40:18, 25; Jer. 10:6).

Israel can rightfully and only be designated as a unique people because of the uniqueness of God. They have the distinction of being the sole nation on all the earth whose God intended to redeem for Himself and make a name for Himself (v. 21; Deut. 4:7, 32–34; 33:26–29; Ps. 147:20). This uniqueness required a response of obedience and faithfulness from Israel. They were ever to remember it and renounce any loyalty to the idol gods of other nations (Deut. 4:34; 7:6–8; 9:4–5; Neh. 9:10). To these ends, the Lord performed special things in Israel's past, beginning with liberating from the oppression (v. 21) in Egypt (Exod. 3:7–8; 19:4–6; Deut. 15:15; Ps. 111:9; Isa. 63:9). Verse 22 affirms the relationship between the Lord and Israel is an incessant one because of

God's sovereign purposes and promises (Exod. 19:5–6; Jer. 31:31–34; Rom. 9:4–6, 25–26; 11:1–12). God indeed is the Lord of all nations. Yet He has an exceptional relationship with Israel, in the fullest sense of the name *Israel* in the Scriptures.

That there was, is, and always will be a special relationship between the Lord and Israel resides in the intentionality of the Lord. David expresses this in verse 22, "For You have made Your people Israel Your very own people forever; and You, LORD, have become their God" (NKJV). Israel's "chosen people" status is the result of the grace, or steadfast love, of the Lord. This concept was conveyed clearly to Israel in the time of Moses: "For you are a holy people to the LORD your God; the LORD your God has chosen you to be a people for Himself, a special treasure above all the peoples on the face of the earth. The LORD did not set His love on you nor choose you because you were more in number than any other people, for you were the least of all peoples; but because the LORD loves you, and because He would keep the oath which He swore to your fathers," (Deut. 7:6–8, NKJV).

III. David's Prayer: Petitions to God for Him and Israel (1 Chronicles 17:23–29)

David turns his attention in this final section to some specific petitions for Israel in relation to God's promises to David and Israel. David's requests here are essentially that the Lord will complete that which He had begun among His people and expressed in His promises. Part of the petitions is related to David himself and "his house," that is his reign and lineage. Thus, he can pray: "And now, LORD, let the promise you have made concerning your servant and his house be established forever" (v. 23). Verses 25–26 indicate why David can not only pray such a prayer, but why he can do so with both confidence and expectation: "O LORD Almighty, God of Israel, you have revealed this to your servant, saying, 'I will build a house for you.' So your servant has found courage to offer you this prayer. O Sovereign LORD, you are God! Your words are trustworthy, and you have promised these good things to your servant." God's revelation and His reliability provide David with the basis for his prayer.

In verses 23 and 24, David seeks something additional in his petitions. One is for the purpose of ongoing praise to the Lord, "that your name will be great forever." The essence of the petition is that as God maintains and fulfills His promises, David, His people Israel, and their successors will always offer praise to God. For to recognize the name of God as great is to recognize God Himself as great (Pss. 21:13; 72:19). Another closely connected aspect to David's petition is here—as God fulfills His promises, people will give testimony to the unique relationship between Yahweh and Israel. David expresses it in vese 24, "Then men will say, 'The LORD Almighty, the God over Israel, is Israel's God!'" Perhaps primarily David speaks here of the people of Israel offering such a testimony concerning the Lord. But he in fact speaks more inclusively of all who witness God's faithfulness to His promises bearing that testimony. "The Lord Almighty," *El Shaddai*, underlines the power of God to bring His word to fulfillment.

The final verse in David's prayer is a

doxology, an expression of praise. The *New Living Translation* provides clear expression of David's intention: "And now, it has pleased you to bless the house of your servant, so that it will continue forever before you. For when you grant a blessing, O LORD, it is an eternal blessing!"

The Lesson Applied

Prayer is an absolutely indispensable experience in the life of the Lord's people. That is true, in part, because it is the primary means of communication with the Lord. Just as ongoing communication is important in one's horizontal relationships, prayer is vital in one's vertical relationship—the relationship with God. To be sure, the communication is and must be dialogical. That is, prayer is as much, and often more, about being silent, listening to the Lord, as it is speaking to Him. Authentic prayer cannot be one-sided. Those who pray need to hear from the Lord in addition to the quest to have the Lord hear from the one offering prayer. Of equal significance is that authentic prayer can never be monolithic. That is, it cannot be one type of prayer.

Let's Talk About It

1. **Recall and then discuss with class members, if you wish, some instances in which a prayer or season of prayer was prompted by the Lord's correction in your life.**
2. **What are some things for which you should give thanks at this point of your life?**
3. **What are some things for which you should praise God and how would you express that praise?**

David's prayer is instructive on this point. In what can be considered a rather short prayer, he includes at least three forms of prayer. He expresses gratitude and praise and makes some specific requests. The foundation of all those, and the entirety of David's prayer, is the unequaled character of God who works redemptively with individuals and groups. His actions and His promises prompt occasions of praise and thanksgiving. Those blessed by Him receive all they do exclusively out of the abundance of His grace and love. None deserves or can earn His favor. That in and of itself should inspire praise and gratitude. As importantly, such praise and gratitude should be expressed in loyalty to the Lord, as well as in words.

David's prayer begins by expressing gratitude for personal blessings, opportunities, and prospects. Yet he soon transitions to God's providence to Israel. Prayer should therefore have a private and a corporate focus.

Home Daily Devotional Readings
December 30, 2019–January 5, 2020

Monday	Tuesday	Wednesday	Thursday	Friday	Saturday	Sunday
Heavenly Vision of the Ark	An Orderly Worship Service	The Law Is Read at Booths Festival	The Ark Brought to the Temple	Priests Praise God with Music	All Temple Furnishings Completed	Preparing to Dedicate the Temple
Revelation 11:15–19	1 Corinthians 14:26–33	Deuteronomy 31:9–13	2 Chronicles 5:2–7	2 Chronicles 5:11–14	2 Chronicles 4:19–5:1	1 Kings 8:1–13

A PLACE FOR THE ARK

ADULT TOPIC:
A LONG–ANTICIPATED CELEBRATION

BACKGROUND SCRIPTURE:
1 KINGS 8:1–13; 2 CHRONICLES 5:1–14

1 KINGS 8:1–13

King James Version

THEN Solomon assembled the elders of Israel, and all the heads of the tribes, the chief of the fathers of the children of Israel, unto king Solomon in Jerusalem, that they might bring up the ark of the covenant of the LORD out of the city of David, which is Zion.

2 And all the men of Israel assembled themselves unto king Solomon at the feast in the month Ethanim, which is the seventh month.

3 And all the elders of Israel came, and the priests took up the ark.

4 And they brought up the ark of the LORD, and the tabernacle of the congregation, and all the holy vessels that were in the tabernacle, even those did the priests and the Levites bring up.

5 And king Solomon, and all the congregation of Israel, that were assembled unto him, were with him before the ark, sacrificing sheep and oxen, that could not be told nor numbered for multitude.

6 And the priests brought in the ark of the covenant of the LORD unto his place, into the oracle of the house, to the most holy place, even under the wings of the cherubims.

7 For the cherubims spread forth their two wings over the place of the ark, and the cherubims covered the ark and the staves thereof above.

8 And they drew out the staves, that the ends of the staves were seen out in the holy place before the oracle, and they were not seen without: and there they are unto this day.

9 There was nothing in the ark save the two tables of stone, which Moses put there at

New Revised Standard Version

THEN Solomon assembled the elders of Israel and all the heads of the tribes, the leaders of the ancestral houses of the Israelites, before King Solomon in Jerusalem, to bring up the ark of the covenant of the LORD out of the city of David, which is Zion.

2 All the people of Israel assembled to King Solomon at the festival in the month Ethanim, which is the seventh month.

3 And all the elders of Israel came, and the priests carried the ark.

4 So they brought up the ark of the LORD, the tent of meeting, and all the holy vessels that were in the tent; the priests and the Levites brought them up.

5 King Solomon and all the congregation of Israel, who had assembled before him, were with him before the ark, sacrificing so many sheep and oxen that they could not be counted or numbered.

6 Then the priests brought the ark of the covenant of the LORD to its place, in the inner sanctuary of the house, in the most holy place, underneath the wings of the cherubim.

7 For the cherubim spread out their wings over the place of the ark, so that the cherubim made a covering above the ark and its poles.

8 The poles were so long that the ends of the poles were seen from the holy place in front of the inner sanctuary; but they could not be seen from outside; they are there to this day.

9 There was nothing in the ark except the two tablets of stone that Moses had placed there at

MAIN THOUGHT: I have surely built thee an house to dwell in, a settled place for thee to abide in for ever. (1 Kings 8:13, KJV)

1 Kings 8:1–13

King James Version	*New Revised Standard Version*
Horeb, when the Lord made a covenant with the children of Israel, when they came out of the land of Egypt.	**Horeb, where the Lord made a covenant with the Israelites, when they came out of the land of Egypt.**
10 And it came to pass, when the priests were come out of the holy place, that the cloud filled the house of the Lord,	**10 And when the priests came out of the holy place, a cloud filled the house of the Lord,**
11 So that the priests could not stand to minister because of the cloud: for the glory of the Lord had filled the house of the Lord.	**11 so that the priests could not stand to minister because of the cloud; for the glory of the Lord filled the house of the Lord.**
12 Then spake Solomon, The Lord said that he would dwell in the thick darkness.	**12 Then Solomon said, "The Lord has said that he would dwell in thick darkness.**
13 I have surely built thee an house to dwell in, a settled place for thee to abide in for ever.	**13 I have built you an exalted house, a place for you to dwell in forever."**

LESSON SETTING

Time: circa 920 B.C.
Place: Jerusalem

LESSON OUTLINE

I. The Processional of the Ark (1 Kings 8:1–9)
II. The Glory of the Lord Appears (1 Kings 8:10–13)

Unifying Principle

People have dedication ceremonies or grand openings for many different things. How are these ceremonies or grand openings celebrated? When King Solomon called an assembly to celebrate the dedication of the temple, the glory of the Lord filled the house of God.

Introduction

First and 2 Kings, the eleventh and twelfth books of the Christian canon, originally were one book and formed part of a larger history of Israel. A near consensus in Old Testament scholarship is that the division of the original work into two parts occurred in the Greek translation of the Hebrew Scriptures, the Septuagint. There, 1 and 2 Kings were known as 3 and 4 Kings. The books we now know as 1 and 2 Samuel originally were 1 and 2 Kings, and the original 1 and 2 Samuel were a single work. Tradition holds the prophet Jeremiah is the author of 1 and 2 Kings. There are some affinities between the theology contained in the Books of Kings and that in the Book of Jeremiah. The Books of Kings give no indication as to their authorship; therefore, determining authorship with certainty is impossible.

While 1 and 2 Kings are historical books that cover a span of time from early in the tenth century B.C. to the fall of Jerusalem, (circa 586 B.C.), the presentation of a pure history was not the authors' purpose. Rather, the authors painted the history of Israel in broad contours from a theological perspective. Episodes, main characters, and details appear in the Books of Kings in relation to how they served the authorial purposes of presenting and evaluating the extent to which they measured up to the requirements of the Mosaic and Davidic covenants. The events recorded by the authors appear because they are essential to understanding what happened to Israel.

With Deuteronomy 28 (esp. vv. 1–14) ever in mind, the authors were concerned that the people maintain consciousness regarding the fulfillment of God's Word. To these ends, 1 and 2 Kings reflect three concerns in Israel's theological history. First, the authors meticulously noted every aspect of God's word would be fulfilled: the promises and blessings, the consequences of disobedience, and God's warnings. The word of God had been articulated clearly in the Deuteronomic codes. It was articulated just as definitively by the classical prophets—Nathan, Elijah, Elisha, Isaiah, and others. The emphasis on the dynamic character of *davar* (or *dabar*), the word of God, could not be ignored.

Second, the authors of the historical books had great concern to maintain the purity of Israel's liturgical life. Two aspects of this were emphasized. One was absolute loyalty to strict monotheism. The requirement of the daily recitation of the Shema (Deut. 6:4–9) and its emphasis on the oneness of God was more than a thoughtless, perfunctory recitation of words. It was, in effect, a confession of faith by which Israel acknowledged the one true God and His immutable commandments for them. Absolute loyalty to the one true God also expressed itself in worship offered only to Him in a place dictated by Him. Ultimately, this meant worship was centered in Jerusalem, which was distinguished from sites associated with paganism.

Finally, the authors of 1 and 2 Kings had a concern there be hope for Israel's future. This rested upon the authority of the oracles and commands of Yahweh and a sense of His salvific purposes through Israel. The foibles and failures of the Patriarchs and kings of Israel did not dismantle God's purposes. The tragedies that befell Israel in retribution for their spiritual depravity did not dismantle God's purpose, and neither would the divided kingdom of Israel nor the Exile to Babylon. Through a faithful remnant and the Messianic Age, God would create a hopeful future.

Today's lesson belongs to the first major section of 1 Kings, the focus of which is the reign of Solomon and includes 1 Kings 1:1–11:43. More narrowly, the lesson passage belongs to 8:1–9:9, which is concerned with the dedication festival of the temple. Verses 1–11 deal with the procession of the Ark of the Covenant. Verses 12–13 are taken from the context of verses 12–21 that presents the blessing on the assembly.

Exposition

I. The Processional of the Ark (1 Kings 8:1–9)

The dedication of the temple is contained in 1 Kings 8:1–9:9, a narrative containing three major parts. First is the procession of the Ark of the Covenant to its final location in the Holy of Holies (Most Holy Place) in the temple. Second is an extended speech and prayer given by King Solomon. Finally comes an account of the festival. Somewhat of an addendum to the dedication narrative is a record of the Lord's response to Solomon's prayer.

The dedication of the temple occurred in the twenty-fourth year of Solomon's reign. Although certainty cannot be determined, many Old Testament scholars suggest

Solomon's reign was from 965–925 B.C. Given this, the temple dedication would have occurred about 921–20 B.C.

Verse 1 of the lesson provides a general summary of the royal summons from Solomon in preparation for transporting the Ark from Bethlehem to Jerusalem. The event was to be inclusive of all the people of Israel—the elders of Israel, leaders of the tribes, and the leaders of families. First Kings 8:65 (NKJV) records of the inclusiveness: "At that time Solomon held a feast, and all Israel with him, a great assembly from the entrance of Hamath to the Brook of Egypt, before the LORD our God, seven days and seven more days—fourteen days." All the people, from the northernmost to the southernmost borders of Israel, were included.

The balance of verse 1 indicates the throng gathered to move the Ark of the Covenant from Zion. Originally, Zion was the hill David took from the Jebusites (2 Sam. 5:6–10). The "City of David," or Zion in Old Testament times, referred to Jerusalem. Zion eventually came to refer to the temple area northward. In New Testament times, "City of David" referred to Bethlehem, David's birthplace, as well as that of Jesus.

The authors provide further insight into the festival of dedication setting. It occurred in the seventh month of the Jewish calendar, Ethanim, meaning "always flowing with water," likely due to overflowing streams from heavy rainfalls. The month also is known as Tishri. The festival coincided with the Feast of Tabernacles (2 Chron. 8:13; Ezra 3:4; Zech. 14:16), and also was called the Feast of Ingathering (Exod. 23:16; 34:22), the Feast to the Lord (Lev. 23:39; Judg. 21:19), or simply The Feast, as in the lesson text and in 2 Chronicles 5:3; 7:8. It was an ancient agricultural new year festival that also placed emphasis on the kingship of the Lord (Pss. 24:7–10; 132).

Solomon and his subjects were diligent to conduct the procedures regarding the Ark of the Covenant in a way that was consistent with the instructions from the days of Moses. Verse 3 (NRSV) explains "all the elders of Israel came, and the priests carried the ark." The priests and the Levites brought up the Ark, the tent of meeting, and all the furnishings (v. 4). Moses previously had instructed Israel's spiritual leaders on the appropriate way to carry the Ark: "When Aaron and his sons have finished covering the sanctuary and all the furnishings of the sanctuary, as the camp sets out, after that the Kohathites shall come to carry these, but they must not touch the holy things, or they will die" (Num. 4:15, NRSV). Deuteronomy 31:9 indicates Moses wrote this law and gave it to all the elders of Israel and to the priests who carried the Ark. That the priests and Levites had responsibility for the maintenance and movement of the Ark of the Covenant and the things associated with it was widely known and observed in Israel (Josh. 3:3,6; 1 Chron. 15:14–15).

When David moved the Ark of the Covenant from the home of Obed-Edom in Gath to Jerusalem, an act of worship was included shortly after the journey began. When those carrying the Ark of the Lord had gone six paces, David sacrificed an ox and fattened sheep (2 Sam. 6:13). First Kings 8:5 indicates Solomon performed a similar act of voluntary worship as they walked in front of the Ark. The worshipers were quite lavish in their sacrifices, offering "so many sheep and oxen that they could not be counted or numbered" (v. 5, NRSV).

Verse 6 relates the Ark of the Covenant was situated in its permanent location—the innermost court of the temple, the Most Holy Place or Holy of Holies. The Ark was placed beneath the wings of the cherubim, one of the classes of winged angels in Jewish thought. Along with the many other sections of the temple constructed, King Solomon contracted Hiram (or Huram), a skilled craftsman from Tyre (1 Kings 7:13–45), to complete the furnishings of the inner sanctuary, including the cherubim (1 Kings 6:23–30). The expanse of the cherubim wings was such they encompassed the entire Ark and the poles on which it had been carried (v. 7).

Original instructions regarding the construction of the poles appear in Exodus 25:13–15. The poles, made of acacia wood and overlayed with gold, were inserted into rings on the sides of the Ark to carry it. The poles were not to be taken from the Ark. (Also see Ex. 37:4–5.) In compliance with those instructions, the poles remained in place, "And they are still there to this day" (v. 8b), meaning they were in place at the time 1 Kings was written.

Verse 9 describes the contents of the Ark of the Covenant. This holy vessel, requiring the utmost attention to detail in its transport, contained only the two tablets of stone Moses had placed there at Horeb, when the Lord made a covenant with the children of Israel (Ex. 25:16, 21; 40:20; Deut. 10:2–5). The mention of the covenant the Lord made with Israel and embodied in the Ten Commandments on the stone tablets gave the name to the chest, Ark of the Covenant.

II. The Glory of the Lord Appears (1 Kings 8:10–11)

The statement in verse 10 concerning the cloud filling the house of the Lord is reminiscent of Moses' experience in Exodus 40:34–35 when the glory of the Lord filled the tabernacle. Moses could not enter the tent of meeting because the cloud had settled upon it and the glory of the Lord filled the tabernacle. The typical term for God's glory in the Old Testament is *kavod*. It actually refers to that which is heavy in weight (1 Sam. 4:18; Prov. 27:3). Figuratively, it was applied to designate large numbers or good fortune (Gen. 13:2; Ex. 12:38; Num. 20:20; 1 Kings 10:2). Elsewhere in the Old Testament, *kavod* was associated with honor (Ex. 20:12; 1 Sam. 15:30; Ps. 15:4; Prov. 4:8; Is. 3:5).

In reference to God, it is associated with the recognition of the shining majesty of God's presence and His worthiness to be praised (Pss. 22:23; 86:12; Isa. 24:15). *Shekinah* ("that which dwells"), a non-biblical term present in many Jewish writings during the Old Testament era, is synonymous with *kavod* in reference to God's glory. Association of God's glory with a cloud occurs frequently in the Old Testament (Exod. 13:21–22; 40:38; Num. 11:25; 12:5; Ps. 99:7). The cloud was a visible reminder of the Lord's presence and presumed to confirm His blessing upon what Solomon had done. The cloud also shrouded His essence from those who saw the cloud. The Lord declared Himself to be too awesome for anyone—even Moses—to see fully (Exod. 33:17–23).

Verse 11 of the lesson text indicates the worship had to cease because of the overwhelming power of the glory of the Lord. Solomon appears to recognize the people are awestruck, and he responds with the opening words of his extended speech and prayer by affirming God's presence in the cloud (v. 12). The Lord had similarly appeared and spoken to Moses (Exod. 19:9). Solomon then turns to a prayer, the opening words of which focus on the place he has built for the presence of God. That statement also would remind the people of the formation of the covenant people at Sinai, the place where the Lord had spoken to Moses from the dense cloud.

The Lesson Applied

Several hundred years had elapsed between the time of Abraham and the time of Moses and the giving of the Law at Sinai. A few millennia had elapsed between the time of Moses and the days of David and his quest to build the temple and Solomon who actually built it. Countless people had been participants in the statement of the Lord's promises about blessings, the defeat of enemies, a permanent land of extreme fertility, and a permanent house of worship dedicated to Him. Yet in keeping with God's purposes and timing, all of that became reality and was celebrated by Solomon and Israel. The message is forthright: The Lord is faithful to His word. Nothing and no one can negate or impede God's plans or His word. Solomon and the entire nation recognized God's faithfulness as they celebrated the Ark of the Covenant reaching its sacred resting place. There had been challenges in getting the Ark to a proper home, but God allowed them to see that day come. So to every generation in every place where His Word and promises are declared, the recipients must maintain unswerving faith and obedience.

Let's Talk About It

1. **What are some religious festivals or celebrations that have special meaning to you and/or your faith community?**
2. **Why are the festivals and celebrations important to the members of your congregation?**
3. **In what ways can you help preserve and promote the importance of those events for others?**

Israel was regularly reminded of the Lord's promises and had heard testimonies of His actions in their past. That inspired them in the present and motivated their future. An understanding of what the Lord has done feeds the faith and hope of people in the now and the coming days.

Home Daily Devotional Readings

January 6–12, 2020

Monday	Tuesday	Wednesday	Thursday	Friday	Saturday	Sunday
A House of Prayer	Forgive and Restore Broken Relationships	Send the Rain	Welcome the Stranger	Forgive and Restore the Captive	Plea for God's Steadfast Love	Solomon Reviews Temple Developments
2 Chronicles 6:12–21	2 Chronicles 6:22–25	2 Chronicles 6:26–31	2 Chronicles 6:32–33	2 Chronicles 6:34–39	2 Chronicles 6:40–42	1 Kings 8:14–21

SOLOMON'S SPEECH

ADULT TOPIC:
I PROMISE!

BACKGROUND SCRIPTURE:
1 KINGS 8:14–21; 2 CHRONICLES 6

1 KINGS 8:14–21

King James Version

AND the king turned his face about, and blessed all the congregation of Israel: (and all the congregation of Israel stood;)
15 And he said, Blessed be the LORD God of Israel, which spake with his mouth unto David my father, and hath with his hand fulfilled it, saying,
16 Since the day that I brought forth my people Israel out of Egypt, I chose no city out of all the tribes of Israel to build an house, that my name might be therein; but I chose David to be over my people Israel.
17 And it was in the heart of David my father to build an house for the name of the LORD God of Israel.
18 And the LORD said unto David my father, Whereas it was in thine heart to build an house unto my name, thou didst well that it was in thine heart.
19 Nevertheless thou shalt not build the house; but thy son that shall come forth out of thy loins, he shall build the house unto my name.
20 And the LORD hath performed his word that he spake, and I am risen up in the room of David my father, and sit on the throne of Israel, as the LORD promised, and have built an house for the name of the LORD God of Israel.
21 And I have set there a place for the ark, wherein is the covenant of the LORD, which he made with our fathers, when he brought them out of the land of Egypt.

New Revised Standard Version

THEN the king turned around and blessed all the assembly of Israel, while all the assembly of Israel stood.
15 He said, "Blessed be the LORD, the God of Israel, who with his hand has fulfilled what he promised with his mouth to my father David, saying,
16 'Since the day that I brought my people Israel out of Egypt, I have not chosen a city from any of the tribes of Israel in which to build a house, that my name might be there; but I chose David to be over my people Israel.'
17 My father David had it in mind to build a house for the name of the LORD, the God of Israel.
18 But the LORD said to my father David, 'You did well to consider building a house for my name;
19 nevertheless you shall not build the house, but your son who shall be born to you shall build the house for my name.'
20 Now the LORD has upheld the promise that he made; for I have risen in the place of my father David; I sit on the throne of Israel, as the LORD promised, and have built the house for the name of the LORD, the God of Israel.
21 There I have provided a place for the ark, in which is the covenant of the LORD that he made with our ancestors when he brought them out of the land of Egypt."

MAIN THOUGHT: And he said, Blessed be the LORD God of Israel, which spake with his mouth unto David my father, and hath with his hand fulfilled it, saying, (1 Kings 8:15, KJV)

LESSON SETTING

Time: circa 920 B.C.
Place: Jerusalem

LESSON OUTLINE

I. Solomon's Preparation to Bless the People (1 Kings 8:21)
II. Solomon's Blessing: Recalling God's Faithful Promises to David (1 Kings 8:15–19)
III. Solomon's Blessing: Stating God's Faithful Promises to Him (1 Kings 8:20–21)

UNIFYING PRINCIPLE

Many people make promises they are unable to fulfill because of unforeseen circumstances. How should people respond when they *do* succeed in fulfilling their promise? Solomon thanked God for fulfilling the promise made to his father, King David, when God enabled Solomon to build the temple in which the Ark could be placed.

INTRODUCTION

Today's lesson passage is a continuation of the narrative of the placement of the Ark of the Covenant in the Holy of Holies in the temple. The priests had just completed the placement of the Ark in the inner sanctuary, beneath the wings of cherubim (1 Kings 8:6–7). Just as the priests began to withdraw from the area, a theophany, a manifestation of the Lord's presence, occurred in a cloud (1 Kings 8:10). The glory of the Lord, indicated by the cloud, was so overwhelming the priests were unable to continue their service. The Lord's presence pervaded the entire temple, and the awe of that experience elicited a response of reverence from the priests as well as the people.

These circumstances set the stage for the present lesson passage, Solomon's address to the gathered assembly (1 Kings 8:12–21). The manifestation of the Lord's glory also provides the context of Solomon's prayer of dedication of the temple (8:22–53). Solomon's speech to the people begins with words from ancient Jewish book, the *Book of Jashar,* a non-canonical work cited in the words of some Old Testament personalities. Solomon's words of his address in 1 Chronicles 6 reflect a citation from Jashar. The Septuagint (LXX, Greek translation of the Old Testament) includes Solomon saying: "The Lord has set the sun in the heavens." That line precedes the king's statement: "The LORD said He would dwell in the dark cloud" (1 Kings 8:12). Joshua also cited excerpts from Jashar in his address to the sun and moon (Josh. 10:12–13). David included an extended quote from the *Book of Jashar* in his lament over Jonathan and Saul (2 Sam. 1:17–27). Solomon's emphasis on the Lord dwelling in the dark cloud recalls such occasions of God's glory in the time of Moses, and it accentuates the fact there is some "hiddenness" to God.

Solomon then expresses what had been his intention in the construction of the Temple. He says to the Lord in 1 Kings 8:13: "I have surely built You an exalted house, And a place for You to dwell in forever." That was seen in contrast to the mobile tabernacle and Ark and the sporadic cloud that revealed God's glory. From that address to the Lord, Solomon then turns to speak to the gathered worshipers.

Exposition

I. Solomon's Preparation to Bless the People (1 Kings 8:21)

The opening verse of the lesson passage indicates: "Then the king turned around and blessed the whole assembly of Israel, while all the assembly of Israel was standing" (NKJV). Solomon previously had been facing the altar, away from the people. Having completed his statements to the Lord, he then turned to face the crowd of people. The author of 1 Chronicles includes an additional detail about Solomon's preparation to address the people. Just prior to the record of Solomon's prayer, the Chronicler indicates: "For Solomon had made a bronze platform seven and a half feet long, seven and a half feet wide, and four and a half feet high and put it in the court. He stood on it, knelt down in front of the entire congregation of Israel, and spread out his hands toward heaven" (2 Chron. 6:13, HCSB).

The platform has been described as a sort of a super bowl. The top was squared, but it may have had an oval base. Some expositors think that the Chronicler invented the platform in order to avoid the impression given the Kings account (especially 1 Kings 8) that Solomon is standing before the altar functioning like a priest. However, the platform was probably recorded in the Chronicler's source and was quite necessary for the occasion if Solomon was to be seen and heard by the great crowd of witnesses..

II. Solomon's Blessing: Recalling God's Faithful Promises to David (1 Kings 8:15–19)

The ceremony of the dedication of the temple and the placement of the Ark of the Covenant signaled for Solomon and the people that God had been faithful to and now fulfilled His promises made to David. Those promises are reflected in David's prayer after he had successfully located the Ark of the Covenant in Jerusalem, after having moved it from the home of Obed-Edom in Gath.

David prayed in 2 Samuel 7:24–29: "You have established your people Israel as your very own forever, and you, O Lord, have become their God. And now, Lord God, keep forever the promise you have made concerning your servant and his house. Do as you promised, so that your name will be great forever. Then men will say, 'The Lord Almighty is God over Israel!' And the house of your servant David will be established before you. O Lord Almighty, God of Israel, you have revealed this to your servant, saying, 'I will build a house for you.' So your servant has found courage to offer you this prayer. O Sovereign Lord, you are God! Your words are trustworthy, and you have promised these good things to your servant. Now be pleased to bless the house of your servant, that it may continue forever in your sight; for you, O Sovereign Lord, have spoken, and with your blessing the house of your servant will be blessed forever." This prayer reflects God's promises of the perpetuity of David's "house" and lineage.

But Solomon also had in mind other

promises the Lord had made to David about the construction of the house of the Lord being accomplished by a descendant and son of David. In His reprimand to David for David's planned intention to build the temple, the Lord both corrected and assured him: "When your time comes and you rest with your fathers, I will raise up after you your descendant, who will come from your body, and I will establish his kingdom. He will build a house for My name, and I will establish the throne of his kingdom forever" (2 Sam. 7:12–13, HCSB).

Yet verse 15 also sets the tone of the entire address to the people as well as the prayer that follows. It does so with its emphasis on praise to God for His faithfulness. It is by "His own hand" (note v. 24) the fulfillment of promises has occurred. God and God alone has made that happen. Therefore, He alone is worthy of the praise Solomon encourages the people to offer God (1 Chron. 29:10, 20; Neh. 9:5; Pss. 41:13; 72:18; 115:18; 117:1–2).

Verse 16 continues with part of the reprimand the Lord had given to David concerning the construction of a temple by David. The Lord had spoken through Nathan that despite David's enthusiastic desire to build a house for the Lord, at no time through the generations had the Lord Himself expressed a desire for such a place (2 Sam. 7:6–7).

Another significant insight is contained in verse 16. It corrects the perspective of both David and Solomon, and perhaps others of their generation, regarding the purpose of the Lord's house. That is the mention by the Lord of "my name." The Lord's name is a dominant motif in Solomon's prayer, as it occurs no less than fourteen times (1 Kings 8:16–20, 29, 33, 35, 41–43, 48). The Lord's intention for the temple was not for it to be a place in which He would "reside." Rather, it was to be a place in which His name would dwell. It would be a place that stood as witness to His character and presence. That would preclude glory for anyone except the Lord, including David and Solomon.

Solomon had detailed knowledge of his father David's desires to build the house of the Lord and the Lord's responses to David. Perhaps father and son had discussed this part of David's experiences. Perhaps David's prophet–advisors had provided such insights to Solomon. There is even the possibility that such knowledge was commonplace among the populace of Israel. Such is likely, due to the public prayers David had offered. Nonetheless, David's experiences regarding the temple significantly informed and instructed Solomon, shaping his theology. Solomon knew that building a house for the Lord had a prominent place in the thoughts of David (v. 17; 2 Sam. 7:2–3; 1 Chron. 17:1–2). And Solomon had even more intimate knowledge of discussions between David and the Lord. He knew the Lord had commended David for such noble desires (v. 18)

Solomon provides two reasons as to why David was forbidden to build the temple. The overriding reason was that such was not the will of God. The Lord wanted David to concentrate on serving as the ruler-shepherd of His people. God's plan was for Solomon to build the temple. But in addition to a theological understanding for David not being able to build the Lord's house, Solomon also had a pragmatic understanding, which he expressed in 1 Kings 5:3 (NKJV), "You know how my father David could not build a house for the name of the LORD his God because of the wars which were fought against him on every side, until the LORD put his foes under the soles of his feet." From this perspective, David was too preoccupied with military campaigns and had no time for the building campaign.

David himself related the military campaigns as perhaps a pragmatic reason he was not allowed to build the temple. First Chronicles 22:7–9 (NKJV) declares: "And David said to Solomon: 'My son, as for me, it was in my mind to build a house to the name of the LORD my God; but the word of the LORD came to me, saying, "You have shed much blood and have made great wars; you shall not build a house for My name, because you have shed much blood on the earth in My sight. Behold, a son shall be born to you, who shall be a man of rest; and I will give him rest from all his enemies all around. His name shall be Solomon, for I will give peace and quietness to Israel in his days."' Both David and Solomon understood the promise that the latter would build the temple and rested in God's faithful promises and their fulfillment.

III. Solomon's Blessing: Stating God's Faithful Promises to Him (1 Kings 8:20–21)

Verse 20 of the lesson focuses on God's faithfulness and fulfillment of promises to Solomon in two ways. One is that in keeping with God's promises, Solomon succeeded his father David and occupies the throne as Israel's king (v. 20a; 1 Chron. 28:5–6). The other is that Solomon has been permitted to build the temple. Solomon again expresses clarity of understanding about the actual purpose of the temple——a place to honor the name of Yahweh, the covenant God of Israel (v. 20).

Solomon emphasizes the covenant between Yahweh and Israel by noting he has provided a permanent place for the Ark. It has historical and theological significance. The historical significance is that the covenant emerged from the deliverance of Israel from Egypt. Also of historical, but more of theological significance, were the contents of the Ark Nothing was in the Ark except the two stone tablets Moses put there at Horeb, when the Lord made a covenant with the children of Israel, when they came out of Egypt (1 Kings 8:9). God's Law, expressed in the Ten Commandments, made the covenant relationship possible. Its presence in the Ark was an ongoing reminder to Israel of that fact.

The Lesson Applied

People do not, and cannot, live in isolation from their family roots. Every generation of a family or of people in general is inextricably linked with the previous, present, and succeeding generation. Such a relationship is analogous to a relay race. One generation possesses and then "passes off the baton" to the next. That baton includes good and bad and positive and negative things. It includes the family story, traditions, memories, values, and morals and ethics. The recipients of the baton then will modify it to an extent and pass it on their progeny. And so the process continues. This metaphor is essentially what this lesson speaks of. Solomon can relate the part of the relay others before him ran because he was familiar with it. He had invested the time to listen to and learn about his past. And then he interpreted and applied that knowledge to his own generation and for his individual life. He completed his part of the race by preserving and passing on the knowledge he had received. Every generation must do the same, particularly in spiritual matters. For only in so doing can we perceive clearly the promises, provisions, and faithfulness of God as they span the years.

Let's Talk About It

1. **How many generations of your family can you recall, either personally or through family stories or memories? What are some of the highlights of your recollections?**
2. **What are some promises of God in the Scriptures that you have seen fulfilled in your time? How have they influenced your journey of faith?**
3. **Discuss the spiritual legacy you wish to pass on to the succeeding generation in your life.**

It is important to note Solomon's prayer does not confine God to the temple. In 1 Kings 8:27, Solomon acknowledges that this "house" cannot contain God, and in several verses he speaks of God's "dwelling place" being in heaven, from where God can hear prayers and act in mercy towards those who pray (1 Kings 8:30-49). Although the temple is central to Israel's worship for many centuries, it is not essential. When it is destroyed (twice), God is still present with and attentive to His people.

Finally, it is important to note that we who are Gentiles are also people of promise in this text. In verses 41–43, Solomon speaks of the "foreigner" who will pray "towards this house." He asks God to heed the prayer of the foreigner "so that all the peoples of the earth may know your name and fear you, as do your people Israel" (8:43). We Gentiles are included in God's mercy and have access to God even at this early stage of Israel's history. Such inclusion is reason for thanksgiving and humility.

God is present with God's people in cloud, in fire, at Mount Sinai, in the tabernacle, in the temple, and most fully in Jesus Christ. God hears the prayers and petitions of His people and will respond to our cries with mercy. Such is the Gospel in this text. The Temple is a sign and a means of that communion with God, and thus deserves to be remembered with honor in both synagogue and church.

Home Daily Devotional Readings
January 13–19, 2020

Monday	Tuesday	Wednesday	Thursday	Friday	Saturday	Sunday
Pray for all Secular Leaders	Forgiveness of Sin Against Another	Forgive Each Other Generously	Encourage Each Other in Facing Difficulties	A House of Prayer for All Peoples	Captives Receive God's Gifts	God's Promises Are Kept
1 Timothy 2:1–6	1 Kings 8:31–32, 41–44	Colossians 3:8–13	1 Corinthians 15:1–11	Isaiah 56:3–8	Ephesians 4:1–8, 11–16	1 Kings 8:22–30, 52–53

SOLOMON'S DEDICATION PRAYER

ADULT TOPIC:
A BRIGHT FUTURE

BACKGROUND SCRIPTURE:
1 KINGS 8:22–53; 2 CHRONICLES 6:12–42

1 KINGS 8:22–30, 52–53

King James Version

AND Solomon stood before the altar of the LORD in the presence of all the congregation of Israel, and spread forth his hands toward heaven:

23 And he said, LORD God of Israel, there is no God like thee, in heaven above, or on earth beneath, who keepest covenant and mercy with thy servants that walk before thee with all their heart:

24 Who hast kept with thy servant David my father that thou promisedst him: thou spakest also with thy mouth, and hast fulfilled it with thine hand, as it is this day.

25 Therefore now, LORD God of Israel, keep with thy servant David my father that thou promisedst him, saying, There shall not fail thee a man in my sight to sit on the throne of Israel; so that thy children take heed to their way, that they walk before me as thou hast walked before me.

26 And now, O God of Israel, let thy word, I pray thee, be verified, which thou spakest unto thy servant David my father.

27 But will God indeed dwell on the earth? behold, the heaven and heaven of heavens cannot contain thee; how much less this house that I have builded?

28 Yet have thou respect unto the prayer of thy servant, and to his supplication, O LORD my God, to hearken unto the cry and to the prayer, which thy servant prayeth before thee to day:

29 That thine eyes may be open toward this house night and day, even toward the place

New Revised Standard Version

THEN Solomon stood before the altar of the Lord in the presence of all the assembly of Israel, and spread out his hands to heaven.

23 He said, "O LORD, God of Israel, there is no God like you in heaven above or on earth beneath, keeping covenant and steadfast love for your servants who walk before you with all their heart,

24 the covenant that you kept for your servant my father David as you declared to him; you promised with your mouth and have this day fulfilled with your hand.

25 Therefore, O LORD, God of Israel, keep for your servant my father David that which you promised him, saying, 'There shall never fail you a successor before me to sit on the throne of Israel, if only your children look to their way, to walk before me as you have walked before me.'

26 Therefore, O God of Israel, let your word be confirmed, which you promised to your servant my father David.

27 "But will God indeed dwell on the earth? Even heaven and the highest heaven cannot contain you, much less this house that I have built!

28 Regard your servant's prayer and his plea, O LORD my God, heeding the cry and the prayer that your servant prays to you today;

29 that your eyes may be open night and day toward this house, the place of which you said,

MAIN THOUGHT: And hearken thou to the supplication of thy servant, and of thy people Israel, when they shall pray toward this place: and hear thou in heaven thy dwelling place: and when thou hearest, forgive. (1 Kings 8:30, KJV)

1 Kings 8:22–30, 52–53

King James Version

of which thou hast said, My name shall be there: that thou mayest hearken unto the prayer which thy servant shall make toward this place.

30 And hearken thou to the supplication of thy servant, and of thy people Israel, when they shall pray toward this place: and hear thou in heaven thy dwelling place: and when thou hearest, forgive.

• • • • • •

52 That thine eyes may be open unto the supplication of thy servant, and unto the supplication of thy people Israel, to hearken unto them in all that they call for unto thee.

53 For thou didst separate them from among all the people of the earth, to be thine inheritance, as thou spakest by the hand of Moses thy servant, when thou broughtest our fathers out of Egypt, O Lord God.

New Revised Standard Version

'My name shall be there,' that you may heed the prayer that your servant prays toward this place.

30 Hear the plea of your servant and of your people Israel when they pray toward this place; O hear in heaven your dwelling place; heed and forgive.

• • • • • •

52 Let your eyes be open to the plea of your servant, and to the plea of your people Israel, listening to them whenever they call to you.

53 For you have separated them from among all the peoples of the earth, to be your heritage, just as you promised through Moses, your servant, when you brought our ancestors out of Egypt, O Lord God."

LESSON SETTING

Time: circa 920 B.C.
Place: Jerusalem

LESSON OUTLINE

I. Solomon's Dedication Prayer: God's Covenant With David (1 Kings 8:22–26)

II. Solomon's Dedication Prayer: God's Attention to Prayers (1 Kings 8:27–30)

III. Solomon's Dedication Prayer: God's Attention to His Special People (1 Kings 8:52–53)

Unifying Principle

People begin new undertakings with anticipation of a better future. How can we mark such important times? Solomon presided at the dedication of the temple by calling upon God to receive Israel's worship and to continue to be their God.

Introduction

Today's lesson passage and the parallel in 2 Chronicles 6:12–42 are Solomon's prayer of dedication of the temple in Jerusalem. The passage can be viewed as part of a larger emphasis on the temple as a house of prayer that includes 1 Kings 8:22–53. That larger context embraces seven distinct petitions or requests Solomon makes to the Lord.

In the first petition (1 Kings 8:31–32), Solomon seeks the Lord's intervention in cases of offense of one person against another. If a person had been accused of sinning against his neighbor, the defendant could take an oath at the temple altar and the Lord would declare whether or not the man was innocent. This was as means of ensuring justice in the land.

In the second petition (8:33–34), Solomon sought forgiveness of the people when Israel had experienced military defeat brought on by their disloyalty to the Lord.

There were times when the Lord withheld rain as a punitive measure, resulting in drought and hence devastation of crops and livestock and hunger or death to humans. So in his third request, Solomon asks that the Lord would restore rain to the earth once Israel had learned the lesson of its disobedience and had returned to the Lord.

The Lord sometimes sent famine as a corrective to the errant behavior of His people, Israel. Certainly famine could be the result of drought. But here Solomon has in mind famine that ensued from blight, mildew, locusts, grasshoppers, other disasters or diseases, or even the invasion of human enemies. Based on the penitent pleas of the people, Solomon's fourth request was that God would hear the prayers and forgive them.

In his fifth petition (1 Kings 8:41–43), Solomon intervenes for "the foreigner who does not belong to your people Israel but has come from a distant land because of your name." When such persons offered prayer to the Lord, Solomon asks God to hear and answer the foreigners' prayers as a witness to others who might thereby be drawn to the God of Israel.

In petition six (8:44–45), Solomon seeks the Lord's empowerment of the armies of Israel when they go to war against their enemies. There is a corollary to this petition in the seventh and final request Solomon makes of the Lord (8:46–53). Solomon knew there would be times when Israel persisted in their sinfulness to the point the Lord would deliver them to their enemies. Yet when they recognized their defeat is the result of their sins, repented, and called to the Lord, Solomon asked for the Lord's forgiveness and freedom to His captive people.

Three major topics are in the lesson text portion of the prayer. Verses 22–26 focus on the promises the Lord had made to David. Verses 27–30 are concerned with the Lord being attentive to the temple and the prayers that will be offered there. This same concern appears in verses 52–53, specifically seeking the Lord's listening ear whenever His people call to Him. There is also a brief but important emphasis on Israel as God's unique people, as evidenced by their selection from among all the other nations of the earth and the Lord's liberation of them from Egypt.

Exposition

I. Solomon's Dedication Prayer: God's Covenant With David (1 Kings 8:22–26)

Detailed discussion was provided in the introductory section of the previous lesson regarding the special platform from which Solomon prayed and addressed the people (2 Chron. 6:12–13). The author of 1 Kings provides additional information regarding Solomon's posture in prayer in the text. He writes at verse 22: "Then Solomon stood before the altar of the LORD in the presence of all the assembly of Israel, and spread out his hands toward heaven." Although kneeling or lying prostrate or facedown on the ground are frequently mentioned in the Old Testament, standing in prayer was the typical posture among Jewish people. The text here and the parallel in 2 Chronicles seem to suggest Solomon both stood and knelt for the dedication prayer (1 Kings 8:54; 2

Chron. 6:13). What is unmistakably clear is he prayed with his eyes open, looking up toward heaven, and with his arms reaching up, palms open. Others would do so looking in the direction of Jerusalem and the temple. Open hands expressed their need and their expectancy as they awaited the Lord's reply to their prayers (1 Kings 8:38; Exod. 9:29, 33; Pss. 63:4; 88:9; 143:6). This standing, outstretched hands, and gazing into heaven posture was apparently the norm in the early church (1 Tim. 2:8)

The prayer begins with a doxology, an expression of glorification or praise to the Lord for His uniqueness (Exod. 15:11; Deut. 4:39; 2 Sam. 7:22) and His covenant of love (Deut. 7:9). The original term for *love* (translated "mercy" in some places) is *hesedh*. It is the Lord's "steadfast," "unchanging," or "faithful" love that is the foundation for His covenant with His people Israel. The Queen of Sheba testified to the Lord's unique love for Israel in her laudatory words to Solomon (1 Kings 10:9): "Praise be to the LORD your God, who has delighted in you and placed you on the throne of Israel. Because of the LORD's eternal love for Israel, he has made you king, to maintain justice and righteousness."

Concerning Solomon's remarks about the uniqueness of God and his overall prayer, one Old Testament exegete submits: "The basis of all true prayer is the character of God ('There is none like thee.') The practical monotheism of the Mosaic covenant is moving in the direction of an explicit monotheism (8:60; Deuteronomy 4:35). The covenant relation is the gracious saving act of a loving God, keeping his promise to David. Promise in the Davidic covenant is unconditional to the dynasty, but to each holder of its throne it is conditioned on his obedience." Solomon acknowledged the faithfulness of the Lord's promise to David in the fact of the temple's existence (v. 24).

The balance of Solomon's emphasis on the Lord's covenant with David combines both confession and petition. He made confession about the Lord's fidelity to His promises in the previous verse. In the latter portion of verse 25, Solomon confesses the conditional nature of the security of each of the descendants of David's reign, based on their obedience (1 Kings 2:4; 2 Sam. 7:27–29). At the same time, Solomon prays the Lord will maintain His promise to David in Solomon's life and for his sake (v. 25). Thus there is an emphasis on the faithfulness of Solomon and succeeding kings, as well as an emphasis on the faithfulness of the Lord. Solomon reemphasizes the request about the fulfillment of the promise to David in verse 26.

II. Solomon's Dedication Prayer: God's Attention to Prayers (1 Kings 8:27–30)

As evidenced by verse 27, Solomon is overwhelmed at the concept of God's awesomeness in relation to the finiteness of the temple. He expressed amazement at the contrast between the greatness of God and the relative insignificance of the work he had done in constructing the temple. How could the Almighty God, the God who created everything, and who is eternal, dwell in a building made by the hands of men? Solomon had expressed this same truth to King Hiram prior to beginning construction (2 Chron. 2:6). The prophet

Isaiah expressed the same sentiment (Isa. 66:1), as do other passages (Ps. 139:7–16; Jer. 23:24; Acts 7:49; 17:24).

The truth of the previous notwithstanding, Solomon proceeds to ask the Lord that the temple, limited and inadequate though it might be in relation to the majesty of God, will be a place from which prayers will be offered and heard. Solomon begins by requesting the Lord will hear and answer his own prayer (2 Chron. 6:19; Ps. 141:2). What Solomon requests of his prayer at the time, he also desires for all time. He asks for God's watchful eyes and attentive ears toward the temple (1 Kings 8:52; Neh. 1:6). Elsewhere, the Lord assured Solomon He indeed would maintain a watchful eye and a hearing ear to the prayers offered in the temple, if the people met certain conditions (2 Chron. 7:14–15).

Of special note in verse 29 is Solomon's recognition of the purpose of the temple. It is a place of which the Lord said, "My name shall be there." In a subsequent time of prayer, the Lord assured Solomon: "I have heard the prayer and plea you have made before me; I have consecrated this temple, which you have built, by putting my name there forever. My eyes and my heart will always be there" (1 Kings 9:3).

The temple as the "house of prayer" is indicated in another manner this passage. Varied terminology for *prayer* appears here. When Solomon asks the Lord to "give attention to" or "regard" the prayer of His servant, the term for *prayer* is one that indicates all kinds of prayers. However, the same term at times intended prayers of intercession—prayers for oneself or others (1 Kings 19:4; Jer. 11:14). In verse 28, Solomon asks the Lord to "regard the prayer of Your servant and his supplication" (NKJV). The word for *supplication* here is a distinct term from the previous one and signifies pleading with God on the basis of His grace. Also in verse 28, there is the mention of the "cry and the prayer" Solomon offers. The original term for *cry* usually designates a loud outcry of praise to the Lord. In the present context, however, it means a strong appeal of request.

There is significant instruction from this summary about the meaning of the temple as the place of prayer. Dr. Roy L. Honeycutt suggests, "The sanctuary is the house of prayer, toward which the prayers of the people should be symbolically directed, confident that the Lord, from his heavenly dwelling, hears the prayers of his worshipers."

III. Solomon's Dedication Prayer: God's Attention to His Special People (1 Kings 8:52–53)

There is a sense in which verse 52 is a repetition (or reemphasis) of an earlier part of Solomon's prayer (vv. 29–30). However, although the language at points is nearly verbatim, the context is different. That context is 1 Kings 8:46. Verse 46 speaks almost prophetically as a prayer and could have been applicable to the time of Tiglath–pileser and the Assyrians (730s B.C., 2 Kings 17–18) or the time of Nebuchadnezzar and the Babylonians (598, 587/86 B.C., 2 Kings 24–25). Both eras involved the deportation of Jews from Israel, with the worst, of course, being the latter era, the Exile. Solomon's prayer at verse 46 (NIV) is: "When they sin against You—for there is no one who does not sin—and and you become angry with them and give them over to their enemies, who take them captive to their own lands, far away or near." That is followed by the anticipated conviction, repentance, and prayers of the exiled people to the Lord. Given that reality, Solomon makes the request that the Lord who had brought Israel from Egypt would open His eyes to Solomon's pleas and those of the Lord's people Israel whenever they called on Him (v. 52). The basis of Solomon's request is the status of Israel as the Lord's special people, chosen from among all the nations on the earth, and in a covenant relationship with Him. That special relationship had its origins in what God had spoken to Moses, and expressed in the Exodus from Egypt (Exod. 19:5–6; Deut. 9:26, 29; 14:2).

The Lesson Applied

Prayer is the primary means God's people communicate with Him. It is a privilege, even a responsibility, He makes available to all His people. In its simplest and perhaps purest form, prayer is a conversation with God. Yet authentic prayer, in distinction from mere words expressed to God, requires some things of those who pray. Prerequisite to acceptable prayer to God is the correct perception of who He is. That involves reverence and respect for the uniqueness of the Lord. Solomon expressed it this way: "O Lord, God of Israel, there is no God like you in heaven above or on earth below." Multiple passages in the Old Testament confirm the same affirmation. Only as one has proper regard for the Lord can one have a relationship with Him and pray to Him.

Let's Talk About It

1. **What are some ways in which you perceive and express the uniqueness of God. How did you come to be aware of that kind of perception?**
2. **To what extent are you content with your prayer life?**
3. **What are some ways in which you can improve your prayer life?**
4. **Identify some impediments to your prayer life and how you manage them.**

Perhaps the most notable expression of the necessity of a proper view of God are the words of Jesus in His instructions about acceptable prayer. To hallow, honor, and revere the name of God is to give God the proper respect He deserves. And that is not a formulaic expression in prayer. It is a constant disposition toward the Lord. Prayer is in the direction of God as the means and route to be closer to God. The desire to grow closer to God requires prayer. Authentic prayer reveals our total dependence on God to provide for our needs.

Home Daily Devotional Readings

January 20–26, 2020

Monday	Tuesday	Wednesday	Thursday	Friday	Saturday	Sunday
Hezekiah Restores the Temple	Solomon Seeks Wisdom to Govern	Solomon's Success Based on His Obedience	Solomon and God's Glory Compared	Temple Completed and Dedicated	Festivities Ended, People Return Home	Solomon Blesses the People, Urges Faithfulness
2 Chronicles 29:3–11	1 Kings 3:5–14	1 Kings 9:1–9	Matthew 6:25–30	2 Chronicles 7:1–6	2 Chronicles 7:8–11	1 Kings 8:54–61

SOLOMON'S BLESSING

ADULT TOPIC:
COMMITMENT TO SUCCESS

BACKGROUND SCRIPTURE:
1 KINGS 8:54–66

1 KINGS 8:54–61

King James Version

AND it was so, that when Solomon had made an end of praying all this prayer and supplication unto the LORD, he arose from before the altar of the LORD, from kneeling on his knees with his hands spread up to heaven.
55 And he stood, and blessed all the congregation of Israel with a loud voice, saying,
56 Blessed be the LORD, that hath given rest unto his people Israel, according to all that he promised: there hath not failed one word of all his good promise, which he promised by the hand of Moses his servant.
57 The LORD our God be with us, as he was with our fathers: let him not leave us, nor forsake us:
58 That he may incline our hearts unto him, to walk in all his ways, and to keep his commandments, and his statutes, and his judgments, which he commanded our fathers.
59 And let these my words, wherewith I have made supplication before the LORD, be nigh unto the LORD our God day and night, that he maintain the cause of his servant, and the cause of his people Israel at all times, as the matter shall require:
60 That all the people of the earth may know that the LORD is God, and that there is none else.
61 Let your heart therefore be perfect with the LORD our God, to walk in his statutes, and to keep his commandments, as at this day.

New Revised Standard Version

NOW when Solomon finished offering all this prayer and this plea to the LORD, he arose from facing the altar of the LORD, where he had knelt with hands outstretched toward heaven;
55 he stood and blessed all the assembly of Israel with a loud voice:
56 "Blessed be the LORD, who has given rest to his people Israel according to all that he promised; not one word has failed of all his good promise, which he spoke through his servant Moses.
57 The LORD our God be with us, as he was with our ancestors; may he not leave us or abandon us,
58 but incline our hearts to him, to walk in all his ways, and to keep his commandments, his statutes, and his ordinances, which he commanded our ancestors.
59 Let these words of mine, with which I pleaded before the LORD, be near to the LORD our God day and night, and may he maintain the cause of his servant and the cause of his people Israel, as each day requires;
60 so that all the peoples of the earth may know that the LORD is God; there is no other.
61 Therefore devote yourselves completely to the LORD our God, walking in his statutes and keeping his commandments, as at this day."

MAIN THOUGHT: The LORD our God be with us, as he was with our fathers: let him not leave us, nor forsake us: That he may incline our hearts unto him, to walk in all his ways, and to keep his commandments, and his statutes, and his judgments, which he commanded our fathers. (1 Kings 8:57–58, KJV)

LESSON SETTING

Time: circa 920 B.C.
Place: Jerusalem

LESSON OUTLINE

I. **Solomon's Benediction: God's Promises Fulfilled (1 Kings 8:54–57)**
II. **Solomon's Benediction: Israel's Obedience (1 Kings 8:58)**
III. **Solomon's Benediction: God's Remembrance of Solomon's Prayer (1 Kings 8:59–61)**

Unifying Principle

People often mark the start of new ventures with special ceremonies or observances because they have high hopes for success. How can we know that what we propose to do will succeed? After dedicating the temple, Solomon prayed for God's continued faithfulness toward Israel while calling on his people to renew their commitment to God.

Introduction

The passage for today is a segment of the rituals of dedication for the temple in Jerusalem (1 Kings 8:1–9:9) and is also another portion of Solomon's prayer. First Kings 8:22–53 is the dedicatory prayer, and the current passage is specifically a benediction. In Old Testament times (and usually also now) a benediction was a prayer at the end of a worship experience that sought the Lord's blessings on the worshipers or affirmed the nearness of His blessings. Undoubtedly, the most notable benediction in the Old Testament is the Aaronic Benediction, which the Lord instructed Moses to give to Aaron and the priests to bless Israel (Num. 6:22–23). They were to say to the people: "The LORD bless you and keep you; The LORD make His face shine upon you, And be gracious to you; The LORD lift up His countenance upon you, And give you peace" (vv. 24–26). The Aaronic Benediction served as a reminder to Israel that all their blessings were from the graciousness of God.

Typically priests gave the benediction. Yet on special occasion, the king could do so, as Solomon's did in this lesson. David also provided the benediction at the worship celebrating the return of the Ark of the Covenant to Jerusalem (2 Sam. 6:18). Solomon's benediction began with an expression of praise to God for His blessings to Israel. He seeks the continued presence of the Lord with Israel. He asks for Israel's continuing loyalty to the Lord. Solomon also seeks blessings for himself as king, to the ends that the entire earth will recognize the Lord for who He is. His blessing concluded with a challenge to Israel.

Exposition

I. Solomon's Benediction: God's Promises Fulfilled (1 Kings 8:54–57)

Up to the point of today's lesson text, Solomon had been in a posture of prayer on a special platform built for such an occasion and to be visible to the gathered worshipers (2 Chron. 6:13). That posture and position allowed him to be seen by the people but also to speak to the Lord on the behalf of the people and himself. Having completed his prayer Solomon then arose and stood to face the assembly and speak the benediction over them. One immediately notices some affinities between the prayer of benediction here and the prayer of blessing Solomon prayed earlier in the temple and recorded in 1 Kings 8:12–21. It has been observed about the two prayers: "This blessing concludes as Solomon's previous blessing (8:12–21) had introduced it, with covenant language. Whereas the covenant promises there were Davidic, these are Mosaic." Standing and addressing the gathered assembly in a loud voice (or, "blessing them at the top of his lungs," MSG), Solomon points to the Mosaic covenant in verse 56.

He identifies the blessing of the completion of the temple and the opportunity to worship there as "rest." Yet the mention of that rest (sabbath) also included the gift of the Promised Land to Israel, securing that land by means of the successful military conquests of David and finally the peacetime and temple construction under Solomon. Certainly when the people heard the word *rest* from Solomon, they recalled the Lord's words to Moses: "But you will cross the Jordan and settle in the land the LORD your God is giving you as an inheritance, and he will give you rest from all your enemies around you so that you will live in safety" (Deut. 12:10).

Reminiscing about the history of Israel and the Lord's dealings with them across the span of several centuries, Solomon reached the only logical conclusion: Not one word has failed of all the good promises He gave through his servant Moses (v. 56, NIV). Of the continuity of the motif of God's faithfulness to His word from the time of Moses to the time of Solomon, one Old Testament interpreter states: "Fulfillment of the divine promises is a strong binding theme within the Deuteronomic history and a strong motivation for retelling the mighty saving deeds of Yahweh." Solomon portrayed, and Israel perceived, Yahweh as the promise-making and the promise-keeping God. Their identity as a nation from time immemorial, as well as their hope for the future, was founded on the immutability and perpetuity of the Lord's promises.

Solomon especially emphasized a frequently repeated promise God originally gave to the patriarchs—that the Lord would never leave nor forsake His people. God was with Abraham during his life, and He likewise promised to be with Isaac (Gen. 26:3, 24–25). The Lord had promised to be with Jacob (Gen. 28:10–15; 31:3; 46:1–4). In subsequent generations, the Lord renewed this promise to Moses (Exod. 3:11–12; 33:12–14). Moses in turn repeated it to his successor, Joshua (Deut. 31:6–8). The Lord Himself also directly gave the promise to Joshua (Josh. 1:1–5, 9; 3:7). The Lord gave it to Gideon (Judg. 6:15–16), and the prophet Samuel conveyed it to the nation (1 Sam. 12:22). David encouraged his son Solomon with the words of the promise when in his discussions about the temple construction (1 Chron. 28:20).

The prophet Isaiah (41:10, 17; 42:16; 44:21; 49:14–16) declared the certainty of the Lord's promises to Israel and encouraged the captive people with them. The Lord used the words of His promises to encourage Jeremiah personally, as well as the nation of Judah through him (Jer. 1:8, 19; 20:11). The same motif of promise and fulfillment appear in the New Testament through the words of Jesus and New Testament writers.

Based on the Lord's past faithfulness to the ancestors of Israel, Solomon asks that the Lord likewise will continue to be as faithful to him, his current generation, and the coming generations (v. 57). Such a request embraces both the promises of the Lord and Israel's unique connection to Him as His people ((Deut. 31:6; Josh. 1:5; 1 Sam. 12:22).

II. Solomon's Benediction: Israel's Obedience (1 Kings 8:58)

Solomon's benediction then expresses a fundamental theological principle in the Old Testament and its record of Israel's relationship with God as well as His relationship as portrayed in the New Testament. That is, the blessings and privileges the Lord graciously provides require obedience on the part of His people. Recollection of the Lord's blessings and faithfulness to the previous generations was (and is) significant. In some ways it is indispensable. Concomitantly, however, awareness of the how the Lord's people are to respond to Him is equally indispensable. The covenant remains intact only to the extent to which God's people honor and are as loyal to their responsibilities as the Lord is faithful to His promises and provisions. There is always a conditional character to a covenant relationship. Just as blessings, security, and prosperity were promised given the obedience of the people, so God's displeasure and punishment were guaranteed in response to their infidelity (Josh. 23:15–16; Lev. 26:14–33; Deut. 28:15).

Therefore, Solomon just as loudly and passionately asks in his dedicatory prayer at verse 58: "May he give us the desire to do his will in everything and to obey all the commands, decrees, and regulations that he gave our ancestors" (NLT). Perhaps the Lord's own words concerning Israel's desires to be obedient inspired Solomon's plea, "Oh, that they had such a heart in them that they would fear Me and always keep all My commandments, that it might be well with them and with their children forever!" (Deut. 5:19, NKJV).

III. Solomon's Benediction: God's Remembrance of Solomon's Prayer (1 Kings 8:59–61)

Part of what Solomon expresses in this section of his dedicatory prayer is just how much value his prayer has for him and for the people of Israel. He essentially seeks that what he has prayed will remain close to the heart of God incessantly. Such is what he means in the words: "And may these words of mine, with which I have made supplication before the Lord, be near the Lord our God day and night." Solomon further intends to indicate the sincerity of his words with this request. Only that which is sincere and authentic merits God's constant notice of it.

Such sincerity occasions another request from Solomon—that the Lord will support the king and his subjects in proportion to their daily needs (v. 59). It also is noteworthy that Solomon asks that his prayers will "be near to the Lord our God." The same original word for *near* here appears in the description of the sacrifices to the Lord by the priests and worshipers. Both sacrifices and prayers, as Solomon understood them, were required to be authentic, which was validated in their presentation to the Lord.

The last petition of the prayer of blessing speaks to the purpose and destiny of Israel as a nation chosen from among all the other nations, most of which were of far greater fame. The desire is that Israel will be a witness to all the other nations of the world that Israel's God, Yahweh, is the one and only true God. That would be evidenced in their chosen status, their obedience, and the genuineness of their worship. Israel had encountered things that convincingly indicated to them the uniqueness of God, as passages such as Deuteronomy 4:35 indicate: "To you it was shown, that you might know that the LORD Himself is God; there is none other besides Him." The same truth is expressed in Joshua 4:24: "He did this so that all the peoples of the earth might know that the hand of the LORD is powerful and so that you might always fear the LORD your God." What Israel knows from its unique experiences and relationship, it must convey to others (1 Kings 8:43; 2 Kings 19:19).

First Kings 8:41-43 asks that even foreigners who pray toward God's house have their prayers heard and answered. Throughout the prayer the frequent repetition of the phrase "your people Israel" emphasizes the identity of Israel as God's chosen covenant community. The focus on these verses about foreigners should not detract from the fact that Solomon's prayer understands Israel alone is God's chosen people. In fact, the prayer ends with the declaration that "you have separated them from among all the peoples of the earth, to be your heritage" (1 Kings 8:53). This petition also proclaims that even those "not of your people Israel" will hear of the greatness of the Lord and come to the temple to offer prayers. By heeding the prayers of foreigners as well as Israelites, according to Solomon's rationale, God will cause the peoples of the earth to know and fear the God of Israel, and "they may know that your name has been invoked on this house that I have built" (1 Kings 8:43). In other words, reverence from foreigners helps to show that out of all the national deities being claimed by various peoples, the God of Israel is the most powerful one, and the house Solomon has built is where that God dwells. Solomon's own international reputation is tied up with God's; if Solomon's God is a winner, so must be Solomon.

Reflection on the role of non-Israelites in the glorification of Israel's God in resonates with similar language in Isaiah 40–55, the portions of Isaiah dating immediately before the Judeans' return from Babylonian exile that describes Israel as "a light to the nations, that my salvation may reach to the end of the earth" (Isa. 49:6).

God's work in Israel promotes God's glorification and salvific work in the rest of the world. The text goes on: "Thus says the LORD, the Redeemer of Israel and his Holy One, to one deeply despised, abhorred by the nations, the slave of rulers, 'Kings shall see and stand up, princes, and they shall prostrate themselves, because of the LORD, who is faithful, the Holy One of Israel, who has chosen you'" (49:7). Again, God's actions with Israel showcase both the glory of God and the status of God's chosen people in the world.

Solomon's final words of his benediction are a commission to Israel: "Let your heart therefore be loyal to the LORD our God, to walk in His statutes and keep His commandments, as at this day." Due to the distinctive character of these words in relation to the rest of the prayer of dedication, what is a conclusion perhaps also was expressed each time Israel had a ceremony of covenant renewal. They constantly needed to be reminded of their responsibilities to Yahweh. Loyalty to Him cannot be for a day or seasonal—it must be perpetual.

The Lesson Applied

God's people always must keep a consciousness of God's blessings close to the forefront of their minds and memories. A part of doing that involves constant awareness that God is the exclusive source of one's blessings. Otherwise, the fatal flaw of human pride can lead one to place far too much emphasis on one's own efforts or accomplishments. Or there will be an undue focus on means through which the Lord has provided blessings.

A focus on passages such as Psalm 103 can help one remain centered on the graciousness of God: "Praise the LORD, O my soul; all my inmost being, praise his holy name. Praise the LORD, O my soul, and forget not all his benefits." And then, just as the psalmist does here, one should take mental and spiritual inventory of as many of God's blessings as one can possibly recall. Shortly after that exercise, a look at Psalm 116 will prove helpful. Again, after meditating on the words of the author, the reader should arrive at the same question the author asks at verse 12: "How can I repay the LORD for all his goodness to me?" The responses one provides might differ from those of the psalmist, but a response will be unavoidable due to God's goodness.

Let's Talk About It

1. **Identify people the Lord has used to shape you spiritually. What contributions have they made in your life?**
2. **Discuss how you testify to unbelievers of your relationship with God.**
3. **How does being in a community of faith equip you for ministry?**

Reflection on God's faithfulness result in praise and thanksgiving. Yet, of equal importance is a sense of obligation to the Lord. Thinking, meditating, reflecting on the Lord's graciousness inevitably lead to gratitude and worship. Yet these exercises also inevitably lead one to determine legitimate ways in which to express gratitude and praise in obedient service to God. The most persuasive testimony to the world of a relationship with the Lord is in a lifestyle that is consistent with His way, will, and Word.

Home Daily Devotional Readings

January 27–February 2, 2020

Monday	Tuesday	Wednesday	Thursday	Friday	Saturday	Sunday
Don't Test the Lord	Angels Guard Tempted Believers	Do Not Forget the Lord	Jesus' Priestly Ministry	Jesus, God's Beloved Son	The Kingdom of Heaven Is Here	Jesus Rejects Satan's Temptations
Deuteronomy 6:16–25	Psalm 91	Deuteronomy 8:11–20	Hebrews 4:14–5:10	Matthew 3:13–17	Matthew 4:12–17	Matthew 4:1–11

Single-minded Obedience

Adult Topic:
Passing the Tests

Background Scripture:
Matthew 4:1–11

Matthew 4:1–11

King James Version

THEN was Jesus led up of the Spirit into the wilderness to be tempted of the devil.

2 And when he had fasted forty days and forty nights, he was afterward an hungred.

3 And when the tempter came to him, he said, If thou be the Son of God, command that these stones be made bread.

4 But he answered and said, It is written, Man shall not live by bread alone, but by every word that proceedeth out of the mouth of God.

5 Then the devil taketh him up into the holy city, and setteth him on a pinnacle of the temple,

6 And saith unto him, If thou be the Son of God, cast thyself down: for it is written, He shall give his angels charge concerning thee: and in their hands they shall bear thee up, lest at any time thou dash thy foot against a stone.

7 Jesus said unto him, It is written again, Thou shalt not tempt the Lord thy God.

8 Again, the devil taketh him up into an exceeding high mountain, and sheweth him all the kingdoms of the world, and the glory of them;

9 And saith unto him, All these things will I give thee, if thou wilt fall down and worship me.

10 Then saith Jesus unto him, Get thee hence, Satan: for it is written, Thou shalt worship the Lord thy God, and him only shalt thou serve.

11 Then the devil leaveth him, and, behold, angels came and ministered unto him.

New Revised Standard Version

THEN Jesus was led up by the Spirit into the wilderness to be tempted by the devil.

2 He fasted forty days and forty nights, and afterwards he was famished.

3 The tempter came and said to him, "If you are the Son of God, command these stones to become loaves of bread."

4 But he answered, "It is written, 'One does not live by bread alone, but by every word that comes from the mouth of God.'"

5 Then the devil took him to the holy city and placed him on the pinnacle of the temple,

6 saying to him, "If you are the Son of God, throw yourself down; for it is written, 'He will command his angels concerning you,' and 'On their hands they will bear you up, so that you will not dash your foot against a stone.'"

7 Jesus said to him, "Again it is written, 'Do not put the Lord your God to the test.'"

8 Again, the devil took him to a very high mountain and showed him all the kingdoms of the world and their splendor;

9 and he said to him, "All these I will give you, if you will fall down and worship me."

10 Jesus said to him, "Away with you, Satan! for it is written, 'Worship the Lord your God, and serve only him.'"

11 Then the devil left him, and suddenly angels came and waited on him.

MAIN THOUGHT: Then saith Jesus unto him, Get thee hence, Satan: for it is written, Thou shalt worship the Lord thy God, and him only shalt thou serve. (Matthew 4:10, KJV)

LESSON SETTING

Time: circa A.D. 30
Place: Jerusalem

LESSON OUTLINE

I. The Setting of Jesus' Temptations (Matthew 4:1–2)
II. The Experience of Jesus' Temptations (Matthew 4:3–10)
III. The Strength for Jesus' Temptations (Matthew 4:11)

Unifying Principle

People are tempted in many ways to turn aside from what they know is right. How can we resist such temptations? Jesus resisted the devil's temptations by quoting the Scriptures, thus demonstrating His single-minded obedience to God.

Introduction

The narrative of Jesus' temptation in the wilderness is what New Testament interpreters call a triple-tradition narrative. That is, the narrative occurs in all three Synoptic Gospels. Luke records it in 4:1–12. Mark summarily mentions the temptation of Jesus in 1:12–13, although there is not a narrative as there is in Matthew and Luke. All the Synoptic writers set the temptations of Jesus immediately following his baptism (Matt. 3:13–17; Luke 3:21–22; Mark 1:9–11). That momentous occasion endorsed the ministry of John the Baptist on the one hand. On another hand, Jesus' baptism served as sign of His "immersion" into the role of God's Messiah, the "Anointed One," for Israel and the world. Furthermore, it also affirmed the unique relationship between the Heavenly Father and Jesus. Jesus was the Son of God in that He was conceived by the Holy Spirit. He was publicly declared to be so initially at His baptism. That relationship would prove to be the basis of the tempter's strategy against Jesus.

Christology is that area of systematic theology concerned with the person and work of Jesus Christ. Its primary questions are: Who was Jesus? What did He do? In constructing Christology, one may emphasize either the humanity or the deity of Jesus. There is sometimes a tendency primarily to emphasize the deity of Jesus. This is certainly appropriate. Jesus was incontrovertibly divine. An adequate Christology, however, is guided by the declaration of the ancient Creed of Chalcedon: Jesus was "very God and very man." He truly was divine, and He truly was man. The writers of the Gospels compellingly portray the humanity of Jesus in a variety of ways. The first of these is the temptation narratives. Noted New Testament scholar Dr. Frank Stagg suggests, "It is significant that the two Gospels which tell of the virgin birth of Jesus also emphasize his temptations. They are as certain of his real humanity as of his divine origin. They nowhere represent the choices Jesus made as easy. Jesus endured the cross; he did not desire it. He did not relish his cup, but he did drink it (26:39)."

One would do well to heed further words from Dr. Stagg when considering the temptations of Jesus. "The temptations of Jesus are to be taken at face value. They were not sham battles but real struggles."

Exposition

I. The Setting of Jesus' Temptations (Matthew 4:1–2)

The opening word of the temptation narrative, "then," makes a clear connection with the narrative of Jesus' baptism. One also notes the emphasis on the role of the Holy Spirit in the experience. The Holy Spirit led Jesus into the wilderness. There was complete awareness that temptation would occur there. Mark employs the Greek word *ekballō* to describe the Spirit's influence over Jesus to the wilderness. The word literally means "to cast, or thrust out." The NKJV captures it: "Immediately the Spirit drove Him into the wilderness." The Spirit, who appeared as a dove as a sign of God's empowerment for Jesus' mission, now takes Him to the gruesome testing place and experience.

That gruesome testing place, the "wilderness," is a term that refers to one of several vast expanses of rocky, dry, wasteland in Israel. Most of it lay south, east, and southwest of the inhabitable land of Israel in the Negeb, Transjordan, and the Sinai. Specifically, the place of Jesus' temptation probably was located on the eastern slopes of the Judean mountains in the rain shadow leading down to the Dead Sea. This area is sometimes called Jeshimon and was a refuge for David during his flight from Saul. The wilderness for Jesus was also a place without human companionship as He faced the tempter.

Matthew indicates the temptations were associated with a forty-day fast of Jesus. It seems Matthew intends for the reader to understand the temptations commenced at the end of this period of fasting. Mark makes it plain the temptations occurred during a forty-day period: "and he was in the desert forty days, being tempted by Satan" (Mark 1:13). Luke concurs with this perspective (Luke 4:2).

Fasting, the self-deprivation of water and food, was a noted spiritual discipline in Israelite religion. Moses was known to fast for forty-day periods, a time span associated with completion. He did so prior to engraving the Ten Commandments on stone tablets (Exod. 34:28). He also fasted for forty days in a time of intercession for Israel's sinfulness (Deut. 9:18). The symbolic representative of Israel's prophetic tradition, Elijah, traveled for a forty-day period without food or drink (1 Kings 19:8). Understandably, Jesus, who is the fulfillment of both the Law and the prophets, would spend this period of a personal spiritual focus in anticipation of His mission.

Matthew provides a significant editorial comment: "and afterward he was hungry." Although this perhaps is something the reader would assume, it sets the stage for the first proposition of the tempter.

II. The Experience of Jesus' Temptations (Matthew 4:3–10)

Most English translations of this passage identify Jesus' nemesis in the wilderness as "the devil" (v. 1). The Greek term for *devil* here, *diabolos*, also means "slanderer." *Diabolos* also occurs in verses 5, 8, and 11. Two other terms appear in this temptation narrative to designate Jesus' wilderness enemy. One is *peirazōn*, occurring at verse 3. This term primarily means "tempter." The Greek term, *satana*, easily recognized as *Satan*, appears in verse 10. Typically, this term means "adversary." The distinctive terms and nuances of meaning all describe the same nefarious personage who seeks to divert Jesus from His mission. In Israelite lore, the wilderness was particularly the domain of this personage and of demons.

The tempter, functioning as one who put Jesus to the test, offers what appears to be a reasonable proposition. Based on the declaration of Jesus' Sonship to God, and upon the hunger following a forty-day fast, Jesus should turn some of the plentiful wilderness stones into bread. The battleground of each of the temptations is the mind of Jesus. It is perhaps significant there are various subjunctives, conditional sentences, in Greek. One is a first-class condition, such as occurs in verse 4.

The subjunctive in the text should be construed: *Since you are God's Son.* The tempter's purpose was not so much to cause Jesus to doubt He was God's Son as it was for Jesus to presume upon that relationship for His own purposes. The tempter called upon Jesus to be something other than the completely obedient Son who is pleasing to His Father.

The starting point was Jesus' own hunger, of course. Yet one of the popular expectations of the Messiah was that He would repeat the miracles from the time of Moses, especially the provision of manna (Exod. 16; John 6:30). To be sure, multitudes of persons in Israel were clamoring for the "bread and water" needs of life. The tempter's proposition was consistent with his purposes to mislead Jesus to meet immediate goals or to employ the wrong methods to meet valid human need.

Guided by His own commitment and obedience, and strengthened by the Scriptures, Jesus responded based on a different perspective on human need. He cites a portion of Deuteronomy 8:3, which recounted the Lord's provisions for Israel: "He humbled you, causing you to hunger and then feeding you with manna, which neither you nor your fathers had known, to teach you that man does not live on bread alone but on every word that comes from the mouth of the LORD."

Herein, Jesus acknowledged the validity of physical needs. The basic necessities of life—food, water, clothing, shelter and such—must be met. Jesus made this abundantly clear in His teachings (Matt. 25:31-46). Yet there were also other needs. There were other aspects to God's Word beside meeting physical needs. Jesus personally, as well as all humanity, must be nourished by all God's self-revelation in Scripture.

R. V. G. Tasker captivatingly summarizes the second proposition of the tempter to Jesus in verses 5–6. "Jesus is tempted … to imagine Himself seated on the pinnacle of the temple with the crowds assembled in the courts beneath, perhaps at the time of the evening sacrifice, and to contemplate jumping down among them—a leap which in the case of everyone else who attempted it would be suicidal, but from which upheld by angels' hands He would escape unscathed."

Satan's first proposition to Jesus had been rebuffed with the Scriptures. Therefore, the devil seeks to substantiate the second test with a citation from Psalm 91:11–12. Shakespeare memorably observed that even the devil can quote Scripture for his own purposes. The devil did so here to strengthen his proposition to Jesus. The Psalm was not an invitation to risk-taking. Rather, it was an assurance to the faithful of God's protection wherever the journey of faith and obedience might lead.

The devil was calling for Jesus to respond to the fervor among the people for miraculous signs. The dramatic, the association of signs and wonders with the coming of Messiah, was consistent with Jewish expectations of the day. This was especially true in relation to the appearance of Messiah in the temple (Mal. 3:1–2).

Jesus responded again from the Scriptures, specifically Exodus 17:2 and Deuteronomy 6:16. Jesus here differentiates between "faith" that seeks to manipulate God to act on one's selfish behalf and faith that relies on God's will as well as His provisions.

Dr. Stagg says of the third and final temptation of Jesus in the wilderness: "Jesus was forced to make a decision with respect to Jewish hopes for messianic deliverance from Rome. Without justifying Roman rule or denying the legitimacy of Jewish longings for national freedom, he refused to interpret the messianic function in political terms or equate the kingdom of God with the kingdom of Israel."

Upon the screen of the mind of Jesus, the devil projected an image of the kingdoms of the world and their splendor (v. 8). The devil offered the political power and wealth of all the world's kingdoms on the condition Jesus would worship him. The devil sought ultimate allegiance to himself from Jesus. Such was an alluring proposition to many, as the Caesars of Rome, the pharaohs of Egypt, Alexander the Great of Greece, and many modern-day governmental leaders have demonstrated. Political power is seductive for many.

Jesus yet again appealed to Scripture for His reply after sternly rebuffing Satan: "Away from me, Satan!" Appealing to Deuteronomy 6:13–14, Jesus insisted worship must be given to the Lord God exclusively. At the same time, Jesus refused to succumb to the temptation of a temporary, limited kingdom. Even this early in His mission, He fully knew His was a kingdom "not of this world" and was eternal. He would come to have all authority in heaven and on earth.

III. The Strength for Jesus' Temptations (Matthew 4:11)

Verse 11 indicates this particular season of temptation ended for Jesus with the departure of the devil. With that departure, but also because of His responses to the tempter, Jesus found spiritual and physical renewal of strength in the ministry of angels. To be sure, the tempter would return over and over in attempts to distort Jesus' view of messiahship and His overall ministry. Nonetheless, now Jesus was victorious over the tempter and would continue to be by reliance on God's provisions.

The Lesson Applied

Noted "father" of the Protestant Reformation, Martin Luther, is purported to have said about one's response to temptation: "You cannot stop a bird from flying over your head, but you can stop it from building a nest in your hair." Encounters with temptation are unavoidable. But, despite what many think, surrender to temptation is not inevitable. One can keep birds from building nests in one's hair; one can overcome temptation. It was at the point of Jesus' humanity that He was tempted. It was also at the point of His humanity, not by divine exercise of power or a miracle, that He was victorious. Jesus' victory came from sheer obedience of the will and reasoned, resolved response from the Scriptures.

The lesson also provides insight about the nature of temptations and their occurrence in one's life. Addressing the proximity of Jesus' baptism and its spiritual ecstasy and the timing of the temptations, Stagg writes: "Moments of great vision and exaltation are precisely those in which one is most subject to assault. The higher life is keyed to the potentiality for truth and good, the more open it is to temptation." In other words, moments of spiritual ecstasy or intense spiritual intimacy with God also may be the time in which temptations are most acute. The moment of one's greatest strength can be the potential for one's greatest weakness. The moment of one's most authentic spiritual commitment also might be the season of one's highest vulnerability.

People often sense God's summons to some special service for Him. Opportunities for ministry come especially to those who previously have proven themselves. Yet the call to service brings with it the issue of how ministry is to be done. The method and the ultimate outcome are always critical. One must always be vigilant regarding the persons or expectations that will shape one's ministry. It is possible to do the right thing by the wrong means and bring reproach rather than glory to God.

Let's Talk About It

1. **What strategy or strategies do you possess and practice for managing temptation?**
2. **What have been some of the more intense seasons of temptation for you? Why was this so?**
3. **How do you prepare for service for the Lord?**
4. **Discuss the role of the Scriptures on your faith journey for maintaining loyalty to God.**

Identity is the focus of the tempter in the scene of Jesus' temptation. "If [Since] You are the Son of God," Satan begins. He desires to tempt Jesus into departing from His mission and purpose with the lure of earthly pleasure or gain. Jesus stands on the Word and refuses to establish His worth and identity on His own terms. Jesus knows who He is by remembering Whose He is. Jesus invites us to find both hope and courage in the God who named not only Him, but all of us, beloved children so we too will discover who we are.

In life we will cross paths with many forms of temptation that can easily set us off course from our true mission and purpose in Christ. By staying closely aligned to God's Word, as Jesus did, we can be sure and secure in our God-given identity and mission.

Home Daily Devotional Readings

February 3–9, 2020

Monday	Tuesday	Wednesday	Thursday	Friday	Saturday	Sunday
Listen and Act with Integrity	Work and Play Are God's Gifts	Express Your Faith Through Actions	A Doxology of Praise to God	Forgive from the Heart	God's Will and Our Needs	Piety That God Expects of Us
Ecclesiastes 5:1–6	Ecclesiastes 5:18–20	Isaiah 1:11–17	1 Chronicles 29:10–13	Matthew 18:21–35	Matthew 6:16–21	Matthew 6:1–8

PIETY THAT HONORS GOD

ADULT TOPIC:
THE PITFALLS OF SHOWING OFF

BACKGROUND SCRIPTURE:
ECCLESIASTES 5:1–6; MATTHEW 6:1–8

MATTHEW 6:1–8

King James Version

TAKE heed that ye do not your alms before men, to be seen of them: otherwise ye have no reward of your Father which is in heaven.

2 Therefore when thou doest thine alms, do not sound a trumpet before thee, as the hypocrites do in the synagogues and in the streets, that they may have glory of men. Verily I say unto you, They have their reward.

3 But when thou doest alms, let not thy left hand know what thy right hand doeth:

4 That thine alms may be in secret: and thy Father which seeth in secret himself shall reward thee openly.

5 And when thou prayest, thou shalt not be as the hypocrites are: for they love to pray standing in the synagogues and in the corners of the streets, that they may be seen of men. Verily I say unto you, They have their reward.

6 But thou, when thou prayest, enter into thy closet, and when thou hast shut thy door, pray to thy Father which is in secret; and thy Father which seeth in secret shall reward thee openly.

7 But when ye pray, use not vain repetitions, as the heathen do: for they think that they shall be heard for their much speaking.

8 Be not ye therefore like unto them: for your Father knoweth what things ye have need of, before ye ask him.

New Revised Standard Version

"BEWARE of practicing your piety before others in order to be seen by them; for then you have no reward from your Father in heaven.

2 "So whenever you give alms, do not sound a trumpet before you, as the hypocrites do in the synagogues and in the streets, so that they may be praised by others. Truly I tell you, they have received their reward.

3 But when you give alms, do not let your left hand know what your right hand is doing,

4 so that your alms may be done in secret; and your Father who sees in secret will reward you.

5 "And whenever you pray, do not be like the hypocrites; for they love to stand and pray in the synagogues and at the street corners, so that they may be seen by others. Truly I tell you, they have received their reward.

6 But whenever you pray, go into your room and shut the door and pray to your Father who is in secret; and your Father who sees in secret will reward you.

7 "When you are praying, do not heap up empty phrases as the Gentiles do; for they think that they will be heard because of their many words.

8 Do not be like them, for your Father knows what you need before you ask him.

MAIN THOUGHT: Take heed that ye do not your alms before men, to be seen of them: otherwise ye have no reward of your Father which is in heaven. (Matthew 6:1, KJV)

LESSON SETTING

Time: circa A.D. 30
Place: Galilee

LESSON OUTLINE

I. Jesus' Instructions About Charitable Giving (Matthew 6:1–4)
II. Jesus' Instructions About Prayer (Matthew 6:5–8)

Unifying Principle

Eager to be well thought of, people are pulled in a multitude of contradictory directions. How can we be true to the highest principles we have been taught? In Matthew 5, Jesus taught the disciples the Beatitudes; and in Matthew 6, He warned them against practicing their piety in order to be praised by others.

Introduction

This lesson passage belongs what many New Testament exegetes designate as the second major division of Matthew's Gospel. That section, of course, is the Sermon on the Mount, which includes Matthew 5:1–7:29.

Following an introduction to the Sermon on the Mount, so designated since the time and terminology of Augustine, there are five major divisions leading up to lesson text. The Beatitudes appear in 5:3–12. The portrayal of disciples in the metaphors of salt, light, and a city on a hill appears in 5:13–16. Jesus presents His relationship with and approach to the Law in 5:17–20. In Matthew 5:21–48, Jesus articulates the intention of the Law by the presentation of six antitheses: murder (5:21–26), lust and adultery (5:27–30), divorce (5:31–32), the meaning of oaths (5:33–37), overcoming evil with the power of good (5:38–42), and love for one's enemies (5:43–48).

In a more narrow context in the Gospel of Matthew, the current lesson passage belongs to Jesus' discussion regarding motives in one's acts of piety. Discussions follow pertaining to the three major expressions of piety in Judaism (and among Jesus' disciples). Jesus discusses the matter of almsgiving or charitable giving in Matthew 6:1–4. The wrong and right methods of prayer appear in 6:5–15. The final topic, fasting, is discussed in 6:16–18.

In His discussions about the three acts of piety, so valued in the religious culture of which He was a part, Jesus sought first of all to correct the faulty motives and methods so common among a segment of Jewish society. The insights of the New Testament scholar, Frank Stagg, provide an illuminating summary of Jesus' teaching on the subject. He writes: "The primacy of motive in religious life is illustrated in the areas of almsgiving, prayer, and fasting. Jesus esteemed all three and assumed that his followers would practice them. His point was that the motive behind religious expression gives it its meaning. Religion as performance designed to impress God, other people, or self is false and futile." He continues with a principle for all acts of piety. "The proposition developed in the three illustrations is set forth in v. 1, 'practicing your piety' is to think of righteousness as outward performance. The fallacy stems from failure to recognize that moral, ethical, or spiritual value is not inherent in things done or said."

In His instructions about the practice of piety, Jesus first confronts His listeners (specifically His disciples) with a contrast to how the particular act of piety should be conducted. He identifies the incorrect practitioners as "hypocrites," insincere members of legitimate religion, such as Judaism. Or He identifies the incorrect practitioners as "pagans," devotees of a god or gods other than the one true God of the Scriptures. Jesus then sets forward the outcome of the incorrect approach and follows that with instruction about the proper practice of the acts of piety.

Exposition

I. Jesus' Instructions About Charitable Giving (Matthew 6:1–4)

There are many special topics of emphasis in the Gospel of Matthew, any one of which could be designated as the theme of the Gospel. Based on a comprehensive perspective of the content of Matthew, a significant segment of New Testament scholars point to the topic of righteousness as the overriding theme of the book. Matthew's Gospel concerns itself with the question: "What does it mean to be righteous, as Jesus Christ defines and exemplifies it?" Jesus discusses this topic throughout the Gospel of Matthew and often challenged various Jewish religious groups regarding their understanding and practice of righteousness. He frequently had discussions, or even debates, with the Pharisees and scribes (3:7; 12:24, 28, 38; 21:45; 22:34–35). Jesus often referred to God's judgment on the Pharisees in Matthew (15:12–13; 23:1–36).

At the same time, however, Jesus recognized the perception among His contemporaries that many, if not most, of the Pharisees were sincere in their religious piety and embodied the ideals of the Mosaic Law. So one should not be surprised to find Jesus appealed to the Pharisees as a standard of righteousness which His own followers should surpass if they were to belong to the Kingdom of heaven. Matthew 5:20 is a clear example of that as well as a statement of the theme of the Gospel of Matthew: "For I say to you, that unless your righteousness exceeds the righteousness of the scribes and Pharisees, you will by no means enter the kingdom of heaven" (NKJV).

The teachings of Jesus in today's lesson passage are illustration of the primary principle of the "surpassing righteousness" of which Jesus speaks. That principle is that acts of piety or righteousness must be motivated by one's relationship with God and be authentic expressions of worship and service to Him.

Jesus begins with a general statement about any and all devotional acts: "Be careful not to do your 'acts of righteousness' before men, to be seen by them. If you do, you will have no reward from your Father in heaven" (v.1, NIV). Other biblical translations refer to acts of righteousness as "good deeds" (NLT), "charitable deeds" (NKJV), and "righteousness" (HCSB). The original term from the Greek, *eleēmosunē,* can indicate any "act of mercy." Or it can specifically indicate charitable giving or almsgiving, donations to help the needy. The context determines which meaning is intended. In verse 1, Jesus speaks of any act of mercy or compassion.

In His warning, Jesus urges the listeners to "hold the mind together," the literal meaning of "take heed" or "beware," about the motivation of their compassionate acts. There is a temptation to do compassionate acts merely as a performance. The term *theathēnai* is "to be seen," or for "an impressive performance," and is the origin of the English word *theatrical*. If putting on a theatrical-like performance is one's motivation for one's compassionate deeds, there will be no approval from the Father, who stands alongside the one doing the deeds. The term for "reward," *apachein*, is a business term meaning "to give a receipt." There is no approval or acknowledgment from God for impure motives for giving.

Jesus's instruction about giving using a negative example in verse 2 is also the use of hyperbole, exaggeration, or overstatement. That was an effective teaching methodology Jesus used to make a significant point (Matt. 18:23–30; 19:24; 23:24). Jesus' statement about not announcing giving with a trumpet is a description of how hypocrites ("pretenders," "play-actors," theatrical performers") give. But it is also an exaggerated way of doing so in order to imprint the importance of the lesson in the learners' minds. There could have been a historical point of reference to the sounding of the trumpet. Trumpets (rams' horns) were sounded to signal times of fast during drought. Or it might have been that a trumpet was sounded in the synagogue to indicate the time in the liturgy to receive alms for the needy.

Jesus was not condemning or challenging either of those. He used an event familiar to His hearers to establish His lesson objective. The behavior to be avoided is "to be honored by men."

In the context of His lesson on authentic acts of compassion, Jesus also employs another overstatement as to how His followers are to give: Do not let your left hand know what your right hand is doing. What an impressive and memorable way to instill in His students the necessity of privacy and authenticity in giving! Giving that the Lord honors, "rewards," is done out of the right motivation. And that motivation is to be a practitioner of true righteousness, which in this case is compassion expressed by a truly compassionate heart and out of devotion to the Lord. It is not an attempt to impress people and gain their acknowledgment or commendation.

The passage as paraphrased in *The Message* is helpful: "When you help someone out, don't think about how it looks. Just do it quietly and unobtrusively. That is the way your God, who conceived you in love, working behind the scenes, helps you out" (vv. 3–4).

II. Jesus' Instructions About Prayer (Matthew 6:5–8)

Jesus whole-heartedly endorsed general acts of mercy and specific acts of compassion as desirable, good, and legitimate expressions of piety or spiritual discipline. The abuse of them by insincere people who had turned them into a spiritual stage show had provoked reprimand and instruction from Jesus. Jesus insisted on authenticity of actions and motives.

Of equal concern to Jesus, for the same reason, and an additional one, was prayer. For just as acts of compassion could, prayer could (and can) be distorted into something that is an exercise in human egotism and totally unacceptable to God. Comments from New Testament exegete Frank Stagg on the character and value of prayer assist in grasping the urgency of the authentic practice of prayer. He writes: "Prayer is communion with God in which we are brought into new relationships and new attitudes, thus opening the way for blessings which God already purposed to impart. The English word for prayer means to ask, and it reflects our unfortunate tendency to reduce prayer to asking. Prayer includes asking, but it is far more. It is more like opening oneself to God in trust and praise, that we may freely receive His gifts and yield to His demands" (*Matthew: Broadman Bible Commentary*, (Nashville: Broadman, 1969) All of this is jeopardized when prayer is offered in the incorrect ways Jesus discusses in the lesson text.

Jesus addresses two concerns in His instructions on prayer. The first is the problem of prayer degenerating into a performance by hypocrites. How and why do the false-face folks, the mask-wearers, pray? Jesus warned, "They love to pray standing in the synagogue and on the street corners to be seen by men" (v.5, NKJV).

In Jesus' lifetime, prayer in the synagogue was offered by a layman as he stood at the front before the worshipers. Often, prayers were offered in the streets at the time of afternoon sacrifices in the temple. There were also three daily times of prayer among the Jews. People would sometimes stop their activities and face Jerusalem to pray at each time. Moreover, the synagogue and the street corners were sites of social interaction among people, especially men. Should the hour of prayer arrive during such times of socializing, Pharisees would assume the attitude of prayer so people might see they were pious.

Jesus does not wholesale condemn these public prayers, or any public prayers. As with the wrongly motivated charitable giving, Jesus' condemnation here is for those who pray "to be seen by men." It is consistent with His intentions to add "to be heard by men and women." As with those who do acts of compassionate out of wrong motives, those who pray also receive what they set out to receive, the commendation of humans. Or as the NLT expresses verse 5, "I tell you the truth, that is all the reward they will ever get."

The ultimate audience for our prayers, according to Jesus, is God Himself. We pray to Him. We address Him. We speak to Him. And if others hear our prayers to Him, they are eavesdropping. "But when you pray, go into your room, close the door and pray to your Father, who is unseen. Then your Father, who sees what is done in secret, will reward you." Jesus then elaborates on and illustrates the meaning of privacy in prayer. He urges those who pray to enter their *tamieion*, translated variously in English versions of the New Testament as "your room," "your private room," "your secret closet." *Tamieion* originally indicated a storehouse, a separate apartment, one's private quarters, a closet, or what is in modern times a den. Jesus meant it as a place where one can retreat from and shut out the world and commune with God.

However, Jesus also addresses another concern in His instructions on prayer. Jesus admonishes His followers not pray like an *ethnikos*. The term is variously translated in the New Testament as "Gentile" (especially when it has an article, "the"), "pagans," "heathens," "idolaters." These keep babbling, saying empty, meaningless phrases as they plead with their gods.

They do so, according to Jesus, because they think the more they say, the longer their prayers, the louder their prayers, the more effective their prayers would be. The pagans believed that through their verbiage, calling the name of the deity frequently enough or the use of formulaic phrases, they could influence the deity to do what they requested (1 Kings 18:25–29; Acts 19:32–34).

Jesus both corrects and encourages His followers: "Do not be like them, for your Father knows what you need before you ask him"(v.8, NKJV). Jesus explicitly indicates loquacious prayers whose purpose seems to be to apprise God of the concerns of the one praying are worthless. God has full knowledge of everything. At the same time, Jesus indicates it is equally unnecessary to attempt to persuade God to comply with the wishes of those who pray. It is the Lord who makes the privilege of prayer possible in the first place. His thorough knowledge of those who pray includes graciousness on His part to answer prayers appropriately.

The Lesson Applied

As one seeks to grasp what Jesus says in the teachings in this passage, it is essential to hear what He does not say. Jesus does not intend to censure all public giving or prayer. Jesus assumed His followers would comply with the Scripture of their day, the Old Testament, and give financially. He expected them to follow the teachings of Deuteronomy 15:7–8, 10–11 which commanded generous sharing with the needy. Such opportunities and responsibilities always would be available, because there always would be needy people. In the time of Jesus, such giving was usually a part of corporate worship. Jesus' principles applied: Motive determined the value of the act of giving.

Let's Talk About It

1. **Some suggest practicing private prayer over public prayer and that not to do so is wrong. Do you agree or disagree with that point of view? Why or why not?**
2. **Discuss the role and importance of a "secret closet" in your prayer and meditation life.**

Jesus does not condemn the public practice of prayer. Nor does He commend private prayer to the exclusion of public prayer. It is possible that even in the "secret closet," one might attempt to impress God rather than sincerely communicate with Him. Any act of service or worship that is not presented on the basis of an authentic relationship with and understanding of God, and from pure motives, is unacceptable to the Lord.

Home Daily Devotional Readings
February 10–16, 2020

Monday	Tuesday	Wednesday	Thursday	Friday	Saturday	Sunday
God's Name Is "Our Father"	The Adopted Children of God	Enticed by Temptation	Forgive the Sins of Fellow Believers	Forgive the Offender	Forgive Like God in Christ Forgives	Praying and Living the Lord's Prayer
Isaiah 63:15–16; 64:8–9	Romans 8:12–17	James 1:12–15	Luke 17:1–4	2 Corinthians 2:5–11	Ephesians 4:25—5:2	Matthew 6:9–15

THE PRAYER OF JESUS

ADULT TOPIC: ASK FOR WHAT REALLY MATTERS	BACKGROUND SCRIPTURE: MATTHEW 6:9–15

MATTHEW 6:9–15

King James Version	*New Revised Standard Version*
AFTER this manner therefore pray ye: Our Father which art in heaven, Hallowed be thy name.	**"PRAY then in this way: Our Father in heaven, hallowed be your name.**
10 Thy kingdom come, Thy will be done in earth, as it is in heaven.	**10 Your kingdom come. Your will be done, on earth as it is in heaven.**
11 Give us this day our daily bread.	**11 Give us this day our daily bread.**
12 And forgive us our debts, as we forgive our debtors.	**12 And forgive us our debts, as we also have forgiven our debtors.**
13 And lead us not into temptation, but deliver us from evil: For thine is the kingdom, and the power, and the glory, for ever. Amen.	**13 And do not bring us to the time of trial, but rescue us from the evil one.**
14 For if ye forgive men their trespasses, your heavenly Father will also forgive you:	**14 For if you forgive others their trespasses, your heavenly Father will also forgive you;**
15 But if ye forgive not men their trespasses, neither will your Father forgive your trespasses.	**15 but if you do not forgive others, neither will your Father forgive your trespasses.**

LESSON SETTING

Time: circa A.D. 30
Place: Galilee

LESSON OUTLINE

I. God's Character and His Kingdom (Matthew 6:9–10)
II. God's Care For His People (Matthew 6:11–15)

UNIFYING PRINCIPLE

The unpredictable challenges and changes of life place demands on our faith, and we often are discouraged in the face of the negative circumstances over which we seem to have no control. In such instances, how do we manage our expectations and emotions to work for a more positive outcome? How can we experience the positive transformations we long for in life? Jesus taught the disciples to pray for God's Kingdom to be manifested in their lives and in all creation.

INTRODUCTION

This lesson passage belongs to the context of the Gospel according to Matthew that many New Testament exegetes designate as the second major division of the book. That section, of course, is the Sermon on the Mount, which includes Matthew 5:1–7:29. Following an introduction to the Sermon on the Mount, so

MAIN THOUGHT: Thy kingdom come, Thy will be done in earth, as it is in heaven. (Matthew 6:10, KJV)

designated since the time and terminology of Augustine, there are five major divisions leading up to the lesson text. The Beatitudes appear in 5:3–12. The portrayal of disciples in the metaphors of salt, light, and a city on a hill appears in 5:13–16. Jesus presents His relationship with and approach to the Law in 5:17–20. In Matthew 5:21–48, Jesus articulates the intention of the Law by the presentation of six antitheses: murder (5:21–26), lust and adultery (5:27–30), divorce (5:31–32), the meaning of oaths (5:33–37), overcoming evil with the power of good (5:38–42), and love for one's enemies (5:43–48).

In a more narrow context in Matthew's Gospel, the current lesson passage belongs to Jesus' discussion regarding motives in one's acts of piety. Discussions follow pertaining to the three major expressions of piety in Judaism (and among Jesus' disciples). Jesus discusses the matter of almsgiving or charitable giving in Matthew 6:1–4. The wrong and right methods of prayer appear in 6:5–15. The final topic, fasting, is discussed in 6:16–18.

In the scriptural context, having most immediately established the warning against inauthentic prayers as expressed in Matthew 6:6–8, Jesus then turns His attention to instruction of the correct approach to prayer. New Testament scholar F. W. Beare (*The Gospel According to Matthew*, Harper and Row, 1982) offers insights about the setting and the instructions in Matthew in relation to what appears in Luke. "This warning against the wrong kind of praying, introduced as a supplement to the warning against ostentation and the desire to win a reputation for piety, is now itself supplemented by a model prayer for the disciples of Christ to use. The Matthean setting is obviously artificial. A more plausible setting is suggested in Luke, where it is said that Jesus gave this prayer in response to a direct request made by the disciples: 'Lord, teach us to pray, as John taught his disciples' (Luke 11:1). It is evident that the Prayer was widely used in the early church, and in this devotional use there would be no mention, of the circumstances in which it was first spoken by Jesus. The Lukan setting is plausible enough—it was not uncommon for Jewish teachers to compose forms of prayer for their disciples—but it is [nonetheless] the framework devised by Luke."

It would appear Matthew positions the Model Prayer in his Gospel account because he is discussing the other acts of piety (charitable giving and fasting). The Model Prayer is consistent with the topical treatment of those pious acts Jesus is teaching His disciples. It also is natural follow-up to the teachings concerning prayer, as well as a natural strategy for instructing believers how to pray.

There is both a unique character and purpose (or purposes) to the prayer in the Gospel according to Matthew, as compared to the parallel in the Gospel according to Luke. "The marvellous [sic] prayer … has depths we shall never plumb. It comes in a rather different form in Luke's account (11:1). There is certainly a different thrust to it. Luke's account is focused on people who needed to know how to pray (11:1) because most of his readers were Gentiles. Matthew's account is primarily directed towards Jewish people who already practiced prayer, but need to know how to pray with the simplicity and directness which

Jesus longs to see in his disciples. And the Prayer shows them. It is not, of course, the 'Lord's Prayer.' Our Lord did not use it: He told them to use it. He never needed to pray, 'Forgive us our debts'. No, it is really the Disciples' Prayer and it is only as we enter into the life of discipleship that we can appreciate the meaning of this prayer."

Throughout the discussion here, the prayer will alternately be called the Model Prayer and the Disciples' Prayer.

Exposition

I. God's Character and His Kingdom (Matthew 6:9–10)

Some New Testament interpreters designate the opening words of the prayer, "Our Father in heaven," as an invocation that is then followed by the "Thou" petitions and the "we" petitions. Jesus entered a religious and theological milieu that was accustomed to addressing God as *Father*. However, there is a sense in which Jesus totally transformed the understanding and the usage of the term *Father* for God.

The concept of God as Father was fairly common in Old Testament theology and appears in several genres of Old Testament Literature. In the Pentateuch, Deuteronomy 32:6 is a representative example: "Is this the way you repay the LORD, O foolish and unwise people? Is he not your Father, your Creator, who made you and formed you?" In the poetic literature or writings, Psalm 89:26 contains references to God's Fatherhood. Verse 26 launches the topic there: "He will call out to me, 'You are my Father, my God, the Rock my Savior.'" Passages in the Prophets, such as Isaiah 1:2; 63:16 and Malachi 3:17 also refer to God as Father.

The Scriptures convey the Fatherhood of God in a universal sense because, as the Creator, God is the Father of all persons. Malachi 2:10 puts forward the question: "Have we not all one Father? Has not one God created us?" Paul expresses the universal Fatherhood of God in Ephesians 3:14–15 (NKJV): "For this reason I bow my knees to the Father of our Lord Jesus Christ, from whom the whole family in heaven and earth is named." And he affirms it in a sermon in Athens, "He has made from one blood every nation of men to dwell on all the face of the earth.…we are the offspring of God" (Acts 17:26, 29). More notably, God is Father to those who have a relationship with Him through Jesus Christ: "Yet, to all who received him, to those who believed in his name, he gave the right to become children of God) (John 1:12, NIV; also see 1 John 2:1, 2).

The four Gospel accounts all record Jesus referring to God as Father no less than sixty times. And He does so at least ten times in times Matthew 6:1–18. But He presents the privilege of "daring intimacy" with God as Father in the Model Prayer, for He has the disciples address God not as "Father," "the Father" or "Heavenly Father." Rather, the disciples are to use the Aramaic term of endearment and intimacy of a child, *Abba*, which nearly equates to the contemporary English "Daddy."

Yet, Jesus also instructs His disciples to include "in heaven," or "which art in heaven" (KJV). This expression, according to Frank Stagg, "preserves the balance between recognizing the nearness and transcendence of God. With the family-like intimacy, God may be addressed as Father, but he remains the transcendent God, always to be approached in awe and reverence.... To deism, God is distant and out of reach; to pantheism, God is everything and everything is God; to the sentimentalist, God may be 'the man upstairs.' To Jesus, God is none of those things. He is Father and He is God, ever near and ever to be held in reverence."

This fact is the basis of the first petition of the Model Prayer, that the name of God will be hallowed or kept holy. The Hebrew *kadosh* and the Greek *hagios* for "holy" mean the same thing and indicate that which is "different," "unique," "other," "separate," or "distinct." The name of God actually means God Himself in biblical thought. God and His name are holy and are to be related to as such by human beings. Leviticus 22:31–33 is an overview of the concept and its implications: "Keep my commands and follow them. I am the LORD. Do not profane my holy name. I must be acknowledged as holy by the Israelites. I am the LORD, who makes you holy and who brought you out of Egypt to be your God. I am the LORD." Isaiah 6:3 is representative of multiple passages in that prophet that frequently calls God "the Holy One." God Himself declares His uniqueness from humans in Hosea 11:9, "For I am God, and not man—the Holy One among you." Relating to God in His holiness is the foundation of the privilege of prayer.

Interpreting the petitions about God's Kingdom and His will as synonymous parallelism, stating the same truth in a similar manner, some New Testament exegetes consider them one truth. The expression about the coming of God's Kingdom issues from the perception of the Kingdom as God's rule within a person's life rather than a geographical area. It is first of all a commitment to be in the Kingdom for oneself. It is living under the rule of God and seeks to do so more and more. And there is an intercessory aspect to the petition in that it desires the reign of God will be extended to embrace more and more people as subjects in His Kingdom. Stagg notes there is both a present and a future dimension to the petition. "The prayer that God's kingdom come looks both to the ultimate triumph of God's rule at the *Parousia* and to immediate and increasing submission to his rule on earth."

The petition about God's will is necessarily and inextricably linked with the one about His Kingdom. It actually seeks to have what God wills (desires and/or plans) realized on the earth to the same extent it is in heaven. To a real extent, the Kingdom comes whenever and wherever people acknowledge and obey God's will on earth. The authenticity and sincerity of expressing that petition, of living it out continually, can occur only as one actively and intentionally lives within the Lord's will. And it is likewise the desire to see God's desires and plans fulfilled throughout the earth, with heaven and its total submission to His will as the standard. Undoubtedly, the third petition essentially has to do with the ongoing desire and quest within the Lord's disciples to become more and more like Him.

Those who correctly understand the holiness of God have a disposition of respect to that. More significantly, however, they will live in such a way that they evidence their perception of His holiness. It will be a life of sharing His holiness in one's day–to–day life. A desire for the extension of God's rule and the quest for His will inevitably follow comprehension of His holiness. What one prays in all three of the petitions regarding God are possible and empowered by a relationship with the One who is the loving, gracious, trustworthy Father.

II. God's Care For His People (Matthew 6:11–15)

One immediately notes about the four petitions having to do with human needs that they are inclusive. They are expressed in the first person plural, "us," "we," "our." There is the implicit instruction one cannot pray properly—or conduct a proper prayer life—apart from concern for others. One also notices a present–tense character to all these petitions. What persons are to pray here are concerns of everyday life. Michael Green suggests about these petitions, "With marvellous (sic.) succinctness Jesus teaches us how to pray for ourselves. We are to pray daily for forgiveness, and for deliverance from evil. All human life is there in those three petitions."

"Give us today our daily bread" is how the first petition is translated in most Bible versions. The original term for "daily" is *epiousios*, a rare word in biblical times. Outside the appearance in Matthew and Luke, which both might have taken from what is known as *Quelle* ("source," an early collection of sayings), the term only appears in one other early papyrus fragment. The term also actually can mean "for tomorrow," "sufficient," or "necessary." Malcolm O. Tolbert probably captures the actual and intended meaning when he says of the parallel in Luke 6:11, "We may interpret Luke's request as follows: 'Give us day by day the bread necessary for that day.' By contrast, most of us want bread laid up for the next ten or twenty years." Jesus acknowledges human beings' need for bread, everything required for physical sustenance. Simultaneously, He assures His disciples that the Father to whom they pray provides for those needs.

Green suggests concerning the petition for forgiveness, "And 'Forgive us…' How vital that is. The disciple never gets to the point where he [or she] does not need daily, hourly forgiveness." As one seeks God's forgiveness for one's indebtedness to God ("trespasses" against Him), one has a right to do so because one has extended forgiveness to those who are indebted to him or her. The term for "debts" (where Luke has "sins," from *hamartias,* 11:4), is *opheilēmata*. It originally was an accounting term for legal debts and here connotes having an "unpaid account" in a relationship due to moral and spiritual matters.

Earlier Jesus taught that the one who provides mercy also will receive it (Matt. 5:7). With forgiveness, the principle is the same. Stagg comments, "It is not God is unwilling to forgive the unforgiving but that the condition of the unforgiving is such that they are incapable of receiving forgiveness. When a door is closed, it is closed from both sides. What blocks the flow of mercy or forgiveness from us blocks its flow to us." (See vv. 14–15.)

The final words of the Disciples' Prayer in verse 13 are viewed by many as one petition, expressed in what is known in Semitic thought as antithetic parallelism.

That is the expression of a single, positive principle by means of two contrasting statements. "Do not lead us into temptation" can be understood as "Don't allow us to be led." There is absolutely no hint in the words of Jesus, nor in the teachings of all the Scriptures, that God ever places us in temptations that could possibly result in disloyalty to God. Jesus actually teaches that His disciples are dependant on God for power to overcome evil, or more likely the Evil One *(ho ponēros*, masculine or *ho ponēron*, neuter, "evil thing").

The Lesson Applied

The privilege and the responsibility of prayer are based in a posture of reverence for God, His holiness, and on a relationship with Him as gracious, loving Father. Given that, one who prays also seeks to live in such a way as to exemplify reverent obedience and plea that others will also.

What Jesus taught, He exemplified. Perhaps a singular prayer of His demonstrates all He taught in the lesson passage. "Then He said to them, 'My soul is exceedingly sorrowful, even to death. Stay here and watch.' He went a little farther, and fell on the ground, and prayed that if it were possible the hour might pass from Him. And He said, 'Abba, Father, all things are possible for You. Take this cup away from Me; nevertheless, not what I will, but what You will'" (Mark 14:36, NKJV).

In this prayer of Jesus, one sees all He conveyed in the Model or Disciples' Prayer. He embraces the uniqueness and Fatherhood of God. He is fully submissive to what the Father desires. He expresses total dependence on the Father and trusts Him explicitly for where the Father's will leads Him—even to the dreaded experience of death. Such is the essence of authentic prayer.

Let's Talk About It

1. **What are some implications of the uniqueness (holiness) of God for your journey of faith?**
2. **In what ways has your experience with prayer developed over the years?**
3. **Describe a few significant things that have contributed to your developing prayer life.**

Prayer is an indispensable component of the life of followers of Jesus Christ. As with all spiritual matters, especially privileges and responsibilities, prayer can be experienced negatively or positively, illegitimately or legitimately. The lesson text for today establishes the positive, legitimate experience of prayer with a paradigm, a pattern, for all prayers.

Home Daily Devotional Readings

February 17–23, 2020

Monday	Tuesday	Wednesday	Thursday	Friday	Saturday	Sunday
Daniel Prays Despite Legal Prohibition	God Forms the Holy Nation	Jesus Prays for Future Believers	The Holy Spirit Empowers Believers	Justice for Those Who Pray Fervently	Ask and It Is Yours!	Ask, Search, and Knock!
Daniel 6:6–13	Ezekiel 36:22–28	John 17:20–26	Acts 1:6–11	Luke 18:1–8	Matthew 7:7–11	Luke 11:5–13

PERSEVERANCE IN PRAYER

ADULT TOPIC:
MAKING THE REQUEST

BACKGROUND SCRIPTURE:
LUKE 11:1–13

LUKE 11:5–13

King James Version

NOW when Daniel knew that the writing was signed, he went into his house; and his windows being open in his chamber toward Jerusalem, he kneeled upon his knees three times a day, and prayed, and gave thanks before his God, as he did aforetime.

11 Then these men assembled, and found Daniel praying and making supplication before his God.

12 Then they came near, and spake before the king concerning the king's decree; Hast thou not signed a decree, that every man that shall ask a petition of any God or man within thirty days, save of thee, O king, shall be cast into the den of lions? The king answered and said, The thing is true, according to the law of the Medes and Persians, which altereth not.

13 Then answered they and said before the king, That Daniel, which is of the children of the captivity of Judah, regardeth not thee, O king, nor the decree that thou hast signed, but maketh his petition three times a day.

14 Then the king, when he heard these words, was sore displeased with himself, and set his heart on Daniel to deliver him: and he laboured till the going down of the sun to deliver him.

15 Then these men assembled unto the king, and said unto the king, Know, O king, that the law of the Medes and Persians is, That no decree nor statute which the king establisheth may be changed.

16 Then the king commanded, and they brought Daniel, and cast him into the den of

New Revised Standard Version

ALTHOUGH Daniel knew that the document had been signed, he continued to go to his house, which had windows in its upper room open toward Jerusalem, and to get down on his knees three times a day to pray to his God and praise him, just as he had done previously.

11 The conspirators came and found Daniel praying and seeking mercy before his God.

12 Then they approached the king and said concerning the interdict, "O king! Did you not sign an interdict, that anyone who prays to anyone, divine or human, within thirty days except to you, O king, shall be thrown into a den of lions?" The king answered, "The thing stands fast, according to the law of the Medes and Persians, which cannot be revoked."

13 Then they responded to the king, "Daniel, one of the exiles from Judah, pays no attention to you, O king, or to the interdict you have signed, but he is saying his prayers three times a day."

14 When the king heard the charge, he was very much distressed. He was determined to save Daniel, and until the sun went down he made every effort to rescue him.

15 Then the conspirators came to the king and said to him, "Know, O king, that it is a law of the Medes and Persians that no interdict or ordinance that the king establishes can be changed."

16 Then the king gave the command, and Daniel was brought and thrown into the den of

MAIN THOUGHT: My God hath sent his angel, and hath shut the lions' mouths, that they have not hurt me: forasmuch as before him innocency was found in me; and also before thee, O king, have I done no hurt. (Daniel 6:22, KJV)

DANIEL 6:10–22

King James Version	*New Revised Standard Version*
lions. Now the king spake and said unto Daniel, Thy God whom thou servest continually, he will deliver thee.	**lions. The king said to Daniel, "May your God, whom you faithfully serve, deliver you!"**
17 And a stone was brought, and laid upon the mouth of the den; and the king sealed it with his own signet, and with the signet of his lords; that the purpose might not be changed concerning Daniel.	**17 A stone was brought and laid on the mouth of the den, and the king sealed it with his own signet and with the signet of his lords, so that nothing might be changed concerning Daniel.**
18 Then the king went to his palace, and passed the night fasting: neither were instruments of musick brought before him: and his sleep went from him.	**18 Then the king went to his palace and spent the night fasting; no food was brought to him, and sleep fled from him.**
19 Then the king arose very early in the morning, and went in haste unto the den of lions.	**19 Then, at break of day, the king got up and hurried to the den of lions.**
20 And when he came to the den, he cried with a lamentable voice unto Daniel: and the king spake and said to Daniel, O Daniel, servant of the living God, is thy God, whom thou servest continually, able to deliver thee from the lions?	**20 When he came near the den where Daniel was, he cried out anxiously to Daniel, "O Daniel, servant of the living God, has your God whom you faithfully serve been able to deliver you from the lions?"**
21 Then said Daniel unto the king, O king, live for ever.	**21 Daniel then said to the king, "O king, live forever!**
22 My God hath sent his angel, and hath shut the lions' mouths, that they have not hurt me: forasmuch as before him innocency was found in me; and also before thee, O king, have I done no hurt.	**22 My God sent his angel and shut the lions' mouths so that they would not hurt me, because I was found blameless before him; and also before you, O king, I have done no wrong."**

LESSON SETTING

Time: A.D. 26–28
Place: Galilee

LESSON OUTLINE

I. A Parable About Persistence in Prayer (Luke 11:5–8)
II. Jesus' Application of the Parable (Luke 11:9–13)

UNIFYING PRINCIPLE

It is hard to press on with a task or routine when doing so does not seem to produce any positive changes. How can we persevere in the absence of tangible progress? Jesus taught the disciples to continue to ask, seek, and knock, confident that God would graciously provide..

INTRODUCTION

Luke 9:51–13:30 is the scriptural context of today's lesson. That larger context contains the first part of Luke's narrative of the transition of Jesus from Galilee to Jerusalem (9:51). The immediate context of today's lesson is Luke 11:1–13, which contains the teachings of Jesus on prayer. Portions of the teachings here have parallels in Matthew 6:9. This is particularly true of Jesus' presentation of the Model Prayer (Luke 11:2–4; Matt 6:9–13). Luke

11:5–13 is an elaboration on the Model Prayer as Luke presents it. Matthew sets the origin of this paradigm for authentic prayer in the topical context of several lessons on true piety (Matt 6:1–4, 5–13, 16–18). In the Gospel according to Luke, the Model Prayer resulted from a request of Jesus' disciples: "One day Jesus was praying in a certain place. When he finished, one of his disciples said to him, 'Lord, teach us to pray, just as John taught his disciples'" (Luke 11:1).

The theme of prayer in general is prominent in the Gospel according to Luke. Luke indicates prayer is prominent in Jesus' teaching ministry. In addition to today's lesson, prayer is the subject of some of Jesus' parables, such as the Parable of the Persistent Widow (18:1–8) and the Parable of the Pharisee and the Tax Collector (18:9–14).

Prayer is particularly prominent in the life of Jesus in the third Gospel. Luke alone relates that Jesus was praying during His baptism by John (3:21), the calling of the Twelve (6:12), the question about His identity among the populace (9:18), and during His Transfiguration on the mountaintop (9:28). Luke also highlights prayer in the ministry of Jesus, including a prayer of rejoicing over the success of the disciples' mission (10:21), an intercession for Peter (22:32), and prayers from the cross (23:34, 46).

The close relationship, contextually and theologically, between the pattern for prayer, or Model Prayer, in 11:1–4 and the Parable of the Insistent Friend is unmistakable. Whereas in the Model Prayer Jesus provided guidelines by which to lead a life of authentic prayer based on a relationship with God the Heavenly Father, the parable that follows serves as an encouragement to prayer. Furthermore, the parable promotes the concept that persistent prayer, even in the face of what appears to be the lack of a response, will be rewarded.

New Testament exegete Dr. Malcolm O. Tolbert provides an insightful overview of the meaning of Luke 11:5–13: "The parable of the insistent friend teaches the need for persistence in prayer. The problem is not that man has to overcome the reluctance of God to hear and answer prayers. To the contrary, the problem is located in the one who prays. If God does not respond immediately and on the person's particular and specific terms, then the individual is apt to lose faith, either in God's existence or in God's character as a loving Father. Persistence in prayer is an act of faith, a testimony to our belief in a loving, personal God" (*Luke-John: The Broadman Bible Commentary*. Nashville: Broadman Press, 1970).

Exposition

I. A Parable About Persistence in Prayer (Luke 11:5–8)

Jesus' most frequent methodology of instruction was parables, brief, story-like comparisons used to declare truth about the Kingdom of God in a picturesque manner. Jesus establishes contact with His audience (His disciples) in this passage, He lures them to listen by posing a rhetorical question: "Suppose one of you has a friend." This introduction appears in several of Jesus' parables in Luke (11:11; 12:25; 14:28; 15:4; 17:7; cf. 14:5). By the phrasing, Jesus asks a rhetorical question that He proceeds to answer. The balance of the introductory lines further draws in the listeners: "And he goes to him at midnight and says, 'Friend, lend me three loaves of bread, because a friend of mine on a journey has come to me, and I have nothing to set before him.'" The details to this point are true enough to life to rivet the attention of the listeners to Jesus.

Travel in the Middle East, particularly during times of intense heat, typically would be conducted during either the early morning hours or late in the evening, thus avoiding the hottest part of the day. It was such a common occurrence that persons were known to arrive at their destinations late at night. People usually baked bread daily and prepared enough bread only for the day's anticipated needs. Few would have bread available after the last people in the household had eaten the evening meal.

The plight of the unfortunate man who lacked sufficient bread was not uncommon. A premium was placed on hospitality in that culture, especially to those who were traveling. The man's request, then, is an urgent one: "A friend of mine has just arrived for a visit, and I have nothing for him to eat" (NLT). Or as *The Message* expresses the urgency: "An old friend traveling through just showed up, and I don't have a thing on hand."

The potential lender is apparently aggravated and displays such in that he does not return the greeting, "friend." Rather, he responds: "Don't bother me. The door is locked for the night, and we are all in bed. I can't help you this time." After a long day, the family has gone to bed for the night in the one-room sleeping accommodations. To get up and answer the door, much less to get the bread, would be quite an inconvenience. The man must get out of bed; carefully step over the children (and his spouse) to get to the door, then unbolt it. Such actions likely would have awakened the entire family. Given all this, it is easy to understand the potential lender-friend's insentience that he cannot help his neighbor is actually an unwillingness to do so. Jesus most likely intended, and His listeners clearly would have perceived, much humor in the details of the picture part of the parable.

Verse 8 indicates the persistence of the needy neighbor. Jesus expresses it: "I tell you, though he will not get up and give him the bread because he is his friend, yet because of the man's boldness he will get up and give him as much as he needs." That the men are friends is not sufficient motivation for the man to open the door and grant the needy man's requests. However, he does respond positively due to the boldness of the neighbor. The Greek word translated "boldness" here, *anaideian*, can also mean "shamelessness," "impudence," or "persistence," and occurs in the New Testament only in this passage. The man possesses indomitable persistence Tolbert observes, "Finally, of course, the poor man has to arise, unbolt the door, awakening all the children in the process, and gives the friend whatever he needs, not necessarily just what he has requested."

II. Jesus' Application of the Parable (Luke 11:9–13)

Having given the parable about prayer, Jesus then proceeds to articulate something of an application of the parable. He gives instructions about persistence in prayer.

The transition from a story to a succinctly stated set of imperatives makes the application all the more impressive. The words of Jesus in the Greek are present imperatives. They carry the meaning, "Keep asking; keep seeking; keep knocking." The imperatives also can be understood as imperatives of condition. So construed, the commands actually are, "if you keep asking," "if you keep seeking," "if you keep knocking."

Here again, Jesus employs synonymous parallelism, expressing the same thing in a similar fashion, to express His lesson in prayer. The suggested actions are not necessarily three different actions. They are actually motifs extracted from the parable of the needy friend at midnight. He engaged in asking, seeking, and knocking. The original term for "asking" is the most frequent term for *prayer* in the Scriptures. "Seeking God" is a common expression, particularly in the Old Testament (Deut. 4:29; Isa. 55:6; 65:1). "Seeking God's face" means to pray (2 Sam. 21:1; Pss. 24:6; 27:8; Hos. 5:15).

The balance of the imperatives is a word of assurance. Just as the command to persistence is in synonymous parallelism, so too is the assurance of answered prayer. That God will answer prayer is expressed as receiving, finding, and having a door opened.

In verses 11–12, Jesus provides another parabolic saying to reinforce the truths already proclaimed. He employs an approach popular among the rabbis of the day in which they reasoned from the "lesser to the greater" in declaring a truth. The rationale is that if one thing is true, how much more will another thing be true. Jesus reasons from the certain graciousness of an earthly father to the more certain graciousness of the Heavenly Father. In this context, if Luke 11:11–12 is true, then 11:13 is all the more true.

The argument in verses 11–12 is set in the context of rhetorical questions. "You fathers—if your children ask for a fish, do you give them a snake instead? Or if they ask for an egg, do you give them a scorpion?" The anticipated response to the rhetorical questions is a resounding no! Sinful, earthly fathers are knowledgeable and gracious enough to provide their children with the necessities of food, such as fish and eggs. That being true, it is much more true that God, the all-loving and thoroughly gracious Heavenly Father, will respond to one's asking, seeking, and knocking.

In Matthew's version of the same comparison, he indicates the Father will give His children "good gifts" (7:11). Luke employs the words "Holy Spirit" as the gift the Father will give. This is not contradictory to what appears in Matthew. Rather, it is in keeping with Luke's emphasis on the Holy Spirit in his writings. For Luke, the superlative gift of God is the Holy Spirit. As Tolbert expresses it, "Of all the good gifts that God can give his children, the Holy Spirit is considered in Luke to be the greatest of all. Through the Spirit man is able to live in fellowship with God and joyously anticipate the full consummation of his salvation."

The Lesson Applied

Robert H. Stein makes extremely insightful comments about the meaning of Luke 11:5–13 when he writes: "The believer is encouraged to pray because of the Father's gracious character. If inhospitable neighbors and unjust judges [Luke 18:1–8] will eventually grant the requests of those entreating them, how much more will a loving Heavenly Father. As a result the believers are to persist in prayer not in order to overcome God's reluctance but because they know God will hear and answer (11:9–13). When one wonders if it is really worthwhile to pray when it seems the prayer goes unanswered, when the believer walks through the valley of the shadow of death and heaven seems deaf, the believer nonetheless persists in prayer due to the character and the promises of the one they call 'Abba'—Father."

There also is a place for the importance of one's faith in experiencing God's responses to prayer. And that, too, is inherent with Jesus' teachings here. Norval Geldenhuys (*Commentary on the Gospel of Luke*, Eerdmans, 1971) speaks to this in his concluding comments on the parable in Luke 11:5–13. "No regenerate child of God should ever doubt that when he prays to God out of real need his prayer will be answered. He who doubts this does Him the greatest dishonour [sic], for by not believing that He will give what we really need we in fact appear to regard Him as less sympathetic and less faithful than an ordinary earthly father or even an ordinary earthly friend. Therefore unbelief in relation to the answering of prayer is not only a weakness, but a serious sin and utter folly."

Let's Talk About It

1. **Provide and discuss your own definition of prayer.**
2. **Share some of your more memorable experiences with prayer.**
3. **What assumptions does one who prays make? Why are these important?**
4. **In this lesson, God is portrayed as the ultimate Parent. What are some other images of God in the New Testament that especially speak to you?**

Jesus teaches that prayer is so much more than a list of requests or a one-time wish expression. Prayer is an ongoing experience. Believers are to be persistent in regard to a particular prayer. They also are to be persistent in the ongoing practice of prayer. Believers are to keep asking, keep seeking, keep knocking. Believers do not attempt to coerce or persuade God in their persistence. That is not necessary since He offers the privilege of prayer in the first place. To whatever extent an earthly father is graciously responsive, the Heavenly Father is exponentially more so. Persistence in prayer is for the benefit of the one who prays and is a reminder of the privilege and necessity of prayer.

Home Daily Devotional Readings
February 24–March 1, 2020

Monday	Tuesday	Wednesday	Thursday	Friday	Saturday	Sunday
The Coming Day of the Lord	Judgment Coming to the Nation	Seek the Lord, Establish Justice	Injustice Leads to Ruin	Lord of Creation and Judgment	God Loves All Peoples	Justice for the Poor and Distressed
Zephaniah 1:14–18	Amos 5:1–3, 16–17	Amos 5:4–5, 14-15	Amos 5:6–7, 10–13	Genesis 1:4–9; Amos 5:8–9	Hosea 2:14–23	Amos 5:18–24

THIRD QUARTER

March

April

May

CALLED TO ACCOUNTABILITY

ADULT TOPIC:
SEEKING JUSTICE

BACKGROUND SCRIPTURE:
AMOS 5

AMOS 5:18–24

King James Version

WOE unto you that desire the day of the LORD! to what end is it for you? the day of the LORD is darkness, and not light.
19 As if a man did flee from a lion, and a bear met him; or went into the house, and leaned his hand on the wall, and a serpent bit him.

20 Shall not the day of the LORD be darkness, and not light? even very dark, and no brightness in it?
21 I hate, I despise your feast days, and I will not smell in your solemn assemblies.
22 Though ye offer me burnt offerings and your meat offerings, I will not accept them: neither will I regard the peace offerings of your fat beasts.
23 Take thou away from me the noise of thy songs; for I will not hear the melody of thy viols.
24 But let judgment run down as waters, and righteousness as a mighty stream.

New Revised Standard Version

ALAS for you who desire the day of the LORD! Why do you want the day of the LORD? It is darkness, not light;
19 as if someone fled from a lion, and was met by a bear; or went into the house and rested a hand against the wall, and was bitten by a snake.
20 Is not the day of the LORD darkness, not light, and gloom with no brightness in it?

21 I hate, I despise your festivals, and I take no delight in your solemn assemblies.
22 Even though you offer me your burnt offerings and grain offerings, I will not accept them; and the offerings of well-being of your fatted animals I will not look upon.
23 Take away from me the noise of your songs; I will not listen to the melody of your harps.

24 But let justice roll down like waters, and righteousness like an ever-flowing stream.

LESSON SETTING

Time: Middle Eighth Century B.C.

Place: Israel

LESSON OUTLINE

I. Judgment not Grace (Amos 5:18–20)

II. Unacceptable Worship (Amos 5:21–23)

III. The Deeds God Seeks (Amos 5:24)

UNIFYING PRINCIPLE

Often people ignore or disregard the plight of the disenfranchised. How will the cause of these disadvantaged be addressed? The prophet Amos confirmed that justice and righteousness of God always champions the poor and oppressed.

INTRODUCTION

Amos is one of the twelve minor prophets mentioned in the Old Testament.

MAIN THOUGHT: But let judgment run down as waters, and righteousness as a mighty stream. (Amos 5:24, KJV)

The biblical record reveals Amos was a prophet who lived in Judah but was called by God to go and prophesy against Israel, Judah's northern neighbor.

In the oracle that comprises today's lesson, Amos confronted Israel about their wrong interpretation of what "the day of the Lord" means. Israel believed that because of its military might and economic prosperity it already was experiencing the Lord's favor. The day of the Lord was seen as another occasion for the Israelites to celebrate God's favor on them. Charles Kraft, in the *Interpreter's One-Volume Commentary on the Bible,* notes that "the year of the Lord was viewed as an annual celebration of the new year. It was a festive time that included ceremonies, such as celebrations of victories over enemies, renewal of the promise of prosperity as well as the re-enthronement of the king. The year of the Lord always carried with it the idea of blessing and bliss."

However, the nation's prosperity had led to greed by an elite class that took advantage of the poor. The foundation of a just society that God intended for His chosen people had collapsed, and Israel's leadership saw no need for change. Israel believed the nation's economic well-being was sufficient confirmation that nothing was wrong. Many Christians wrongly interpret financial prosperity as a sign of God's approval. Certainly, financial well-being can be a true blessing from the Lord, yet it is not the sole barometer of His approval. God's mercy is abundant, and His patience always abounds.

Amos the prophet denounced the ways society had been ordered. The rich live in extreme opulence at the expense of others living in poverty and need. Wealth is inequitably distributed. Workers barely were receiving starvation wages. The masses of people were perishing on what Dr. Martin Luther King called in his "I Have a Dream" speech: "a lonely island of poverty in the midst of a vast ocean of material prosperity."

It is amazing that a people who rose from the injustice of human bondage could, in just a few generations, become so corrupt themselves, oppressing one another for financial gain. Nevertheless, it is from within this context that Amos delivered what may be his most famous oracle in a call for Israel's return to justice.

Exposition

I. Judgment not Grace (Amos 5:18–20)

The government of a king brought to pass what Samuel had warned: The king would use his privileged position as a means to advance his personal needs and concerns above the things of God. Yahweh's kingship over the nation now was challenged by a new system that was aligned with a privileged class—a small but powerful group—at the expense of the poor and vulnerable.

The sanctuary at Bethel was being served by a priesthood that was hostile to Yahweh and His prophets. The temple priests also were accommodating toward the Canaanite culture that had a large influence on Israel. Despite these realities, Israel still expected the day of the Lord to be one of continued blessings for the nation and her king. There was no concern in the populace's view for how the poor were being treated by a system of government devoid of justice for the community.

Amos declared the day of the Lord would not be a day of blessing, but rather a day of judgment. Yahweh would confront the unjust system oppressing the poor by condemning those in power. Amos used two metaphors to describe the day of the Lord. The first metaphor was darkness. The day of the Lord would not be a day of light, but one of darkness. There would be nothing to rejoice about on that day because the day of the Lord would bring only disaster.

The second metaphor Amos used was that of a person fleeing danger. The image was held in stark contrast to that of a feast. There would be nothing to celebrate on the day of the Lord; there would be only danger. The day of the Lord would be so terrible that those who attempted to flee would not be able to escape no matter how hard they tried.

During the time of Amos, incidences of animal attacks were not uncommon. Amos noted that a person runs into danger during the normal routine of life by encountering a lion. However, when the person escapes the lion he meets a bear. The comparison to meeting a lion and bear give witness to a constant threat of danger on the day of the Lord. Though it appears the person has escaped the threat of danger in one place, danger finds him or her in the next place.

Furthermore, a person's home would not provide security from the coming judgment. There would be no escape. There is no grace to be found on the day of the Lord that Amos described. The absence of justice in the community and the continued oppression of the poor would not go unpunished for those who are to represent Yahweh's justice in the community. Amos declared what could be expected was darkness instead of light and judgment rather than grace.

This declaration from the prophet was a terrible surprise. Imagine planning for a great celebration only to have it turn into an unimaginably horrific event.

II. Unacceptable Worship (Amos 5:21–23)

Israel continued its ritualistic worship celebration while still oppressing the poor and denying justice to the most vulnerable. Under their then-current system in the text, the vulnerable constantly were in danger of losing their land, as in the case of Naboth's vineyard. Members of the elite class were able to use their position to gain large land holdings and turn the population into vassals and peasants. Yet all the while they were praising God. They believed God was satisfied with them and therefore had blessed them with economic prosperity. Amos clarified that God hated their religious actions toward Him. None of their forms of worship were acceptable: their ritual festivals, solemn assemblies, burnt offerings, grain offerings, well-being offerings, songs, and music all were rejected by God.

The expansive list of the worship forms that were rejected by God excluded no form of worship as a public ritual. Public worship would not be allowed to serve as a mask for the nation's deeper issues. Public worship would provide no cleansing for a nation bent on the oppression of the most vulnerable. The declaration of God's hatred for their worship served notice to the nation and its leaders for their need to repent. Israel was not free to use worship as a means of avoiding the responsibility of measuring justice in the community. Praise that disregards the God who cares about our relationships within our communities is praise that is unacceptable to God. God is under no obligation to accept the people's praise, including when they follow the practices established by Moses.

God's rejection of their worship exposed the vulnerability of the nation's leaders. Those who were believed to be powerful are shown as vulnerable. God said no to the thing that defines the nation more than anything else—its worship of Yahweh. What Amos revealed is the connection between worship of God and relationship to humanity. Our relationships—especially with those who are vulnerable—inform and influence our relationships to God. Praise that is acceptable to God never occurs in a vacuum. Worship is far more than ritual and ceremony. It is, in part, an indication of how God's will is made known via acts of justice and our willingness to participate as agents of justice. Worship that is acceptable to God reflects a right relationship with others as well as right relationship with God. At the center of that relationship is justice—where justice reflects the peace and good will of God for all of creation.

III. The Deeds God Seeks (Amos 5:24)

Amos called the leaders and the nation to return to justice. Author David Pleins, in *The Social Visions of the Hebrew Bible* (Westminster John Knox Press, 2000), said, "God's vision for creation is one that is centered on justice where justice is the absence of abuse and oppression as well as complete obedience to God." Throughout Israel's history, they had leaders who called them to be a community that was different from the communities around, as evidenced by their commitment to justice. The great human need that may be able to keep the coming judgment of God at bay is justice.

Amos did not seek a negotiated form of justice that makes concessions to those in power. Amos declared the justice that God seeks is ever-flowing—flowing like waters in mighty streams. The listeners immediately would understand what Amos had in mind because most of the nation was desert, and without water the people would perish. Just as the nation needed water to survive, the people needed justice to prevail. Every person needed access to justice to ensure his or her survival and the ability to thrive in the land.

Justice, in the case before Israel, would mean a change in actions by the king and the elite class. First, justice meant the restoration of all that was lost through fraud and deceit. Authentic justice begins with a restorative component intended to make others whole. Much of the wealth of the elite class was obtained by fraud. Therefore, people who were defrauded were to be given reparations as a sign of confession and repentance through deeds that yielded change in the community.

Second, justice would involve the establishment of a fair and equitable structure for all future activities, encompassing every facet of life. Third, justice would provide for dignity for all people, regardless of station in life. Finally, justice would acknowledge the need for compassion as a moral and community value central to faith in and fidelity to Yahweh.

Amos not only called for justice, but also declared the need for righteousness, which is the embodiment of what it means to belong to the Lord. Israel was chosen by Yahweh to be distinct from the nations around them. Israel was delivered from bondage to be a witness to the nations of how a people loyal to Yahweh live their faith. Israel had abandoned that responsibility, however. Their current structure of government simply mirrored the nations of idol worshipers. Their rejection of a righteous state had made the nation dark and corrupt. They were on a collision course with judgment—and God's judgment would prevail. Their only hope lay in a return to righteousness.

Just as the brooks were overrun with water during the rainy season and flowed to the valleys below, sustaining life in the process, likewise does God's righteousness flow, giving life to the nation. God seeks justice and is just and righteous. The good news is that Israel still has time if the people would heed the prophet's declaration. Despite His judgment, God's mercy is evident to the nation He chose as His own. He continued to give the people warning, through His prophet, offering yet another opportunity to repent and return to Him.

The Lesson Applied

The words of Amos need to be heard afresh in America. We have adopted the symbol of Lady Justice to symbolize our nation's commitment to equitable treatment, especially in the court system. Although the United States has countless worship centers and elected leaders who are quick to claim they are people of faith, the vulnerable continue to suffer. Injustice abounds. Public education across the land continues to be defunded. Infant mortality rates, especially among African Americans, is the highest among developed nations. Gun violence claims thousands of victims, from the very young to the very old. Law enforcement officials often show little regard for black lives, thus giving birth to such movements as Black Lives Matter.

The United States, established on the premise of equity and freedom, is fast becoming a nation structured solely for the benefit of the wealthy while holding the poor in disdain. The tax cut approved by Congress in 2018 created record corporate profits, yet worker's wages have been all but flat since 1973, when adjusted for inflation. Home ownership among people of color lags pitifully behind that of whites. Furthermore, the religious fervor from those who claim to be fighting for God has not changed the tribalism that makes up the nation's politics. Meanwhile, the vulnerable suffer because of an absence of justice and righteousness.

The need for affordable housing, criminal justice reform, a livable wage, and fair treatment regardless of class, race, gender, or religious affiliation speak to what Dr. Martin Luther King Jr. had in mind when he notoriously quoted Amos 5:24: "Let justice roll down like water and righteousness like an ever-flowing stream."

It is likely that many who expect to receive great rewards at the judgment may be surprised. In several Gospel passages, Jesus warned that those who are first in this world shall be last in our eternal world while those who are last now shall be first in the eternal world (see Matt. 19:30; 20:16; Mark 10:31; and Luke 13:30). Each time Jesus used the phrase, it referred to the fact that a person's position in this life does not give him or her an advantage in gaining eternal life or salvation. Jesus' message was consistent: It does not matter who we are in this world or what we have done. Eternal life is for those who believe in Him, who repent of their sins and commit themselves and their lives to Him and His glory.

Let's Talk About It

1. Why do Christians tend to equate God's favor and approval with economic prosperity?

Why do people think participation in religious ritual is enough to appease God? Many times, a person who claims to be a Christian accepts the philosophy of Gnosticism without realizing it. The Gnostics held a view that separated the body from the spirit. Thus, it did not matter what one did with the body, for the spirit was separate and apart. This view justified conduct that was in conflict with what God desires for His people. What we do on this temporal plane matters to God. We are to serve God with our bodies through justice and equity in our relationships. When we do so, we bear witness to the God in whom we believe.

2. What place does conversation about the judgment of God hold in the church today?

Though grace is a cornerstone of our faith, we must remember God will judge sin and sinners. In the lesson, Israel is given the opportunity to repent and change; without change judgment is sure to come. Judgment finally came to Israel with its collapse in the battle against the Assyrians. Judgment is the price paid for declining grace amid disregard for God's commands.

3. How are we to understand justice as Amos envisioned it?

Justice begins and ends with healthy relationships free of abuse and oppression. Any time people are seen as less valuable than others, the reality of them being treated unjustly is a powerful threat to their well-being. Israel's king and elite class perceived themselves to be above others and therefore entitled to take advantage of the vulnerable if it advanced their agendas. Justice seeks a level playing field on which everyone plays by the same rules, and those rules are supplied by God. In fact, the justice of God goes even further, because the strong must bear the infirmities of the weak (Rom. 15:1). Additionally, in Acts 2–4, the church picks up the slack for the marginalized in society. The ministry of the Hellenistic diaconate is a case in point. Justice Amos' style is only the starting point.

Home Daily Devotional Readings
March 2–8, 2020

Monday	Tuesday	Wednesday	Thursday	Friday	Saturday	Sunday
Job's Cry for Justice Frustrated	The Rock's Work Is Justice	God's People Ravaged for Sin	Chaldeans to Ravage the Nations	The Destructive Character of the Enemy	Assyrians Punished for Arrogance	Why, Lord, Does Injustice Prevail?
Job 19:1–7	Deuteronomy 32:1–4	Jeremiah 5:14–19	Habakkuk 1:5–11	Habakkuk 1:15–17	Isaiah 10:12–14	Habakkuk 1:1–4, 12–14

A PRAYER FOR JUSTICE

ADULT TOPIC:
ENDING INJUSTICE

BACKGROUND SCRIPTURE:
HABAKKUK 1

HABAKKUK 1:1–4, 12–14

King James Version

THE burden which Habakkuk the prophet did see.

2 O LORD, how long shall I cry, and thou wilt not hear! even cry out unto thee of violence, and thou wilt not save!

3 Why dost thou shew me iniquity, and cause me to behold grievance? for spoiling and violence are before me: and there are that raise up strife and contention.

4 Therefore the law is slacked, and judgment doth never go forth: for the wicked doth compass about the righteous; therefore wrong judgment proceedeth.

• • • • • •

12 Art thou not from everlasting, O LORD my God, mine Holy One? we shall not die. O LORD, thou hast ordained them for judgment; and, O mighty God, thou hast established them for correction.

13 Thou art of purer eyes than to behold evil, and canst not look on iniquity: wherefore lookest thou upon them that deal treacherously, and holdest thy tongue when the wicked devoureth the man that is more righteous than he?

14 And makest men as the fishes of the sea, as the creeping things, that have no ruler over them?

New Revised Standard Version

THE oracle that the prophet Habakkuk saw.

2 O LORD, how long shall I cry for help, and you will not listen? Or cry to you "Violence!" and you will not save?

3 Why do you make me see wrongdoing and look at trouble? Destruction and violence are before me; strife and contention arise.

4 So the law becomes slack and justice never prevails. The wicked surround the righteous—therefore judgment comes forth perverted.

• • • • • •

12 Are you not from of old, O LORD my God, my Holy One? You shall not die. O LORD, you have marked them for judgment; and you, O Rock, have established them for punishment.

13 Your eyes are too pure to behold evil, and you cannot look on wrongdoing; why do you look on the treacherous, and are silent when the wicked swallow those more righteous than they?

14 You have made people like the fish of the sea, like crawling things that have no ruler.

MAIN THOUGHT: Thou art of purer eyes than to behold evil, and canst not look on iniquity: wherefore lookest thou upon them that deal treacherously, and holdest thy tongue when the wicked devoureth the man that is more righteous than he? (Habakkuk 1:13, KJV)

LESSON SETTING

Time: Seventh Century B.C.
Place: Judah

LESSON OUTLINE

I. **Habakkuk's Complaint Before God (Habakkuk 1:1–4)**
II. **The Role of Enemies in the Plan of God (Habakkuk 1:12–13)**
III. **Is Mercy No Longer Available? (Habakkuk 1:14)**

Unifying Principle

People wonder about the seeming prevalence of injustice. How will justice and fairness be established for all? Habakkuk appealed to God to end wickedness and injustice.

Introduction

Habakkuk was a prophet from Judah who questioned God about the raging injustices in the society of his day. Though Yahweh intended for Judah to be known for a commitment to Yahweh and His ways of justice for all people, the society had fallen into a tailspin of injustice and wicked behavior. Habakkuk was different from other prophets in that he raised the question of injustice with God rather than God raising the issue of the people's injustices with the prophet. Habakkuk was discontent and impatient, and that impatience led to his complaint to God. Habakkuk's questions to God came in the form of complaint because the prophet expected more from God for His people. He expected God to act by restoring justice in the nation.

God's response to Habakkuk was not of comfort but of concern, for God declared things would get worse before they got better. God would act, but not in the ways Habakkuk expected and hoped. Although Habakkuk was free to question God, God had the sovereign authority to respond according to His choosing, including when it was not what the prophet anticipated. Habakkuk's queries/complaints about injustice eventually led him to a deeper understanding of God and God's authority to use sources the prophet had not considered in order to restore a desire for justice and a dependence on Yahweh alone.

Exposition

I. Habakkuk's Complaint Before God (Habakkuk 1:1–4)

Habakkuk's questions to God most often are viewed as complaints because they reveal the prophet's perplexity about why God appeared quiescent in the face of gross injustice. Habakkuk operated from the assumption that a just God was required to act in the face of unending and unbridled injustice. Habakkuk had no confidence the nation's leaders would be able to restore justice. The only answer seemed to be divine intervention.

To Habakkuk, all that was needed to restore order was for God to act. Thus, Habakkuk's questions and complaints were his appeal for God to take action. The questions were Habakkuk's way of reminding God what was expected of Him. This form of complaint also is known as *lament*. Such expressions of grief are present in many of the psalms as the psalmist complained to God about conditions, circumstances, or situations in which the mercy of God was needed to bring change. Lament never looks to answers beyond those God is able to provide because the person offering the lament has come to terms with the limitations of human frailty. Only God can change the outcome, and with confidence in the steadfast mercy of God there is hope change *will* come.

As a member of a faith community, Habakkuk wanted to see his faith rewarded by God responding as he thought suitable—a return to justice in the land. Habakkuk's questions revealed his willingness to wait on God for a response. Though the wait appeared unbearable, Habakkuk was willing to endure it because he believed the waiting would be rewarded with a divine response. An important aspect of faith in God is persistence, and Habakkuk would not allow the lapse of time to deter him from seeking an answer from God. Habakkuk was certain God would respond. The description of the desperate position in which Habakkuk found himself included widespread violence, misery, misuse of the Torah, and tribalism that had made community harmony impossible.

For Habakkuk, the condition of his people was reason enough for God to act swiftly. The prophet argued that these conditions were a means of motivating God to act quickly. Widespread evil and injustice are conditions that trouble most people, especially people of faith, and they want to see it annihilated. When people lose confidence in the systems established to govern them, chaos replaces order and puts community well-being in jeopardy.

Noted historian and scholar, the late Dr. Vincent G. Harding considered the torment of Nat Turner as he observed the conditions of his enslaved people: "Nat claimed that his most profound lessons came in his own lonely, personal struggles with the spirit, whom he identified as 'the Spirit that spoke to the prophets'" (*There Is a River: The Black Struggle for Freedom in America.* Harcourt Brace Jovanovich, 1981). After years of watching and wrestling with the harsh treatment of his people at the hands of the powerful who professed to believe in the God of justice, Turner was moved to orchestrate the only sustained slave rebellion in U.S. history.

II. The Role of Enemies (Habakkuk 1:12–13)

When God answered Habakkuk's questions and complaints about injustice, God informed him He would use a foreign nation, Babylon, as a means of discipling Judah. The people of Judah would be carried away into captivity, and the nation's independence would be lost. Judah would become a vassal state, paying tribute to a nation that did not recognize Yahweh.

Habakkuk's perplexity about the injustice was exchanged for his confusion about God using Babylon—a pagan nation—to discipline Israel, God's chosen people. A new set of questions emerged from Habakkuk. The first question was about God's plan for the nation. Had Judah's ungodly conduct caused the people to forfeit the promises God made to them long ago? Could God still be expected to honor His commitment to David?

Surely the One who is holy and eternal would remain faithful to His promise. The planned discipline at the hands of an enemy army would not wipe out the entire nation. Long before the emergence of remnant theology, Habakkuk expressed his belief there would be a remnant from among the people who would remain in the land.

In the midst of discipline, Habakkuk's questions revealed his unending conviction in the goodness of God and the reality of *chesed* (חֶסֶד). God's lovingkindness gives evidence of His faithfulness to the nation.

Habakkuk's second question raised the concern of comparative righteousness: Would God punish Judah, yet not punish Babylon for its wickedness? Though they were corrupt apostates, Judah still acknowledged Yahweh as the one true God. Conversely, Babylon was a nation of idol worshipers who practiced evil. Surely one who acknowledged Yahweh could not be punished without the unbelieving nation being punished, as well!

Bible scholar and author Elizabeth Achtemeier offered a helpful analysis of this passage when she said international relations always are under God's sovereignty. "World history does not take place by chance, according to Scripture, nor are human beings ever the sole effectors of it. Human actions result in particular events to be sure, but human actions always also accompanied by God's effective actions as he works out his purpose" (*Nahum—Malachi: Interpretation: A Bible Commentary for Teaching and Preaching*. Westminster John Knox Press, 2002, p. 39). God gave Habakkuk no response about His plans for Babylon except that they would be used to punish Judah. The nation's enemy was an instrument in the hand of God to work out His purposes to prove His holiness and His faithfulness.

The Creator God has given us free will to ask questions about His decisions and actions. However, that does not mean He owes us a response. God may remain silent toward our questions so we may continue to relate to Him in faith and trust in His sovereignty.

III. Is Mercy No Longer Available? (Habakkuk 1:14)

The question of mercy points to the concern of the helpless position of Judah against the evil of a strong and powerful nation such as Babylon. What happens when God's people are fish in a barrel? Is the nation without help from Him? Are the people of God not more important to Him than the fish in the sea? Habakkuk was attempting to come to terms with the approaching reality in light of what he believed about God's mercy. At the heart of Jewish theology is the belief that God is merciful and long-suffering. The Psalms declare His mercy endures forever. Where was the witness to God's mercy in light of impending evil?

Habakkuk's questions continued to appeal to God through the lens of faith and his convictions about Yahweh. God's plan to use Babylon to discipline Israel did not make Habakkuk shrink from God and protest in anger. Habakkuk remained engaged with his Creator, seeking to understand God and test his beliefs about God. The problem of relentless evil was not enough to keep Habakkuk away from God. Similar to Job before him, Habakkuk continued to trust God. The prophet refused to believe Judah was not without a leader. Though the nation may not have followed their leader or obeyed him, Yahweh is still the ultimate Leader of the land and the people. Habakkuk came to the position of trusting God though he did not have the answers to all his questions. His continued engaging

God, hoping it would be enough to sustain him in these difficult times. Habakkuk discovered that God keeps His promises because He is with him always.

Mercy may come in many forms, and the mercy we receive is determined by the God who offers it to us. Mercy may not always mean deliverance, however. Sometimes mercy is God's presence with us as we walk through the darkest valleys.

The Lesson Applied

In 1785, poet Robert Burns wrote a poem titled *For Man Was Made to Mourn: A Dirge*. Within that poem is the phrase, "man's inhumanity to man." In the poem, this expression presents the idea that humans were created in order to be sad. It addresses oppression and cruelty that human beings cause and, consequently, humanity suffers.

Since the Fall of humanity, injustice and suffering have been a part of the human experience. Yet in the face of injustice, we are called to put our trust in God. This is not an excuse to avoid taking a stand, for God uses human hands to act on His behalf. Few would argue that the work of Dr. Martin Luther King Jr. and the Southern Christian Leadership Conference was not divinely inspired and sanctioned. Still taking a stand against injustice always has its risks, for power does not concede voluntarily.

We serve a God who is so great that no human being can understand Him fully. No matter how earnestly we seek to know Him, the fullness of His identity and nature will elude us. Isaiah 55:8-9 confirms God is not like us. There Yahweh explains to the prophet Isaiah: "For my thoughts are not your thoughts, nor are your ways my ways, says the Lord. For as the heavens are higher than the earth, so are my ways higher than your ways and my thoughts than your thoughts" (NRSV). There always will be times and situations that confound human understanding. That's when we must place total and complete trust in the One who created us. We sometimes are forced through lack of options to trust in His sovereignty and retreat to the song of our childhood, "He's Got the Whole World in His Hands."

We must not forget that though world events sometimes catch us off guard, perhaps that's exactly the way God intended to move human history into His ultimate plan. God has a way of orchestrating life events in order to bring His plans to fruition. Sometimes it means God uses what appear to be unconventional methods to accomplish His goals.

Sometimes enemies may be used as tools of God's justice. The fall of Judah and the exile that came at the hands of the Babylonians took place in order to usher in a time of rededication to covenant loyalty and the ways of Yahweh. The injustice of the Babylonians' treatment of Israel was an eye-opening experience for a community that had abandoned its First Love. Further reading of the Old Testament reveals that from the ruins of exile would emerge some of the most powerful witnesses to faith recorded in the Bible.

Let's Talk About It

1. **What may be some reasons why God allows injustice to persist?**

   Fair-minded people want the rules of life to be applied even-handedly. There should not be one set of rules for the privileged and another set of rules for the poor. However, what we often see is a justice system that is anything but blind and impartial. African Americans often fall victim to crimes and are made to suffer for their perceived actions without the benefit of due process under the law. Countless incidents of injustice at the hands of authority figures have been recorded on video, yet the courts still fail to deliver justice—from Rodney King to Tamir Rice.

The biblical concept of justice calls the American and any other system of "so-called" justice into question and demands that justice God's style be implemented immediately, that the standard for human justice erupt from the commandments and standards established by God. Amos' rules of fair play must no longer be ignored and dismissed because one possesses wealth, affluence, and education.

2. How difficult is it to stay engaged with God when God does not give you the answer you expect?

There always is a temptation to give up on faith when God does not respond the way we hope. To Habakkuk's credit, he would not turn his back on God or abandon his convictions about the nature of God. In our humanness, we sometimes are tempted to question God's identity and nature. Why does God allow children and the elderly to be abused? Why does God not step in when laws are implemented to keep the poor in poverty while making the rich more wealthy? Why are people so mean to one another, and their wickedness only seems to be rewarded? Rather than question the nature and character of God, we are to find new strength for every challenge of life as we stay engaged with God. His strength is made perfect in our weakness. In the words of one contemporary gospel song: "Don't give up on God, 'cause He won't give up on you. He's able!"

3. Why are arguments about comparative righteousness often made during hard times?

It's tempting to question God about our difficult times when those who live unrighteously seem to be having easy times. Such comparative righteousness fails to acknowledge we all have come short of the glory of God (see Rom. 3:23). How our lives compare to others is not the standard by which we should consider our circumstances. The sinless model of Jesus is the standard by which we are called to live, yet our righteousness is but filthy rags (see Isa. 64:6). We are to practice complete obedience to God; and in doing so, we allow Him to gain the glory from our lives.

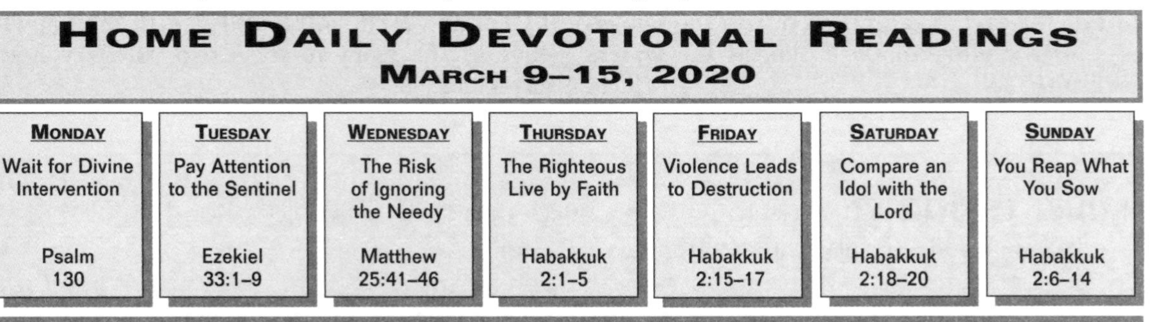

Home Daily Devotional Readings

March 9–15, 2020

Monday	Tuesday	Wednesday	Thursday	Friday	Saturday	Sunday
Wait for Divine Intervention	Pay Attention to the Sentinel	The Risk of Ignoring the Needy	The Righteous Live by Faith	Violence Leads to Destruction	Compare an Idol with the Lord	You Reap What You Sow
Psalm 130	Ezekiel 33:1–9	Matthew 25:41–46	Habakkuk 2:1–5	Habakkuk 2:15–17	Habakkuk 2:18–20	Habakkuk 2:6–14

CONSEQUENCES FOR INJUSTICE

ADULT TOPIC:
GETTING WHAT THEY DESERVE

BACKGROUND SCRIPTURE:
HABAKKUK 2

HABAKKUK 2:6–14

King James Version

SHALL not all these take up a parable against him, and a taunting proverb against him, and say, Woe to him that increaseth that which is not his! how long? and to him that ladeth himself with thick clay!

7 Shall they not rise up suddenly that shall bite thee, and awake that shall vex thee, and thou shalt be for booties unto them?

8 Because thou hast spoiled many nations, all the remnant of the people shall spoil thee; because of men's blood, and for the violence of the land, of the city, and of all that dwell therein.

9 Woe to him that coveteth an evil covetousness to his house, that he may set his nest on high, that he may be delivered from the power of evil!

10 Thou hast consulted shame to thy house by cutting off many people, and hast sinned against thy soul.

11 For the stone shall cry out of the wall, and the beam out of the timber shall answer it.

12 Woe to him that buildeth a town with blood, and stablisheth a city by iniquity!

13 Behold, is it not of the LORD of hosts that the people shall labour in the very fire, and the people shall weary themselves for very vanity?

14 For the earth shall be filled with the knowledge of the glory of the LORD, as the waters cover the sea.

New Revised Standard Version

"WILL not all of them taunt him with ridicule and scorn, saying, "'Woe to him who piles up stolen goods and makes himself wealthy by extortion! How long must this go on?'

7 Will not your creditors suddenly arise? Will they not wake up and make you tremble? Then you will become their prey.

8 Because you have plundered many nations, the peoples who are left will plunder you. For you have shed human blood; you have destroyed lands and cities and everyone in them.

9 "Woe to him who builds his house by unjust gain, setting his nest on high to escape the clutches of ruin!

10 You have plotted the ruin of many peoples, shaming your own house and forfeiting your life.

11 The stones of the wall will cry out, and the beams of the woodwork will echo it.

12 "Woe to him who builds a city with bloodshed and establishes a town by injustice!

13 Has not the LORD Almighty determined that the people's labor is only fuel for the fire, that the nations exhaust themselves for nothing?

14 For the earth will be filled with the knowledge of the glory of the LORD as the waters cover the sea.

MAIN THOUGHT: Woe to him that buildeth a town with blood, and stablisheth a city by iniquity! (Habakkuk 2:12, KJV)

LESSON SETTING

Time: Seventh Century B.C.
Place: Judah

LESSON OUTLINE

I. Profiting by Taking Advantage of Others (Habakkuk 2:6–8)
II. Promised Punished for Wrongdoing (Habakkuk 2:9–11)
III. Power that Brings Real Change (Habakkuk 2:12–14)

UNIFYING PRINCIPLE

People seem not to suffer for unjust actions. When will acts of the unjust be punished? The psalmist affirmed God would reward the just, and Habakkuk declared the unjust would be punished for their wickedness.

INTRODUCTION

Habakkuk, Obadiah, and Malachi were the only three of the Minor Prophets about which nothing is known except their names. Habakkuk plainly identified himself as a prophet in the first verse of his book of prophecy. Some scholars associate Habakkuk's name with that of an Assyrian plant; however, church father Hieronymus (who translated the Bible into Latin) translated the prophet's name as "embraced" or "embracer." Martin Luther, a seminal figure of the Protestant Reformation, observed: "Habakkuk bears the right name to his commission. For Habakkuk means, 'to hug.' He does so with his prophecy by hugging or embracing his people. He comforts them and takes them into his arms as one does with a crying child or adult.

A contemporary of Jeremiah, Habakkuk bears similarities with Jeremiah, including his sensitive nature and his grief regarding the condition of God's people.

In chapter 2, Habakkuk responds to the news that God would use the Babylonians (also referred to as the Chaldeans) to punish Israel with a taunting song reflecting that a just God who punishes Israel for wrongdoing would punish the Babylonians as well. Although Babylon would be an instrument of punishment in the hands of God, that people group would not escape their own wrongdoing. The song was referred to as the "oracles of woe."

Such oracles were used by multiple prophets to reflect how the current injustice in the community had gained God's attention and that God was about to act with punishment and judgment. The woe oracles from this prophet—a series of five woes are outlined in Habakkuk 2:6–20—served as a source of warning for what was to come because the action had been ordained by God. For those suffering under oppression, the woe oracles were good news that God had not forgotten them. Divine justice, although delayed, would not be denied. God cannot allow sin to go unpunished; therefore, He demands justice.

Habakkuk revealed his belief through these woe oracles that God is not a neutral Observer in the affairs of humanity. God, in fact, has taken a stance and has chosen to side with the weak rather than the powerful who would deny justice and oppress the poor. Biblical scholar and theologian Dr. James Cone, in his classic work, *God of the Oppressed* (Orbis Books, 1997), said: "to know God is to experience the acts of God in the concrete affairs and relationships of people, liberating the weak and the helpless from pain and humiliation."

Exposition

I. Profiting by Taking Advantage of Others (Habakkuk 2:6–8)

The economic system on which the wealth of the privileged class was built resulted from taking advantage of various economically disadvantaged groups. The most common method employed involved an abuse of the pledge system. This system allowed a borrower to pledge as collateral an item of daily use or importance, such as a cloak, tool, or animal used for farming or food. Israel had strict rules governing the pledge system to guard against abuse by creditors and to ensure that borrowers did not needlessly suffer harm. One example of such restrictions was that the creditor had to give back the borrower's cloak at sundown so he would not be exposed to the cold. The restrictions on the pledge system were put in place to keep creditors from becoming rich at the expense of borrowers. The restrictions also were put in place to prevent the establishment of a permanent underclass. Babylon had abolished all the rules governing the pledge system, however, and borrowers were losing everything because of their inability to repay creditors. Excessive interest rates and extended time or lack of time to repay the loans effectively eradicated what few protections and resources the poor had.

The five woes are specific infractions against the Commandments, for which God promised to punish them. This consoled Habakkuk to know the Babylonians would not get away with ravaging Judah. The prophet was reassured of his faith and confidence in the God he knew, believed in, and understood. The Babylonians would get what they deserved.

Verses 6–8 detail the first woe. The Babylonians had obtained dishonest gain by oppression, which is a violation of the eighth commandment. In short, the Babylonians were stealing. To make a bad situation worse, they were oppressing people and plundering their goods as they advanced through the conquered nations. In verse 5, the prophet introduced the woes by depicting an ugly image of their greed. Their desire to consume more and more was unquenchable. Their lust for more was unquenchable and was at the expense of the most vulnerable among them.

The prophet declared the day would come when Babylon's economy would be exposed to the same abusive practices they had imposed on others. On that day there would be no mercy for Babylon, just as they had been merciless toward Israel. Habakkuk revealed God held individuals and nations accountable for abusive economic practices that take advantage of others. Unfair lending practices were at the heart of the housing collapse that created the great recession of 2008. Many people lost not only their homes, but also their economic footing. Whereas the banks received government bailouts, countless Americans were left victimized by an economic system that took advantage of them. These systems of injustice will have to give account to a just God.

Habakkuk's prophecy of doom against Babylon was fulfilled not long after Babylon invaded Judah, when the Medo-Persian Empire overtook Babylon with little violence. Babylon was defeated easily simply because of its arrogance. Those whom the Babylonians had abused would rise up and gain revenge. Meanwhile, those who had been asleep (unaware), at some point would become fed up and take a stand.

Babylon's wealth had been built by taking everything of value from the people it conquered, but they would lose all of their ill-gotten gains and more as those called to rise up would take revenge upon them.

II. Promised Punishment for Wrongdoing (Habakkuk 2:9–11)

Habakkuk, in the second woe oracle, continued the theme of wealth and power obtained by unjust means through covetousness. The Babylonians had a false sense of security in wealth gained unjustly. Through their actions, they had broken the tenth commandment: "You shall not covet your neighbor's house. You shall not covet your neighbor's wife, or his male or female servant, his ox or donkey, or anything that belongs to your neighbor" (Ex. 20:17, KJV).

Babylon's wealth is described as big houses built upon nests. The symbol of a nest reveals the arrogance and perceived invincibility of the Babylonians as compared to other nations. The Babylonians were confident of their power and position. It never occurred to them their security could be breached by an enemy force. This was a promise of punishment; there was no escape or fleeing from the pursuit of a just God. He was able to reach the Babylonians no matter where they fled.

Their unbelief in the God who created all things was evident as their actions indicated they placed their security in their wealth. However, God was not impressed with their efforts to secure their corrupt fortunes by placing them out of the reach of others. Fortunes obtained through violence and injustice ensured the same violence would be returned upon the Babylonians. Instead of establishing their houses and the future of their names with their fortunes as they intended, the Babylonians had done the opposite. Fortunes that had been obtained through violence never should be celebrated; rather, they are seen as a reason for shame.

In the absence of repentance, the shame of their abusive activities meant the Babylonians had forfeited their lives. The houses the Babylonians had built as signs of their prestige and power would become places of protest, as the stones and wood used to build the houses cried out against them. The phrase "cutting off" (see v. 10) referred to selling fabric that purposely had been cut short in order to cheat the customer. This was but one example among the many that demonstrate their sinful behavior. Their homes, built with the proceeds of ill-gotten gain, were testimonies to their wickedness. When others saw their houses, they would not be impressed by the grandeur and finery; rather, they would be observing structures that were built on shame. The rocks from which their houses were built would cry out in testimony against them. The huge, expensive timber that spanned the ceilings of great rooms would call out an opulence derived from stolen property.

The crying out of natural resources in protest to being abused is akin to the ground crying out with the blood of

Abel. There was no escape. There was no place to flee where they would be free of witnesses to their crimes against humanity and God. Big houses built on foundations of dishonest gain cannot stand.

III. Power that Brings Real Change (Habakkuk 2:12–14)

In their greedy quest for material wealth and power, the Babylonians killed indiscriminately, wiping out entire villages and tribes. The crime of bloodshed can be paid for only with blood. Their murderous ways were a violation of God's sixth commandment, "You shall not murder" (Ex. 20:13, NRSV). Furthermore, their cities were built on perversity, crimes that deserved a death penalty.

As horrible as the Babylonians' actions were, they were merely a repeat of prior corrupt regimes. Babylon conquered Judah because of Judah's own corrupt practices. Regime change had made no difference in how the oppressed and the poor were treated. The great cities of the day all were built on the backs of oppressed people. Habakkuk visualized a future that would be different, not because of a new and just regime, but rather because of the actions of a just God. Yahweh would act to demonstrate the transitory nature of the nations' wealth by making it useless. God turned their wealth into ashes.

All of creation would return to the earth from which it came, including the wealth that some nations thought would last forever. No amount of human effort would change this reality. Regimes may work as hard as they can to build their strength by expanding their power and becoming more abusive, but the wealth will not last. Habakkuk affirmed the only thing that would last is the glory of the Lord. God's glory should be the true focus of the nations and individuals, never ill-gotten gain.

The glory of the Lord, for the prophet, was in the community's awareness of God in ways that lead to their just dealings with one another. God's glory yielded right relationships in creation, void of the influence of sin and selfishness. The power to bring about real change belongs to God alone.

Verse 14 speaks to the issue that inspired Habakkuk's queries: Does God punish the wicked, or does He allow them to prosper in their sin? God revealed His purpose is larger than merely taking sides among warring nations. God's purpose is that those who place their faith in Him ultimately will be preserved. Those who do not ultimately will be judged to condemnation. Habakkuk prophesied of a time when all people would know of God and His purpose. At this time, the power of God's Word was known by relatively few; however, His Word would be as evident to all people as the waters above are to the seabed. The glory of God would be revealed one day—a time when every knee will bow and every tongue confess that Jesus is Lord and salvation comes through faith in His name.

Habakkuk never lost confidence in God's ability to bring justice, even in the midst Babylonian oppression. Habakkuk's confidence in God's sovereign authority to bring change for the oppressed is akin to a traditional saying in the Black Church: "I'm so glad that trouble don't last always!"

The Lesson Applied

Governments and individuals often participate in corrupt economic policies that take advantage of certain classes of people. Tax cuts for the wealthy and government bailouts for corporations many times place ordinary wage earners at disadvantages. High interest rates are levied on people based on factors that require them to pay outrageous sums to obtain basic life essentials. Food deserts force those living in underserved communities to travel far from their communities to secure healthy food options. Student loan debt accrues long after graduation, at times limiting employment options. Middle-class wages have been nearly flat since 1973, while corporations enjoy record profits. These are the conditions Habakkuk spoke against. Justice surely will come because these are the actions that gain God's attention. God will not be silent forever. He will take action that brings justice.

Let's Talk About It

1. **How does Habakkuk demonstrate the ways people can cope with injustice in the world?**

   Habakkuk provided two ways to cope with injustice in the world. First, Habakkuk held to a vision of the reliability and sovereignty of God's rule. Second, Habakkuk believed in the ultimate power of justice. Habakkuk was convinced injustice could not stand forever before a God of justice.

2. **What does this lesson say to us about nations or individuals who abuse others for economic gain?**

   The primary problem Habakkuk cried out against was an unjust economic system. The text reveals that while there may be short-term gains for those who take advantage of or oppress others, they only secure their demise by their actions. The witness of history is seen in how nations and people have stood up to change their condition and usher in a day of justice.

3. **Do words of warning effectively motivate people to change?**

   The woe oracles of Habakkuk speak to a future judgment. These warnings came as a means of leading the people to repentance, if they were willing to change. We can create a different future when we are willing to heed warnings in life and govern ourselves accordingly. One of the greatest warnings of our time is global warming. Scientific evidence points to the impact of greenhouse gases causing climate change. If we continue to ignore the warnings and abuse the earth for financial gain, we only secure our own demise.

Home Daily Devotional Readings
March 16–22, 2020

Monday	Tuesday	Wednesday	Thursday	Friday	Saturday	Sunday
The Lord Acts Justly	The Results of Social Injustice	Justice Actions by the Expected Messiah	Prophets Fail on Their Watch	Remember God's Righteous Actions	Cheating and Violence Will Be Punished	God Requires Justice for All
Psalm 146	Isaiah 5:18–24	Isaiah 11:1–5	Micah 3:5–8	Micah 6:1–5	Micah 6:9–16	Micah 3:1–3, 9–12; 6:6–8

CORRUPT LEADERS

ADULT TOPIC:
DOING JUSTICE

BACKGROUND SCRIPTURE:
MICAH 3–6

MICAH 3:1–3, 9–12; 6:6–8

King James Version

AND I said, Hear, I pray you, O heads of Jacob, and ye princes of the house of Israel; Is it not for you to know judgment?

2 Who hate the good, and love the evil; who pluck off their skin from off them, and their flesh from off their bones;

3 Who also eat the flesh of my people, and flay their skin from off them; and they break their bones, and chop them in pieces, as for the pot, and as flesh within the caldron.

• • • • • •

9 Hear this, I pray you, ye heads of the house of Jacob, and princes of the house of Israel, that abhor judgment, and pervert all equity.

10 They build up Zion with blood, and Jerusalem with iniquity.

11 The heads thereof judge for reward, and the priests thereof teach for hire, and the prophets thereof divine for money: yet will they lean upon the LORD, and say, Is not the LORD among us? none evil can come upon us.

12 Therefore shall Zion for your sake be plowed as a field, and Jerusalem shall become heaps, and the mountain of the house as the high places of the forest.

• • • 6:6–8 • • •

6 Wherewith shall I come before the LORD, and bow myself before the high God? shall I come before him with burnt offerings, with calves of a year old?

New Revised Standard Version

THEN I said, "Listen, you leaders of Jacob, you rulers of Israel. Should you not embrace justice,

2 you who hate good and love evil; who tear the skin from my people and the flesh from their bones;

3 who eat the flesh of my people, flay their skin off them, break their bones in pieces, and chop them up like meat in a kettle, like flesh in a caldron.

• • • • • •

9 Hear this, you leaders of Jacob, you rulers of Israel, who despise justice and distort all that is right;

10 who build Zion with bloodshed, and Jerusalem with wickedness.

11 Her leaders judge for a bribe, her priests teach for a price, and her prophets tell fortunes for money. Yet they look for the LORD's support and say, "Is not the LORD among us? No disaster will come upon us."

12 Therefore because of you, Zion will be plowed like a field, Jerusalem will become a heap of rubble, the temple hill a mound overgrown with thickets.

• • • 6:6–8 • • •

6 With what shall I come before the Lord and bow down before the exalted God? Shall I come before him with burnt offerings, with calves a year old?

MAIN THOUGHT: He hath shewed thee, O man, what is good; and what doth the LORD require of thee, but to do justly, and to love mercy, and to walk humbly with thy God? (Micah 6:8, KJV)

MICAH 3:1–3, 9–12; 6:6–8

King James Version	*New Revised Standard Version*
7 Will the LORD be pleased with thousands of rams, or with ten thousands of rivers of oil? shall I give my firstborn for my transgression, the fruit of my body for the sin of my soul?	**7 Will the LORD be pleased with thousands of rams, with ten thousand rivers of olive oil? Shall I offer my firstborn for my transgression, the fruit of my body for the sin of my soul?**
8 He hath shewed thee, O man, what is good; and what doth the LORD require of thee, but to do justly, and to love mercy, and to walk humbly with thy God?	**8 He has shown you, O mortal, what is good. And what does the LORD require of you? To act justly and to love mercy and to walk humbly with your God.**

LESSON SETTING

Time: 735–725 B.C.
Place: Judah

LESSON OUTLINE

I. **An Indictment of Leaders (Micah 3:1–2)**
II. **A Corrupt Community (Micah 3:9–12)**
III. **The Way of Change (Micah 6:6–8)**

UNIFYING PRINCIPLE

Leaders often struggle with expectations of being examples of justice. How can leaders become models of justice worthy of emulation? Micah confronted the leaders of Israel for their failure to pursue justice and suggested that acting justly should be the basis of their lives.

INTRODUCTION

Micah was an eighth century prophet from a small village twenty miles southwest of Jerusalem, near the border of the Philistines. The prophet's name is likely an abbreviation of Micaiah, meaning "who is like Jehovah?"

Micah's time as a prophet coincided with that of Isaiah. Whereas Isaiah's ministry was primarily in Jerusalem and centered on the temple, Micah was more concerned with the daily conditions of the poor. Micah's prophetic utterances cover the reign of three kings of Judah: Jotham, Ahaz, and Hezekiah. Despite limited reforms instituted primarily by Hezekiah, the nation was marred in corruption. Micah focused on the social and economic condition of the poor as his primary concern. For Micah, the plight of the poor revealed the heart of the nation and the failure of leadership. Any nation that would abuse poor people and not care for them was not following the ways of Yahweh. Micah made no distinction between the social, political, and religious responsibilities of the nation. The increasing number of refugees and the demands from Assyria on Judah as a vassal state to pay tribute made the poor vulnerable to abuse by its leaders. Micah cried out against these abuses and warned Judah of coming judgment.

When the prophet Jeremiah announced Judah's captivity at the hands of the Babylonians about one hundred years later, the oldest inhabitants among them were familiar with Micah's prophecy at the time of King Hezekiah in Micah 3:12 (see Jer. 26:18).

EXPOSITION

I. AN INDICTMENT OF LEADERS (MICAH 3:1–2)

A critical question that impacts every person at some point in life is: When is it an appropriate time to speak up against an issue and take a stand? Are we to continue to witness the injustices that affect the most vulnerable in the community and say nothing? Are we to ignore the obvious suffering taking place at the hands of corrupt leaders? Micah answered these questions with a resounding no.

Although Micah, similar to many other prophets, was not from a ruling class, he would not allow his lower position on the social ladder to determine his right to speak on behalf of the people. Micah voiced a harsh indictment on the leaders of Israel and the ways they took advantage of the people. Israel's leaders were operating from a position of entitlement, using their offices to enrich themselves as opposed to serving the people. Micah began his description of the leaders' abuse by calling out their failure to act justly. Their decisions lacked any sign of justice. The laws and the offices of the elected leaders were used to benefit the privileged class at the expense of the rest of the society. Here, Micah also could be describing the decline of civility and decency as guides for public dialogue and action.

Micah may be referring to career politicians who were so focused on re-election they never focused on meeting the needs of the people whom they were to represent. Whatever the case, Micah observed a level of cruelty at which the leaders treated the people as prey to feed their personal agendas. In their time in office, the leaders were willing to denigrate the people through policies and actions that led to their demise.

The scene of a hungry animal consuming is prey is an imagine that speaks to an absence of power (v. 2). The only concern of a hungry animal is finding its prey and consuming it. The animal has no concern for the plight of his prey. Where is the concern for the poor and under served? Where is the mercy for the helpless and hopeless? Where is the help leaders are to extend to those whom they serve? The actions of the leaders have left the people in a state of fear and frustration. Hating good and doing evil leads to judgment for those who think they are safe.

II. A Corrupt Community (Micah 3:9–12)

Micah declared that a community built on corruption cannot last. The corruption of the community was so widespread that every area of society was engrossed in wrongdoing: business, government, and religion. A corrupt community that functions for the benefit of a select elite would be destroyed. What was built by violence would be destroyed by violence.

Micah did not pronounce the destruction of the city without detailing why. The Book of Micah affirms that people will pay for the wrong they do to others. There is no escaping the justice God will bring on a community that refuses to change. Micah clearly outlined the community's misdeeds, and he began with the role money plays in deeds of injustice.

Money has become a tool used to keep the elite in power at the expense of the poor. Officers of the court accept bribes and give positions of advantage to those with cases that come before the courts. Priests work only for those who are able to pay for their services. Prophets are more concerned about payment than faithfulness to their tasks. Because of their thirst for money, there is an effort at every level to maintain the status quo, even if it means the people are neglected.

Faith in money had replaced the leaders' dependence upon God. Money and its potential to help leaders amass more power in the community has become the goal. Micah declared that when money becomes the goal of leaders, they no longer can declare their dependence on God. Nothing was to come between Judah and their loyalty to a covenant-keeping God. The corruption within the community was so vast the leaders were unaware they had allowed money to be such a determining factor in obtaining their personal goals. Corruption had become the norm; injustice no longer was questioned. Therefore, the leaders believed no harm would come to them or to the city they had built on a foundation of corruption.

III. The Way of Change (Micah 6:6–8)

Micah's prophesy of impending judgment led the people to question what could be done to make things right with God. Was there a way to change the mind of God and avoid the coming judgment? Micah made it clear God could not be appeased with religious rituals and ceremonies.

Sometimes the easy thing to do was to participate in some type of religious ritual or activity and think enough had been done to atone for past wrongdoing. To regard religious ritual in those terms is wrong and corrupts its meaning. They are not interested in repentance. They simply want to avoid punishment through perfunctory acts of worship. The role of religious ritual is to make people aware of God's presence and His claim on us as His people. Religious ritual is intended to remind us for whom we are making life choices and decisions every day.

Religious ritual had lost its true meaning among the people of Judah and had become an exercise in futility. Participation in religious ritual was not the answer to the problem Judah faced. What God desired most of Judah was acts of justice. He desires that His people do good toward others and love mercy (v. 8).

God sought right relationships between the leaders and the people in which the leaders no longer were using the people for their selfish gain but were serving the people. God was seeking a form of justice that ensured the weak, poor, and powerless were not exploited. Whenever leaders exploit those they are called to serve for personal gain, it is a sign of sin at work. Acts of justice are testaments to the fact sin is removed and people are able to live faithfully. God's overarching concern is justice because He is just.

On the heels of restoring justice, the community is to love mercy, which is demonstrated through acts of kindness that hold greed at bay. Mercy reminds the community what it means to live in loving relationship to one another and to God. Mercy is to be ever-flowing because mercy is a core attribute of Israel's faith. The prophet told the people to walk humbly with God. Humility is the virtue that reminds people of their frail nature and just how prone they are to sin unless God's presence and power helps them. The way to change is to replace greed, selfishness, and hatred with justice, mercy, and humility. When we do these things, we demonstrate our real love for God.

The Lesson Applied

The role of money in politics, the legal system, and the church still can have undue influence today. Lobbyists pay politicians large sums of money to influence laws. The legal system's fee structure and bailout policies often cause those who can least afford them to spend more time in prison than they should. Churches are forced to have conversations about direction and values to keep growing and pay institutional expenses. Money never should replace our values as people of God or as a nation that professes to be "under God." Rather, we all should work to ensure serving the needs of people comes first. Money should not prevent people from having equal protection under the law simply because they have little or no financial resources.

Money had become a negative factor within Micah's community, and it opened the door for widespread corruption. We are to hold our leaders accountable at every level to prevent our values from being replaced. We have a responsibility to speak up and say, "Enough," and work to monitor and maintain a just government as well as just relations among church members. It always seems easier to go along to get along, but the God we serve is a God of justice who demands more of His people. He is a God who demands and expects His children to love justice and mercy just as much as He does.

Let's Talk About It

1. How do we know when is the appropriate time to speak out?

Micah was from a small community southwest of Jerusalem. His rural upbringing put him in close association with the poor. Micah had an upfront view of the struggles and concerns of those living on the margins of life. Therefore, Micah was able to give voice to those concerns as well speak of God's desire for justice.

Micah was willing to speak out because of the injustices he witnessed in his community. Micah saw the poor being abused and the absence of justice regarding their plight. Micah knew God expected better from the nation's leaders. It is always time to speak out when we see injustice. Without the voice of those who speak out, it becomes easy for injustice to become the norm.

2. Why is religious ritual not enough to appease God?

The Lord wants hearts that are dedicated to Him. Religious substance that is void of true devotion through acts of justice, mercy, and humility are meaningless. Going through the motions can become a form of idolatry if one thinks the actions will excuse him or her from their true responsibility and accountability to God.

Home Daily Devotional Readings

March 23–29, 2020

Monday	Tuesday	Wednesday	Thursday	Friday	Saturday	Sunday
Offer Sacrifice of Thanksgiving to God	Bring Acceptable Offerings to the Lord	God's Name Is Great Among Nations	Be Faithful to One Another	Messenger of Judgment Coming	God's Blessings and Delights Await	Leading in Troubled Times
Psalm 50:1–15	Leviticus 22:17–25	Malachi 1:11–14	Malachi 2:10–16	Malachi 2:17–3:4	Malachi 3:7–12	Malachi 2:1–9; 3:5–6

LEADING JUSTLY

ADULT TOPIC:
JUSTICE FOR ALL

BACKGROUND SCRIPTURE:
MALACHI 2–3

MALACHI 2:1–9; 3:5–6

King James Version

AND now, O ye priests, this commandment is for you.

2 If ye will not hear, and if ye will not lay it to heart, to give glory unto my name, saith the LORD of hosts, I will even send a curse upon you, and I will curse your blessings: yea, I have cursed them already, because ye do not lay it to heart.

3 Behold, I will corrupt your seed, and spread dung upon your faces, even the dung of your solemn feasts; and one shall take you away with it.

4 And ye shall know that I have sent this commandment unto you, that my covenant might be with Levi, saith the LORD of hosts.

5 My covenant was with him of life and peace; and I gave them to him for the fear wherewith he feared me, and was afraid before my name.

6 The law of truth was in his mouth, and iniquity was not found in his lips: he walked with me in peace and equity, and did turn many away from iniquity.

7 For the priest's lips should keep knowledge, and they should seek the law at his mouth: for he is the messenger of the LORD of hosts.

8 But ye are departed out of the way; ye have caused many to stumble at the law; ye have corrupted the covenant of Levi, saith the Lord of hosts.

New Revised Standard Version

"AND now, you priests, this warning is for you.

2 If you do not listen, and if you do not resolve to honor my name," says the LORD Almighty, "I will send a curse on you, and I will curse your blessings. Yes, I have already cursed them, because you have not resolved to honor me.

3 "Because of you I will rebuke your descendants; I will smear on your faces the dung from your festival sacrifices, and you will be carried off with it.

4 And you will know that I have sent you this warning so that my covenant with Levi may continue," says the LORD Almighty.

5 "My covenant was with him, a covenant of life and peace, and I gave them to him; this called for reverence and he revered me and stood in awe of my name.

6 True instruction was in his mouth and nothing false was found on his lips. He walked with me in peace and uprightness, and turned many from sin.

7 "For the lips of a priest ought to preserve knowledge, because he is the messenger of the LORD Almighty and people seek instruction from his mouth.

8 But you have turned from the way and by your teaching have caused many to stumble; you have violated the covenant with Levi," says the LORD Almighty.

MAIN THOUGHT: If ye will not hear, and if ye will not lay it to heart, to give glory unto my name, saith the LORD of hosts, I will even send a curse upon you, and I will curse your blessings: yea, I have cursed them already, because ye do not lay it to heart. (Malachi 2:2, KJV)

MALACHI 2:1–9; 3:5–6

King James Version

9 Therefore have I also made you contemptible and base before all the people, according as ye have not kept my ways, but have been partial in the law.

• • • 3:5–6 • • •

5 And I will come near to you to judgment; and I will be a swift witness against the sorcerers, and against the adulterers, and against false swearers, and against those that oppress the hireling in his wages, the widow, and the fatherless, and that turn aside the stranger from his right, and fear not me, saith the LORD of hosts.

6 For I am the LORD, I change not; therefore ye sons of Jacob are not consumed.

New Revised Standard Version

9 "So I have caused you to be despised and humiliated before all the people, because you have not followed my ways but have shown partiality in matters of the law."

• • • 3:5–6 • • •

5 "So I will come to put you on trial. I will be quick to testify against sorcerers, adulterers and perjurers, against those who defraud laborers of their wages, who oppress the widows and the fatherless, and deprive the foreigners among you of justice, but do not fear me," says the LORD Almighty.

6 "I the LORD do not change. So you, the descendants of Jacob, are not destroyed.

LESSON SETTING

Time: Fifth Century B.C.
Place: Judea

LESSON OUTLINE

I. The Penalty of a Bad Priest (Malachi 2:1–4)
II. The Blessings of a Good Priest (Malachi 2:5–7)
III. The Impact of Ungodly Leadership (Malachi 2:8–9)
IV. The Promised Day of Accountability (Malachi 3:5–6)

UNIFYING PRINCIPLE

Just leaders act honorably toward constituents. How do just leaders act toward others? Malachi admonishes the priests to turn from their wickedness, revere God, and reap a rich harvest for promoting godly justice.

INTRODUCTION

Malachi, the name of the last book of the Old Testament, means "my messenger." The name may be an abbreviation of *Malachjah,* which means "messenger of Jehovah.. Some biblical scholars do not hold Malachi as a first name, but rather as a designation. We are given no personal details of Malachi, a minor prophet. He is charged to speak to a mixed community of Jews comprised of those who never left Jerusalem after the fall of the city to Babylon as well as Jews who are returning from Exile.

The current state of Jerusalem and the rebuilt temple did not meet the expectations of a people that longed for the return of the city's glory days during the reign of David. In the absence of a functioning monarchy, the temple priests and Levites became the new leaders. The new leadership group was known as the Zadokite priesthood. With the backing of the Persian Empire, the Zadokite priesthood members were willing to repress certain aspects of Israel's religious faith in Yahweh. Particularly, among the items repressed, were components of temple worship that called for full fidelity to Yahweh. The religious leaders used their newly-acquired positions to take advantage of the people and distort temple worship. God's standards for sacrifice often were compromised, and the people were led into sin. The capture of Jerusalem by the Babylonians had led many to believe God had failed His people. The purpose of the religious system that guided the nation's understanding was being questioned. Malachi spoke a word of rebuke to this corrupt system and sought to return God's people to covenant loyalty.

Exposition

I. The Penalty of a Bad Priest (Malachi 2:1–4)

Many scholars believe Malachi was part of an opposition group comprised of loyalists to the Yahwistic tradition. His words of condemnation against the reigning priests reflect a movement for the opposition to be heard and change to come. The indictment made by Malachi is striking. The central problem is a priesthood that will not listen to God, who is speaking to the priests just as He has in the past. However, the current group of priests will not listen. The priests have allowed other concerns to guide their service to the people rather than the voice of God. Because the priests will not listen to Yahweh, they have no way of knowing how to bring glory to Him. Personal profit, political influence, and the interests of Persia have been their main considerations, in order that they might remain in power.

Malachi declares that God has passed judgment upon such priests by cursing them. The efforts of the priests who have abandoned the ways of Yahweh will not be rewarded as they think. The things they expect to bless them will curse them (v. 2). The promise to curse their blessings also could be a reference to the gifts or blessings brought to the priests by the people, or the priestly blessings they gave to the people.

Malachi provides no specific details of the curse, only that when the events happen, the priests will recognize they have been cursed by God. What is clear is the curse intends to bring personal and public shame. The ancient world regarded shame as something to be avoided at all costs. The thought that a group of leaders, who believed they should be honored for their privileged positions, actually would be brought to shame was inconceivable. Malachi declares the shame the priests will experience at the hand of God includes the punishment of their children.

This punishment comes in some form of rejection by God, who denies the children of these wicked priests the opportunity to ascend to the position of priest when they become of age. Every male child of a priest was eligible to become a priest; however, God would intervene to prevent the wicked priests' children from becoming priests in the future.

Next, God would take the manure of the offerings the priests made and place it on their faces. This is the ultimate sign of shame because the manure would not be on their garments, but on their faces. Manure on the faces of the priests would be an indication of what the men could not hide about themselves and their rejection by God. Bad priests run the risk of encountering both judgment and shame.

II. The Blessing of a Good Priest (Malachi 2:5–7)

The contrast is provided in a good priest from a bad priest. Malachi declares God's intention for the priestly office to demonstrated how far Israel's current priesthood had strayed off course. Levi is used as an example of God's intent for the priesthood through a covenant relationship based upon fidelity to God.

God had promised Levi his descendants would be scattered in Israel. This was turned into a wonderful blessing when Levi was designated as the priestly tribe and the priests were sprinkled throughout Israel. Nowhere does the Old Testament give an accounting of this covenant being made. However, there are numerous scriptural references that such a covenant was made. What we have are indications that one did exist (see Deut. 33:8–10, Neh. 13:29, and Jer. 33:20–21).

The ideal model for the priest begins with reverence and awe of God. When God is revered, the actions one takes are informed by the sense of reverence. Genuine reverence will not allow one to abuse the responsibility God has placed upon a person, nor will he abuse the people of God. When the priest is in the right relationship with God, the blessings of God open up to the priest in order for the priest to bless the people.

The primary way the priest blesses the people is through the work of intercession. The priest offers his prayers to God on behalf of the people and seeks the welfare of the people as he leads them to obedience to God's will in the community. The priest also provides the people with the word of God as he communicates to the people all that God has told him.

Therefore, the priest was required to speak the truth even if the truth was harsh. If the priest spoke the truth, the people would know how to respond, and if the response called for repentance, the priest would lead the way in confession and repentance. A good priest never forgets he is the Lord's messenger.

III. The Impact of Ungodly Leaders (Malachi 2:8–9)

The prophet charges the priests with corrupting the covenant of Levi (v. 8). He reveals they had encouraged gross impertinence to God in the matter of sacrificial worship (1:6–2:3) and had undermined the authority and impartiality of covenant law. Had they been faithful to their sacred duty as priests, the people would have received God's blessings of life and peace. But as they were in the days of King Asa, Israel was "without a teaching priest and without law" and so in her life was "without the true God" (2 Chron. 15:3, KJV).

The failure of the current priesthood was not simply the problem of priests following interests that were separate from God's interests. The current priesthood's failure had led to the moral, social, and religious collapse of an entire community. Because the priests had turned away from God's expectations of them, a different standard emerged from within the community and cheapened their worship and opened the door for the moral decay of the entire society. Israel suffered from a crisis of belief in the efficiency of God. Therefore, Israel saw no need to follow the responsibilities of covenant loyalty in the sacrifices they offered nor their social and economic responsibility to justice in their dealings with others.

The priests, through their bad examples, had created a problem that went beyond temple worship and created a space for injustice to thrive. Ungodly leaders can set a community on a course of decline that can take generations to correct. The priests who were to be a source of blessing to the people have made them stumble and fall. There will be no blessings for a community that is directed by ungodly leaders.

Because the priests have fallen so far short of God's ideal, the people held them in contempt.

IV. The Promised Day of Accountability (Malachi 3:5–6)

The day of accountability Malachi envisions is a day that is not reserved just for priests who have led the community astray. Much of what Malachi sees in the day of accountability deals with social and economic injustices in the community. Lack of fidelity to Yahweh has led to infidelity in marriage, in legal proceedings, and in employment. The community is coming apart because of lost fidelity to Yahweh. An institution cannot hold when God is not at its center. The day of accountability is addressed in legal terms, a court proceeding where God is both prosecutor and judge. The current situation cannot continue. God will have to act soon.

Malachi concludes with the reminder that God does not change. Whereas the priests change and the community changes, God does not. Thus, it is the responsibility of the priests and the community to return to covenant loyalty.

The Lesson Applied

A striking parallel to Malachi's experience can been seen today in the church of the Western world. Over the last two centuries, and to a great degree during the past fifty years, the truth of God's Word has been dismantled progressively by those whose duty it was and is to maintain it. As a result, society has reduced the Bible to a book like any other, containing some important historical facts and useful insights of wisdom for living. Fewer people hold to the belief the Bible is the inspired and inerrant Word of God.

Words seem to have disappeared from our vocabulary, even within our churches. We seemingly disregard the need for words like *regeneration* and *atonement*. *Justification* and *sanctification* are long words that are glossed over in search of a more palatable message. Morality is watered down to living in love without the need to conform to God's demands. Meanwhile, our leaders often fail to speak out from the pulpit for fear of losing their position in the church or their status in the community.

There are times when the church suffers because of religious leaders who have interests that differ from the priorities of God. Churches should not become so associated with a political agenda, economic position, or a cultural position that they lose their primary focus of what it means to have unwavering fidelity to God. Such devotion to God should inform our every decision as we seek to bear witness to our faith in Christ. The Church is to always listen to the voice of God rather than the competing voices of the world.

Let's Talk About It

1. How do we maintain reverence and awe of God in an age of growing secularism?

An issue that contributed to the problems caused by a corrupt priesthood that compromised temple worship was the generations of people who had not been instructed in the true ways of Yahweh. The community served by the priests included exiles who never had participated in temple worship prior to their return to Judah. Their time spent in a foreign land had removed all institutional knowledge of how God was to be worshiped and served.

The church always is to guard the institutional knowledge of the faith and pass it to each new generation. The danger today lies in incorporating secular beliefs into the faith in order to make it more appealing to those who have no knowledge of the church. Many sincere leaders grapple with how to attract an unchurched generation, so they look to secular appeals. Further exacerbating the problem today are compromised religious leaders who are more concerned with maintaining popularity in the community, television ratings, book sales, or offerings in the collection plate. God's Word is not always popular, but it will be heard and heeded by those who have an ear to listen.

2. What does it mean to listen to God?

We need the Holy Spirit to help us discern God's message when He speaks. The Holy Spirit bears witness to the truth and will guide us if we will heed His direction. Being able to hear His still, small voice means taking time to push away the cares and concerns of the world to focus on His voice. Listening for the voice of God means preparing our hearts to receive His message.

3. Are there witnesses to the things that Malachi mentioned as a justice concern to God at work in today's world?

Yes. The treatment of immigrants, elderly, and the poor; the sexual abuse of children by religious leaders; the blatant disregard for Black life by some law enforcement officers; and the uneven sentencing meted out in our justice system are just a few examples. These vulnerable groups often suffer unnecessary hardship because of policies that harm them and limit their opportunities. Meanwhile, those in power are slow to take action for fear of losing their own positions.

Home Daily Devotional Readings

March 30–April 5, 2020

Monday	Tuesday	Wednesday	Thursday	Friday	Saturday	Sunday
Faith Heroes Acted Justly	Your King Comes Humbly	House of Prayer for All Nations	Neglect Justice at Your Peril	Jesus, God's Servant Messiah	God Will Not Forsake the People	God's Servant to Establish Justice Everywhere
Hebrews 11:29–35	Matthew 21:1–11	Mark 11:15–19	Luke 11:42–44	Matthew 12:15–21	Isaiah 42:10–17	Isaiah 42:1–9

GOD'S JUST SERVANT

ADULT TOPIC:
SEEKING A CHAMPION OF JUSTICE

BACKGROUND SCRIPTURE:
ISAIAH 42

ISAIAH 42:1–9

King James Version

BEHOLD my servant, whom I uphold; mine elect, in whom my soul delighteth; I have put my spirit upon him: he shall bring forth judgment to the Gentiles.

2 He shall not cry, nor lift up, nor cause his voice to be heard in the street.

3 A bruised reed shall he not break, and the smoking flax shall he not quench: he shall bring forth judgment unto truth.

4 He shall not fail nor be discouraged, till he have set judgment in the earth: and the isles shall wait for his law.

5 Thus saith God the LORD, he that created the heavens, and stretched them out; he that spread forth the earth, and that which cometh out of it; he that giveth breath unto the people upon it, and spirit to them that walk therein:

6 I the LORD have called thee in righteousness, and will hold thine hand, and will keep thee, and give thee for a covenant of the people, for a light of the Gentiles;

7 To open the blind eyes, to bring out the prisoners from the prison, and them that sit in darkness out of the prison house.

8 I am the LORD: that is my name: and my glory will I not give to another, neither my praise to graven images.

9 Behold, the former things are come to pass, and new things do I declare: before they spring forth I tell you of them.

New Revised Standard Version

"HERE is my servant, whom I uphold, my chosen one in whom I delight; I will put my Spirit on him, and he will bring justice to the nations.

2 He will not shout or cry out, or raise his voice in the streets.

3 A bruised reed he will not break, and a smoldering wick he will not snuff out. In faithfulness he will bring forth justice;

4 he will not falter or be discouraged till he establishes justice on earth. In his teaching the islands will put their hope."

5 This is what God the LORD says—the Creator of the heavens, who stretches them out, who spreads out the earth with all that springs from it, who gives breath to its people, and life to those who walk on it:

6 "I, the LORD, have called you in righteousness; I will take hold of your hand. I will keep you and will make you to be a covenant for the people and a light for the Gentiles,

7 to open eyes that are blind, to free captives from prison and to release from the dungeon those who sit in darkness.

8 "I am the LORD; that is my name! I will not yield my glory to another or my praise to idols.

9 See, the former things have taken place, and new things I declare; before they spring into being I announce them to you."

MAIN THOUGHT: Behold my servant, whom I uphold; mine elect, in whom my soul delighteth; I have put my spirit upon him: he shall bring forth judgment to the Gentiles. (Isaiah 42:1, KJV)

LESSON SETTING

Time: Seventh Century B.C.
Place: Judah

LESSON OUTLINE

I. **The Appearance of God's Servant (Isaiah 42:1–4)**
II. **The Reminder of God's Ability (Isaiah 42:5–6)**
III. **The God Who Is to Be Praised (Isaiah 42:7–9)**

Unifying Principle

People seek a champion of justice. Who can and will defend and uphold the cause of justice? In Matthew 21, Jesus upholds God's justice in the temple, fulfilling Isaiah 42's vision of the Messiah.

Introduction

Many scholars hold that the book of Isaiah consists of three distinct sections, possibly written by different authors. Isaiah 40–66 is the second section. The passage for this lesson comprises one of the Servant Songs. These songs speak of a future God has planned for Israel to restore justice, fidelity, and the blessings of *chesed*, the undying faithfulness of Yahweh. Scholars hold differing views regarding the identity of the servant in the Servant Songs. Some hold the servant is the nation of Israel as God's chosen people. Other scholars assert the position that the servant is an actual person but make no clear determination of who the person may be. Finally, there are scholars who maintain the servant is the Messiah, Jesus Christ.

Conservative scholarship has long noted Isaiah as the book that makes more references to Jesus Christ than any other Old Testament book. The writer of Isaiah 40–66, referred to as *Deutero-Isaiah,* faced a problem not unlike contemporary religious leaders. The prophet spoke to exiled Jews in Babylonia, most of whom had never been to their homeland. Having little connection to the faith practices of their forebears, some of them doubted whether God still loved the Jewish people and whether they had any future as a people. Others wondered whether the God of Israel really was the Creator of the world and, thus, powerful enough to defeat the seemingly powerful Babylonian gods. Deutero-Isaiah attempts to comfort the exiles, to explain the reasons for their plight, and to convince them the Babylonian Empire soon would collapse, freeing them to return to their ancient homeland.

Deutero-Isaiah is known for his characteristic form of pronouncing salvation as a determined fact by the actions of Yahweh. Deutero-Isaiah offers hope, not judgment. Isaiah's message reminds the people of God's delivering power and how that power would be made known again, even for a people who had been in exile.

Exposition

I. The Appearance of God's Servant (Isaiah 42:1–4)

God sends a spirit-filled servant, not a conqueror or tyrant to His people. "A bruised reed he will not break," (v. 3, NRSV). This agent of God is a liberator assigned to bring justice, not domination, which is so familiar to Israel having suffered under Babylonian rule. The appearance of the servant of God is described in a court scene. The servant of the Lord is an official for the Kingdom, making his desires known to the people. By describing the servant of the Lord in the language of a court scene, Isaiah makes clear the legal responsibility the people have to heed the king's servant. God grants His unwavering support to His servant.

The support of the servant is mentioned in several ways. First, God promises to uphold His servant. God's power would be with His servant in ways that would allow the servant to stand against all who might resist the servant and the message he proclaimed. Second, God informs the community the servant among them is the one whom God has chosen. God had decided who He wanted to represent Him. God's selection reinforces God's sovereign authority to enter into covenant relationships with those whom God wants to use for His purposes. Third, God's delight in the servant is an indication of the servant's complete obedience to God. Disobedience by the nation had been the cause of their exile and punishment. The servant's obedience to God would restore the people and bring peace between the Israel and God. Fourth, the servant would have the Spirit of God upon him. The power of the Spirit's ongoing presence leads many to believe the servant mentioned in this passage is Jesus. The Spirit in the Old Testament did not have the role of constant indwelling in believers. God's Spirit, in the Old Testament, would appear upon a person for a task or a moment, but did not abide upon them continually. It is this continued presence of the Spirit that separates this servant from all others.

Thus, the servant of the Lord, at his appearing, would be equipped to do what no one prior to his appearance could. This unique equipping means the servant of the Lord would not just bring justice to Israel, but he would bring justice to the nations. The servant of the Lord is the one who shows God's concern of justice for all through compassion, mercy, and grace.

II. The Reminder of God's Ability (Isaiah 42:5–6)

The prophet is challenged to encourage a people who had been abandoned to their enemies. How could a mighty Deliverer allow this to happen? Did He not have the power to stop this? Did He have the power to restore them? Had God abandoned them? They had been removed from access to the temple and to the land. Were they still considered God's people? Was God still God? While living in exile, they could only conclude God had withdrawn His favor and allowed the Babylonians to punish them for their sins and disobedience.

Deutero-Isaiah helps the people know the God of their forebears who had chosen them and delivered them from bondage. The prophet informs them of what God already has done to make them aware of what God can and will do in the future. The most common reminder of what God has done refers to God's creative acts. God created the heavens and the earth and all that comes from it. The proof of God's power is witnessed in the everyday affairs of life.

The prophet provides an awareness of God that should not be taken for granted in the space human beings occupy. Recognition of the creative activity of

God is also confessional, for the prophet gives God glory for what He has done. No other deity could have done what the God of Israel has done in His creative work in the world. Israel and all of humanity are the receptors of God's gracious action on their behalf. Moreover, God, who created the heavens and the earth, has provided life to people on the earth.

Again, the prophet is calling the community to think about the ways God already has shown His power at work. God is alive and active in the here and now. It is easy for exiles living under bondage to think God has forgotten them. The hardships of the Exile made the people wonder where God was and how this could have happened to Israel if God was able to prevent it. The words of the prophet rekindle and re-imagine God in times of hardship to call humanity to know God is present and powerful in the world He created.

The work of re-imagining is a main focus for Deutero-Isaiah because he asks his community to think about a future that is different from their current reality. Punishment and exile are not permanent despite the power of Babylon and the weakened state of Israel. God will rise up and remember His covenant and bring forth a different future, a hopeful one.

For the prophet, the reality of a different future is assured by the God who keeps covenant. Therefore, the prophet reintroduces covenant theology by telling Israel they have been called to be light to the nations. Jesus parallels this message in Matthew 5:14–16 (NRSV), when He tells His disciples, "You are the light of the world.… let your light shine before others, so that they may see your good works and give glory to your Father in heaven." The Servant calls for God's people to be light in both the Old and New Testaments. God has chosen Israel to demonstrate to the nations of the world what fidelity to the one true God can accomplish in the world. Just as God created the world, God has chosen Israel. Punishment and exile do not change the reality that Israel was chosen by God. The time will come when Israel will fulfill God's intent, planned long ago for them, by being the light to the nations.

The model of servant continues from Isaiah to Matthew. In Jesus, God sends a Servant who will bring justice, who God anoints "to bring good news to the poor ... proclaim release to the captives, and recovery of sight to the blind, to let the oppressed go free, and declare the year of the Lord's favor" (Luke 4:18–19, NRSV).

III. The God Who Is to Be Praised (Isaiah 42:7–9)

In these three verses the prophet gives great hope through God's promises. God will open the eyes of those who are blind to His name and His purpose (v. 7). Their many years of ignorance about the God who had chosen them as His people would be lifted.

The use of God's name in connection with God's actions in creation and history is a call for Israel to praise God. Israel knows God's name, and knowledge of this God is to inform their relationship with God. Israel is not to act in the same manner as the nations that do not know God. Because Israel knows the name of God and shares a unique relationship with God, they are to praise God. Israel is to give God glory in all things.

God establishes His identity (v. 8): "I am the Lord." His position is sovereign and unwavering. He is the God who has all life in and of Himself, and He gives life to His creation. He is the everlasting, unchangeable, and omnipotent God who both can and will fulfill all of His promises. God's capacities have not been diminished. He is who He has been and always will be.

Here the prophet employs a call to praise similar to that found in the Psalms. Israel is not permitted to withhold praise from God simply because their condition may not be ideal. In many of the psalms, particularly those that start as lament, the psalmist discovers the presence of God in the midst of sorrow. And without a clear answer to his lament, the psalmist moves to praise of God because of his awareness of God's presence with him.

In like manner, the prophet calls on his community to not lose their sense of need to praise God. The praise of God is not connected to a condition within the community. Israel is called upon to praise God because of who He is, not simply because of things happening in the present moment. God's revelation to the world makes praise necessary for those who know His name. Also, God will not share His praise with others, whether human or idol. Israel is to remain focused upon the God whose name they know and praise Him. In the midst of praising God, Israel will discover God already has done a new thing. Punishment for past wrongs is about to give way to new hope.

In the past (v. 9), Yahweh had spoken of things that would come to pass—and they did. God's Word is powerful and reliable. Now, God declares a new thing the people have not heard before. Yahweh challenged the idols in the preceding chapter: "Let them bring them, and tell us what is to happen. Tell us the former things, what they are, so that we may consider them, and that we may know their outcome; or declare to us the things to come" (Isa. 41:22, NRSV). Now God says He will do what the idols could not do—tell of new things "before they spring forth." The metaphor used here is taken from the actions of plants and flowers. The Hebrew word צמח *tsâmach* refers to plants springing from the ground or sending out shoots, buds, or flowers. The phrase literally means, "before they begin to germinate."

In like manner, God tells of future events before there is anything that indicates such occurrences would take place. His knowledge is not the result of heightened perception to the ways of humanity. People sometimes can predict future events with great probability by taking note of certain political, economic, or societal indications or developments. God foretells events and gives His people reason to hope even when there are no indicators. His words are given by pure omniscience. God's foretelling word differs from the conjectures of mortals in that He is not guessing or speculating. What God says will come to pass. God distinguishes Himself from the idols so familiar to the exiles. He is the creator God. What have the idols created? He is the all-knowing God who foretells what the idols do not even know.

The Lesson Applied

There are times when we look for someone with more power than we possess to right a wrong, to correct some injustice, and/or to ensure fairness in the treatment of all people. For many years, Thurgood

Marshall and Walter White held such positions for people of color through the work of the NAACP. The legal victories won by the NAACP Legal Defense team brought desegregated schools, voting rights, fair housing, and a host of legal changes that made life better for people of color and for society in general. Indeed, these men and the team that stood behind them were champions of justice, serving a people who had no voice or the means to secure one through their own resources.

The prophet Isaiah promises a day when the servant of the Lord will appear and return the land to a nation of justice and compassion for all people. God provides the help humanity needs to return to the just world He envisions for all.

Let's Talk About It

1. **How are we to understand the identity of the servant mentioned in the Servant Songs of Isaiah?**

   Most popular scholarship makes Israel the servant that Isaiah has in mind in the Servant Songs of Isaiah. The basis for this position is the role Israel was to play in human history as light to the nations of the world. Israel introduced the world to monotheism and the personal nature of a God who would enter a covenant relationship with His people. However, other scholars hold the servant in the Servant Songs of Isaiah to be a direct reference to the Messiah. The connection of Jesus to Isaiah is reflected in the Gospels when Jesus quoted Isaiah and identified Himself as the One upon whom the Spirit of God was bestowed to bring salvation to the people.

2. **Why do we need to be reminded about what God has done?**

   Life's difficulties can cause us to become so focused on our challenges that we fail to acknowledge the power of God to bring about change. What is difficult for us is not difficult for God because He is Sovereign. When we acknowledge God is in control, we also acknowledge things may change for the better at any moment.

3. **In what way does the prophet reveal the compassion of the servant?**

   The prophet used the metaphor of a bruised reed the servant would not break. A reed often was used as a flute to play music. However, reeds were fragile and would crack easily. Because reeds were so plentiful, however, people simply discarded them and made a new flute from a new reed. The compassion of the servant of the Lord is revealed in His willingness to mend the bruised reed rather than discard it. Whether or not the bruised reed plays less than perfectly, the servant of the Lord will not dispose it.

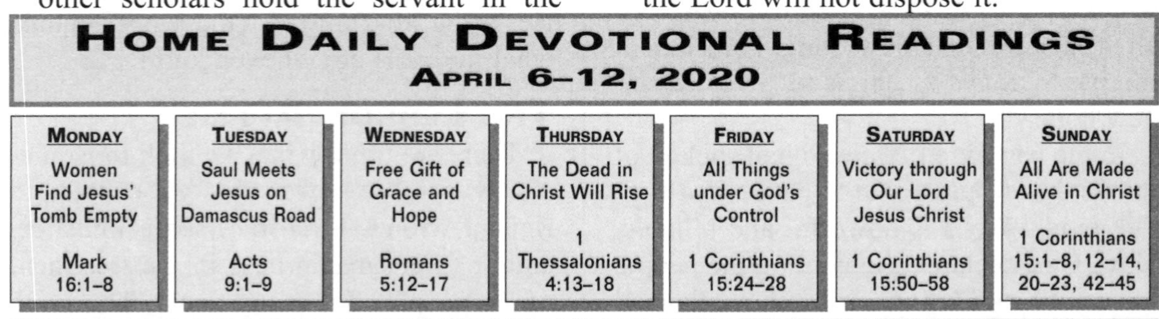

Home Daily Devotional Readings

April 6–12, 2020

Monday	Tuesday	Wednesday	Thursday	Friday	Saturday	Sunday
Women Find Jesus' Tomb Empty	Saul Meets Jesus on Damascus Road	Free Gift of Grace and Hope	The Dead in Christ Will Rise	All Things under God's Control	Victory through Our Lord Jesus Christ	All Are Made Alive in Christ
Mark 16:1–8	Acts 9:1–9	Romans 5:12–17	1 Thessalonians 4:13–18	1 Corinthians 15:24–28	1 Corinthians 15:50–58	1 Corinthians 15:1–8, 12–14, 20–23, 42–45

RESURRECTION HOPE

ADULT TOPIC:
HOPE FOR A BETTER LIFE

BACKGROUND SCRIPTURE:
MARK 16; 1 CORINTHIANS 15

1 CORINTHIANS 15:1–8, 12–14, 20–23, 42–45

King James Version

MOREOVER, brethren, I declare unto you the gospel which I preached unto you, which also ye have received, and wherein ye stand;

2 By which also ye are saved, if ye keep in memory what I preached unto you, unless ye have believed in vain.

3 For I delivered unto you first of all that which I also received, how that Christ died for our sins according to the scriptures;

4 And that he was buried, and that he rose again the third day according to the scriptures:

5 And that he was seen of Cephas, then of the twelve:

6 After that, he was seen of above five hundred brethren at once; of whom the greater part remain unto this present, but some are fallen asleep.

7 After that, he was seen of James; then of all the apostles.

8 And last of all he was seen of me also, as of one born out of due time.

• • • • • •

12 Now if Christ be preached that he rose from the dead, how say some among you that there is no resurrection of the dead?

13 But if there be no resurrection of the dead, then is Christ not risen:

14 And if Christ be not risen, then is our preaching vain, and your faith is also vain.

• • • • • •

New Revised Standard Version

NOW, brothers and sisters, I want to remind you of the gospel I preached to you, which you received and on which you have taken your stand.

2 By this gospel you are saved, if you hold firmly to the word I preached to you. Otherwise, you have believed in vain.

3 For what I received I passed on to you as of first importance: that Christ died for our sins according to the Scriptures,

4 that he was buried, that he was raised on the third day according to the Scriptures,

5 and that he appeared to Cephas, and then to the Twelve.

6 After that, he appeared to more than five hundred of the brothers and sisters at the same time, most of whom are still living, though some have fallen asleep.

7 Then he appeared to James, then to all the apostles,

8 and last of all he appeared to me also, as to one abnormally born.

• • • • • •

12 But if it is preached that Christ has been raised from the dead, how can some of you say that there is no resurrection of the dead?

13 If there is no resurrection of the dead, then not even Christ has been raised.

14 And if Christ has not been raised, our preaching is useless and so is your faith.

• • • • • •

MAIN THOUGHT: If in this life only we have hope in Christ, we are of all men most miserable. But now is Christ risen from the dead, and become the firstfruits of them that slept. (1 Corinthians 15:19–20, KJV)

1 Corinthians 15:1–8, 12–14, 20–23, 42–45

King James Version	*New Revised Standard Version*
20 But now is Christ risen from the dead, and become the firstfruits of them that slept.	**20 But Christ has indeed been raised from the dead, the firstfruits of those who have fallen asleep.**
21 For since by man came death, by man came also the resurrection of the dead.	**21 For since death came through a man, the resurrection of the dead comes also through a man.**
22 For as in Adam all die, even so in Christ shall all be made alive.	**22 For as in Adam all die, so in Christ all will be made alive.**
23 But every man in his own order: Christ the firstfruits; afterward they that are Christ's at his coming.	**23 But each in turn: Christ, the firstfruits; then, when he comes, those who belong to him.**
••••••	••••••
42 So also is the resurrection of the dead. It is sown in corruption; it is raised in incorruption:	**42 So will it be with the resurrection of the dead. The body that is sown is perishable, it is raised imperishable;**
43 It is sown in dishonour; it is raised in glory: it is sown in weakness; it is raised in power:	**43 it is sown in dishonor, it is raised in glory; it is sown in weakness, it is raised in power;**
44 It is sown a natural body; it is raised a spiritual body. There is a natural body, and there is a spiritual body.	**44 it is sown a natural body, it is raised a spiritual body. If there is a natural body, there is also a spiritual body.**
45 And so it is written, The first man Adam was made a living soul; the last Adam was made a quickening spirit.	**45 So it is written: "The first man Adam became a living being"; the last Adam, a life-giving spirit.**

LESSON SETTING

Time: A.D. 55
Place: Corinth

LESSON OUTLINE

I. Eyewitnesses to the Resurrection (1 Corinthians 15:1–8)
II. Why the Resurrection Matters (1 Corinthians 15:12–14)
III. Paul's Explanation of the Resurrection (1 Corinthians 15:20–23, 42–45)

Unifying Principle

People struggle with the probability of life after death. How can resurrection from death provide life that is different from what is experienced before death? In First Corinthians and Mark, only life through the resurrection of Christ engenders hope for authentic justice.

Introduction

First Corinthians is one of two books written to the church at Corinth. Most scholars hold that 1 and 2 Corinthians actually are fragments from as many as four letters Paul wrote to the Corinthian believers. The two letters of the canon provide the largest amount of material in the New Testament written by Paul to a single church. The Apostle seeks to address practical and theological matters for the church.

In the lesson today, Paul provides a theological lesson on the resurrection. In this passage, Paul confronts Gnosticism and its influence in the life of the church. Gnosticism held the position that body and soul were separate; the soul was good, but the body and all material things were bad. Therefore, the Gnostics denied the reality of a bodily resurrection. A cornerstone to the church's faith in Jesus Christ is the resurrection of the body from the grave and eternal life with Christ. Paul informs the Corinthians that the resurrection is not an opinion, speculation, or legend but a fact that is substantiated by eyewitnesses.

Since the Corinthians apparently were accepting of the Gnostic view that the body held no value, some of the Corinthians must have chafed at the idea of a God who raises corpses. Why would God want these bodies? The Corinthians must have resisted Paul's teachings, wondering why they couldn't believe God is all-powerful and follow Jesus's teaching to love one another. Did they really need to believe God raised Jesus from the dead? What was the importance of living in the hope of Christ's return?

On this issue, Paul is unyielding. If there is no resurrection, then there is no hope. If there is no resurrection, everything we thought we knew about God is not true. In Paul's estimation, without the resurrection, all we have is this earthly life, and the Gospel we preach contains no Good News.

Chapter 15 can be divided into three sections: (1) details of Jesus' post-resurrection appearances (15:1-11); (2) the resurrection of believers as a consequence of Jesus' resurrection (15:12-34); and (3) a reflection on how the dead are raised and what the resurrection body is like (15:35–58).

Exposition

I. Eyewitnesses to the Resurrection (1 Corinthians 15:1–8)

In these first eight verses, Paul recounts the resurrection story as part of a Gospel that has been passed on to him. Paul makes clear the resurrection story is not a theological position he established as means to teach about the meaning of Jesus' life. The resurrection is an actual occurrence because there is eyewitness proof of its reality. There are many witnesses to the resurrection of Jesus. Whereas the appearance of Jesus after the resurrection, as stated by Paul, begins with Peter and the apostles to affirm their authority as leaders of the Church, Jesus' appearances do not end with the apostles.

Jesus appears to many in His post resurrection state and provides instruction for how the Church is to move forward in the world, bearing witness to Him. Being able to see the resurrected Christ transformed a once-frighten band of followers into faithful witnesses who proclaim what God has done in Jesus Christ for all of humanity.

The resurrection of Jesus is central to Paul because the apostle includes his own experience with the resurrected Christ as the basis for his ministry. The resurrection is a story that needs to be repeated as a means of reminding the Church of how far God has gone to redeem a people back to Himself. The Church is never to forget how important the resurrection is to the Christian faith. By establishing the resurrection as central to the message of Jesus, Paul is formulating what will become Christian doctrine. Whereas particular stories about Jesus may not be passed down to each generation, the importance and the central role of the resurrection will be passed down to each succeeding generation to hold firm as a part of the vital beliefs of the church. The building of a tradition that can be taught to every generation is one of Paul's greatest contributions to the Church.

In verse 8, Paul emphasizes the impact of the resurrection upon his own life. The apostle's recognition of the great privilege he has of being counted worthy to see the resurrected Savior inspires deep humility, which was always stoked by the painful awareness of his having once persecuted the Church. In recognition of this, Paul expresses his strong sense of unworthiness to hold this honor by describing himself as an untimely birth. It would be nearly impossible for the apostle to abase himself more than he does by this single moniker. Paul literally describes himself as an abortion (לפנ *nephel*) that is not worthy of the name of a man, so he affirms himself as unworthy of the name of an apostle. Before Christ entered his life, Paul counts his life as meaningless, as though he never had lived.

II. Why the Resurrection Matters (1 Corinthians 15:12–14)

At the heart of Paul's preaching and teaching is the cross and the resurrection. When Paul first arrived in Corinth, he declared he was determined to know nothing among them but Jesus Christ and Him crucified. C.H. Dodd in his classic work *Apostolic Preaching and Its Developments* (Hodder & Stoughton Ltd., 1936) states: "in the preaching attested by Paul although it was similarly addressed to the wider public, there does not seem to be any such comprehensive summary of the facts of the ministry of Jesus as distinct from the facts of is death and resurrection." Paul chooses to make the death and resurrection of Jesus central to all of his preaching. Jesus died for the sins of the world, God raised Him from the dead, and through faith in Him all believers can receive eternal life.

For the resurrection to be questioned by the Corinthians, or those who may have had influence over them, brought all of Paul's preaching into question. Paul says that if what the Corinthians suggest about the resurrection is true, then his preaching and his entire ministry has been in vain. Paul does not preach Jesus as a moral teacher or a philosopher who, if followed, will allow believers to have a better life. Countless philosophies in the Roman Empire sought to influence human behavior, but Paul has no interest in presenting Jesus simply as another good teacher to follow. Jesus is the Son of God who died on the cross for the sins of the world. God is doing in Jesus the new thing the prophets of old had spoken. There is no Good News for Paul outside of the cross and the resurrection of Jesus Christ. Without the resurrection, Paul declares not only has his preaching been in vain, their faith is useless as well.

The resurrection matters because it is the manifestation of how God has dealt with sin and separation in the world by the power of redemption. Resurrection is redemptive work. The resurrection is the way God makes clean the slate that has been soiled by sin. The resurrection provides a new display of God's power at work in the world by raising Christ from death and in so doing making it possible for all who have died in faith to be raised by the same power.

III. Paul's Explanation of the Resurrection (1 Corinthians 15:20–23, 42–45)

Paul begins his explanation of the resurrection beginning with the resurrection of Jesus Christ. The resurrection of Jesus provides a window for understanding the resurrection. What can be seen in the resurrection of Jesus is how God raised Him from the dead. The power of God was on display in the resurrection of Jesus and demonstrated that the power of God is greater than the power of death. Through the resurrection, God had sided with life, and death could not hold its victim.

In using the term "firstfruits," Paul uses a Jewish term with a Gentile audience. The firstfruits refer to the harvest festival that celebrated the grain and barley harvest from the fields. The firstfruits celebration was a reminder of God's faithfulness through the season of planting until the season of harvest. William Barclay in his commentary *Corinthians: William Barclay's Daily Study Bible* (Saint Andrew Press, 1953) states: "the first fruit was a sign of the harvest to come and the resurrection of Jesus was a sign of the resurrection for all believers which was to come. Just as the new barley could not be used until the first fruit had been offered so the new harvest of life could not come until Jesus had been raised from the dead."

Next Paul provides a contrast between Adam and Jesus. Adam's disobedience to God ushered in the age of sin, and along with it the presence of death. In his use of Adam, Paul is explaining why death exists. There is no arguing the reality of death, and Paul says it is because of the choices of one man. If death then is possible by one man's choice, then life also should be possible by another man's choice—that man is Jesus Christ. His death and resurrection now open the door for all persons to know eternal life by faith in Him.

Paul uses a farming metaphor to conclude his explanation about the resurrection. Paul points out that what is planted is not the same thing that comes up out of the ground at harvest. What is planted is a seed of some kind, but what comes from the ground is the fruit of the seed planted. If we are able to receive the fruit that comes from a seed planted in the ground, why is hard to believe God can raise persons from the dead in a body suited for His purpose? The resurrection is not simply an idea or philosophy for Paul or the church; it is a reality accepted by faith that has been passed down for generations.

The Lesson Applied

Today the Church celebrates its most sacred day—Easter. Resurrection Day is an occasion for the Church to pause and reflect on the most central tenet of the Gospel—the death and resurrection of Jesus Christ. It is the death and resurrection of Christ that makes the Gospel Good News for a sinful and hopeless humanity. The Church must be careful not to lose its way in stressing other issues on the banner of relevance so that the significance of Easter becomes lost. The death and resurrection of Jesus must be passed down to every generation as the component that matters most. The Church must never fail in its teaching to tell the story that has been passed down from generation to generation about what God has done in Jesus Christ. Death has been defeated and eternal life has been secured.

Just as Paul was unwavering in his letter to the Corinthians regarding the significance of the bodily resurrection of Christ, we must be unmovable in the pivotal tenet of our faith. In our attempts to appeal to the masses, we cannot offer a weakened and watered down Christ who simply lived a good life on earth and taught profound truths to His followers. In fact, the late Dr. James Cone once noted the story of Jesus Christ and the resurrection is a story of human failure. Without the resurrection and the victory over death that it wrought, the historical Jesus is little more than a smart Jewish man who had the potential to lead an insurrection against Rome and restore the nation, but He failed because of the crucifixion. Thankfully, there is more to the story of Jesus. The resurrection brings victory to what otherwise might have been a tragic story.

Let's Talk About It

1. Why does Paul have to remind the Corinthians about the importance of the resurrection, given it was such a large part of his preaching at Corinth?

Corinth was a large metropolitan city and a center for commerce. People from all over the Roman Empire came to Corinth, and its citizens were exposed to many different ideas about philosophy and religion. Paul's attempt to reinforce his teaching amid their widespread exposure to competing ideas and beliefs impacted the Corinthian church to the point of their questioning what they had been taught.

2. Why does Paul stress the resurrection as a part of a tradition that had been passed down to him?

Paul wants to ensure the Corinthians do not view the resurrection as an idea of Paul's creation. Paul wanted the church to understand what was most central to faith in Christ.

3. Why Paul does use Jewish illustrations to teach a Gentile audience about the resurrection?

Paul uses Jewish illustrations to teach lessons about the resurrection to further connect Gentile churches with their Jewish brothers and sisters through Christ. The Church is born within Judaism. Yet, as it spreads out among the Gentiles, it becomes less influenced by ideas centered around Judaism, but never cuts itself off from the witness of God's actions among the Jews.

Home Daily Devotional Readings

April 13–19, 2020

Monday	Tuesday	Wednesday	Thursday	Friday	Saturday	Sunday
Mordecai Refuses to Bow to Haman	Haman Sets Decree to Destroy the Jews	Haman Builds Gallows to Hang Mordecai	Decree against Jews Struck Down	Festival of Purim Established	Mordecai Advances Welfare of the Jews	Esther's Plea and Haman's Punishment
Esther 3:1–6	Esther 3:7–11	Esther 5:9–14	Esther 8:3–8, 16–17	Esther 9:18–23, 29–32	Esther 10:1–3	Esther 7:1–10

Injustice Will Be Punished

Adult Topic:
Justice Prevails

Background Scripture:
Esther 3; 5; 7

Esther 7:1–10

King James Version

SO the king and Haman came to banquet with Esther the queen.

2 And the king said again unto Esther on the second day at the banquet of wine, What is thy petition, queen Esther? and it shall be granted thee: and what is thy request? and it shall be performed, even to the half of the kingdom.

3 Then Esther the queen answered and said, If I have found favour in thy sight, O king, and if it please the king, let my life be given me at my petition, and my people at my request:

4 For we are sold, I and my people, to be destroyed, to be slain, and to perish. But if we had been sold for bondmen and bondwomen, I had held my tongue, although the enemy could not countervail the king's damage.

5 Then the king Ahasuerus answered and said unto Esther the queen, Who is he, and where is he, that durst presume in his heart to do so?

6 And Esther said, The adversary and enemy is this wicked Haman. Then Haman was afraid before the king and the queen.

7 And the king arising from the banquet of wine in his wrath went into the palace garden: and Haman stood up to make request for his life to Esther the queen; for he saw that there was evil determined against him by the king.

8 Then the king returned out of the palace garden into the place of the banquet of wine; and Haman was fallen upon the bed whereon Esther was. Then said the king, Will he force

New Revised Standard Version

SO the king and Haman went in to feast with Queen Esther.

2 On the second day, as they were drinking wine, the king again said to Esther, "What is your petition, Queen Esther? It shall be granted you. And what is your request? Even to the half of my kingdom, it shall be fulfilled."

3 Then Queen Esther answered, "If I have won your favor, O king, and if it pleases the king, let my life be given me—that is my petition—and the lives of my people—that is my request.

4 For we have been sold, I and my people, to be destroyed, to be killed, and to be annihilated. If we had been sold merely as slaves, men and women, I would have held my peace; but no enemy can compensate for this damage to the king."

5 Then King Ahasuerus said to Queen Esther, "Who is he, and where is he, who has presumed to do this?"

6 Esther said, "A foe and enemy, this wicked Haman!" Then Haman was terrified before the king and the queen.

7 The king rose from the feast in wrath and went into the palace garden, but Haman stayed to beg his life from Queen Esther, for he saw that the king had determined to destroy him.

8 When the king returned from the palace garden to the banquet hall, Haman had thrown himself on the couch where Esther was reclining; and the king said, "Will he even assault

MAIN THOUGHT: So they hanged Haman on the gallows that he had prepared for Mordecai. Then was the king's wrath pacified. (Esther 7:10, KJV)

Esther 7:1–10

King James Version

the queen also before me in the house? As the word went out of king's mouth, they covered Haman's face.

9 And Harbonah, one of the chamberlains, said before the king, Behold also, the gallows fifty cubits high, which Haman had made for Mordecai, who spoken good for the king, standeth in the house of Haman. Then the king said, Hang him thereon.

10 So they hanged Haman on the gallows that he had prepared for Mordecai. Then was the king's wrath pacified.

New Revised Standard Version

the queen in my presence, in my own house?" As the words left the mouth of the king, they covered Haman's face.

9 Then Harbona, one of the eunuchs in attendance on the king, said, "Look, the very gallows that Haman has prepared for Mordecai, whose word saved the king, stands at Haman's house, fifty cubits high." And the king said, "Hang him on that."

10 So they hanged Haman on the gallows that he had prepared for Mordecai. Then the anger of the king abated.

LESSON SETTING

Time: 486–465 B.C.
Place: Persian Capital, Susa

LESSON OUTLINE

I. **The King's Question (Esther 7:1–2)**
II. **The Courage to Speak (Esther 7:3–7)**
III. **Haman's Fate (Esther 7:8–10)**

Unifying Principle

Ignoble people often seem to attain great power and wealth. What evidence is there that people will receive the recompense their evil deeds deserve? The story of Esther's triumph over Haman provides assurances that evil does not prevail.

Introduction

The book of Esther is unique in many aspects. First, Esther is one of only two books of the Bible named for a woman. Second, the book of Esther makes no direct mention of the name of God, nor does the storyline reference the covenant to remind exiles of their relationship to Yahweh. A primary character in the book appears to be Mordecai, the relative and apparent foster parent to Esther. Some translations refer to him as Esther's uncle, while others refer to him as her cousin. She obviously has high regard for her elder, as Esther allows him to direct her in what she should do. Mordecai guides her carefully; however, it is actually Haman's disregard for Mordecai that puts into action the plans that ultimately lead to Haman's demise on the gallows he had built for Mordecai.

Jealousy, racial hatred, and abuse of power all are critical parts of the Esther narrative. Haman has no idea the queen is of Jewish descent because Esther has kept her identity hidden until the time when she needs to expose it to deliver her people. Hiding in plain sight was the source of deliverance that God had arranged for a people threatened by an abuse of power and racial hatred. Esther had been fully prepared for the day when she had to exercise courage and take a daring step for the sake of her people. Justice prevails in the lives of Esther and her people because of a God who is concerned about justice.

Exposition

I. The King's Question (Esther 7:1–2)

The scene where the king asks Esther what she desires is a banquet that Esther has prepared for the king and Haman. It is the second of such banquets that Esther has hosted for the king and Haman. Before the first banquet, Esther took the risk of going before the king without first being summoned by him. This action could have led to Esther's death because Persian law did not allow anyone, even the queen, to come before the king without being summoned first. Only if the king agreed to see a person, as indicated by waving his royal scepter, would the person be spared.

During the first banquet, Esther requests that the king and Haman return the following day for a second feast. In the second banquet scene, Esther again arranges for Haman, the enemy of her people, to be present. Haman is unaware of Esther's true identity and believes he has been invited to dinner with the king and queen to receive some type of honor. The second banquet is when Esther will share her request with the king.

Esther plans her strategy well. She ensures her husband is in a relaxed mood from drinking wine (v. 2). She is slow to reveal her request, coaxing the king until he promises to give Esther up to half of the kingdom as a sign his commitment to honor the queen's request. The second banquet created the right setting for the king to affirm that commitment to Esther and for her to make her request known.

The law of timing is set into motion—the people, the situation, and the opportunity align. The law of timing allowed the queen's request to open the door for justice to come to a people under threat of extinction because of jealousy, racial hatred, and an abuse of power.

II. The Courage to Speak (Esther 7:3–7)

The king's request of Esther is made in the presence of Haman. If Esther makes her request known to the king, it will mean speaking in the presence of the enemy. Haman is not without power, and he is willing to use his power to influence the king. If Esther makes her request in Haman's presence, she will have to overcome any fear of what Haman may be able to do to harm her and her people.

Esther displays remarkable courage to expose her identity when her people are under the threat elimination. Courage to confront one's enemy with the truth comes from a conviction that God is on the side of truth. God is not a disinterested third party simply observing human affairs from a distance. God has placed His weight on the side of truth and justice. God supplies the courage Esther and all those like Esther have needed to speak truth to power.

When Esther does speak, she is careful to honor the king yet still make her condition known in ways that would move the king to act on her behalf. What confronts her people is worse than anything the Jews have ever experienced, including their enslavement and exile. Esther's own appearance in Susa is a direct result of the Exile. Esther also affirms that Jews have been sold. Not all Jews lived in the Persian Empire as a result of the Exile. Some Jews have been sold into slavery. However, what threatens the Jews now is complete annihilation because of ethnic and religious hatred and jealousy. If Haman's plans were to advance, not even the queen would be spared. Esther makes her situation and that of her people known, thus petitioning for the king's intervention. Esther contextualizes her request as if she already has found favor from the king. Assuming the king's favor begs the question of whether the king cares more for Esther than he does power and wealth. Haman has promised the king money in his plan to eliminate the Jews by taking the resources of his victims as spoils of war.

Esther's request is challenging on multiple fronts. First, the king is challenged as to whether or not he will protect his queen. The prestige of the royal family in the eyes of the citizens of the kingdom is under attack. Second, the king is challenged with a political concern. Will racial exclusion become the new way Persia governs all of its foreign citizens? Then, the king is challenged by the courage of a woman speaking truth to power. Will Esther's gender become a reason to disregard her request? Courage is not confined to a gender. God provided Esther the courage to speak.

III. Haman's Fate (Esther 7:8–10)

Upon hearing Haman's plot would mean the death of the queen and her people, King Xerxes (NRSV: Ahasuerus) is overwhelmed. He retreats to process what he has heard. Haman is a trusted advisor to Xerxes (Esther 3:1), and the king is uncertain how to respond when he hears the news.

While the king seeks to process the news from Esther, Haman immediately recognizes he is in peril and pleads for mercy from Esther. Haman is hopeful Esther will extend to him mercy he would deny Esther or her people. Esther remains silent on Haman's request.

Some scholars applaud Esther's courage to speak up and save her people, but question her lack of compassion for Haman. Because Esther is a woman, she is expected to behave in ways that reflect a conservative view of women as sympathetic and compassionate. Hebrew Bible scholar Dr. Sidnie White Crawford observes in *The Woman's Bible Commentary* that Esther is locked in a life-and-death struggle that is not of her making. The outcome seems to be either the life of the Jews or that of Haman. Were he to be spared, there are no guarantees Haman would repent of his hatred of the Jews and his attempt to make them suffer. Esther does not have the freedom of taking that chance. She allows justice to take its course.

When the king returns to the room and finds Haman in close quarters with the queen, he is enraged. It is doubtful Haman was making undue advances toward the queen, but the king's claim of such actions seals Haman's fate. The king is given to making snap judgments throughout the Esther narrative, and at the prompting of a servant, he decides to hang Haman on the gallows he had built for Mordecai.

Haman's death does not end the challenge facing the Jews because the king had signed a law to eliminate the Jews, and the law could not be changed. Thus, the king issued a new law that allowed the Jews to defend themselves against those who sought to eliminate them. Haman's fate made the new law possible and secured the Jews from being eliminated throughout the Persian Empire.

The Lesson Applied

Racial hatred, jealousy, and abuses of power have been part of human existence practically since the beginning of time. Distorted beliefs about ethnic superiority/inferiority have led to countless suffering worldwide. History records a wealth of such human abuses—from the slave trade in the Western world to the Holocaust and other acts of violence perpetrated for the purposes of genocide and ethnic cleansing in Eastern Europe, Bosnia and Herzegovina, and most recently, Rwanda. Whenever one group uses their position of power to oppress the less powerful, it violates the justice God desires for all people.

Prolonged injustice cannot succeed ultimately. God gives us the courage to fight injustice. Chosen ones among us will speak truth to power. Rosa Parks was a woman in the mold of Esther whose witness for justice ushered in a new world of freedom. According to the late theologian Dr. James Cone, God has taken sides in the battle of injustice, and God is on the side of the oppressed. Scores of men and women marched for freedom during the Civil Rights Movement, singing, "We Shall Overcome" as an expression of what God would do, even in the face of overwhelming odds. Justice will prevail because we are ruled by a just God who cares for the plight of the oppressed.

Let's Talk About It

1. Why did Haman despise Mordecai?

Haman hated Mordecai because of his religious convictions and his difference. Mordecai was not like others and could not be intimidated by Haman and his position of power.

2. Why did Esther have two banquets before asking the king what she wanted?

The first banquet was to get an audience with the king in attempt to determine how the king felt about Esther. The second banquet was held in order to make her case to the king. Esther makes her request known in the presence of both the king and her enemy, Haman.

3. Should Esther have shown mercy toward Haman?

Haman's continued influence in the kingdom might have continued to make life hard for Jews even if he did not have them killed. Personalities like Haman have the capacity to create a culture built upon hatred that can last for generations. Such was the case with Adolf Hitler. Although he has been dead for almost seventy-five years, his racist philosophies continue to infect and influence those who espouse racial supremacy today. Only the king could have given Haman mercy; the matter was out of Esther's hands.

Home Daily Devotional Readings

April 20–26, 2020

Monday	Tuesday	Wednesday	Thursday	Friday	Saturday	Sunday
Solomon Makes a Just Decision	Jesus Issues His Platform for Justice	The Year of Jubilee Established	A Light to the Nations	A New Vision for the People	Zion Welcomes the Redeemed Home	The Lord Brings the People Justice
1 Kings 3:16–28	Luke 4:14–21	Leviticus 25:8–17	Isaiah 49:1–7	Isaiah 61:1–7	Isaiah 62:5–12	Isaiah 61:8–11; 2:2–4

LESSON IX

APRIL 26, 2020

THE LORD LOVES JUSTICE

ADULT TOPIC:
WHAT GOES AROUND COMES AROUND

BACKGROUND SCRIPTURE:
ISAIAH 61:8—62:12

ISAIAH 61:8–11; 62:2–4

King James Version

FOR I the LORD love judgment, I hate robbery for burnt offering; and I will direct their work in truth, and I will make an everlasting covenant with them.

9 And their seed shall be known among the Gentiles, and their offspring among the people: all that see them shall acknowledge them, that they are the seed which the LORD hath blessed.

10 I will greatly rejoice in the LORD, my soul shall be joyful in my God; for he hath clothed me with the garments of salvation, he hath covered me with the robe of righteousness, as a bridegroom decketh himself with ornaments, and as a bride adorneth herself with her jewels.

11 For as the earth bringeth forth her bud, and as the garden causeth the things that are sown in it to spring forth; so the LORD God will cause righteousness and praise to spring forth before all the nations.

• • • 62:2–4 • • •

2 And the Gentiles shall see thy righteousness, and all kings thy glory: and thou shalt be called by a new name, which the mouth of the LORD shall name.

3 Thou shalt also be a crown of glory in the hand of the LORD, and a royal diadem in the hand of thy God.

4 Thou shalt no more be termed Forsaken; neither shall thy land any more be termed Desolate: but thou shalt be called Hephzibah, and thy land Beulah: for the LORD delighteth in thee, and thy land shall be married.

New Revised Standard Version

FOR I the LORD love justice, I hate robbery and wrongdoing; I will faithfully give them their recompense, and I will make an everlasting covenant with them.

9 Their descendants shall be known among the nations, and their offspring among the peoples; all who see them shall acknowledge that they are a people whom the LORD has blessed.

10 I will greatly rejoice in the LORD, my whole being shall exult in my God; for he has clothed me with the garments of salvation, he has covered me with the robe of righteousness, as a bridegroom decks himself with a garland, and as a bride adorns herself with her jewels.

11 For as the earth brings forth its shoots, and as a garden causes what is sown in it to spring up, so the LORD God will cause righteousness and praise to spring up before all the nations.

• • • 62:2–4 • • •

2 The nations shall see your vindication, and all the kings your glory; and you shall be called by a new name that the mouth of the LRD will give.

3 You shall be a crown of beauty in the hand of the LORD, and a royal diadem in the hand of your God.

4 You shall no more be termed Forsaken, and your land shall no more be termed Desolate; but you shall be called My Delight Is in Her, and your land Married; for the LORD delights in you, and your land shall be married.

MAIN THOUGHT: For I the LORD love judgment, I hate robbery for burnt offering; and I will direct their work in truth, and I will make an everlasting covenant with them. (Isaiah 61:8, KJV)

LESSON SETTING

Time: 539 B.C.
Place: Judah

LESSON OUTLINE

I. **God's Promises to a Just Nation (Isaiah 61:8–9)**
II. **Rejoicing in Salvation (Isaiah 61:10–11)**
III. **A New Position and a New Name (Isaiah 62:2–4a)**

UNIFYING PRINCIPLE

When people feel helpless and angry, they seek help from others. What hope is there that the conditions of the powerless will be addressed? God loves justice, and Isaiah affirms that the righteous will be vindicated.

INTRODUCTION

Today's lesson is from a portion of what scholars call Third Isaiah, or Trito-Isaiah. It is widely believed by scholars that Trito-Isaiah was written during the return of the exiles to Jerusalem to rebuild the temple. Cyrus, the king of Persia, issued an edict in 538 B.C. that allowed for rebuilding the temple, and he gave back the temple vessels that were carried to Babylon when Jerusalem was captured. By 537 B.C., the returning exiles had laid the foundation for the new temple before the work ceased due to economic and political uncertainty within the Persian Empire.

Claus Westermann in *The Old Testament Library: Isaiah 40–66* (Westminster John Knox Press, 1966) states the nucleus of Third Isaiah, as contained in chapters 60–62, is a message of salvation. The proof of salvation is in the return of the exiles home to Jerusalem. Israel's time of punishment had come to an end and new dawn had come—a time filled with hope and possibility. In this season of hope, with the return from exile, Israel is to remember the importance of justice and how actions of injustice played a role in their exile. God desires justice to be the foundation for the nation. Israel is never to forget the God whom they serve loves justice.

EXPOSITION

I. GOD'S PROMISES TO A JUST NATION (ISAIAH 61:8–9)

The promises of God to a just nation begin with God's declaration to judge those that had abused Israel. Not even a nation that served as God's instrument for punishing Israel will be able to avoid the judgment of God for their treatment of Israel. The witness that God loves justice is reflected in a deity that will not turn the other way at signs of injustice that take place in His created world. Wrongdoing is never justified with the God who loves justice. As Judge of those who promoted injustice, God will pay them back for their misdeeds. Injustice will not go unpunished. Whether committed at the hands of Israel or Babylon, God will punish injustice. The recompense of God is not limited to punishment of those who have acted with injustice. God's recompense also includes the restoration of Israel. The time of suffering is now over, and God will reestablish His covenant with His people. Israel is reminded of the faithfulness of God in this act of restoration for a nation that once lived in exile.

The everlasting covenant is the covenant God made with Abraham. Just as God had promised to bless Abraham and his seed, God would uphold that promise with the descendants of Abraham who have returned to Israel. What Israel had endured during its season of exile, and having been able to return home to rebuild the temple, would be the indication to surrounding nations of God's favor upon Israel. The nation did not have the power within itself to overthrow Persian rule. Neither could Israel have anticipated finding favor with Cyrus to the extent he would allow them to return home and rebuild the temple.

The temple, for Israel, is not only a religious symbol and institution, the temple also is a social and political symbol that spoke to Israel's sole allegiance to Yahweh. The act of rebuilding the temple reinforced religious fervor that could have manifested in open rebellion to the Persian Empire. However, despite all these risks, Cyrus allowed the exiles to return home and rebuild their most important national symbol. Third Isaiah interprets these actions as a clear sign God has given Israel favor among the nations. In turn, these nations acknowledge the hand of God is with Israel. God's promise of a just nation is that all nations will know there is something different about Israel, and that difference is their God.

II. Rejoicing in Salvation (Isaiah 61:10–11)

This section of Third Isaiah is a hymn of praise and thanksgiving for the act of God's deliverance of a people who once lived in exile. The hymn is seen as the natural response to the recognition of what God had done. The hymn places the focus upon God. There is nothing Israel has done to cause Cyprus to change his mind about conquest. The people fully recognize God has moved on Israel's behalf and brought salvation and deliverance to His people. Israel has a new status because of God's actions on their behalf. The change in status—from exiles to free persons able to fully participate in their religious practice without interference from the Persian Empire—is reason to rejoice.

As the prophet continues to offer praise and thanksgiving, he uses the imagery of clothing to further reveal the change in Israel's status. To be clothed with garments of salvation, covered with the robe of righteousness, decked with garland, and provided jewels all are signs of being held in honor. The ancient world placed a high value on being held in positions of honor. To their understanding, honor revealed a privileged class that was afforded a lifestyle not available to everyone. Honor reflected access to power and opportunity.

The prophet rejoices because Israel's deliverance from exile has brought honor to the people. Honor also is the opposite of what Israel experienced while in exile. Because of their ouster from their homeland, Israel experienced the shame of a nation whose God had allowed its enemy to be used as a tool of their punishment. While in exile, Israel was forced to compromise its culture, its religious practices, and its community values, which further brought shame upon the people. This hymn of thanksgiving is the prophet's way of celebrating Israel's return to honor because their God had delivered them.

Israel's elevated status of honor opens new possibilities that are described as a young plant just breaking the soil. As much as Israel has to celebrate already, what has happened is just the beginning of what is possible because their God is working on their behalf. They have reasons to continue rejoicing. There will be new signs of God's blessings that are yet to come—but the sign of coming blessings is reason enough to rejoice and praise God in the current moment.

III. A New Position and a New Name (Isaiah 62:2–4a)

Israel's new status, which has come as the result of returning home from exile, introduces other signs of newness. These signs actually are part of the historic witness God had planned for Israel in the promise made to Abraham—that the nations would recognize Israel and call it blessed. God's plan was for Israel to be a light to the nations of the world, teaching them there is but one true God (see Isa. 42:6). Israel's covenant relationship with Yahweh was intended to order a society built upon a social and religious ethic of justice—one that would show pagan nations how to be just in their relationships within their own communities. When Israel lives up to the principles of justice that God planned for them, its righteousness will shine so brightly the nations of the world will not be able to avoid its witness nor deny its power. Restoration to their homeland now provides the opportunity for Israel to fulfill its mission of justice. Israel is to make sure they take advantage of this new opportunity, lest their failure leads to a second removal from the land God promised.

In this new position of opportunity to be a light to the nations, the prophet declares God will give the nation a new name. There is no actual name given by the prophet to reflect this change in status. Westermann states, "the contrast evidenced by the old and the new names is due to God's having once turned away from Jerusalem and his turning toward her now." There indeed may be no literal new name, but declaring a new name becomes a way to understand a new identity that has been made possible by God's grace toward Israel. The nation can no longer conduct itself in the ways it did in the past; but rather, it must reflect a commitment to this new identity built upon a commitment to justice in the community because its God loves justice.

This new self-understanding and identity allows Israel to put its mistakes behind it. In the past, they were known as a forsaken people because the land their God had given them lay desolate because of their idolatry and disobedience. However, the Lord now has restored them and committed Himself to using Israel as an instrument of grace to the nations of the world. God will hold Israel in His hand as a royal scepter, displaying the sovereign rule of God in the world. *The Old Testament Commentary* by Keli Dectushie states: "Zion is not the ancient crown which the Eternal wears upon His head, but the crown wrought out of time which He holds in His hands because He is seen in Zion by all creation. Never again will Jerusalem be called the forsaken city for the blessing of God will reside with his people in the holy city of God."

The nation is ready to put the badge of shame behind them and move forward with a new identity. It will be the light that shines the justice of a just God to the nations that do not know Him. It will be a living example of the God of redemption, for He has redeemed His people, bringing them from shame to honor.

The Lesson Applied

God is always able to bring about the change we seek, even when the odds appear to be stacked against us. God moved upon the heart of the king of Persia to allow a conquered people exiled to a hostile land to return home and rebuild the communities that had been destroyed during the Babylonian invasion of Israel. But then God took further steps to redeem His people. Israel had no resources except those that Cyrus provided, yet they were able to return to Jerusalem and establish their communities anew. Because of God's commitment to justice and His desire to see the world operate justly, the conqueror of Israel's oppressor provided the means for its liberation.

We may never know who God will use or how God will use them to be instruments of deliverance and blessing. All we can know by faith is that God often uses unexpected participants, and sometimes even hostile forces, to be our tools for blessings. We must accept God's discipline when He renders it, as He demands justice. Nevertheless, we can rejoice, as Israel did, as His loving mercy brings restorative power to accomplish His purposes.

Let's Talk About It

1. **Why does the prophet use the metaphors about new beginnings, such as a young plant coming from the soil?**

   The ancient world made use of metaphors to draw mental images to help people visualize events or the possibilities for life. People usually are able to relate to what they can see. The use of metaphors about new beginnings helped Israel visualize its own new beginning as a nation. They could see themselves as more than a people wearing a badge of shame.

2. **Do the concepts of shame and honor carry the same impact today as they did in Isaiah's world?**

   Given the lack of civility in the public square of the nation's political debate and growing violence in houses of faith, our world appears to be moving in a direction that is absent of shame as a means of impacting behavior.

3. **What does it mean in today's lesson to be "blessed by God"?**

   The blessing of God is defined here as restoration to the land as well as to the nation's role of being a witness of justice for the world. Justice is a critical virtue for God, and His people are to demonstrate to the world what it means to act in just relationships that build peace. No justice, no peace.

Home Daily Devotional Readings
April 27–May 3, 2020

Monday	Tuesday	Wednesday	Thursday	Friday	Saturday	Sunday
God Promises Restoration of Israel's Fortunes	God Will Shepherd the People	God Will Strengthen the People	Christ's Forgiveness of Israel's Sins	Leaders, Priests, and Prophets Don't Listen	God Will Preserve a Remnant	Rejoice in God's Glory and Salvation
Deuteronomy 30:1–6	Ezekiel 34:11–16	Zechariah 10:6–12	Acts 5:27–32	Zephaniah 3:1–7	Zephaniah 3:8–13	Zephaniah 3:14–20

A VISION OF RESTORATION

ADULT TOPIC:
THE RETURN OF JOY

BACKGROUND SCRIPTURE:
ZEPHANIAH 3

ZEPHANIAH 3:14–20

King James Version

SING, O daughter of Zion; shout, O Israel; be glad and rejoice with all the heart, O daughter of Jerusalem.

15 The LORD hath taken away thy judgments, he hath cast out thine enemy: the king of Israel, even the LORD, is in the midst of thee: thou shalt not see evil any more.

16 In that day it shall be said to Jerusalem, Fear thou not: and to Zion, Let not thine hands be slack.

17 The LORD thy God in the midst of thee is mighty; he will save, he will rejoice over thee with joy; he will rest in his love, he will joy over thee with singing.

18 I will gather them that are sorrowful for the solemn assembly, who are of thee, to whom the reproach of it was a burden.

19 Behold, at that time I will undo all that afflict thee: and I will save her that halteth, and gather her that was driven out; and I will get them praise and fame in every land where they have been put to shame.

20 At that time will I bring you again, even in the time that I gather you: for I will make you a name and a praise among all people of the earth, when I turn back your captivity before your eyes, saith the LORD.

New Revised Standard Version

SING aloud, O daughter Zion; shout, O Israel! Rejoice and exult with all your heart,

15 The LORD has taken away the judgments against you, he has turned away your enemies. The king of Israel, the LORD, is in your midst; you shall fear disaster no more.

16 On that day it shall be said to Jerusalem: Do not fear, O Zion; do not let your hands grow weak.

17 The LORD, your God, is in your midst, a warrior who gives victory; he will rejoice over you with gladness, he will renew you in his love; he will exult over you with loud singing

18 as on a day of festival. I will remove disaster from you, so that you will not bear reproach for it.

19 I will deal with all your oppressors at that time. And I will save the lame and gather the outcast, and I will change their shame into praise and renown in all the earth.

20 At that time I will bring you home, at the time when I gather you; for I will make you renowned and praised among all the peoples of the earth, when I restore your fortunes before your eyes, says the LORD.

MAIN THOUGHT: Behold, at that time I will undo all that afflict thee: and I will save her that halteth, and gather her that was driven out; and I will get them praise and fame in every land where they have been put to shame. (Zephaniah 3:19, KJV)

LESSON SETTING

Time: 630 B.C.
Place: Jerusalem

LESSON OUTLINE

I. From Lament to Praise (Zephaniah 3:14–15)
II. The Promise of Victory of Every Foe (Zephaniah 3:16–18)
III. The Blessing of Restoration (Zephaniah 3:19–20)

UNIFYING PRINCIPLE

Oppression of the poor and powerless seems pervasive in our world. Is there any hope for reversal of this condition? The prophet Zephaniah proclaims the day of restoration when God's people shall be returned to righteousness, justice, and peace.

INTRODUCTION

Zephaniah is the ninth of the twelve Minor Prophets. The prophet's full name is Zephaniah ben Cushi. The reference to Cush indicates the prophet has African ancestry. Zephaniah lived during the reign of the righteous young King Josiah (from 640 to 609 B.C.). However, the worship of false gods prevailed in Jerusalem at the time, and Zephaniah warned of impending destruction in the day of the Lord.

Zephaniah cautions that the day of the Lord would not be one of celebration but rather a day of judgment. Judah would not be spared, and their covenant relationship with Yahweh would not make them exempt from divine judgment. Zephaniah encourages his community to repent, to restore justice, and to embrace humility. Although judgment could not be avoided, God was willing to restore His people and return them to land He had given them.

In Zephaniah, a remnant theology emerges. Remnant theology says God will not be left without a witness of faithfulness to His people and even in the midst of judgment there is hope for the future. Zephaniah provides an example of what Gerhard von Rad said in his work, *The Message of the Prophets* (HarperCollins, 1972): "The prophets never spoke of judgment without pointing to a future with hope because of the faithfulness of Yahweh to his people—his mercy endures forever."

EXPOSITION

I. FROM LAMENT TO PRAISE (ZEPHANIAH 3:14–15)

The prophet tells the community to sing and praise God because judgment will not be a permanent condition. God will again move with grace and mercy among the people, removing their hardship and replacing it with joy. Zephaniah's words are similar to Isaiah's in that they speak tenderly to Jerusalem and cry to her that her warfare is over. God's judgment is never intended to be permanent; but rather, judgment comes to bring repentance and return to God. When the judgment has passed, there is no need for further lament. The prophet declares God is in their midst (v. 16). What greater assurance can any believer have than to know God is with them?

The call for praise is a call to acknowledge God for who He is and for the deliverance He has wrought for His people. The entire community is called upon to participate in this act of praise because everyone has benefited from the blessing of God's deliverance. The ritual of praise is a reminder to the community of God's gracious actions on their behalf. The deliverance that will be enjoyed is not the result of Judah's ability to obtain it on its own merit. Instead, deliverance comes as the result of a God who would not forget His people nor deny His promise to their forebear, Abraham.

Whereas much of Zephaniah has focused upon the day of the Lord as a day of judgment, God is still present and active on the behalf of His people. That divine activity is reason enough for Judah to praise God.

Zephaniah identifies several ways God will prove His actions on behalf of the people. The Lord will remove Judah's enemies. The Lord will live among the people, and all of the people's troubles will be over. The actions of God will address every area that afflicts Judah that gives witness to judgment. The new reality for Judah will be one of blessing and hope. The blessings and hope that come from God are reasons to praise Him. The sentence of judgment has been removed, making a new and hopeful future possible. Judah will be free again to live in the land God had provided for them and worship the God who made it possible for them to be free from danger. God changes their lament to praise, their judgment to restoration, and their despair to hope.

II. The Promise of Victory over Every Foe (Zephaniah 3:16–18)

The admonishment not to fear is an indication of God's presence among the people to bring them victory over every foe. The threat and power of the powerful Babylonian Empire was more than Judah could withstand alone. Israel to the north already had collapsed under the conquest of Assyria, and without divine intervention the same would happen to Judah.

Zephaniah speaks of a time to come when Judah will no longer fear the power of other nations to overtake them by conquest. God's presence will provide Judah the strength they need. They will no longer be looked upon as weak. "Do not let your hands grow weak" (v. 16, NRSV) is Zephaniah's way of telling Judah not to give in to the temptation to see itself as a nation without resources of support. For the hands to grow weary would be to deny the power of God to provide and fulfill His promise of salvation. The Lord's salvation will empower Judah in ways that will ensure its victory. In the language of a battle, Zephaniah calls God a warrior. The Hebrew word for warrior is *gibbor,* and it is used to describe actions related to the military. The God in Judah's midst is the God who fights for Judah and banishes every foe.

The promise of victory is reason enough to for continued praise. Judah is to rejoice and be glad. God's actions require a community response in recognition of what God has done. The entire community is to act differently, and by doing so they embrace what God has done in ways that return them to just actions with one another. Achieving victory is always invigorating. One of the effects of Judah's victory over every foe is that the people will be renewed. God's renewal of Judah is one that brings the nation back to covenant relationship with God. Judah is reminded of how they are to be different from the pagan nations around them because they have been set aside for God's purpose. The people of Judah are not free to do as they please because they belong to God. Through renewal, Judah is reminded of its responsibility to God and to one another. Renewal will make Judah aware of the depths of God's love for His people, and this love is to always be celebrated.

III. The Blessing of Restoration (Zephaniah 3:19–20)

The final words of Zephaniah focus upon themes of restoration and redemption. Zephaniah's concern about restoration places the outcast at center stage. God will gather the lame and the outcast and give them a station of honor. The lame and the outcast reveal God's concern about justice and that the needs of the most vulnerable be met. God's restoration will leave no one out. Even those who may not appear to be able to contribute to the well-being of the community have a place of protection under God's umbrella of love. God establishes a societal safety net; He elevates the vulnerable and protects them.

The image of God restoring the vulnerable carries with it the faithful shepherd who leads his flock to where none go missing. In John 10:11-18, Jesus identifies Himself as the Good Shepherd who will not abandon them, but rather, will lay down His life for His sheep. He cares for the vulnerable over whom He has been given charge. In biblical times, the shepherd tended his flock both day and night. They were never left unprotected. At night, the shepherd would gather the sheep into a sheepfold for their protection. The sheepfold was a pen, cave, or area backed by stone walls. Since there were no doors, the shepherd often would sleep or sit at the opening, ready to protect his sheep from predators.

When the vulnerable are provided for, it reveals the inclusive provision of God in leading His people. The restoration God promises makes room for everyone. God's promise of restoration involves giving back what was lost in past judgments. God gives Judah back the land from which they had been exiled for seventy years. The promises made by Zephaniah find their fulfillment in the return of the exiles after seven decades of bondage in Babylon.

God's promise of restoration includes the fortunes of Judah. The nation's captivity by conquest had meant the loss of their wealth as well as their freedom. Yet, when God returns Judah to its homeland, He restores the lost wealth. God's final promise of restoration is the return of Judah as a nation of honor among the nations of the world. Judah will no be identified as a people in bondage. The blessing of God will establish Judah as nation of honor. Their past shame will have been removed and the fulfillment of restoration will be seen in the reversals God has orchestrated. Their restoration will occur in the plain sight of all the nations, and nothing would be able to suppress or prevent it. Because Judah's restoration will take place in plain sight, the glory and honor will belong to God for what He has done.

The Lesson Applied

A key component of the lesson today is restoration and how God makes it possible in spite of conditions and circumstances that seek to prevent it. Our nation needs the restoration that reminds us that all persons have value and the most vulnerable need protection. Zephaniah makes clear that when the least are provided for, it assures no one will be left behind. Restoration always involves a return to a set of values, to some prior condition that was beneficial, or the recovery of which provides meaning and purpose to a community. For the United States to truly be one nation under God will require the restoration of the value and worth of all persons, regardless of their color, gender, or class. When this restoration comes, our nation will exemplify what the founders had mind with the American experiment.

Our move toward being a just nation will not be without God's blessings. The exile had caused Judah to doubt God was still with them. They questioned whether God had abandoned them (despite the fact they had abandoned His demand for justice). Zephaniah affirms God stands in the midst of a just people (v. 14).

When we endure hardship, whether of our own making or at the hands of another, we tend to question whether God has abandoned us. However, like the poem *Footprints in the Sand*, when we look back we can see God's presence. He does not exempt us from trouble or discipline; nevertheless, He does not abandon us in times of trouble.

Let's Talk About It

1. **What may be some reasons why Zephaniah's African ancestry is seldom mentioned? Could his heritage possibly have affected his worldview?**

   Most biblical scholarship avoids racial identity as being significant to biblical interpretation; however, Dr. Cain Hope Felder of Howard Divinity School disagrees. Race, he asserts, provides a social construct for understanding God's presence in the world. If not significant during his time, certainly the acknowledgement of Zephaniah as a man of color who proclaims the liberating power of God in times of oppression offers hope to persons of color in the struggle.

2. **What role do enemies play in Zephaniah's prophecy?**

   The enemies are the nation state that God uses to discipline Judah for its lack of fidelity to Yahweh. Enemies also are the persons whom God deals with to restore Judah and reestablish the bonds of covenant loyalty.

3. **Why does singing play such a significant part of what Zephaniah admonishes the community to do?**

   Singing is praise that celebrates the power of God at work among the people. Singing gives witness to the life we hope to receive and gives glory to God for what He has done.

Home Daily Devotional Readings

May 4–10, 2020

Monday	Tuesday	Wednesday	Thursday	Friday	Saturday	Sunday
God's Worldwide Covenant with Abraham	A New Covenant of the Heart	Divided Peoples to Become One	Just Living in Church and World	Cultivate Peaceful and Just Relations	Joyful Feasts Draw Newcomers	Enjoy Fruits of Peace and Justice
Genesis 12:1–8	Jeremiah 31:31–34	Ezekiel 37:15–23	Romans 12:9–21	1 Thessalonians 5:12–22	Zechariah 8:18–23	Zechariah 8:1–8, 11–17

PEACE AND JUSTICE REIGN

ADULT TOPIC:
A NEW DAY IS COMING!

BACKGROUND SCRIPTURE:
ZECHARIAH 8

ZECHARIAH 8:1–8, 11–17

King James Version

AGAIN the word of the LORD of hosts came to me, saying,

2 Thus saith the LORD of hosts; I was jealous for Zion with great jealousy, and I was jealous for her with great fury.

3 Thus saith the LORD; I am returned unto Zion, and will dwell in the midst of Jerusalem: and Jerusalem shall be called a city of truth; and the mountain of the LORD of hosts the holy mountain.

4 Thus saith the LORD of hosts; There shall yet old men and old women dwell in the streets of Jerusalem, and every man with his staff in his hand for very age.

5 And the streets of the city shall be full of boys and girls playing in the streets thereof.

6 Thus saith the LORD of hosts; If it be marvellous in the eyes of the remnant of this people in these days, should it also be marvellous in mine eyes? saith the LORD of hosts.

7 Thus saith the LORD of hosts; Behold, I will save my people from the east country, and from the west country;

8 And I will bring them, and they shall dwell in the midst of Jerusalem: and they shall be my people, and I will be their God, in truth and in righteousness.

• • • • • •

11 But now I will not be unto the residue of this people as in the former days, saith the LORD of hosts.

12 For the seed shall be prosperous; the vine shall give her fruit, and the ground shall give her increase, and the heavens shall give their

New Revised Standard Version

THE word of the LORD of hosts came to me, saying:

2 Thus says the LORD of hosts: I am jealous for Zion with great jealousy, and I am jealous for her with great wrath.

3 Thus says the LORD: I will return to Zion, and will dwell in the midst of Jerusalem; Jerusalem shall be called the faithful city, and the mountain of the LORD of hosts shall be called the holy mountain.

4 Thus says the LORD of hosts: Old men and old women shall again sit in the streets of Jerusalem, each with staff in hand because of their great age.

5 And the streets of the city shall be full of boys and girls playing in its streets.

6 Thus says the LORD of hosts: Even though it seems impossible to the remnant of this people in these days, should it also seem impossible to me, says the LORD of hosts?

7 Thus says the LORD of hosts: I will save my people from the east country and from the west country;

8 and I will bring them to live in Jerusalem. They shall be my people and I will be their God, in faithfulness and in righteousness.

• • • • • •

11 But now I will not deal with the remnant of this people as in the former days, says the LORD of hosts.

12 For there shall be a sowing of peace; the vine shall yield its fruit, the ground shall give its produce, and the skies shall give their dew;

MAIN THOUGHT: So again have I thought in these days to do well unto Jerusalem and to the house of Judah: fear ye not. (Zechariah 8:15, KJV)

King James Version

dew; and I will cause the remnant of this people to possess all these things.
13 And it shall come to pass, that as ye were a curse among the heathen, O house of Judah, and house of Israel; so will I save you, and ye shall be a blessing: fear not, but let your hands be strong.
14 For thus saith the Lord of hosts; As I thought to punish you, when your fathers provoked me to wrath, saith the Lord of hosts, and I repented not:
15 So again have I thought in these days to do well unto Jerusalem and to the house of Judah: fear ye not.
16 These are the things that ye shall do; Speak ye every man the truth to his neighbour; execute the judgment of truth and peace in your gates:
17 And let none of you imagine evil in your hearts against his neighbour; and love no false oath: for all these are things that I hate, saith the Lord.

New Revised Standard Version

and I will cause the remnant of this people to possess all these things.
13 Just as you have been a cursing among the nations, O house of Judah and house of Israel, so I will save you and you shall be a blessing. Do not be afraid, but let your hands be strong.

14 For thus says the Lord of hosts: Just as I purposed to bring disaster upon you, when your ancestors provoked me to wrath, and I did not relent, says the Lord of hosts,
15 so again I have purposed in these days to do good to Jerusalem and to the house of Judah; do not be afraid.
16 These are the things that you shall do: Speak the truth to one another, render in your gates judgments that are true and make for peace,
17 do not devise evil in your hearts against one another, and love no false oath; for all these are things that I hate, says the Lord.

LESSON SETTING

Time: 520 B.C.
Place: Judah

LESSON OUTLINE

I. God's Promised Return to Jerusalem (Zechariah 8:1–3)
II. God's Blessings to His People (Zechariah 8:4–8)
III. God's Love Multiplied (Zechariah 8:11–17)

Unifying Principle

Sometimes people respond to evil conditions in the world with a sense of hopelessness, regret, and doom. Where can they find motivation for continuing? The prophet Zechariah delivers God's promise of a new world of peace and prosperity for God's people.

Introduction

Zechariah is the eleventh of the twelve Minor Prophets. Zechariah ministers to a people who have returned to Judah from exile. The small band of returnees started the work of rebuilding their community, and their first efforts focused on the temple. However, the progress of rebuilding fades as Judah gives in to the ridicule and oppression they experience from neighboring nations. Zechariah calls his community to return to God and offers a vision of hope in the work of rebuilding.

Many scholars believe the book of Zechariah consists of perhaps three different writers. The book is attributed to one prophet; however it is clearly separated into two parts in style and content First

Zechariah (chapters 1–8) is written with the return from Babylonian Exile as background, and the name of the prophet and the dates of his prophecy are clear. The writings of Second Zechariah (chapters 9–14) are of an eschatological nature and are written in an obscure style with allusions to unclear backgrounds. First Zechariah's work is closely aligned with Haggai and its focus upon the completion of the Temple restoration project in order to restore proper worship. First Zechariah gives a number of visions. The oracles that Zechariah offers as a result of his visions are extended sermons that provide inspiration and hope in the community's rebuilding efforts. God has promised a new day that will be filled with blessings and possibility for a fragile community. God's new day will usher in a reversal of Judah's circumstance. The small community of exiles will know the joy of an expanding community where both young and old dwell in peace and prosperity.

Exposition

I. God's Promised Return to Jerusalem (Zechariah 8:1–3)

God's return to Jerusalem restores the fallen city as the place of God's dwelling. Traditional lore says when Jerusalem fell to the Babylonian invasion and the temple vessels were removed as trophies of Israel's defeat, the Spirit of the Lord vacated the Temple and the city. Zechariah now states God's promise to restore the city by dwelling there once again. Jerusalem again will be the place where the presence of God is made known among the people of God. He restores Jerusalem because of His love for the city. Zechariah interprets God's love as being not reserved for people only; God can and does love places. Jerusalem is the city where God has chosen as the place to make His name known.

The returning exiles could not envision what Zechariah was saying about God or Jerusalem given how ruined the city was and the small number of inhabitants that had been permitted to return. Yet, what appears impossible for the returning exiles is not impossible for God. He is able to accomplish whatever He wills. God is not limited by the constraints of human achievement. Whereas God's power is not in question for Zechariah, what the prophet seeks to communicate to the returning exiles is God's love for the city. Because of His love, God is willing to do what may appear impossible. God's love is revealed in His power, and God's power is used to redeem and restore the city. The restoration of Jerusalem by the love and power of God causes the city to be known as the Faithful City. The emphasis of *faithful* is reflected in what God will do for a city that was in ruins. He will reverse the fortunes of the city and make it glorious again.

II. God's Blessings to His People (Zechariah 8:4–8)

Zechariah's vision of God's blessings to His people in the city He has restored is multigenerational. The vision of blessing begins with the elderly men and women having freedom to move about in the city without fear or opposition. The city square will be a place of activity that speaks to the life of the city. This view is upheld in contrast to a city that is now in ruins with only a few inhabitants, most of whom are of working age, healthy and well enough to travel and capable of manual labor. A city with elderly walking on canes suggests persons at the twilight of life with no ability to assist with the manual labor needed to rebuild the city. The point of Zechariah's vision is that this is the day that is coming. This is the day the builders are working toward, and God's promise is that the day will come. God will fulfill the day of their hopes and dreams.

The city streets also will have children playing again. The witness of children is important because it means the city and the people will continue to thrive as there are generations yet to come. The city will not become dormant because of a failure to repopulate. Although the current residents reflect only a remnant, it is the remnant that God will bless that will make contributions to countless future generations. What starts small will increase and grow to be inclusive of multiple generations because of the blessings of God are upon His people. Careful consideration also should be given to the fact that the children are playing in the streets. Play is always associated with leisure and means the work is complete. There could be no better sign of hope than children playing to encourage the builders to know God will honor their labor with success.

The returning exiles also are told God will gather those still living in exile and return them home to Judah. The God that restores a city will restore a people as well. God's people, no matter where they are located, will be brought back to Jerusalem. This is welcome news because some of the current returnees may have had relatives still living in exile. The promise of more exiles returning to Jerusalem was motivation to continue the work of rebuilding.

III. God's Love Multiplied (Zechariah 8:11–17)

God's love is the basis for the change in how God will relate to the returning exiles. God will not deal with their idolatry and acts of in justice as He did their forebears. The time of punishment is over. A day of peace and prosperity has come. The witness of peace and prosperity will be seen in how the land yields its produce. The harvest will be so great the people will have more than enough to meet their needs. The abundance of the harvest reveals God decision to have creation cooperate with God's plan to bless the returnees. The earth will yield its crops, and the dew will water the land so the people's needs are met. Zechariah's words about the cooperation of creation to bless the returnees (v. 12) is best understood in light of the words of God spoken to Solomon at the first temple dedication (see 1 Chron. 7:13-14). Only sin could cause creation not to cooperate with Israel's efforts to cultivate the land. However, repentance from sin and returning to God would lead to creation cooperating once again. God's love multiplied begins with the cooperation of creation in an abundant harvest.

Next, God's love is demonstrated in the elevated status Judah holds with the nations of the world. No longer will Judah be known by the shame of exile and defeat. God will bless them in ways that are clear to all nations of the world. The blessing is not specifically mentioned, but rather, the effects of the divine blessing. The effects of the blessing will make Judah a symbol and source of blessing that all nations will acknowledge. The blessing serves in part as continued motivation for rebuilding the temple. Given the magnitude of God's blessing, made possible by His love, Judah has the responsibility to stay faithful to the work until it is finished. God's love comes with the responsibility to respond by finishing the temple and restoring the ritual of temple worship.

Also, there is the responsibility to treat others justly. Judah is not to pick up the old habits that led its exile. The peace and blessing of God are tied to a commitment to justice in the community.

The Lesson Applied

The oracles of Zechariah are dependent upon Zechariah's willingness to accept the interpretation of his visions by the angel. Zechariah has to be willing to trust that although he had the vision, what the intermediary told him was the truth. We all at times have to depend upon others to interpret information for us, whether the information is legal, political, or spiritual. We all have gone through intermediaries at one time or another and trusted the information they gave us is true. The angel provided the truth that Zechariah needed to communicate to his community.

Let's Talk About It

1. How do we build communities that value the young and old, so they may live where they are safe to prosper?

Critical to a community that values young and old is a commitment to be inclusive and ensure no single group benefits at the expense of another. Zechariah's vision of inclusion is fundamental to helping all persons see their value to the community's well-being.

2. How does the power of intervention change outcomes for people or nations?

Judah is not able to deliver itself from Babylonian oppression or rebuild its community with such limited resources. It is only because of divine intervention out of His love for Jerusalem and for His people that change comes. We all have experienced the blessings that come from God's intervention in the affairs of our lives. Such intervention may come through a Sunday School teacher, a neighbor, a friend, or a mentor, but we were made better because they intervened.

3. Why does Zechariah include the role the earth will play in the abundant harvest as a sign of God's blessing?

We never should forget God created the world as well as people. God is concerned about the world, and He wants the land to do what it was intended to do—to be fruitful and provide the blessing of life that made the world the beautiful place it is.

Home Daily Devotional Readings
May 11–17, 2020

Monday	Tuesday	Wednesday	Thursday	Friday	Saturday	Sunday
Seeking Divine Help in Troubled Times	Land Now Belongs to Babylon	Choose to Love and Obey the Lord	Surrender and the People Will Live	Jerusalem Will Fall	Jerusalem Defeated and Zedekiah Exiled	Choose the Life of Justice
Psalm 86:1–13	Jeremiah 27:1–11	Deuteronomy 30:15–20	Jeremiah 38:14–18	Jeremiah 21:1–7	2 Kings 24:20b–25:7	Jeremiah 21:8–14

PRACTICE JUSTICE

ADULT TOPIC:
JUST REWARDS

BACKGROUND SCRIPTURE:
JEREMIAH 21

JEREMIAH 21:8–14

King James Version

AND unto this people thou shalt say, Thus saith the LORD; Behold, I set before you the way of life, and the way of death.

9 He that abideth in this city shall die by the sword, and by the famine, and by the pestilence: but he that goeth out, and falleth to the Chaldeans that besiege you, he shall live, and his life shall be unto him for a prey.

10 For I have set my face against this city for evil, and not for good, saith the LORD: it shall be given into the hand of the king of Babylon, and he shall burn it with fire.

11 And touching the house of the king of Judah, say, Hear ye the word of the LORD;

12 O house of David, thus saith the LORD; Execute judgment in the morning, and deliver him that is spoiled out of the hand of the oppressor, lest my fury go out like fire, and burn that none can quench it, because of the evil of your doings.

13 Behold, I am against thee, O inhabitant of the valley, and rock of the plain, saith the LORD; which say, Who shall come down against us? or who shall enter into our habitations?

14 But I will punish you according to the fruit of your doings, saith the LORD: and I will kindle a fire in the forest thereof, and it shall devour all things round about it.

New Revised Standard Version

AND to this people you shall say: Thus says the LORD: See, I am setting before you the way of life and the way of death.

9 Those who stay in this city shall die by the sword, by famine, and by pestilence; but those who go out and surrender to the Chaldeans who are besieging you shall live and shall have their lives as a prize of war.

10 For I have set my face against this city for evil and not for good, says the LORD: it shall be given into the hands of the king of Babylon, and he shall burn it with fire.

11 To the house of the king of Judah say: Hear the word of the LORD,

12 O house of David! Thus says the LORD: Execute justice in the morning, and deliver from the hand of the oppressor anyone who has been robbed, or else my wrath will go forth like fire, and burn, with no one to quench it, because of your evil doings.

13 See, I am against you, O inhabitant of the valley, O rock of the plain, says the LORD; you who say, "Who can come down against us, or who can enter our places of refuge?"

14 I will punish you according to the fruit of your doings, says the LORD; I will kindle a fire in its forest, and it shall devour all that is around it.

MAIN THOUGHT: O house of David, thus saith the Lord; Execute judgment in the morning, and deliver him that is spoiled out of the hand of the oppressor, lest my fury go out like fire, and burn that none can quench it, because of the evil of your doings. (Jeremiah 21:12, KJV)

LESSON SETTING

Time: 609 B.C. – 598 B.C.
Place: Judah

LESSON OUTLINE

I. **The Choice God Offers (Jeremiah 21:8–10)**
II. **A Mandate for Justice (Jeremiah 21:11–12)**
III. **Misplaced Trust (Jeremiah 21:13–14)**

UNIFYING PRINCIPLE

Evil is pervasive throughout human society. Can people continue to do evil without consequence? Jeremiah tells us God is a God of justice and will recompense evil.

INTRODUCTION

Jeremiah is a major prophet of the Old Testament writings, and this designation is primarily because of the extent of his writings. Jeremiah is from Anathoth, a small rural village northeast of Jerusalem. Jeremiah's ministry covers a period that includes the rise of Babylon as a major military power in the region, replacing the Assyrians. During Jeremiah's ministry, Judah had moments of faithfulness to God, as in the case of Josiah's reign as king. However, Judah more times than not participated in pagan worship as a means to appease its neighbors in a policy of accommodation.

Jeremiah warns Judah of the dangers of pagan worship and calls the nation to repent and turn back to God. The influence of Babylon makes Judah a vassal state that has to pay tribute to the Babylonians, and during the time of Zedekiah's reign, Jeremiah warns the king not to trust Egypt or break the Babylon treaty. Jeremiah informs Judah the nation will fall and the people will be carried into captivity. God's promised punishment for Judah's rebellion and idolatry finally had arrived.

EXPOSITION

I. THE CHOICE GOD OFFERS (JEREMIAH 21:8–10)

God created humankind as freewill beings, giving them choice in how they order their lives. Free will also means people are responsible for the choices they make. If a bad choice is made, there are consequences, and if a good choice is made, there are benefits that make life better. The choice God places before the people of Judah is difficult because it is a choice to surrender to the enemy or resist and experience certain defeat.

Zedekiah wants a different choice for his people, and because he wants to choose differently, he dismisses Jeremiah's words as being those of a false prophet. His desire for a different choice, however, does not change what Judah faces. God has decided there will be only two choices for the nation. Judah can surrender and save its life, or Judah can resist and die.

The combination of words such as "sword," "famine," and "pestilence" reveals the coming judgment and defeat of Judah would be inescapable if they chose to resist. The choice before Judah demonstrates God has decided to turn the people over to their enemies. Judah had refused to trust God and serve only Him. They continued to participate in pagan worship to appease the Babylonians Now they will discover that false gods cannot save them.

God always has been a jealous God. He has no tolerance for people who want to worship Him alongside idol gods. Since the day when God issued the Decalogue to Moses atop Mount Sinai, He declared in the first commandment: "I am the Lord your God, who brought you out of the land of Egypt, out of the house of slavery; you shall have no other gods before me (Ex. 20:2–3, NRSV). Knowing His chosen people eventually would be in close company with nations serving idol gods, He further cautioned, "for I the Lord your God am a jealous God" (Ex. 20:5, NRSV). Despite knowing the nature and character of God from the outset, God's chosen people pursued the temptation to worship other gods. They have dismissed the fact Yahweh had delivered them from bondage at the hand of the Egyptians.

The stance Jeremiah takes in communicating God's choice to Judah is not popular, but prophets are called to deal in truth, even when the truth is hard to receive. This truth motivated the Apostle Paul to advise young Pastor Timothy to be strong in his mission and ministry: "preach the word; be ready in season and out of season; reprove, rebuke, exhort, with great patience and instruction. For the time will come when they will not endure sound doctrine; but wanting to have their ears tickled, they will accumulate for themselves teachers in accordance to their own desires" (2 Tim. 4:2–3, NRSV).

Although the decision to surrender is difficult and unsavory, it is a choice that will save the lives of the people and give them an opportunity to live to see a different outcome in the future. While Judah has come to such a gut-wrenching decision, the mercy of God has sustained them to this point, giving them an opportunity to step away from the their idol worship and injustice and serve God. By the time Jeremiah informs Judah of its choices, there have been multiple opportunities for Judah to change prior to this moment. The prophet had made them aware of that opportunity countless times. For years, Jeremiah warned of what was coming if Judah did not repent and change. Now that day had finally arrived. The enemy is at the city gates, and there is no help from God for a people who have abandoned their God. Yahweh refuses to intervene to save the city.

II. A Mandate for Justice (Jeremiah 21:11–12)

The presence of enemies at the gate does not remove Zedekiah from his responsibility to ensure justice is administered in the city. The first part of the king's day was dedicated to hearing disputes and administering justice. The most famous biblical example of a king hearing cases of dispute among the people is the two mothers who came before Solomon in a dispute over two babies, one dead and the other one alive (1 Kings 3:16-28). Solomon rightly administered justice by ruling to whom the child belonged and gained the esteem of all who heard what happened.

The administration of justice was the highest function a king performed. Jeremiah warns Zedekiah not to neglect his responsibility to provide justice. Perhaps the king is so concerned about the enemy at the gate that he fails to administer justice for those who seek his aid. No matter what, Zedekiah is not to stop doing his duty as king and administer justice fairly. Failure to do his duty would further anger God. The particular forms of justice

Jeremiah mentions concern those who are robbed and those who are oppressed.

Robbery may have been widespread in an environment of political uncertainty. There was no time line regarding how long the city would last before falling to the enemy. Amid such instability, individuals may have looked for ways to take advantage of others, and the normal safeguards in the city could have lapsed. The king's task was to help those persons and restore to them what had been taken falsely.

The second group the king is to protect are those who are oppressed. Although the nature of the oppression is not mentioned, the prophet's charge may have had something to do with fair wages for services provided. Whatever the case, people were being taken advantage of in some form. Moreover, others were benefiting from the marginalized position in which the oppressed have been placed. Zedekiah is to rescue the oppressed and restore them to their rightful place in the community.

When people sense they are in danger, they often move into survival mode. The norms that allow people to relate to one another according to rules of fairness and decency get eroded. In a community under fire, people can become more concerned about their own survival than about God's requirements for justice. The concern for maintaining a just community is so important to God that He allows for no excuses to deny justice or to suspend the need to regard one another justly. Whenever justice is disregarded as a community norm, God is displeased. Even though Judah was under the threat of siege, God still expected them to regard each other according to His commands.

III. Misplaced Trust (Jeremiah 21:13–14)

Judah believed the fortress they had established in Jerusalem could not be breached because the city is elevated and surrounded by hills. The natural geography of the city provided Jerusalem with high ground in any military battle. As a general rule, forces fighting from high ground have a strategic advantage over forces that have to fight uphill. The Babylonian army had never been challenged by a fortress as well-defended as Jerusalem.

Furthermore, Jerusalem was almost unapproachable. The west side of the city had the Judean Mountains as its boundary. The east side was bounded by the Judean dessert. The east, west, and south sides of Jerusalem had steep ravines as much as two hundred to four hundred feet deep. The walls of Jerusalem encircled the city for four miles and were one hundred feet high. There were ninety towers on the city walls, each manned by soldiers who were ready to defend the city as necessary. Given the extent of Jerusalem's fortifications, it is easy to see why Zedekiah and the people feel their city was impenetrable. The king and the people had placed their trust in the defenses of the city to save them.

Despite their false sense of security, Jeremiah informs the king their defenses will not help them because God had decided to fight against them. Judah's real defense always has been the God who protected them, not the defenses of their city. Now that God has turned against them, the various and strategic defenses of the city would prove useless. God had determined they had behaved unjustly long enough. Just as Jericho had fallen a city where the inhabitants thought it could not collapse to military attack (Josh. 6), so too will Judah fall. And as it will be with Jerusalem, Jericho fell because God had determined He would be on the side of Joshua's army: "The Lord said to Joshua, 'See, I have handed Jericho over to you, along with its king and soldiers'" (Josh. 6:2, NRSV). Jericho fell, not because of Israel's military might or strategy, but rather because the Lord was on their side.

Jerusalem will fall to its enemy because of their misplaced trust. We are never to trust the resources God provides more than the God who provides them. Each time we put our faith in temporal things, it reflects misplaced trust.

The Lesson Applied

Life sometimes brings us to a place where our choices are limited and none of the options before us are desirable. However, to be able to move on and experience something better in the future, we have to decide. In such moments, it is important to trust God and lean upon His mercy and grace. We may have to go through a season of difficulty, but hope in God allows us to believe in a better day. Psalm 30:5 assures us that weeping may endure for a night, but joy comes in the morning!

Let's Talk About It

1. **Why did Zedekiah seek a different option than the two Jeremiah provided?**

   It always is difficult to accept news we do not want to hear. Zedekiah wanted to believe there was another option because the choices before him were distasteful. He hoped that surely God would deliver His people again, despite their infidelity to Him.

2. **Why are we prone to trust things more than we trust God?**

   Zedekiah believed the city's natural and planned defenses would protect them from Babylonian attack. People often are willing to trust what they can see more than the God they cannot see. Faith is the pivotal component that allows us to appropriate our trust to the God who has demonstrated His saving power time and again.

3. **How difficult is it to continue to do your job when you do not know how long the job will last?**

   Zedekiah is told to continue to administer justice although the enemy was at the gate. Zedekiah understandably struggled to stay focused on his responsibility to administer justice. Nevertheless, God's demand for justice does not waver because of our circumstances.

Home Daily Devotional Readings
May 18–24, 2020

Monday	Tuesday	Wednesday	Thursday	Friday	Saturday	Sunday
Justice for Aliens, Orphans, and Widows	God Requires Godly Rule by Kings	Who May Enter God's Holy Presence?	God's Justice for the Unjust King	The City Suffers for Its Disobedience	Injustice Ends the Line of David	Repent of Misdeeds and Unjust Actions
Deuteronomy 24:17–22	Deuteronomy 17:18–20	Psalm 15	Jeremiah 22:11–19	Jeremiah 22:20–23	Jeremiah 22:24–30	Jeremiah 22:1–10

REPENT OF INJUSTICE

ADULT TOPIC:
DO THE RIGHT THING

BACKGROUND SCRIPTURE:
JEREMIAH 22

JEREMIAH 22:1–10

King James Version

THUS saith the LORD; Go down to the house of the king of Judah, and speak there this word,

2 And say, Hear the word of the LORD, O king of Judah, that sittest upon the throne of David, thou, and thy servants, and thy people that enter in by these gates:

3 Thus saith the LORD; Execute ye judgment and righteousness, and deliver the spoiled out of the hand of the oppressor: and do no wrong, do no violence to the stranger, the fatherless, nor the widow, neither shed innocent blood in this place.

4 For if ye do this thing indeed, then shall there enter in by the gates of this house kings sitting upon the throne of David, riding in chariots and on horses, he, and his servants, and his people.

5 But if ye will not hear these words, I swear by myself, saith the LORD, that this house shall become a desolation.

6 For thus saith the LORD unto the king's house of Judah; Thou art Gilead unto me, and the head of Lebanon: yet surely I will make thee a wilderness, and cities which are not inhabited.

7 And I will prepare destroyers against thee, every one with his weapons: and they shall cut down thy choice cedars, and cast them into the fire.

8 And many nations shall pass by this city, and they shall say every man to his neighbour,

New Revised Standard Version

THUS says the LORD: Go down to the house of the king of Judah, and speak there this word,

2 and say: Hear the word of the LORD, O King of Judah sitting on the throne of David—you, and your servants, and your people who enter these gates.

3 Thus says the LORD: Act with justice and righteousness, and deliver from the hand of the oppressor anyone who has been robbed. And do no wrong or violence to the alien, the orphan, and the widow, or shed innocent blood in this place.

4 For if you will indeed obey this word, then through the gates of this house shall enter kings who sit on the throne of David, riding in chariots and on horses, they, and their servants, and their people.

5 But if you will not heed these words, I swear by myself, says the LORD, that this house shall become a desolation.

6 For thus says the LORD concerning the house of the king of Judah: You are like Gilead to me, like the summit of Lebanon; but I swear that I will make you a desert, an uninhabited city.

7 I will prepare destroyers against you, all with their weapons; they shall cut down your choicest cedars and cast them into the fire.

8 And many nations will pass by this city, and all of them will say one to another, "Why

MAIN THOUGHT: Thus saith the LORD; Execute ye judgment and righteousness, and deliver the spoiled out of the hand of the oppressor: and do no wrong, do no violence to the stranger, the fatherless, nor the widow, neither shed innocent blood in this place. (Jeremiah 22:3, KJV)

King James Version	*New Revised Standard Version*
Wherefore hath the LORD done thus unto this great city?	**has the LORD dealt in this way with that great city?"**
9 Then they shall answer, Because they have forsaken the covenant of the LORD their God, and worshipped other gods, and served them.	**9 And they will answer, "Because they abandoned the covenant of the LORD their God, and worshiped other gods and served them."**
10 Weep ye not for the dead, neither bemoan him: but weep sore for him that goeth away: for he shall return no more, nor see his native country.	**10 Do not weep for him who is dead, nor bemoan him; weep rather for him who goes away, for he shall return no more to see his native land.**

LESSON SETTING

Time: 588 B.C.
Place: Jerusalem

LESSON OUTLINE

I. A Chance to Change (Jeremiah 22:1–4)
II. The Penalty for Refusing to Change (Jeremiah 22:5–7)
III. An Embarrassed Nation (Jeremiah 22:8–10)

Unifying Principle

Society often ignores and even condones the oppression of the vulnerable. Will righteousness be rewarded, and will evil face retribution? Through the prophet Jeremiah, God exhorts the people either to repent of injustice and deliver those who are oppressed or face destruction.

Introduction

A primary concern of the prophet Jeremiah is the lack of justice and how those living on the margins of life are treated. Judah is to be different from the nations that surround it. One of the ways that difference is to manifest is in the equitable and fair treatment of all persons, especially the powerless. The king of Judah has failed in his responsibility to administer justice, and that failure has placed the nation in peril. If the king will not execute his responsibilities faithfully, God will remove the king and all of those with him who have profited from a system that denies justice to the powerless.

Jeremiah's words are spoken in the form of an either/or proposition that reflects the covenantal relationship of Judah with God. There is a way for Judah to avoid the pending judgment if they return to covenant loyalty. Jeremiah never ceases to hold out hope that Judah will change. The opportunity to repent and return to Yahweh is a sign of God's commitment to Judah. God remained faithful to His covenant with the people, despite their continued disregard for the sacred nature of that relationship. Whereas the prophets all spoke of pending judgment, each one of them held to the hope the nation would change and turn back to God.

Exposition

I. A Chance to Change (Jeremiah 22:1–4)

The central claim of Jeremiah in the oracle to the king is that the kingship and justice are mutually interdependent to the extent one cannot survive without the other. The king of Judah is unlike any other ruler whose only concerns may be political arrangements and military conquests that expand their territory and treasury. Judah's kings were not to be motivated by grand ideas of nation building; rather, the royal line was to ensure the nation treated all persons justly, thus serving as an example to the surrounding pagan nations.

The king's role is vital to the administration of justice. This responsibility consumes a large percentage of the king's time. Judah's judicial structure included an appeal process where the powerless are ensured a fair and impartial hearing. Jeremiah's admonition to the king to "act with justice" (v. 3) is a particular concern for the oppressed, aliens, widows, and orphans. God's concern for these marginalized groups is repeated as a central message of all the prophets. When the Law was given to Moses, before Israel entered the land God promised, they were told their ability to keep the land would depend on how they treated the disadvantaged in their midst.

By Jeremiah's time, Judah's governing system—one God had designed to be built upon justice—had been co-opted by special interest groups and their quest for economic aggrandizement. The needs of the poor and the powerless were ignored by the king as he listened more to lobbyists and advisers seeking to expand personal fortunes and power in the land. This expansion of controlling voices surely had a ripple effect, impacting fair labor rights, land usage, and discriminatory practices, particularly toward immigrants. Within such an environment, particular groups of people can be preyed upon without fear of retribution—either because they have no legal protections or because societal attitudes suggest they can be disregarded.

Jeremiah makes known that the king has an opportunity to reverse their course of action—cease the abuse of justice and restore the justice God intended for the nation. If the king is willing to restore justice, both the nation and the king will experience the blessings of God. His blessing for the king is that someone from the line of David always will sit on the throne.

Succession to the throne was a concern for every ruling monarch. Every king wanted to ensure his bloodline would maintain control of the nation he had governed. God's blessing to the nation, if the king obeyed, is to have the people share in the king's success via the access they would have to a house built upon justice. What Jeremiah makes clear is that God has given the king an opportunity to change and restore justice.

II. The Penalty for Refusing to Change (Jeremiah 22:5–7)

The penalty for refusing to change starts with the destruction of the house/throne of David. Jeremiah's cautionary message of Judah's impending demise is delivered now to Jehoiakim, but also may have crossed the reign of Jehoahaz, who was carried away captive into Egypt. A succession of kings and princes have been exhorted to execute justice and are given Yahweh's assurance that if they did so, the royal line would flourish; otherwise it would be ruined. There will be no one to succeed Jehoiakim because God will bring his rule in the nation to an end. The king's removal will have a cascading impact upon all who have depended upon their relationship with the king to forward their economic interests. No one who has participated in a system that neglects the poor and the oppressed will be left. Anthony Saldarini, in the *New Interpreter's Bible Commentary,* writes: "The reference to Gilead and Lebanon probably is an allusion to the fact that the palace was built of the cedars of Lebanon. It was built with a hall of justice where the king was to pronounce judgment. Since the hall of justice was not used properly the mighty cedars of the royal palace would fall at the hands of an unnamed enemy."

The victory of the approaching enemy will come to fruition because the king has abandoned his responsibility to administer justice. The complete desolation of the city will be evidence of God's disapproval of Judah. When a land is without justice, it impacts the poor and oppressed, in effect making their conditions comparable to that of living in a wasteland. Therefore, God will turn Judah into an actual wasteland as it no longer serves the purpose God intended.

Now the king and Judah must choose. There is a way to escape the pending danger, but it will require immediate action to restore justice in the land. The failure to restore justice will lead God to allow the nation's enemies to conquer it and the kingdom will be lost. God's patience has expired.

III. An Embarrassed Nation (Jeremiah 22:8–10)

The desolation of Judah for its failure to administer justice will be so great that the nations of the world will attribute its ruin to God's actions against them. The prophet in the oracle reveals how the nations that do not worship the God of Judah will view the fall of Judah as God working against it. The ancient world's view was that if the gods were displeased with a people or a nation, those gods would punish them as warning to others.

At the sight of the extent of Judah's demise, other nations will ask, *Why has God done this? Surely there has been some act of rebellion, some form of dishonoring the nation's God that led to such widespread destruction.* Jeremiah provides the answer—they are a people who continually have forsaken their covenant with Yahweh. Beginning at verse 10, the prophet details some of the royal offenders. The prophet laments Jehoahaz, here referred to as Shallum (vv. 10–12). The brother of Jehoiakim, he succeeded Josiah but was almost immediately deposed by Pharaoh Necho (2 Kings 23:31–35). Jehoiakim also is admonished and threatened (v. 13–19). Another message is sent then in the reign of Jehoiachin (Jeconiah), the son of Jehoiakim. He is charged with a stubborn refusal to hear and is threatened with destruction. Jeremiah foretells that under him David's house will fall (vv. 20–30).

When Jeremiah says "the people," he has in mind the ruling class, not the community in general. Judah's government is not a democratic system of electing leaders by the people; kings are appointed leaders who are to rule justly on behalf of the people, following the laws of the covenant. The ruling class has failed to live by the standards of the covenant and its requirements of justice and righteousness that were set forward in the laws given by Moses. Judah's humiliation in full view of other nations is also a sign to future generations of their leaders' responsibility to make justice foundational to the community's well-being.

Because of God's promise to David that his house and kingdom would be established forever (2 Sam. 7:16), future generations of his lineage may have believed they would continue to rule despite their failure to follow God's commands. The closing words of Jeremiah's oracle reveal the prospect of exile, where God will not only leave the land desolate by the enemy's destruction, He also will leave the land vacant of people. Yet the prophet announced that death would be preferable to exile (v. 10) because those taken captive would never again see their homeland.

The Lesson Applied

There always are consequences for unjust actions. When nations allow a privileged class to benefit by denying justice to those at the margins of life, it can lead to civil disobedience, and in extreme cases, revolution. When nations exploit labor and abuse the environment, it can cause unrest in the workplace. Such actions gain God's attention and put the offenders at risk of His judgment. God is concerned about justice in America. Therefore, as a professed Christian nation, we need to restore justice to those who have been denied it for so long.

Let's Talk About It

1. **How are Christians to respond to abuses of power and denial of justice?**

   Christians are to advocate for justice because this is what God desires. God has made justice a centerpiece of human relationships. When we act justly, we demonstrate we value what God's values.

2. **The oracles of the prophet Jeremiah are given to provide accountability to the king and to the nation. Why is accountability so important?**

   Accountability matters because it keeps individuals from acting independently with no regard for their responsibility or of others. We are always to view our roles and responsibilities in relationship to established expectations. We are not free to determine our own life rules as we go. Checks and balances through accountability hold us to what is right according to known standards.

3. **Why do the prophets hope for change when they place choices before the nation and prophesy what will happen if they do not change?**

   The prophets hold out hope because of the mercies of God and God's fidelity to the covenant. This hope in God's faithfulness causes the prophets to hope the people also will see it and be inspired to repent and change.

Home Daily Devotional Readings
May 25–31, 2020

Monday	Tuesday	Wednesday	Thursday	Friday	Saturday	Sunday
Receiving a New Vision of God	Justice for Gentile Believers	The Up or Down Choice	Jesus a Migrant from Egypt	Ephraim Spurns God's Love and Suffers	Once a Slave; Now a Brother	Respond with Love and Justice Daily
Genesis 28:10–17	Acts 15:10–17	Deuteronomy 28:1–6, 15–19	Matthew 2:13–15	Hosea 11:3–6	Philemon 8–21	Hosea 11:1–2, 7–10; 12:1–2, 6–14

RETURN TO LOVE AND JUSTICE

ADULT TOPIC:
MEASURE UP!

BACKGROUND SCRIPTURE:
HOSEA 11–12

HOSEA 11:1–2, 7–10; 12:1–2, 6–14

King James Version

WHEN Israel was a child, then I loved him, and called my son out of Egypt.

2 As they called them, so they went from them: they sacrificed unto Baalim, and burned incense to graven images.

• • • • • •

7 And my people are bent to backsliding from me: though they called them to the most High, none at all would exalt him.

8 How shall I give thee up, Ephraim? how shall I deliver thee, Israel? how shall I make thee as Admah? how shall I set thee as Zeboim? mine heart is turned within me, my repentings are kindled together.

9 I will not execute the fierceness of mine anger, I will not return to destroy Ephraim: for I am God, and not man; the Holy One in the midst of thee: and I will not enter into the city.

10 They shall walk after the LORD: he shall roar like a lion: when he shall roar, then the children shall tremble from the west.

• • • 12:1–2, 6–14 • • •

1 Ephraim feedeth on wind, and followeth after the east wind: he daily increaseth lies and desolation; and they do make a covenant with the Assyrians, and oil is carried into Egypt.

2 The LORD hath also a controversy with Judah, and will punish Jacob according to his ways; according to his doings will he recompense him.

• • • • • •

New Revised Standard Version

WHEN Israel was a child, I loved him, and out of Egypt I called my son.

2 The more I called them, the more they went from me; they kept sacrificing to the Baals, and offering incense to idols.

• • • • • •

7 My people are bent on turning away from me. To the Most High they call, but he does not raise them up at all.

8 How can I give you up, Ephraim? How can I hand you over, O Israel? How can I make you like Admah? How can I treat you like Zeboiim? My heart recoils within me; my compassion grows warm and tender.

9 I will not execute my fierce anger; I will not again destroy Ephraim; for I am God and no mortal, the Holy One in your midst, and I will not come in wrath.

10 They shall go after the LORD, who roars like a lion; when he roars, his children shall come trembling from the west.

• • • 12:1–2, 6–14 • • •

1 Ephraim herds the wind, and pursues the east wind all day long; they multiply falsehood and violence; they make a treaty with Assyria, and oil is carried to Egypt.

2 The LORD has an indictment against Judah, and will punish Jacob according to his ways, and repay him according to his deeds.

• • • • • •

MAIN THOUGHT: Therefore turn thou to thy God: keep mercy and judgment and wait on thy God continually. (Hosea 12:6, KJV)

Hosea 11:1–2, 7–10; 12:1–2, 6–14

King James Version	*New Revised Standard Version*
6 Therefore turn thou to thy God: keep mercy and judgment and wait on thy God continually.	**6 But as for you, return to your God, hold fast to love and justice, and wait continually for your God.**
7 He is a merchant, the balances of deceit are in his hand: he loveth to oppress.	**7 A trader, in whose hands are false balances, he loves to oppress.**
8 And Ephraim said, Yet I am become rich, I have found me out substance: in all my labours they shall find none iniquity in me that were sin.	**8 Ephraim has said, "Ah, I am rich, I have gained wealth for myself; in all of my gain no offense has been found in me that would be sin."**
9 And I that am the LORD thy God from the land of Egypt will yet make thee to dwell in tabernacles, as in the days of the solemn feast.	**9 I am the LORD your God from the land of Egypt; I will make you live in tents again, as in the days of the appointed festival.**
10 I have also spoken by the prophets, and I have multiplied visions, and used similitudes, by the ministry of the prophets.	**10 I spoke to the prophets; it was I who multiplied visions, and through the prophets I will bring destruction.**
11 Is there iniquity in Gilead? surely they are vanity: they sacrifice bullocks in Gilgal; yea, their altars are as heaps in the furrows of the fields.	**11 In Gilead there is iniquity, they shall surely come to nothing. In Gilgal they sacrifice bulls, so their altars shall be like stone heaps on the furrows of the field.**
12 And Jacob fled into the country of Syria, and Israel served for a wife, and for a wife he kept sheep.	**12 Jacob fled to the land of Aram, there Israel served for a wife, and for a wife he guarded sheep.**
13 And by a prophet the LORD brought Israel out of Egypt, and by a prophet was he preserved.	**13 By a prophet the LORD brought Israel up from Egypt, and by a prophet he was guarded.**
14 Ephraim provoked him to anger most bitterly: therefore shall he leave his blood upon him, and his reproach shall his LORD return unto him.	**14 Ephraim has given bitter offense, so his LORD will bring his crimes down on him and pay him back for his insults.**

LESSON SETTING

Time: 793-753 B.C.
Place: Israel

LESSON OUTLINE

I. **Rejected Love (Hosea 11:1–2)**
II. **Extended Mercy (Hosea 11:7–10)**
III. **The Case of Rebellion (Hosea 12:1–2)**
IV. **The Fruit of Rebellion (Hosea 12:6–14)**

Unifying Principle

People often equate prosperity with righteousness. Is prosperity the standard by which people and society should be judged? Hosea reminds us that love and justice are God's standards.

Introduction

Hosea is one of the prophets of Israel whose time span covered the reign of Jeroboam II. Jeroboam's reign included a significant expansion of Israel's territory that brought economic prosperity to a select few. The expansion left many in Israel destitute as the wealth gap between the ruling class and the common people widened. Hosea denounced the social injustices that took advantage of the poor and extended the position of the privilege. However, Hosea is most noted for calling attention to Israel's worship of pagan gods. Israel has forsaken its true love, Yahweh, and pursued idols.

Hosea represents the covenant theology that guided Israel's early relationship to God. At the core of covenant theology is having no other gods before the God who had led Israel out of bondage and the wilderness, through the conquest, and into the land of promise. Second in its importance to covenant theology was just dealings with fellow Israelites and strangers. Under Jeroboam II, Israel had abandoned fidelity to Yahweh and justice in the community as idolatry and greed became the standards of the day. Hosea calls Israel to return to their first love—the God who had forged them into a nation.

Exposition

I. Rejected Love (Hosea 11:1–2)

Hosea starts his case against Israel with a lesson in history. Israel has not arrived in the land of promise on its own. Israel has arrived and flourished in the land because of the love and blessings of Yahweh. His love for Israel was not due to its rich resources. God's love for Israel has its origins in His covenant with Abraham, and was extended to his descendants. When Israel had nothing to offer, God loved them and choose them as His own. God heard the cries of a people in bondage and had mercy upon them. Hosea declares that it was God's love that moved Him to act on Israel's behalf when they had nothing to offer. This is an important point because it counters the popular notion moving through the nation that wealth and prosperity are a sign of God's favor. Material blessings are not the sole barometer sign of God's favor. Material gain may be a sign of greed where the wealthy take advantage of the poor. This was a common occurrence during Jeroboam's reign, as false weights were used to measure crops to increase the sellers' profits.

God's love had brought Israel out of Egypt when they were confronted by the greatest military known. Without a standing army, God through miracles and mercy gave Israel the victory over Egypt and every foe that stood in the way of the people receiving the land of promise. While in the wilderness, God had given the Commandments as rules of the covenant to govern the people's relationships to God and to each other. Every action of God on behalf of the people was an expression of His love for them. Israel was the object of divine love as God had chosen them to be His people.

Yet Israel's response to God's great love was constant rebellion. There were acts of rebellion in route to the Promised Land when the people failed to trust the God of their deliverance because of the report of the ten spies (Num. 13:25–14:10). There were acts of rebellion during the period of conquest through Achan (Josh. 7), who hid items that God said were to be destroyed. By the time of Hosea's prophecy, rebellion against God is nothing new to Israel. The current sign of rebellion that grieves God is idol worship. Israel has begun to worship the fertility god Baal.

II. Extended Mercy (Hosea 11:7–10)

Despite Israel's constant turning away from Yahweh to follow idols, God responds with mercy, not judgment. Hosea presents God as a distraught parent attempting to decide what to do with a rebellious child. The image and metaphor may have been taken from Hosea's personal experience with his unfaithful wife Gomer. God has no desire to do to Israel what was done to Admah and Zebolim (Gen. 18–19; Deut. 29:23), cities in the plains near Sodom and Gomorrah that were destroyed because of their sin.

Although Israel is in danger of judgment, God extends mercy—a part of covenant theology where God's faithfulness is held in contrast to Israel infidelity. Nevertheless, mercy is not a blank check to cover continue wrongdoing. It is the means God uses to pursue Israel in His love. God's love should turn Israel back to Him. God's mercy extended during Israel's rebellion is what holds back God's wrath. He is free to decide how He will respond to Israel because God is not a mortal accountable to someone else for His decisions. God's mercy gives Hosea hope and adds to the prophet's understanding of covenant theology.

Covenant theology at its core is dependent upon the God who chooses to be faithful to the people He has selected as His own. Whereas the people may rebel and turn away from God, He never turns away from the people. Even when judgment comes upon the nation, it is God's way of disciplining the people He loves to draw them back to himself.

III. The Case of Rebellion (Hosea 12:1–2)

Hosea declares the nation's rebellion has led to indictment by God. The language Hosea uses is legal and draws the image of a court scene where the charges are brought against the defendant. Judah is the defendant, and God is both prosecutor and judge. The case is framed by the nation's history, beginning with Jacob. From this starting point, Hosea brings into focus a deceitful nature as an early issue within the nation. Israel is quick to trust more in their ability to deceive than in the bonds of covenant.

Trusting allegiances with other nations more than trusting in God's care and provision is one expression of deceit that Hosea brings as a charge against the nation. Permitting violence against the innocent and the lack of justice in the community are additional charges. Israel will not avoid the accounting God will one day demand. Their continued rebellion will lead to judgment and estrangement similar to what Jacob encountered when he was forced from home and mistreated by others.

IV. The Fruit of Rebellion (Hosea 12:6–14)

Israel has been lured into false security by the nation's current economic success. The triad of worship, righteousness, and compassion have been replaced with idolatry, greed, and selfishness. Economic prosperity has blinded the people to the larger problem in their midst. God's coming judgment promises a return to economic conditions that will force the people to trust Him. They will be forced to live in tents as a reminder of when they were a nomadic people. The prophets' words would bring judgment for sin, not hope and blessings. Their places of sacrifice would lay in ruin because God will be unwilling to accept sacrifices from an unjust people practicing idolatry. The fruit of rebellion will leave no aspect of the community unjudged. Israel's rebellion will have consequences—economic collapse, loss of land, the absence of a spoken word that blesses, as well as the failure of the sacrificial system. The fruit of rebellion is removal of God's protection and care over the community.

The Lesson Applied

It is easy for individuals or nations to trust their economic prosperity more than they trust God. It also is easy to interpret economic prosperity as God's blessing. Christians believe material prosperity without God cannot be sustained, whether in an individual, a family, or a nation. We cannot allow a desire for wealth to lead us to take advantage of others. We are to be as concerned about economic justice as we are other forms. No one should suffer because of economic decisions that benefit only a few. Economic decisions are expressions of our faith and what we believe about a God who desires justice for everyone in all things.

Let's Talk About It

1. **How can history inform us about the decisions we need to make today?**

   History provides a context for understanding how a person or a nation arrived in the position they are in today and how they may respond to the choices before them in their relationship to God and to one another. History can be a valued tool helping us not to make the mistakes of the past or by knowing what path we should take in the present because of the choices of those that came before us.

2. **Given all that God had done for Israel, why would they follow after idols?**

   Israel was surrounded by a Canaanite culture that worshipped the fertility god Baal. In order to find acceptance among them, the compromise of idol worship may have been viewed as a vital option.

3. **How might Hosea's personal experience with marital infidelity influence his understanding about Israel's infidelity?**

   Hosea sees Israel's response to God as one of infidelity, no different than his wife Gomer. However, just as Hosea went to purchase Gomer from the slave block because of his love for her, God was pursuing Israel despite its infidelity because of His love for His people.

Home Daily Devotional Readings
June 1–7, 2020

Monday	Tuesday	Wednesday	Thursday	Friday	Saturday	Sunday
Faith Community Discerns Path of Wisdom	Parents Joyfully Pass on the Faith	Learning the Fear of the Lord	Violence Not a Wise Choice	Vast Scope of Solomon's Wisdom	Prize Wisdom and Insight	Godly Wisdom for Life's Decisions
Acts 6:1–7	2 Timothy 1:3–9a	Psalm 34:11–18	Matthew 26:47–52	1 Kings 4:29–34	Proverbs 4:1–9	Proverbs 1:1–4, 7–8, 10–11, 20–22, 32–33

Fourth Quarter

June

July

August

Lesson material is based on International Sunday School Lessons and International Bible Lessons for Christian Teaching. Copyrighted by the International Council of Religious Education and is used by its permission.

THE CALL OF WISDOM

ADULT TOPIC:
LISTEN UP!

BACKGROUND SCRIPTURE:
PROVERBS 1

PROVERBS 1:1–4, 7–8, 10, 20–22, 32–33

King James Version

THE proverbs of Solomon the son of David, king of Israel;

2 To know wisdom and instruction; to perceive the words of understanding;

3 To receive the instruction of wisdom, justice, and judgment, and equity;

4 To give subtilty to the simple, to the young man knowledge and discretion.

• • • • •

7 The fear of the LORD is the beginning of knowledge: but fools despise wisdom and instruction.

• • • • •

8 My son, hear the instruction of thy father, and forsake not the law of thy mother:

• • • • •

10 My son, if sinners entice thee, consent thou not.

• • • • •

20 Wisdom crieth without; she uttereth her voice in the streets:

21 She crieth in the chief place of concourse, in the openings of the gates: in the city she uttereth her words, saying,

22 How long, ye simple ones, will ye love simplicity? and the scorners delight in their scorning, and fools hate knowledge?

• • • • •

32 For the turning away of the simple shall slay them, and the prosperity of fools shall destroy them.

33 But whoso hearkeneth unto me shall dwell safely, and shall be quiet from fear of evil.

New Revised Standard Version

THE proverbs of Solomon son of David, king of Israel:

2 For learning about wisdom and instruction, for understanding words of insight,

3 for gaining instruction in wise dealing, righteousness, justice, and equity;

4 to teach shrewdness to the simple, knowledge and prudence to the young—

• • • • •

7 The fear of the LORD is the beginning of knowledge; fools despise wisdom and instruction.

• • • • •

8 Hear, my child, your father's instruction, and do not reject your mother's teaching;

• • • • •

10 My child, if sinners entice you, do not consent.

• • • • •

20 Wisdom cries out in the street; in the squares she raises her voice.

21 At the busiest corner she cries out; at the entrance of the city gates she speaks:

22 "How long, O simple ones, will you love being simple? How long will scoffers delight in their scoffing and fools hate knowledge?

• • • • •

32 For waywardness kills the simple, and the complacency of fools destroys them;

33 but those who listen to me will be secure and will live at ease, without dread of disaster."

MAIN THOUGHT: The fear of the LORD is the beginning of knowledge: but fools despise wisdom and instruction. (Proverb 1:7, KJV)

LESSON SETTING

Time: 970–931 B.C.
Place: Israel

LESSON OUTLINE

I. The Purpose for the Proverbs (Proverbs 1:1–4, 7)
II. When Wisdom Calls (Proverbs 1:8, 10, 20–22)
III. Answer and Live (Proverbs 1:32–33)

UNIFYING PRINCIPLE

People feel compelled by something greater than themselves to act wisely when confronted by feelings of inadequacy to complete a task. How can they overcome these feelings of inadequacy and move forward? The wisdom of God instructs us to discern the direction we should go and gives us the insight we need to understand how we are to live in order to please the Lord and enjoy His peace and prosperity.

INTRODUCTION

Solomon is given credit for authoring the majority of the book of Proverbs. However, internal evidence in the text points to the book being a collection of wisdom from a variety of individuals, edited and compiled over a period of time.

Solomon was the son of King David and Bathsheba (see 2 Sam. 12:24–25), and he ruled Israel from 970–931 B.C. The portions of Proverbs written by Solomon would have been written during his reign as king. Solomon was known for his wisdom and wealth, and most scholars believe he wrote these proverbs during the early years of his reign, before "his heart had turned away from Yahweh" (1 Kings 11:9).

The Book of 1 Kings gives us a clear picture of King Solomon's most impressive characteristics. The text says: "God gave Solomon very great wisdom, discernment, and breadth of understanding as vast as the sand on the seashore, so that Solomon's wisdom surpassed the wisdom of all the people of the east.... He was wiser than anyone else.... His fame spread throughout all the surrounding nations. He composed three thousand proverbs.... People came from all the nations to hear the wisdom of Solomon" (1 Kings 4:29–34, NRSV).

The word proverb is a translation of the Hebrew word *maschal*, which means "a saying." Proverbs are short, pithy, memorable sayings that provide advice for living. God used Solomon to pen much of the book of Proverbs, which is full of advice for living successfully from God's perspective. Instead of pursuing foolishness, God's people can heed the lessons found in the proverbs. As we will see in this lesson, Proverbs 1 identifies the purpose for the proverbs, calls wisdom seekers to listen intentionally, and provides tools for successful living for those who choose to respond to wisdom's call.

EXPOSITION

I. THE PURPOSE FOR THE PROVERBS (PROVERBS 1:1–4, 7)

The Book of Proverbs is considered wisdom literature, written in the form of poetry. Generally, the subsequent lines of each proverb compliments or contrasts the thought in the first line of the proverb (*HCSB Study Bible*, p. 1023). Because it fits in the genre of wisdom literature, Proverbs must be interpreted with care. Max Anders notes in the *Holman Old Testament Commentary on Proverbs*: "Proverbs presents general truths often not intended to be taken literally in every situation.... They are not intended to be technically true in all situations, and they do not state everything about a given truth.... Proverbs are not promises but general statements of truth. Rather than being thought of as exacting promises from God, they must be understood as general guidelines for living a successful life" (p. 2). For this reason, we will study Proverbs, not as promises we intend to claim, but through the lens of carefully considered general principles that can be learned and applied in our cultural context.

Proverbs 1:1–7 serves as a prologue or introduction for the entire book. In verse 1, readers learn the book's primary author (Solomon) and the author's family lineage (son of Israel's beloved King David).

Verses 2–3 provide the author's purpose for writing: "For learning about wisdom and instruction"; "For understanding words of insight (v. 2, NRSV); "For gaining instruction" (v. 3, NRSV). It is not enough for a person to have heard knowledge of what would be considered the wise action to take in a situation. In addition to learning about wisdom, one must have discipline to actually do what wisdom requires. Other translations render verse 2 as, "to teach people wisdom and discipline" (NLT) and "for learning what wisdom and discipline are" (CSB). The word *understanding* in verse 2 expresses the idea of knowledge or insight (truth revealed by God) that is so deeply internalized as to permeate and guide one's actions. It is knowing that shows up in one's doing.

The audience for Proverbs is revealed in verses 4–5: "the simple [and] ... the young" along with "the wise ... and the discerning" (NRSV). Solomon was writing to provide guidance to those who are young and inexperienced; those who lack common sense; those who desire the sensibility and discretion required to navigate life successfully; and those who are wise and want more wisdom. Perhaps Eugene Peterson described Solomon's audience best in his translation of verses 4–5 in *The Message*: "To teach the inexperienced the ropes and give our young people a grasp on reality. There's something here also for seasoned men and women, still a thing for two for the experienced to learn."

Although "simplemindedness" often is associated with youth, the two are not necessarily related. That is to say, it is possible for a person who chooses not to learn wisdom's lessons to be an old fool. Likewise, a young person who seeks after and heeds wisdom can have wisdom beyond his or her years.

Proverbs 1:7 is one of the most memorized and referenced proverbs in the book and is considered a motto for this collection of wisdom. Following his purpose for writing, Solomon identified the "beginning" (NRSV) of wisdom, which suggests a starting point or prerequisite. He then identified that starting point as "the fear of the Lord." This fear is not a shaking-in-one's-boots intimidation type of fear. Solomon actually was referring to awe and reverence for the Lord. Honoring and respecting the Lord requires surrendering and giving Him the proper place in one's life.

The Message explains the fear of the Lord in this way: "Start with God—the first step in learning is bowing down to God." Such fear of the Lord results in love for, trust in, and obedience to God. It is giving complete honor and adoration to God in worship.

Solomon contrasted those who fear the Lord with those "fools [who] despise wisdom and discipline" (v. 7, NRSV). The word despise means "to hold in contempt or to view as insignificant" (*BlueletterBible.com*). People who devalue God or His perspective will not seek to live according to His will, often choosing to disregard the discipline and guardrails provided by God's instructions. Solomon described the person who chooses not to fear the Lord as foolish and seemed to suggest only two options in this verse—fear God or be a fool. Summarily, the purpose of the proverbs is to teach readers the way of wisdom, which begins with properly relating to and serving God (see also Prov. 8:13; 9:10; 14:27; 15:33; and 19:23).

II. When Wisdom Calls (Proverbs 1:8, 10, 20–22)

The first seven verses of Proverbs 1 explain wisdom is not hiding, waiting to be found. Instead, its source is God, and we begin to find it when we fear the Lord. In Proverbs 1:8, Solomon shifted his focus to giving advice and instruction, similar to the way parents instruct children. The NRSV translates verse 8 as, "hear, my child, your father's instruction, and do not reject your mother's teaching." Other versions translate it as, "my child, listen when your father corrects you. Don't neglect your mother's instruction" (NLT), and "pay close attention, friend, to what your father tells you; never forget what you learned at your mother's knee" (MSG). Regardless of the translation, readers easily are able to picture a loving parent or other person of authority passing life lessons to the inexperienced and the young (see Prov. 1:4).

Solomon instructed readers to wear these teachings as "a garland of grace on your head" and a "gold chain around your neck" (v. 9, HCSB). This is not the only place in the Bible that speaks to the blessings that come from heeding the wisdom of parents (see Exod. 20:12; Eph. 2:2). Solomon suggested the teachings of our elders (when aligned with Scripture) provide protection from sin and its consequences. When we allow the wisdom of godly people God has placed in our lives to influence our thoughts and actions, we avoid the pitfalls of sin.

Speaking as a loving parent to a child, the writer gave a warning in verse 10: If sinners or those to whom we refer as "the crowd" try to entice or lure a person to dishonor God or the wisdom of godly parents, then the only appropriate response is "do not consent" (NRSV); "turn your back on them" (NLT); "don't be persuaded" (HCSB). Verses 11–14 elaborate on this idea by providing examples of actions sinners might try to persuade us to take, such as: "Come with us! Let's set an ambush and kill someone. Let's attack some innocent person just for fun! Let's swallow them alive, like *Sheol*. We'll find all kinds of valuable property and fill our houses with plunder. Throw in your lot with us, and we'll share our money" (HCSB).

As it is said, sin will take us further than we want to go, keep up longer than we want to stay, and cost us more than we want to pay. Solomon warned against associating with the wrong people for the wrong reasons because "their feet run toward trouble … they set an ambush to kill themselves and attack their own lives" (vv. 16–18). Perhaps the wisdom of my dear grandmother sums this up well: If it starts wrong, it won't end well.

In verses 20–22, the writer personifies wisdom as a woman calling out. Verses 20–21 describe a public outcry from Lady Wisdom to people "in the squares," "at the busiest corner," "at the entrance of the city gate," and "above the commotion." Wisdom is neither hiding nor trying to remain concealed. Instead, wisdom is taking the initiative to offer her services to those who choose to receive and follow her guidance. In verse 22, Lady Wisdom asks two rhetorical questions of those who need her counsel the most, which include the naïve and simpleminded, the scoffers who enjoy mockery, and the fools who hate knowledge. Notice the repeated words in the two questions: "How long?" These words suggest a propensity to ignore the warnings of wisdom, perhaps because there seems to be no immediate consequence for following the way of folly. However, there must be an urgency to turn away from foolishness, an urgency to hear and highly regard the call of Lady Wisdom.

III. Answer and Live (Proverbs 1:32–33)

When wisdom calls, as the title of the previous section suggests, the best response is to answer. Verse 23 provides an excellent reason to answer wisdom's call: "If you respond to my warning, then I will pour out my spirit on you and teach you my words" (HCSB). In addition, responding obediently to Lady Wisdom results in avoiding the waywardness that ultimately will destroy simpleminded, complacent fools (v. 32). A final reward is assured to those who answer Lady Wisdom's call: They will "be secure and will live at ease, without dread of disaster" (v. 32). The wise person will enjoy a good life, one full of security and peace.

A thorough reading of Proverbs 1 in its entirety reveals Solomon's intention is to call for his readers to devote themselves to the pursuit of answering the call of wisdom, listening and responding affirmatively to the advice and wise counsel of godly parents, elders, and teachers.

The Lesson Applied

We live in a time when we often prefer not to answer phone calls. We are bombarded by telemarketers and scammers we prefer to avoid at all costs. Often if we cannot identify who's calling from the caller ID or by the name/number that pops up on our cell phones, we choose not to answer. However, there are some calls we cannot afford to miss or save for later.

Solomon reminded readers in Proverbs 1:20 that wisdom calls out to us, and we must listen carefully and respond appropriately. In fact, we must respond with a sense that obeying wisdom is an urgent duty of God's people. Sometimes our response is to ignore her call so we can continue doing whatever it is we would rather be doing, an example of foolishness at its finest. However, Proverbs 1:32 reminds us that blessings, the kind money can't buy, result when we live according to divine wisdom and embrace a life that prioritizes knowing and doing the will of God.

Let's Talk About It

1. We live in a world full of knowledge, innovation, and technology, yet the wisdom described in Proverbs

has become a rarity, including among God's people. What fresh truth has this lesson revealed to you about the importance of godly wisdom?

The Holy Spirit guides as we seek to uncover the truth of the Scriptures. Perhaps this lesson will remind adults that although wisdom takes the initiative to pursue them, we must choose to follow and obey. The lesson also reminds us we must answer wisdom's call with a sense of urgency rather than waiting as long as we can. Foolishness, not wisdom, leads us to believe we have time to wander in waywardness and need not rush to live according to God's will. However, the opposite actually is true (Prov. 1:22).

2. **We tend to define success based on a variety of worldly indicators. How is success defined in your community? In your family? In your church? How does success look based on the verses from Proverbs 1, and does this match the definition of the members of your community, family, and church?**

Success often is defined based on the level of education a person has achieved, the job a person has, the car a person drives, the titles a person holds inside or outside the church, and so forth. Regardless of how *success* is defined in our communities, families, and churches, Proverbs 1 clearly reveals a successful person is one who fears the Lord and pursues godly wisdom. Pursuing possessions, relationships, education, or any other worldly measure of success will leave us feeling empty and wanting.

3. **The unifying principle for this lesson reminds us that feelings of inadequacy can perpetuate a limiting belief system and/or negative attitude, or they can become an opportunity to renew our minds with Scripture. What general truth from this lesson can we apply to our lives when feelings of inadequacy hinder our growth in the Lord?**

This lesson serves as a reminder that negative and limiting belief systems often result from having a fixed mindset about a situation. Every moment of every day is an opportunity to learn and grow in wisdom and maturity of thought. As a matter of fact, the book of Proverbs was written to help us grow in righteousness and integrity (1:3), knowledge (1:4), discernment (1:5), and understanding (1:6).

Wisdom is pursuing us, and God has given us His Word, His Holy Spirit, prayer, and godly people to steer us in the right direction. Feelings of inadequacy must be replaced by the truth found in God's Word. Let us venture to be open to the pursuit of wisdom and its benefits.

Home Daily Devotional Readings

June 8–14, 2020

Monday	Tuesday	Wednesday	Thursday	Friday	Saturday	Sunday
Work for the Good of All	Live Together in Harmony	Wisdom Is Walking Together in Love	Joseph Resists Temptation	Wisdom Saves from Temptation	Walk on Just and Good Paths	Following Godly Wisdom Pays
Galatians 6:1–10	Romans 15:1–6	2 John 4–11	Genesis 39:6–18	Proverbs 2:12–19	Proverbs 2:20–22; 4:24–27	Proverbs 2:1–11

THE VALUE OF WISDOM

ADULT TOPIC:
SEEKING MEANING

BACKGROUND SCRIPTURE:
GENESIS 39; PROVERBS 2

PROVERBS 2:1–11

King James Version

MY son, if thou wilt receive my words, and hide my commandments with thee;
2 So that thou incline thine ear unto wisdom, and apply thine heart to understanding;
3 Yea, if thou criest after knowledge, and liftest up thy voice for understanding;
4 If thou seekest her as silver, and searchest for her as for hid treasures;
5 Then shalt thou understand the fear of the Lord, and find the knowledge of God.
6 For the LORD giveth wisdom: out of his mouth cometh knowledge and understanding.
7 He layeth up sound wisdom for the righteous: he is a buckler to them that walk uprightly.
8 He keepeth the paths of judgment, and preserveth the way of his saints.
9 Then shalt thou understand righteousness, and judgment, and equity; yea, every good path.
10 When wisdom entereth into thine heart, and knowledge is pleasant unto thy soul;
11 Discretion shall preserve thee, understanding shall keep thee:

New Revised Standard Version

MY child, if you accept my words and treasure up my commandments within you,
2 making your ear attentive to wisdom and inclining your heart to understanding;
3 if you indeed cry out for insight, and raise your voice for understanding;
4 if you seek it like silver, and search for it as for hidden treasures—
5 then you will understand the fear of the LORD and find the knowledge of God.
6 For the LORD gives wisdom; from his mouth come knowledge and understanding;
7 he stores up sound wisdom for the upright; he is a shield to those who walk blamelessly,
8 guarding the paths of justice and preserving the way of his faithful ones.
9 Then you will understand righteousness and justice and equity, every good path;
10 for wisdom will come into your heart, and knowledge will be pleasant to your soul;
11 prudence will watch over you; and understanding will guard you.

LESSON SETTING
Time: 970–931 B.C.
Place: Israel

LESSON OUTLINE
I. **Big IFs: Conditions Must Be Met (Proverbs 2:1–4)**
II. **Rewarding THENs (Proverbs 2:5–11)**

UNIFYING PRINCIPLE

People search for life's meaning through wealth, wisdom, or other worldly things. What is the best method to search for meaning in life? Wisdom's treasure is more valuable than riches because it can center a person's heart, will, and thought toward a knowledge of God.

MAIN THOUGHT: For the LORD giveth wisdom: out of his mouth cometh knowledge and understanding. (Proverbs 2:6, KJV)

Introduction

During last week's lesson, we discovered God used Solomon to pen much of the book of Proverbs, which is full of advice for living successfully from God's perspective. Proverbs 1 identified the purpose for writing the book of Proverbs and challenged its readers to recognize and heed wisdom's call in order to live successfully. In addition, it warned of the eventual consequences that result from ignoring wisdom's call.

As we move into chapter 2, Solomon transitions into celebrating the blessings wisdom can bring. In Hebrew, Proverbs 2:1–22 is one elaborate sentence consisting of 22 lines that correspond to the number of letters in the Hebrew alphabet. During this session, we will examine Proverbs 2:1–11 closely to discover conditions that must be met for God's people to experience the blessings provided by wisdom.

Exposition

I. Big IFs: Conditions Must Be Met (Proverbs 2:1–4)

You might remember studying conditional statements at some point while in school. A conditional statement is set up with the words if and then, and such statements require a condition to be met before the latter part of the statement can be true. For example, a parent might say to his or her child, "If your bedroom is clean, then you will be able to play outside with your friends." For the child to be able to run around the neighborhood, hanging with friends, a certain condition must be met—the bedroom must be clean.

Solomon used conditional statements in Proverbs 2:1–11. The if portions of these statements, found in Proverbs 2:1–4, describe the conditions that must be met by the person who is seeking wisdom and meaning in life.

Speaking as a loving parent to a child, Solomon began with "my son" (v. 1). Although he spoke as a parent, he pointed beyond himself and advised the son to listen to wisdom and understanding, which come from the Lord. The first condition that must be met is found in verses 1–2: "if you accept my words and store up my commands within you, listening closely to wisdom and directing your heart to understanding" (HCSB). The word accept in Hebrew denotes taking and carrying along with you (*BlueletterBible.com*). This first condition implies an admiring child holding on to the father's words and commands as valuable teachings. Notice the verb forms in verses 1–2: accept, store up, listening, and directing. It is clear that seeking wisdom is an active process; passively learning facts pertaining to wisdom is not enough. This requires the student of wisdom to be receptive and attentive, listening not only with one's ears, but also with the heart. Summarily, the first condition for gaining wisdom is having receptive ears and a welcoming heart.

The second condition is found in verse 3, which says, "furthermore, if you call out to insight and lift your voice to understanding" (HCSB). To call out (HCSB) or cry out (NRSV) describes an audible request. (Recall from our last lesson that wisdom was calling and crying out in Prov. 1:20–21.) Verse 3 seems to suggest the second condition for gaining wisdom is asking for it. Parents always know when babies need something, not necessarily because they have the language to express their desires, but because they cry out. In the same way, those who seek wisdom must passionately cry out to the Lord as if receiving wisdom is a desperate and urgent need.

The third condition is found in verse 4: "If you seek it like silver and search for it like hidden treasure" (HCSB). Of course, the pronoun it in verse 4 refers to wisdom, and this verse conjures up the imagery of intensely looking for something precious and prized (such as silver and hidden treasure). Searching for wisdom in this manner requires seekers to be determined and committed, much the same as a person who is looking for something deemed priceless does not give up until it is found.

Notice the word understanding appears twice in these verses (see vv. 2–3). This same word appears later in Proverbs 2:6, 11. In Hebrew, this word for understanding describes "competency at a task or skill required to live successfully in society" (*Holman Christian Study Bible*, p. 1033). This particular word does not mean "deep intellectual understanding." Instead, it refers to the skill of discerning the plans and purposes of God in a way that allows one to live skillfully and successfully in the world. As leader of Israel, Solomon was endowed with such understanding (see 1 Kings 4:29), and this type of understanding is a gift from God. The book of Proverbs tells us the person who acquires this God-given understanding is happy (3:13), slow to anger (14:29), even-tempered (17:27), humble (18:2), and successful (19:8).

II. Rewarding THENs (Proverbs 2:5–10)

Proverbs 2:1–4 illuminated several conditions that must be met by those seeking wisdom. In Proverbs 2:5–10, Solomon concluded the if-then conditional statements. The author elaborated on the rewards and benefits that will result for those who seek wisdom and meaning.

First, Solomon explained those who fulfill the conditions, those who seek wisdom as a priority in life, subsequently will "understand the fear of the LORD and discover the knowledge of God" (v. 5, HCSB). Recall from Proverbs 1:7 that the "fear of the Lord is the beginning of wisdom." This means wisdom is not elusive. Rather, those who seek wisdom certainly will find God and the wisdom only He can provide. Wisdom seekers also find more than what they were searching for because the search for wisdom leads to intimate relationship with the true and living God. Isaiah 55:8 reminds us His ways are nothing like our ways and His thoughts go beyond anything we are able to imagine. There is no greater blessing than knowing God and walking according to His ways.

Verses 6–8 elaborate on the blessings that come from understanding the fear of the Lord and discovering "the knowledge of God" (v. 5). Verse 6 affirms God is the Giver of wisdom, knowledge, and understanding (see previous section for deeper insight regarding the meaning of the word understanding). The book of James echoes this same truth (see 1:5). Proverbs 2:7a says, "He stores up success for the upright" (HCSB). Notice the similar language of Proverbs 2:1, in which Solomon exhorts his son to "store up" (HCSB, NIV) or "treasure" (NRSV) his father's commands. The writer suggested that when wisdom seekers make it a priority to store up and live by God's commands, then He in turn will "store up" success, sound judgment, competence, and resources as reward.

Verses 7b–8 emphasize the protection God bestows on wisdom seekers who meet the aforementioned conditions. These verses refer to God as a "shield for those who live with integrity." He also is the Guard for the "paths of justice"; ultimately, He is the only One qualified to "protect the way of His loyal followers" (HCSB). Yet notice His protection extends to those who "live with integrity" (v. 7) and those who are "His loyal followers" (v. 8). Solomon made it clear a commitment to holy living must accompany one's pursuit of wisdom. A person who is seeking wisdom must prioritize following God's commands. In the New Testament, Jesus affirmed the relationship between loving and obeying God: "If you love Me, keep My commands" (John 14:15).

Verse 9 introduces a second *then* statement. In addition to wisdom seekers who fulfill the if conditional statement, understanding the fear of the Lord (v. 5), they also will "then … understand what is right and just and fair—every good path" (v. 9, NIV). God's wisdom will give us a deeper awareness of right and wrong and a deeper desire to live honorably before the Lord.

Verse 10 explains how this will occur: "for wisdom will enter your heart" (NIV). One's heart refers to his or her innermost being. In Hebrew, the heart (more specifically, the gut) is where decisions are made, and our decisions show what is most important to us (Matt. 6:24). Moses commanded the Israelites to love the Lord with all their hearts (Deut. 6:5), knowing this depth of love for God would result in wholehearted devotion and obedience despite life's circumstances. Jesus echoed the priority of loving God in the Parable of the Good Samaritan (see Luke 10:25–37). Summarily, Solomon said in verse 10 that the more we seek wisdom, the more open we will be to God. As we open our hearts to His will, verse 10 tells us wisdom will "be pleasant to [our] souls." In essence, we experience regeneration, acquiring a taste and desire for wisdom and truth just as we can acquire a taste for food.

Proverbs 2:11 includes a final declaration about the protection that wisdom provides. The text says prudence (NRSV) or discretion (HCSB) and understanding will guard and watch over wisdom seekers. In the same way God protects His children, wisdom watches over and guards those who seek and live by wisdom's principles. Proverbs 2:11 repeats the same idea expressed in Proverbs 1:33, which describes the security that those who listen to wisdom will enjoy.

The Lesson Applied

I recently played hide and seek with my three-year-old niece. She is a rambunctious kid with a big personality and a smile that melts my heart. It was her turn to hide, so I counted to twenty and then went looking for her. The only problem is she did not want to be found this time. I usually can find her because she makes noise and hides in the same places. This time, however, she was silent. My heart sank as I looked for her for more than five minutes because I could not find her. The whole family joined in, but no one could find her. (For those who need to know the rest of the story, my niece finally jumped out of her hiding place and yelled, "Surprise!" I have not played the game with her since that brief scare.) When we look at the condition of our world, we might be lulled into thinking wisdom, similar to my niece's behavior in not wanting to be found, is hiding and trying to make it difficult for people who are searching for her to find her.

Today's text reveals the opposite is true. In fact, the key verse for this lesson reminds us "the LORD gives wisdom" (Prov. 2:6). However, the text also informs us certain conditions must be met in order for us to experience the rewards and blessings only Lady Wisdom is able to provide.

Today's wisdom seekers, similar to the son to whom Solomon referred in Proverbs 2:1, must be open to receiving wisdom; they must cry out, in a sense of urgency and desperation, for they must search for it wholeheartedly. In finding wisdom, we find God, experience intimate fellowship with Him, and enjoy the blessings that come with obedience to God's will.

Let's Talk About It

1. **The unifying principle for today's lesson reminds us people constantly are searching for meaning in life, but they often are looking for it in the wrong places. What are some *wrong* ways or places where people search, hoping to find wisdom's treasures?**

   We often expect to find meaning and significance in activities or things such as money, titles, and other worldly accomplishments or the many and varied ways we can serve and/or perhaps gain notoriety for having done. However, bank accounts with high balances and promotions never will give us what we desperately need from God. In addition, we never will be content or satisfied until our statuses and positions in life are defined by the Holy Spirit and the wisdom only He is able to provide.

   While doing and serving often are good and necessary things in which we can and sometimes should be engaged, our true identities are not edified or satisfied simply by being as busy as we possibly can be. Having unlimited engagements on your calendar is not a badge of honor. Sometimes the truest form of wisdom is displayed in the ability to say no and then rest in the Lord for His renewal.

2. **Proverbs 2:1 begins with the words, "My son, if you accept my words." Verse 2 includes, "If you call out to insight." Verse 3 challenges, "If you seek it ... and search for it." God is the great Initiator, but such admonishment makes it clear we must take action if we want to experience God's wisdom to the fullest. Ask the Lord for insight as you examine your heart and motives. What is keeping you from internalizing and fulfilling the *if* conditions in these verses?**

   Often the guilt of choosing sin leads us to believe we have messed up too much for God to love us and redeem our mistakes. In addition, unrepentance and the lack of a deep desire to please God more than we desire to satisfy our fleshly needs keeps us stuck in the muck and mire.

   Fortunately, 1 John 1:9 reminds us that when we confess our sins, our just and faithful heavenly Father forgives us fully and cleanses us completely. It is the goodness of God that leads us to repentance (Rom. 2:4), which in itself is a gift of His grace, but we must be willing to follow and accept a new set of priorities.

Recall the words of the prophet Isaiah in chapter 55 of the book he penned: "'Let the wicked forsake his way, and the unrighteous man his thoughts; let him return to the LORD, and He will have mercy on him; and to our God, for He will abundantly pardon. 'For My thoughts are not your thoughts, nor are your ways My ways,' says the LORD. 'For as the heavens are higher are higher than the earth, so are My ways higher than your ways, and My thoughts than your thoughts'" (vv. 7–9).

This same principle holds true when it comes to seeking godly wisdom of any type or pertaining to any matter with which we must deal in this life, because the search for wisdom really is a search for deeper fellowship with the true and living God. His ways are beyond what we are able to arrive at in our limited human perspective.

Also, Proverbs 2:2 calls us to turn away from our personal agendas so we are able to listen closely to wisdom and direct our hearts to true and deep understanding. Giving up our desires to do things our way is a necessary requirement for experiencing God's best and for finding meaning in life. Finding wisdom is like discovering the pearl of great price.

3. Bible verses such as Proverbs 2:7 remind us God is storing up many eternal benefits and blessings for faithful wisdom seekers and Christ followers. When or how have you seen God release stored-up success on your life or the life of someone else who's living according to wisdom's principles? How can this verse serve as a reminder of God's unmatched faithfulness?

People often become discouraged when it seems as if there is a delay in receiving the rewards and benefits of wise, faithful, godly living. Waiting is hard work when our hours and days seem to be passing us by with vague or inadequate developments. Nevertheless, we are to be encouraged and know God will reward all who walk in wisdom. The reward might be in storage, but it certainly is on the way. Take comfort in the fact that sometimes miracles lie dormant before bursting forth into full flower. Yet, also be aware that our loving Father knows our exact needs, as well as what brings us true joy. Perhaps He withholds blessings until our hearts shift about the things we desire. He alone knows the inner workings of the human heart, and He alone satisfies. Remember to trust in Him and rely on His promises. That is what it means to walk in divine wisdom and faith. Let us trust in Him.

HOME DAILY DEVOTIONAL READINGS
JUNE 15–21, 2020

MONDAY	TUESDAY	WEDNESDAY	THURSDAY	FRIDAY	SATURDAY	SUNDAY
Christ, the Wisdom of God	God Abundantly Rewards Job's Faithfulness	God Restores Job's Family and Wealth	Wisdom Calls the People to Respond	Wisdom Present and Active During Creation	Choose Wisdom and Live	Wisdom Affects All of Life
1 Corinthians 1:18–25	Job 1:1–5	Job 42:10–17	Proverbs 8:1–7	Proverbs 8:22–31	Proverbs 8:32–36	Proverbs 8:8–14, 17–21

THE GIFTS OF WISDOM

ADULT TOPIC: WISDOM'S REWARDS

BACKGROUND SCRIPTURE: JOB 1; 42; PROVERBS 8

PROVERBS 8:8–14, 17–21

King James Version

ALL the words of my mouth are in righteousness; there is nothing froward or perverse in them.

9 They are all plain to him that understandeth, and right to them that find knowledge.

10 Receive my instruction, and not silver; and knowledge rather than choice gold.

11 For wisdom is better than rubies; and all the things that may be desired are not to be compared to it.

12 I wisdom dwell with prudence, and find out knowledge of witty inventions.

13 The fear of the LORD is to hate evil: pride, and arrogancy, and the evil way, and the froward mouth, do I hate.

14 Counsel is mine, and sound wisdom: I am understanding; I have strength.

• • • • •

17 I love them that love me; and those that seek me early shall find me.

18 Riches and honour are with me; yea, durable riches and righteousness.

19 My fruit is better than gold, yea, than fine gold; and my revenue than choice silver.

20 I lead in the way of righteousness, in the midst of the paths of judgment:

21 That I may cause those that love me to inherit substance; and I will fill their treasures.

New Revised Standard Version

ALL the words of my mouth are righteous; there is nothing twisted or crooked in them.

9 They are all straight to one who understands and right to those who find knowledge.

10 Take my instruction instead of silver, and knowledge rather than choice gold;

11 for wisdom is better than jewels, and all that you may desire cannot compare with her.

12 I, wisdom, live with prudence, and I attain knowledge and discretion.

13 The fear of the LORD is hatred of evil. Pride and arrogance and the way of evil and perverted speech I hate.

14 I have good advice and sound wisdom; I have insight, I have strength.

• • • • •

17 I love those who love me, and those who seek me diligently find me.

18 Riches and honor are with me, enduring wealth and prosperity.

19 My fruit is better than gold, even fine gold, and my yield than choice silver.

20 I walk in the way of righteousness, along the paths of justice,

21 endowing with wealth those who love me, and filling their treasuries.

MAIN THOUGHT: Receive my instruction, and not silver; and knowledge rather than choice gold. For wisdom is better than rubies; and all the things that may be desired are not to be compared to it. (Proverbs 8:10–11, KJV)

LESSON SETTING

Time: 970–931 B.C.
Place: Israel

LESSON OUTLINE

I. **Wisdom's Value (Proverbs 8:8–11)**
II. **Wisdom's Virtue (Proverbs 8:12–14, 17–21)**

UNIFYING PRINCIPLE

People desire wisdom and rightfully expect to be rewarded when they have searched diligently for wisdom and truth. Why is wisdom so desirable? Wisdom's value is more than the tangible material gain of things such as precious metals and stones. True wisdom gives applicable knowledge to those who pursue her, as well as courage, and leads seekers along God's path of justice and righteousness.

INTRODUCTION

Solomon is credited with writing most of the book of Proverbs. Solomon ruled Israel from 970–931 B.C., and the portions of the book that he wrote most likely were written during his reign as king. After having gained some valuable life experience, he shared the wisdom afforded to him through the course of his life on earth.

Most adults are willing to search for something if they believe their searches will be fruitful. For example, it's normal and reasonable to search multiple car lots for a good deal on a new car, as well as search multiple shops to find the perfect outfit for special occasions. Because there is a tangible reward at the end of a search, we don't give up until we've found what we need. The same is true in our searches for wisdom. Those who search diligently will "understand the fear of the LORD and discover the knowledge of God" (Prov. 2:5). There are blessings, spiritual and perhaps sometimes (but not always) material, that result from living according to godly wisdom. This month, we are studying wisdom from the book of Proverbs. Today, we continue studying God's sage advice in Proverbs 8, discovering more about wisdom's value and virtue.

EXPOSITION

I. WISDOM'S VALUE (PROVERBS 8:8–11)

Proverbs 8 includes the Bible's most detailed personification of wisdom. In this chapter, Solomon described wisdom as a beautiful woman of high esteem and value. In the first seven verses, Solomon portrayed wisdom as a woman calling out in the busy city streets to anyone who was willing to listen, to heed her warnings and advice for living well. She extended a public invitation to "people" (v. 4), "mankind" (NIV), the "inexperienced" (v. 5, HCSB), and those who are "foolish" (v. 5, HCSB). In other words, she was inclusive, rejected no one, and called all people groups to herself that they might be blessed with information they would need to live God-honoring lives that please their Creator.

The fact that Lady Wisdom called out in the streets for all to hear seems to indicate she is no respecter of persons but is accessible to all who seek her and are willing to answer her call. Instead of speaking from the perspective of a father to a son (see lessons 1 and 2), the writer allowed wisdom to speak for herself via the literary device of personification.

Through personification, writers give human characteristics to inanimate objects or concepts. Personification can be seen in verses 7–8. Wisdom personifies herself as a powerful speaker, describing her words as "righteous" (v. 8), "clear to the perceptive" (v. 9), and "right to those who discover knowledge" (HCSB).

Verses 8–9 make it clear that whatever a person hears from wisdom is sure to be true and righteous. Because wisdom's source is God, it should be no surprise her words never are "crooked or perverse" (v. 8, NIV). Instead, they are "clear to the perceptive" (v. 9, HCSB) and "upright to those who have found knowledge" (v. 9, NIV).

Proverbs 8:1–9 encourage people to listen to Lady Wisdom's call with open hearts and receptive ears, but verse 10 requires action: "choose my instruction … [and] knowledge" (NIV). The encouragement to make a choice is reminiscent of a similar admonition in Joshua 24:15, which urges, "choose this day whom you will serve" (NRSV). The reason for choosing seems obvious after a close reading of verses 10–11: Wisdom's value far exceeds that of silver, gold, and precious jewels such as rubies.

Gold has held its value or increased since ancient times because it is hard to find in nature. In addition, it is strong enough to maintain its condition for centuries. Gold has been used as money, as a symbol of wealth, and as decoration and jewelry, yet Solomon affirmed wisdom is far more important and priceless. Unlike precious metals and jewels, wisdom cannot be exchanged or traded, only employed by the wise for living well.

Readers can imagine the writer of this proverb using a balance scale with wisdom on one side and precious jewels and metals on the other side. The scale tips in wisdom's favor every time because "nothing desirable can compare with it" (v. 11, HCSB). That is because despite the durability of precious metals, they are components of this world, which are passing away. Nothing material is lasting and eternal. On the final day, when the course of time has reached its end, all that currently is perishing will cease to exist.

Wisdom, however, is eternal. True wisdom includes knowledge about God, as well as knowing God Himself. True wisdom includes life principles that never will change because they align with God's Law, His unchanging Word of Truth. Those who belong to Him seek to live by these principles as outlined in Scripture because doing so provides countless benefits.

To live by godly, scriptural principles reduces our stress, mitigates worry and anxiety, absolves us when falsely accused, produces good fruit in our lives, provides confidence, strengthens us, gives us courage, bolsters our reputations, confirms our good character, and causes others to hold us in high regard and seek us out for counsel.

Wisdom still is calling. The question is: Will we choose to accept and live by wisdom's principles? Our lives, society in general, our communities, our families, and our churches would be remarkably different if we valued wisdom in the way Solomon suggested we should in this text.

II. Wisdom's Virtue (Proverbs 8:12–14, 17–21)

Virtue can be defined as "morally good behavior or godly character." In Proverbs 8:12, Lady Wisdom personified herself as a member of the family of good virtues. In the text, wisdom speaks of "sharing a home" (HCSB) and living with three roommates: prudence, knowledge, and discretion. In the book of Proverbs, the word prudence has a positive connotation and means "sensible behavior or the right use of knowledge in a given situation." The word knowledge refers to more than just book sense; it includes knowledge of what is true and right and will remain right and true. The word discretion refers to "careful choices and behavior that result from clear, godly thinking." These virtues are complementary. The fact that wisdom, prudence, knowledge, and discretion live together in harmony in the same home actually means that when we find one of these virtues, we usually find the others. They are natural by-products of one another and build on one another. Those who are wise practice discretion and prudence, as well as seek knowledge.

Proverbs 8:13 describes a prerequisite for fearing the Lord. Recall from Proverbs 1:7 that the "fear of the LORD is the beginning of knowledge," and finding wisdom requires awe and reverence for the Lord that results in surrendering and giving Him the proper place in our lives.

In verse 13, Lady Wisdom explains a necessary aspect of fearing the Lord is hating anything that dishonors or displeases Him. The wise person loves what God loves and hates what God hates, which according to this verse includes evil conduct, arrogance, pride, and inappropriate speech. Wisdom calls us to turn away from these dispositions because they interfere with our relationship with the Lord.

As we read verse 14, it is helpful to remember wisdom comes from God, and she derives her characteristics from God. Lady Wisdom explains she is powerful and can provide good advice, sound judgment, and insight—all qualities of God and all of which are needed for godly decision-making and success.

Lady Wisdom's power resides in the fact she encompasses truth, and truth never changes. When we are operating in truth and wisdom, we possess power. We do not have to allow life's circumstances to destroy or steal our peace when we know we are acting and living according to godly wisdom and truth. Though we may face trials, including false accusations, misinformation, the disbelief (and sometimes insecurity) of others, we can choose to maintain our integrity by clinging to godly faith and wisdom. God's truth never changes, and He promises to share with us His inexhaustible wisdom.

We are able to live wise, virtuous lives only when (according to v. 17) there is a passionate pursuit. Think about how people who are in love pursue one another, sacrificing time and money to be in the other's presence. In the earlier verses of Proverbs 8, Wisdom seems to offer herself to everyone (see vv. 4–5). However, verse 17 makes it clear that only those who "love and seek" wisdom actually will receive her benefits. James 1:5 seems to echo this same truth: "If you need wisdom, ask our generous God, and He will give it to you. He will not rebuke you for asking." Proverbs 8:17 coupled with James 1:5 provides reassurance that when we come to God seeking wisdom, He will give us what we need.

In verses 18–21, Wisdom promises a variety of gifts to those who passionately search for her, which include riches, honor, wealth, and an inheritance. Bear in mind, though, there is no time line provided for when these benefits, gifts, and promises will become ours. In a sense, they already belong to us. Our Father is storing up treasures for us in heaven; and in our limited vision and understanding, we cannot begin to conceive all the Lord has planned for His children once we return home.

Yet, in another sense, we already possess many blessings and benefits as children of the Most High God. As coheirs with Christ, we already have access to our internal inheritance, including but not limited to assurance of salvation, the peace that surpasses all understanding, and more.

Another example of personification appears in verse 20, where wisdom has the ability to walk. Wisdom walks and leads her followers to where they will be rewarded, but notice that wisdom will lead her followers "in the way of righteousness, along the paths of justice" (v. 20, HCSB). Because wisdom's source is God, she only is able to lead her followers in the ways of God. Following wisdom results in blessings and rewards money cannot buy. That is, the life of wisdom is all about living righteously and justly, and spiritual (and perhaps material) prosperity is the result.

We spend our lives searching for meaning and success. Proverbs 8 affirms we find more than what we are looking for when we search for the right things in the right places. We must value wisdom to search for it; and when we do, we will discover wisdom's value far exceeds anything we can imagine.

The Lesson Applied

Not every pursuit in life is worthy of our time and effort. Wisdom and discernment help us determine when, where, and how we spend our time pursuing education, careers, right relationships, strategic partnerships, investment options, and more. Proverbs 8 reminds us there are no shortcuts to or substitutes for divine wisdom. Today's lesson describes wisdom's value and virtue and challenges us to evaluate our priorities. If we want to experience wisdom's incomparable value, we must choose to pursue wisdom's instruction as a priority (Prov. 8:20).

Let's Talk About It

1. **Paul challenged us to remember and value the power of self-examination in 1 Corinthians 11:27. Reflect on the wisest and most foolish things to which you are committed right now.**

   Read Proverbs 8:17 as a reminder that God wants us to apply to our lives what we are learning from His Word.

   Also, remind the class He will respond affirmatively when we repent and ask for power to walk more closely with Him. Our God is knowable and desires to be known. The whole reason He allowed His Son to die on the cross was in order to bring all who belong to Him home to dwell with Him forever in the home He is building for us. So, from this we can discern and conclude He desires deep and intimate relationships with each of His children. Jesus told His disciples in Matthew 11:28 to, "Come unto me, all ye that labor and are heavy laden, and I will give you rest." To accept His invitation is the epitome of acting wisely and prudently.

2. **Proverbs 8:10 exhorts, "Choose my instruction instead of silver, knowledge rather than choice gold, for wisdom is more precious than**

rubies, and nothing you desire can compare with her." What do you tend to prioritize in your life? How have you experienced the incomparable value of wisdom in your own life? Do you normally find yourself valuing wisdom in the same way Solomon valued it in this text?

Adults may answer the question about their priorities with a variety of responses, including jobs, families, material possessions, major achievements and accomplishments, and so forth. As class members discuss their priorities in their own lives, be sure to affirm the necessity of these good things as being honorable priorities that foster hope and allow us to continue to grow.

However, as good as they are, we must never allow them to get in the way of our devotion to God and our pursuit of wisdom. This is because His wisdom will equip us to live our lives successfully as well as manage our responsibilities in ways that honor God. To allow other priorities to dethrone Him is to enter idolatry. Adults may or may not have found themselves valuing wisdom, but more than likely this unit has challenged learners to think more deeply about wisdom's value and role in their lives.

3. In response to this lesson, what is the most important action you can take to follow wisdom more closely?

You may want to remind your listeners of Lady Wisdom's challenge in Proverbs 8:10: "Choose my instruction instead of silver, knowledge rather than choice gold" (NIV). You also might want to point out Proverbs 8:21: "Those who love me inherit wealth. I will fill their treasuries."

Remind learners true wisdom is eternal while things of this world are temporal, fleeting, and passing away. Encourage them to store up treasure in heaven, for those things that are stored in and with the Father never can be taken away from us or stolen out of His hand. He always and forever will take care of what and who belongs to Him.

4. How important is it for Christians today to pay attention to the wisdom expressed by the writer of Proverbs?

The book of Proverbs was developed and placed in the biblical canon for reproof, correction, inspiration, and discipline like all other Scripture. These words of wisdom enable Christians to manage their lifestyles appropriately. The instructions given here always should be considered as a way to enhance life.

HOME DAILY DEVOTIONAL READINGS
JUNE 21–28, 2020

MONDAY	TUESDAY	WEDNESDAY	THURSDAY	FRIDAY	SATURDAY	SUNDAY
Law Provides the Edge	Wise and Foolish Bridesmaids	Church Proclaims the Wisdom of God	No Wise Person among You?	Wise and Foolish Builders	Benefits of Making the Wise Choice	Wisdom Delivers Many Benefits
Psalm 119:97–104	Matthew 25:1–13	Ephesians 3:7–13	1 Corinthians 6:1–6	Matthew 7:24–27	Psalm 1	Proverbs 9:1–6, 8–10, 13–18

WISDOM'S FEAST

ADULT TOPIC: INVITATION TO WISDOM

BACKGROUND SCRIPTURE: PROVERBS 9

PROVERBS 9:1–6, 8–10, 13–18

King James Version

WISDOM hath builded her house, she hath hewn out her seven pillars:

2 She hath killed her beasts; she hath mingled her wine; she hath also furnished her table.

3 She hath sent forth her maidens: she crieth upon the highest places of the city,

4 Whoso is simple, let him turn in hither: as for him that wanteth understanding, she saith to him,

5 Come, eat of my bread, and drink of the wine which I have mingled.

6 Forsake the foolish, and live; and go in the way of understanding.

• • • • •

8 Reprove not a scorner, lest he hate thee: rebuke a wise man, and he will love thee.

9 Give instruction to a wise man, and he will be yet wiser: teach a just man, and he will increase in learning.

10 The fear of the LORD is the beginning of wisdom: and the knowledge of the holy is understanding.

• • • • •

13 A foolish woman is clamorous: she is simple, and knoweth nothing.

14 For she sitteth at the door of her house, on a seat in the high places of the city,

15 To call passengers who go right on their ways:

16 Whoso is simple, let him turn in hither: and as for him that wanteth understanding, she saith to him,

New Revised Standard Version

WISDOM has built her house, she has hewn her seven pillars.

2 She has slaughtered her animals, she has mixed her wine, she has also set her table.

3 She has sent out her servant-girls, she calls from the highest places in the town,

4 "You that are simple, turn in here!" To those without sense she says,

5 "Come, eat of my bread and drink of the wine I have mixed.

6 Lay aside immaturity, and live, and walk in the way of insight."

• • • • •

8 A scoffer who is rebuked will only hate you; the wise, when rebuked, will love you.

9 Give instruction to the wise, and they will become wiser still; teach the righteous and they will gain in learning.

10 The fear of the LORD is the beginning of wisdom, and the knowledge of the Holy One is insight.

• • • • •

13 The foolish woman is loud; she is ignorant and knows nothing.

14 She sits at the door of her house, on a seat at the high places of the town,

15 calling to those who pass by, who are going straight on their way,

16 "You who are simple, turn in here!" And to those without sense she says,

MAIN THOUGHT: Forsake the foolish, and live; and go in the way of understanding. (Proverb 9:6, KJV)

PROVERBS 9:1–6, 8–10, 13–18

King James Version	*New Revised Standard Version*
17 Stolen waters are sweet, and bread eaten in secret is pleasant.	**17 "Stolen water is sweet, and bread eaten in secret is pleasant."**
18 But he knoweth not that the dead are there; and that her guests are in the depths of hell.	**18 But they do not know that the dead are there, that her guests are in the depths of Sheol.**

LESSON SETTING

Time: 970–931 B.C.
Place: Israel

LESSON OUTLINE

I. Accept the Invitation to Dine with Lady Wisdom (Proverbs 9:1–6)
II. Remember the Theme of the Proverbs (Proverbs 9:8–10)
III. Forego the Invitation to Dine with Folly (Proverbs 9:13–18)

UNIFYING PRINCIPLE

Two competing voices call to us on life's journey: wisdom and folly. Why should we heed the call of wisdom? Wisdom gives instruction to those who are wise to seek her, yet the foolish always will suffer their own downfalls. Recall James 1:5 tells us, "If any of lacks wisdom, let him ask of God, who gives to all liberally and without reproach, and it will be given to him." Therefore, we are able to conclude that if we do not have the wisdom we need, it's our own fault for not asking the Lord to help us understand. The Lord does not withhold wisdom from those who come to Him.

INTRODUCTION

Solomon is credited with authoring the majority of the book of Proverbs, including Proverb 9. Solomon ruled Israel from 970–931 B.C., and the portions written by Solomon most likely would have been written during his reign as king.

We all enjoy receiving invitations to something special. Whether a birthday party, a retirement celebration, a graduation, or a wedding, we feel special when people think enough of us to extend an invitation to us. This is our fourth and final lesson in this unit on the wisdom from Proverbs. As we carefully read Proverb 9, we not only will be reminded of the all-important theme of fearing the Lord, but we also will investigate contrasting invitations from Lady Wisdom and Lady Folly. We may be delighted to receive both invitations; however, in the end, only one is worth accepting.

EXPOSITION

I. ACCEPT THE INVITATION TO DINE WITH LADY WISDOM (PROVERBS 9:1–6)

During last week's lesson, we studied Proverb 8. In verse 12, Solomon alluded to wisdom sharing a home with other virtues. Similarly in Proverb 9, Lady Wisdom has "built her house" (v. 1), and its seven pillars signify that her house is large, spacious, and well-built on sturdy supports. Perhaps similar to homeowners we know today, Lady Wisdom has a flair for hospitality and entertaining. She makes all the necessary preparations for a lavish meal, which include slaughtering and preparing animals to serve for meat, carefully mixing the wine, and setting the table (v. 2). The reference to mixing wine may refer to diluting it with water. For example, Passover wine was mixed with three parts of water to one part of wine. This verse also might refer to the custom of mixing spices into the wine to enhance its flavor (see Ps. 75:8) (*Holman Old Testament Commentary*). After closely reading verses 1–2, one easily is able to detect Lady Wisdom's intentionality and her investment. The imagery in this verse probably reminds modern readers of Thanksgiving or Christmas meals. Symbolically, wisdom is ready to share her valuable instruction with all her guests who desire to partake (*HCSB Study Bible*, p. 1043).

Now that her home is ready and the feast is prepared, Lady Wisdom sends out her servants to act as messengers on her behalf (v. 3). This scene reminds us of Jesus' parable of the large banquet in Luke 14:15-24, in which, He commanded His servants to, "Go out into the highways and hedges, and compel them to come in, that My house may be filled" (14:23).

However, in this case, Lady Wisdom does not fully delegate this responsibility to others; she also plays a critical role in extending a public invitation. Verse 3 tells us, "She [also] calls from the highest places in the town" (NRSV). This is consistent with her character, as we already have observed Lady Wisdom calling out in the streets and public squares (Prov. 1:20–21) and from the hilly areas overlooking the city (Prov. 8:2–3).

It probably is not surprising that wisdom's guest list is not filled with the upper echelon of society. Instead, wisdom actually speaks with her voice saying, "Whoever is inexperienced, enter here! To the one who lacks sense … come, eat my bread and drink the wine I have mixed" (v. 4, HCSB). This feast is reserved for those who realize they need help the most. Wisdom invites the simple and inexperienced to eat and take in all she has to offer. Instead of following the wrong path, Lady Wisdom invites us to pursue wisdom's way so we might enjoy her benefits.

Wisdom's invitation is an offer we cannot refuse. By necessity, accepting wisdom's invitation will require leaving some things behind (as the title of this section suggests), such as immaturity and naiveté, according to verse 6. Those who need wisdom must "lay aside" (v. 6, NRSV) these weights so they may "live and walk in the way of insight" (NRSV). This is similar to the encouragement from the writer of Hebrews 12:1, which urges, "let us lay aside every weight, and the sin which doth so easily beset us" (KJV).

II. Remember the Theme of the Proverbs (Proverbs 9:8–10)

Verses 8–9 seem to shift focus to learning from correction. Correction is one of wisdom's best teaching methodologies; however, not everyone can receive it. Solomon provided contrasting responses to correction in verses 8–9. The mocker, for example in verse 8, hates those who try to correct or rebuke him. On the other hand, a wise person has a teachable spirit and loves correction, instruction, and the people who are willing to try to help him or her. Wise people don't view such advice as criticism, but as information for improvement because in the end, correction makes receptive learners better and stronger. This seems to echo Hebrews 12:6, which reminds us correction, chastisement, and discipline are ways God demonstrates His love for us.

In addition to inviting wisdom seekers to partake of her bountiful blessings, Lady Wisdom speaks again in verse 10, this time reminding her listeners that, "the fear of the LORD is the beginning of wisdom" (see also vv. 1:7 and 8:3). Walking in wisdom requires awe and reverence for the Lord that results in surrendering and giving Him the proper place in one's life. This same fear of the Lord is required for a person to be open to receiving correction (see vv. 8–9). Without relating to God properly, following His wisdom never will be a reality in one's life. It goes without saying that fearing the Lord is a theme of Proverbs, but it also must be the posture of our lives.

III. Forego the Invitation to Dine with Folly (Proverbs 9:13–18)

For every invitation, there is a competing invitation. For example, will you accept the birthday party invitation, or will you accept the invitation to spend your time doing whatever you choose? Will you accept an invitation to go to church, or will you accept the invitation to rest a few more hours? Every invitation has a competing invitation, and every invitation requires a choice.

In Proverbs 9:1–6, Lady Wisdom extended an invitation to all who are open to receiving all she has to offer with one caveat: Those who have chosen to follow wisdom's path must leave behind everything that is not a good fit for the journey. In verses 8–9, Solomon reminded readers about a critical theme of the book: "The fear of the LORD is the beginning of wisdom" (v. 10). In these final verses, Solomon describes a competing invitation from Lady Folly (for a definition of folly, see the glossary below).

Also personified as a woman in verses 13–18, Lady Folly exudes the opposite of Lady Wisdom as she attempts to lure guests into accepting her invitation. She is described as "loud" (NRSV) and "rowdy" (HCSB) in verse 13a. She is just as ignorant as her guests are, and she knows nothing according to verse 13b. She is ignorant when it comes to the things of God, and she "knows nothing" about walking in wisdom, surrendering to God's agenda, or living in light of His will.

Like wisdom, folly positions herself on the highest point so many people can hear her invitation. Recall that Lady Wisdom sent her servants out with invitations to compel people to come to her intricately prepared feast of godly instruction (Prov. 9:1–6). Folly, on the other hand, "sits at the door of her house, on a seat at the highest places of the town, calling to those who pass by, who are going straight on their way" (vv. 14–15, NRSV).

In your sanctified imagination, can you imagine folly shouting to passersby? The phrase, those "who are going straight on their way," more than likely refers to those who are living godly lives (see Prov. 4:25–27). Lady Wisdom is industrious, resourceful, and hardworking (Prov. 9:1–3), and her mission is to align those who accept her invitation with God's purposes. In contrast, Lady Folly sits and yells, and her goal is to lead people away from God's way. It is important to note that chairs as we have today were rare in ancient times. The word seat in verse 14 means a throne or seat of honor fit for a person of power, authority, and royal dignity (*BlueletterBible.com*). Only kings and honored teachers sat on such seats on a regular basis. Lady Folly's sitting symbolically in verse 14 represents her false claim of authority to rule or teach (*HCSB Study Bible*, p. 1044).

Lady Folly names her target audience in verse 16: "the inexperienced" (HCSB) or "the simple" (NRSV) and "the one who lacks sense" (HCSB). Notice that folly extends her invitation to the same invitees as Lady Wisdom (see v. 4), but her lackluster menu does not radiate the same quality. Folly offers only bread and stolen water, whereas wisdom offers meat and wine.

We must remember, though, that these vulnerable people have the ability to choose, just as contemporary Christians are able to make good or bad decisions. We can resist temptation and humbly accept wisdom's invitation, or we can choose to remain foolish. Wisdom's feast leads to maturity, insight, and life. However, verse 18 informs readers that folly's invitation is like the unlucky doors on *Let's Make a Deal.* These unlucky doors may seem appealing at first glance; but in reality, death lies waiting behind the door. When folly seems to be competing for our attention, we must take time to read the fine print and think through the unintended consequences that may result when we choose any path that dishonors God. Indeed, Folly's invitation is one offer that we simply must refuse.

The Lesson Applied

We live in a world where we are intrigued by, yet often leery of, enticing offers and invitations. When it comes to the choice between wisdom and folly, the answer should be a no-brainer. In this unit, we have studied passages from Proverbs 1–9 that present two paths: the path of wisdom leading to life (successful life on earth and eternal life in heaven) and the path of folly leading to death. Throughout the book, God's wisdom is personified as a gracious woman who invites everyone to come and learn from her.

We face myriad choices every day, some that lead to blessings and rewards and some that lead to sin's consequences. In the presence of various options, it is comforting to know wisdom's invitation is a great exchange. We must lay aside immaturity and naïveté in order to follow wisdom and experience God's best. The appropriate response to this lesson is clear. Accept the right invitation and choose wisdom. Sacrificing the mediocre for eternal life and God's best certainly is worth it.

Let's Talk About It

1. **Proverbs 9:3 says Lady Wisdom sends out her servants to invite anyone who will accept her invitation to come. God continues to use people to encourage us to live wisely. Whom has God sent out and used to encourage you to live wisely?**

   God can use anyone to get His message to you. For contemporary wisdom seekers, He specifically uses pastors, teachers, parents, mentors, and other Christians in the body of Christ to encourage us to live wisely. Pray that God will give adults discerning ears so they will be able to distinguish between the invitations of wisdom and folly. Also pray the Holy Spirit will empower them to resist folly's temptation, realizing the appeal is short-lived.

Sometimes there are things we desire so much we are willing to compromise what we know is truly the wise thing to do. More mature Christians are able to restrain themselves and wait on the Lord to act, to change circumstances and/or provide whatever it is we are needing the most. Sometimes, whatever it was we thought we needed actually is a barrier to the greater blessing the Lord wants to provide. It is wise to wait on His perfect timing.

2. **What is the most important thing you can do right now to begin following wisdom more closely?**

The answer to this question will be unique and specific to each person you ask; but, by all means, encourage adults to apply the principles they have learned to all aspects of their lives.

We have choices; so, remaining immature, gullible, naïve, and foolish does not have to be what any of us choose. Remind students the proverbs we have studied have taught us that everyone can find true and eternal life and escape the terrible consequences of foolishness. Far better is it for ourselves, our relationships, and the world when we choose to pay attention to wisdom's call and obey wisdom's advice.

3. **Whose lives are you affecting: spouse, children, grandchildren, neighbors, church members, coworkers? Are others learning from your witness what it means to fear the Lord and live a life of wisdom?**

Most of us probably are able to identify people in our lives whom we consider to be wise and God-fearing. We esteem such people and seek them out when we need to talk through a situation with someone. However, can people say the same is true of us and that they seek us for godly guidance and understanding to a particular situation in which they find themselves? In response to this unit of study from the book of Proverbs, challenge adults to consider whether they have accepted Lady Wisdom's invitation to the point of experiencing transformation. Lead adults to evaluate whether the people in their circles of influence can see wisdom at work in their lives and the extent to which they are modeling lives that have answered wisdom's call.

HOME DAILY DEVOTIONAL READINGS
JUNE 28–JULY 5, 2020

MONDAY	TUESDAY	WEDNESDAY	THURSDAY	FRIDAY	SATURDAY	SUNDAY
Wise Counsel for Defending Your Faith	Wise Deeds of the Coming Messiah	John the Baptist, God's Messenger	The Messiah's Wise Deeds	Woes on Unwise Cities	Wisdom's Invitation to Come and Rest	Wisdom Is Vindicated by Her Deeds
Matthew 10:16–23	Isaiah 35:3–10	Luke 7:24–28	Matthew 11:1–6	Matthew 11:20–24	Matthew 11:25–30	Matthew 11:7–19

WISDOM'S VINDICATION

ADULT TOPIC:
WISDOM IN ACTION

BACKGROUND SCRIPTURE:
MATTHEW 11:1–19

MATTHEW 11:7–19

King James Version

AND as they departed, Jesus began to say unto the multitudes concerning John, What went ye out into the wilderness to see? A reed shaken with the wind?

8 But what went ye out for to see? A man clothed in soft raiment? behold, they that wear soft clothing are in kings' houses.

9 But what went ye out for to see? A prophet? yea, I say unto you, and more than a prophet.

10 For this is he, of whom it is written, Behold, I send my messenger before thy face, which shall prepare thy way before thee.

11 Verily I say unto you, Among them that are born of women there hath not risen a greater than John the Baptist: notwithstanding he that is least in the kingdom of heaven is greater than he.

12 And from the days of John the Baptist until now the kingdom of heaven suffereth violence, and the violent take it by force.

13 For all the prophets and the law prophesied until John.

14 And if ye will receive it, this is Elias, which was for to come.

15 He that hath ears to hear, let him hear.

16 But whereunto shall I liken this generation? It is like unto children sitting in the markets, and calling unto their fellows,

17 And saying, We have piped unto you, and ye have not danced; we have mourned unto you, and ye have not lamented.

18 For John came neither eating nor drinking, and they say, He hath a devil.

New Revised Standard Version

AS they went away, Jesus began to speak to the crowds about John: "What did you go out into the wilderness to look at? A reed shaken by the wind?

8 What then did you go out to see? Someone dressed in soft robes? Look, those who wear soft robes are in royal palaces.

9 What then did you go out to see? A prophet? Yes, I tell you, and more than a prophet.

10 This is the one about whom it is written, 'See, I am sending my messenger ahead of you, who will prepare your way before you.'

11 Truly I tell you, among those born of women no one has arisen greater than John the Baptist; yet the least in the kingdom of heaven is greater than he.

12 From the days of John the Baptist until now the kingdom of heaven has suffered violence, and the violent take it by force.

13 For all the prophets and the law prophesied until John came;

14 and if you are willing to accept it, he is Elijah who is to come.

15 Let anyone with ears listen!

16 "But to what will I compare this generation? It is like children sitting in the marketplaces and calling to one another,

17 'We played the flute for you, and you did not dance; we wailed, and you did not mourn.'

18 For John came neither eating nor drinking, and they say, 'He has a demon';

MAIN THOUGHT: The Son of man came eating and drinking, and they say, Behold a man gluttonous, and a winebibber, a friend of publicans and sinners. But wisdom is justified of her children. (Matthew 11:19, KJV)

King James Version	*New Revised Standard Version*
19 The Son of man came eating and drinking, and they say, Behold a man gluttonous, and a winebibber, a friend of publicans and sinners. But wisdom is justified of her children.	**19 the Son of Man came eating and drinking, and they say, 'Look, a glutton and a drunkard, a friend of tax collectors and sinners!' Yet wisdom is vindicated by her deeds."**

LESSON SETTING

Time: circa A.D. 26–28
Place: Galilee

LESSON OUTLINE

I. The Jews Foolishly Reject John the Baptist (Matthew 11:7–11)
II. Jesus Challenges the Jews to Listen and Accept (Matthew 11:12–15)
III. The Proof Is in His Deeds (Matthew 11:16–19)

UNIFYING PRINCIPLE

People often label unusual or unexpected behavior as eccentric, foolish, or even wrong and sometimes vilify the person whose behavior they condemn. What should we think when someone's behavior is unexpected? In Matthew, Jesus said His and John's behavior, while unusual in their day, eventually would prove wise. This week we transition from studying the wisdom of Proverbs and consider the Gospels' teaching on wisdom.

Christians live counter to culture. It's not easy to be different, especially when others misunderstand our intentions. Yet as we learned from Proverbs, fearing the Lord and walking in wisdom causes us to stick out like sore thumbs because God's holy standards are contrary to culture's. Today we'll learn about two men bold enough to live wise, God-honoring lives when others deemed them odd and eccentric.

INTRODUCTION

The Gospel of Luke informs us John the Baptist's ministry began in the fifteenth year of the reign of Tiberius Caesar, year A.D. 26 (3:1). Jesus began His public ministry shortly thereafter, when He was about thirty years old (3:23).

EXPOSITION

I. THE JEWS FOOLISHLY REJECT JOHN THE BAPTIST (MATTHEW 11:7–11)

To understand the context for today's lesson, we'll review Matthew 11:1–6. Jesus and His disciples had been ministering throughout Galilee. His relative and forerunner, John the Baptist, sat in prison, wondering if Jesus truly was the long-awaited Messiah he had believed Him to be since the womb (Luke 1:41–44).

John had been imprisoned (for details, see Matt. 11:1–4; also 4:12 and Mark 6:16–20), and his imprisonment had been the impetus for Jesus to continue the ministry John had announced. Though he had expressed faith in Jesus, incarceration was taking a toll on John, causing him to need confirmation and clarity of Jesus' identity. John also probably was swayed by popular expectations of the Messiah; most Jews were expecting their Messiah to deliver them from political oppression, which was the reason for John's imprisonment. So,

John sent his disciples with a message to Jesus: "Are you the One … or should we expect someone else?" (Matt. 11:3).

Jesus simply could have said yes; yet, He chose to give evidence and facts to John, proving His Messiahship. He told John's disciples to "report to John what you hear and see" (11:4). There were miraculous healings, the dead had been raised, and the Gospel was reaching the poor.

Matthew's goal in 11:7–19 was to reveal the rejection in the hearts of the Jewish people, first of John the Baptist and then Jesus. Recall Proverbs 8:17, in which Lady Wisdom said: "I love those who love me, and those who seek me diligently find me" (NRSV). Because Jesus did not fit their expectations of the Messiah, many Jews and their religious leaders were unable to receive Jesus' message and ministry. Their rejection should remind us that when we do not understand all that God is doing or His messengers, we should pray for and diligently seek wisdom to understand from God's perspective.

After sending John's disciples back with evidence confirming His identity, Jesus turned His attention to the crowd around Him and used this opportunity to talk about John the Baptist. The people in the crowd probably were familiar with John and his ministry. The primary setting for John's ministry was in the wilderness or desert of Judea (Matt. 3:1), and he certainly had a unique fashion sense and diet (Matt, 3:4). Still, people went out of their way to see and hear John—"from Jerusalem, all Judea, and all the vicinity of the Jordan were flocking to him" (Matt. 3:6)—as they were captivated by his methods and message of repentance.

In verse 7, Jesus asked the crowd a poignant question: What were those who were traveling to the wilderness to hear John expecting to witness? Certainly, they were not expecting to see a "reed swayed by the wind" (v. 7, NIV), a metaphor for a person who lacks wisdom and conviction and is easily swayed by others. They would not have been expecting to see a wealthy teacher (v. 8). It is as if Jesus were telling them they knew what they were seeking when they made the trek into the desert—John the mighty prophet of God—because his reputation preceded him.

In verse 9, Jesus confirmed that regardless of whether they realized it, John exceeded their expectations. He was more than the typical Old Testament prophet. From his miraculous conception to elderly and barren parents, John had been given a mission that set him apart from all other prophets: "he will be filled with the Holy Spirit before he is born. He will return many people of Israel to the Lord their God. He will go on before the Lord … to ready a people prepared for the Lord" (Luke 1:15–17). In verse 10, Jesus quoted Malachi 3:1 to identify John as the prophesied messenger and Himself as the promised Messiah.

Throughout the Gospels, Jesus used verbiage such as, "I assure you" (v. 10), "Truly I tell you" (v. 10), or "Verily I say unto you" (v. 10) to emphasize what He was about to say. Jesus affirmed none was greater than John the Baptist because of his divine purpose and commitment to obedience. Also, notice at the end of verse 11 that Jesus introduced a new measuring stick for greatness to show that success from God's perspective typically does not correspond to society's ideals. John's imprisonment was not the image of success then or today. Yet wisdom in action requires us to see from God's perspective rather than our own. These countercultural Kingdom values and perspectives Jesus was teaching in verse 11 would have been difficult for the Jews to accept.

When we willingly yield our hearts and our hands to God to fulfill His purposes through us, the outcome may not always be success as determined by worldly, cultural standards. However, humility in the Kingdom is great. Matthew 19:30 echoes this truth: "But many who are the greatest now will be least important then, and those who seem least important now will be the greatest then" (NLT).

II. Jesus Challenges the Jews to Listen and Accept (Matthew 11:12–15)

Remember that Matthew's goal in 11:7-19 was to reveal the rejection in the hearts of the Jewish people toward John and Jesus. To this end, Jesus made an interesting comment, explaining that from the beginning of John the Baptist's ministry up to the moment he was addressing the Jewish crowd, "the kingdom of heaven has been forcefully advancing, and violent people are attacking it" (v. 12).

The New King James Version translates this verse in the way many often have quoted this verse: "the kingdom of heaven suffers violence, and the violent take it by force." This verse has been hard for commentators to interpret. The goal of the commentary for this verse is not to take a position on this difficult-to-interpret text, but to consider a possible meaning in the larger context of the passage.

Remember, John had been arrested and imprisoned at this point in his ministry, and Jesus had begun to face major opposition from the Jewish leaders. Given this context, it is plausible to view verse 12 to mean that as Jesus' Kingdom agenda advanced, it has been (and will continue to be) forcefully opposed by hostile people, including the Jewish leaders who did not want to see this happen. Indeed, Jesus' enemies relentlessly sought to silence His message and mission. However, if the grave didn't have the power to stop God's plan of salvation for humanity, nothing on earth could either.

In verse 13, Jesus affirmed the purpose of the Old Testament prophets and the Law was to reveal to humanity God's plan for salvation, and John echoed this same message. Jesus was the turning point in history and the One who came to fulfill the prophesies and Law. He is the Lamb of God who came to take way the sins of the world (John 1:29), the One who gave His life as a ransom for many (Matt. 20:28).

Malachi 4:5–6, which also happen to be the last two verses of the last book of the Old Testament, prophesy that One who is representative of Elijah is coming before the day of God's judgment to provide an opportunity for the Jews to return to the faith of their ancestors. Jesus affirmed John the Baptist fulfilled the role of Elijah. Now that Jesus the Messiah was present among them, they had the opportunity to experience the long-awaited Messiah and His Kingdom. However, there are two requirements of the Jews. First, they must be "willing to accept it" (v. 14). Second, they must listen attentively with open ears and hearts (v. 15).

Wisdom in action requires God's people to be willing to hear and see from His perspective, to pursue His heart, and to have His attitude. When our values, beliefs, and actions collide with God's plan and instructions, we must abandon them in submission to His will rather than hold on tighter to that which He's asking us to release. Many of the Jews were unwilling to let go of their wrong thinking; in fact they preferred to kill Jesus rather than change their minds. We do well to remember the wisdom from Proverbs we studied in lesson 2, that when we struggle to make sense of God's agenda, commands, and expectations: "If you call out for insight and cry aloud for understanding, and if you look for it as for silver and search for it as for hidden treasure, then you will understand the fear of the Lord and find the knowledge of God" (Prov. 2:3–5, NIV).

III. The Proof Is in His Deeds (Matthew 11:16–19)

After paying tribute to John the Baptist and challenging the Jews in the crowd to accept and receive the message He and John proclaimed, Jesus condemned their unbelief. In verse 16, "this generation" refers to hypocritical Jewish people and religious leaders who rejected John and Jesus. Jesus referred to an ancient game similar to Simon Says, in which there is an appropriate response to each action that is called out by a player. To play the game correctly, there must be a response in the form of participation. For example, when a child played a flute, the other children were supposed to dance (see v. 17). Using this illustration, Jesus compared the Jews to spoiled children who pout and whine when they do not get their way.

Similar to the unresponsive, non-participatory children in the game, the Jews were unresponsive to the ministries of John the Baptist and Jesus, and they refused to participate in God's plan of salvation for all humanity. According to verse 18, Jesus said they rejected Him and John for different, yet equally ridiculous, reasons: "For John didn't spend his time eating and drinking, and you say, 'He's possessed by a demon.' The Son of Man, on the other hand, feasted and drunk, and you say, 'He's a glutton and a drunkard, and a friend of tax collectors and other sinners'" (NLT)! The people's hearts were hardened by the fact that John and Jesus did not fit their preconceived expectations, and nothing either did made the general public happy. Instead of repenting, the people persisted in looking for reasons to reject and derail their ministries.

Jesus closed with a nod to wisdom in verse 19. He informed the dissenters that wisdom proves or shows she is right by her "deeds" (NIV) or "her children" (NKJV). The idea is that Jesus' claim to be the Messiah is proven by actions and works—the same actions and deeds John the Baptist had heard about while in prison in Matthew 11:2, the same evidence Jesus instructed John's disciples to report back to him in Matthew 11:4–6. Jesus asserted that anyone who observed either ministry with humble, honest, and receptive hearts would see the righteousness of their work.

Wisdom in action, per our lesson title, requires God's people to be discerning based on what a person produces. Jesus said we easily are able to identify real and false prophets by the fruit they produce (Matt. 7:15–16).

The Lesson Applied

My daughter currently is a middle schooler, and the desire to be like her peers is strong among them all. The same desire creeps into adult lives too. We crave what we see others doing, possessing the same things other people have, and achieving titles that others hold.

The desire to conform and be like everyone else is something we all are able to identify with; however, Jesus and John the Baptist show us that being different in that we are led by a Kingdom agenda is God's plan for His children. We are challenged to prioritize obedience to God. In America, we have just celebrated Independence Day; the example of John the Baptist and Jesus should encourage us to live independently of the world's expectations. Even if people call us out for being odd or different, we must learn to be comfortable with being uncomfortable for the cause of Christ.

Let's Talk About It

1. **The actions of Jesus differed from the actions of John the Baptist, yet both acted and spoke in ways that were considered unusual in their day and wise from God's perspective. Why might we consider these men to be wise in God's economy?**

   Proverb 1:7 reminds us the fear of the Lord is the starting point for wisdom and knowledge. As we relate to God through humble submission, prayer, and Bible study, our desire to live according to biblical expectations will exceed our desire to follow the world's agenda. Wisdom from heaven's perspective always requires us to prioritize holiness and obedience to God's Word.

2. **Why was the ministry of John the Baptist necessary?**

   John served as a forerunner of our Lord Jesus Christ. In the Old Testament, when the king was coming to visit the people, a person who served as the official announcer came to alert and inform the people to prepare for the royal presence. John, in fulfillment of the Old Testament prophecies, came to announce to the world the coming of the predicted Messiah so they might prepare to receive Him properly. That is to say, John came to announce the coming of God's new Kingdom of human salvation that would be ushered in with the preaching of the Christ. Mark tell us Jesus came preaching a Gospel of repentance through obedience and faith (see Mark 1:14–15).

   It is also significant the John came in the way and form of the Old Testament prophets, therefore, linking the prophets to the new dispensation that would take place in the ministry of Jesus.

Home Daily Devotional Readings
July 6–12, 2020

Monday	Tuesday	Wednesday	Thursday	Friday	Saturday	Sunday
Everything Has Its Time and Season	Perform Your God-Given Task	The Firstborn Belong to God	Jesus Presented to the Lord	Simeon Praises God for the Child	Anna Speaks about the Christ Child	The Wise Boy Jesus Amazes Teachers
Ecclesiastes 3:2–8	Ecclesiastes 3:9–15	Numbers 3:11–13	Luke 2:21–24	Luke 2:25–35	Luke 2:36–38	Ecclesiastes 3:1,7; Luke 2:39–52

THE BOY JESUS

ADULT TOPIC:
WISDOM THAT AMAZES

BACKGROUND SCRIPTURE:
ECCLESIASTES 3:1–15; LUKE 2:39–52

ECCLESIASTES 3:1, 7; LUKE 2:39–52

King James Version

TO every thing there is a season, and a time to every purpose under the heaven:

• • • • •

7 A time to rend, and a time to sew; a time to keep silence, and a time to speak;

• • • Luke 2:39–52 • • •

AND when they had performed all things according to the law of the Lord, they returned into Galilee, to their own city Nazareth.

40 And the child grew, and waxed strong in spirit, filled with wisdom: and the grace of God was upon him.

41 Now his parents went to Jerusalem every year at the feast of the passover.

42 And when he was twelve years old, they went up to Jerusalem after the custom of the feast.

43 And when they had fulfilled the days, as they returned, the child Jesus tarried behind in Jerusalem; and Joseph and his mother knew not of it.

44 But they, supposing him to have been in the company, went a day's journey; and they sought him among their kinsfolk and acquaintance.

45 And when they found him not, they turned back again to Jerusalem, seeking him.

46 And it came to pass, that after three days they found him in the temple, sitting in the midst of the doctors, both hearing them, and asking them questions.

47 And all that heard him were astonished at his understanding and answers.

New Revised Standard Version

FOR everything there is a season, and a time for every matter under heaven:

• • • • •

7 a time to tear, and a time to sew; a time to keep silence, and a time to speak;

• • • Luke 2:39–52 • • •

WHEN they had finished everything required by the law of the LORD, they returned to Galilee, to their own town of Nazareth.

40 The child grew and became strong, filled with wisdom; and the favor of God was upon him.

41 Now every year his parents went to Jerusalem for the festival of the Passover.

42 And when he was twelve years old, they went up as usual for the festival.

43 When the festival was ended and they started to return, the boy Jesus stayed behind in Jerusalem, but his parents did not know it.

44 Assuming that he was in the group of travelers, they went a day's journey. Then they started to look for him among their relatives and friends.

45 When they did not find him, they returned to Jerusalem to search for him.

46 After three days they found him in the temple, sitting among the teachers, listening to them and asking them questions.

47 And all who heard him were amazed at his understanding and his answers.

MAIN THOUGHT: And the child grew, and waxed strong in spirit, filled with wisdom: and the grace of God was upon him. (Luke 2:40, KJV)

ECCLESIASTES 3:1, 7; LUKE 2:39–52

King James Version

48 And when they saw him, they were amazed: and his mother said unto him, Son, why hast thou thus dealt with us? behold, thy father and I have sought thee sorrowing.

49 And he said unto them, How is it that ye sought me? wist ye not that I must be about my Father's business?

50 And they understood not the saying which he spake unto them.

51 And he went down with them, and came to Nazareth, and was subject unto them: but his mother kept all these sayings in her heart.

52 And Jesus increased in wisdom and stature, and in favour with God and man.

New Revised Standard Version

48 When his parents saw him they were astonished; and his mother said to him, "Child, why have you treated us like this? Look, your father and I have been searching for you in great anxiety."

49 He said to them, "Why were you searching for me? Did you not know that I must be in my Father's house?"

50 But they did not understand what he said to them.

51 Then he went down with them and came to Nazareth, and was obedient to them. His mother treasured all these things in her heart.

52 And Jesus increased in wisdom and in years, and in divine and human favor.

LESSON SETTING

Time: Ecclesiastes: 970–931 B.C.
Place: Israel
Time: Luke: circa A.D. 7–20
Place: Jerusalem

LESSON OUTLINE

I. There Is a Time for Everything (Ecclesiastes 3:1, 7)

II. Jesus Grew Physically and in Wisdom (Luke 2:39-40)

III. Jesus Demonstrated a Time to Speak and a Time to Be Silent (Luke 2:41-50)

UNIFYING PRINCIPLE

Many young people amaze others with a wisdom that seems beyond their years. How should we respond to precocious wisdom? Ecclesiastes affirms there is a time to speak and a time to be quiet; and Luke records that the teachers in the temple were awed by the wisdom of twelve-year-old Jesus while Mary and Joseph were confused and exasperated.

INTRODUCTION

Scholars who credit Solomon with authoring the book of Ecclesiastes date the writing of this book toward the end of Solomon's life, believing the book to be Solomon's reflection on his life from the perspective of a repentant heart (*HOTC Ecclesiastes*, p. 6).

Most scholars date Jesus' birth around 4 B.C. If we take this to be correct and note the text tells us Jesus was twelve years old (see Luke 2:42) when His family made this trip to Jerusalem to celebrate the Passover, then we can assume this occurred in approximately A.D. 7–10.

Born in 1950, Stevland Hardaway Morris amazed the world when he entered the stage. Better known as Stevie Wonder, he was considered a child prodigy not only because of his ability to play numerous instruments, but also because of his ability to write, produce, perform, and sing at such a young age. At age thirteen, "Little Stevie Wonder" had his first number one hit, making him the youngest artist ever to top the chart and the first artist in history to top the pop and R&B charts simultaneously. His remarkable musicality makes him an amazing talent, but the fact he has been blind since shortly after his birth makes him that much more astounding. If Little Stevie captivated the world in the 1950s and '60s, imagine how people responded to Jesus in first-century Israel. In today's lesson, we will study a text that gives us insight about Jesus in His youth, and we will learn Jesus' wisdom and insight made Him stand out among temple leaders.

Exposition

I. There Is a Time for Everything (Ecclesiastes 3:1, 7)

Throughout June, we studied the God-given wisdom of Solomon in Proverbs. Today, we turn our attention to Ecclesiastes, another book of wisdom literature written by Solomon. Ecclesiastes 3:1 serves as a summary statement for verses 1–9. Solomon affirmed in verse 1 that there is a "season" (KJV), "occasion" (HCSB), or "opportune time" (*The Message*) for everything under heaven. Psalm 103:19 reminds us God sovereignly rules over everything, and every activity under heaven has a God-ordained time for its occurrence. God is the Father of time, and He is not constrained by human limitations on time. For these reasons, walking in wisdom requires that we operate according to God's timetable.

In Ecclesiastes 3:2–9, Solomon elaborates on and lists activities that happen at appropriate times and seasons: birth, death, planting, uprooting, killing, healing, tearing down, building up, weeping, laughing, mourning, dancing, throwing and gathering stones, embracing, searching, counting losses, keeping, throwing away, tearing, sowing, loving, hating, fighting war, and pursuing peace. Verse 7 explains there are times to speak and times to remain quiet.

How can we know the difference between these times? God's wisdom helps us discern when it is appropriate to speak or keep silent. James 3:5–8 says the tongue is powerful and though one of the smallest parts of the body, also perhaps the hardest to tame. We cannot control our tongues without divine power, and this is why we must allow the Holy Spirit to determine when and how to use our words in God-honoring ways. In Proverbs, Solomon gave a clear picture of a wise speaker. First, "the prudent hold their tongues" (10:19); second, "the lips of the righteous nourish many" (10:21); third, "the mouth of the righteous is a fountain of life" (10:11); fourth, "wisdom is found on the lips of the discerning" (10:13, all NIV).

II. Jesus Grew Physically and in Wisdom (Luke 2:39–40)

Today's passage includes a perfect example of knowing when to speak and when to be silent. Jesus was born in Bethlehem (Luke 2:1–7); the shepherds had come to visit Him (Luke 2:8–20); Jesus had been circumcised and presented in the temple in Jerusalem (Luke 2:21–24); and Simeon and Anna had blessed and prophesied about Jesus. Luke 2:39 tells us readers it was time for the family to return home as Joseph and Mary had done everything required by the Law.

Luke 2:40 reminds us Jesus is fully God and fully human. He grew up as other children in Nazareth. As He matured, He became "strong, filled with wisdom, and God's grace was on Him" (HCSB). Jesus grew intellectually and was guided by fear and reverence for His heavenly Father, which is the beginning of wisdom (Prov. 1:7), which filled Him (Luke 2:40). Jesus grew in the same ways as all human children do. Each aspect of His development prepared Him to fulfill His God-given assignment.

III. Jesus Demonstrated a Time to Speak and a Time to Be Silent (Luke 2:41–50)

Luke 2 gives us the only glimpse of Jesus' life between His birth and baptism by His cousin and forerunner, John the Baptist (see Mark 1:9–11). Children love hearing stories about their childhoods, and Luke 2 helps us discover more about Jesus as a child. Verse 2:41 begins with the words, "Every year" (NIV), demonstrating that Jesus' parents were pious Jews who prioritized observing the festivals and requirements of the Law. Joseph and Mary traveled with their family to Jerusalem annually to celebrate Passover.

Adult Jewish males were expected to make a pilgrimage to Jerusalem for the annual feasts of Passover, Pentecost, and Tabernacles (see Exod. 23:14–17; 34:23–24; Deut. 16:16–17). Bar mitzvahs for boys on their thirteenth birthdays mark the time when a Jewish male is recognized as a man. Verse 42 tells us Jesus was twelve years old when His family made this particular trip, so this would have been His final Passover before being considered an adult. During each trip to Jerusalem, Jesus learned more and more about Jewish Law and history, the worship of His heavenly Father, and His people.

When the celebration of Passover ended, everyone said goodbye and returned home. Verse 43 tells us Jesus was not quite ready to leave. The problem was His parents did not know He was not traveling with the caravan. We might wonder, *How could Joseph and Mary leave Jesus in Jerusalem?* Joseph and Mary probably were traveling with a host of friends and relatives, so they probably assumed Jesus was somewhere among the group.

"Assuming He was with the traveling party" (v. 44, HCSB), Joseph, Mary, and the caravan traveled a full day before realizing Jesus was not with them. When they made it to a place where they could rest for the night, they began searching for Jesus, who was nowhere to be found. Imagine the panic they must have felt when they realized they had lost the Son of God! They had to return to Jerusalem to search for Him there (v. 45).

Note they traveled for one day, but verse 46 says, "after three days" they found Him in the temple. What is amazing about this is that Jesus, a twelve-year-old, is "sitting among the teachers, listening to them and asking them questions" (v. 46). Jesus' understanding of Scripture astounded everyone present. The teachers in this verse refer to rabbis, scholars of the Mosaic Law. They were impressed by the questions He asked.

Jesus actively participated in the study and discourse; He was not a typical twelve-year-old boy. It is clear from the text that Jesus had a deep understanding of the Law and prophets. Also, the rabbis and teachers typically did not welcome young people to be part of their interaction. Notice the reaction of the people who were present at the temple that day: "All who heard Him [Jesus] were amazed at His understanding and His answers" (v. 47, NLT).

Verse 48 says Joseph and Mary have a similar reaction. They were astonished when they saw their son interacting with the rabbis and teachers. However, Mary seemed to display confusion. She asked Jesus what any mother would ask after such an ordeal: "Son … why have You done this to us? Your father and I have been searching for You everywhere" (v. 48). Mary seemed to focus more on how losing Jesus had affected her in this moment, not on His divine mission. Because Mary was unable to discern the situation from a heavenly perspective, Jesus responded by asking why she was looking for Him: "Did you not know that I must be about My Father's business?" (v. 49). Jesus' response indicated awareness that His relationship with God was of greater importance than the earthly parental relationship.

Despite this clarification, Joseph and Mary still were confused: "They did not understand what He was saying to them" (v. 50). Jesus was their son; until this point, He probably was similar to most other boys His age. He grew and matured as do other children, but here we begin to see His divine nature.

Joseph and Mary were Jesus' earthly parents, and He returned home with them to Nazareth (v. 51) in obedience, because the time for His public ministry had not arrived. Meanwhile, Mary "treasured all these things in her heart" (v. 51). She was becoming increasingly aware that the angel's words concerning Jesus (see Luke 1:31–33) would be fulfilled. Though He seemed to be an ordinary child in some respects, He actually was the Son of God, Messiah, Savior of the World.

Jesus' growth was not yet complete. Luke 2:52 describes how Jesus continued to grow "in wisdom and stature, and in favor with God and men." Jesus grew in wisdom, meaning He matured intellectually and in practical holiness. In addition, He grew in stature, referring to His physical maturation. Jesus also grew "in favor with God," suggesting spiritual growth and closeness with His heavenly Father. Jesus grew in His social relationships ("favor with men"). That He had favor with people seems to indicate others respected Him.

Jesus' wisdom and understanding as a twelve-year-old was impressive (see vv. 42, 46–47), and He experienced all types of earthly growth so He would be prepared to fulfill His heavenly mission in that He was able to identify with those whom He came to seek and save. The perfect sacrificial Lamb would have to resemble those for whom He would lay down His life.

The subtitle for this section indicates Jesus models for us Ecclesiastes 3:7: there is "a time to keep silence, and a time to speak" (NKJV). It was appropriate for Jesus to speak up in the temple among the rabbis, and it was the appropriate time for Him to begin reminding His parents that His God-given purpose at times would clash with their expectations. However, we also observe Jesus humbly obeying His earthly parents and growing as a normal child. Indeed, there is "a time for every purpose under heaven," and God gives us wisdom to discern such times and seasons.

The Lesson Applied

In Luke 2, everyone began to realize Jesus was not just one of the youth from Nazareth. Though our offspring are not fully God but are fully human, they still bear God's image and have unique purposes. When we recognize God at work in young people, we must pray for wisdom to lead them and provide opportunities for them to use the gifts and abilities God has given them. Don't be that person who throws water on a child's enthusiasm for the Lord, but remember Jesus' words in Luke 18:16: "Let the little children come to Me, and do not hinder them, for the kingdom of God belongs to such as these."

Let's Talk About It

1. **Jesus demonstrated for us that asking good questions signifies godly wisdom. Are you more apt to give an opinion or to ask a poignant question?**

   Often we are quick to give our opinions without taking time to think things through. For example, when people come to us with problems, we share our opinions without praying and sometimes without hearing the entire story. At work when problems arise, we share solutions without considering all the variables. It is easy for us to share our opinions, but in Luke 2:46, Jesus taught that one of the wisest actions we can take is to ask good questions. As the group discusses this question, emphasize the fact we do not always need to feel responsible for providing solutions. Sometimes the Holy Spirit may prompt us to ask a question that will spark someone else's thinking.

2. **What do we learn from the interaction between Joseph, Mary, and Jesus to help us in interacting with precocious children?**

   Parents and other adults must take seriously the responsibility to lead and guide children to reach their God-given potential and purpose. We must walk in wisdom and in the fear of the Lord if we are to lead them to do so. Pray that the Lord will open the eyes of our hearts to see our children and youth from His perspective so we will be able to guide them wisely to have positive impacts on the world.

3. **Why does the writer of the book of Ecclesiastes give us a list of opposite things to consider as we live within the spectrum of life?**

   The list is given to enable understanding that not all things can be done at once. There are times when certain things and/or actions are more appropriate and when we must learn to work within these parameters. The enlightenment of the Scriptures help us to work within and understand these parameters.

Home Daily Devotional Readings

July 13–19, 2020

Monday	Tuesday	Wednesday	Thursday	Friday	Saturday	Sunday
Jesus Restores Leader's Daughter to Life	Samaritans Testify to Wisdom of Jesus	All Wisdom Dwells in Christ	Jesus Denounces Human Traditions	God's Wisdom Trumps Human Commands	The Heart Not the Stomach Defiles	Jesus' Wisdom Astonishes His Hometown People
Mark 5:35–43	John 4:27–29, 39–42	Colossians 2:1–5	Mark 7:1–8	Mark 7:9–15	Mark 7:17–23	Mark 6:1–6

THE WISDOM OF JESUS

ADULT TOPIC:
WISDOM THAT ASTOUNDS AND OFFENDS

BACKGROUND SCRIPTURE:
MARK 6:1–6; 7:1–23

MARK 6:1–6

King James Version

AND he went out from thence, and came into his own country; and his disciples follow him.

2 And when the sabbath day was come, he began to teach in the synagogue: and many hearing him were astonished, saying, From whence hath this man these things? and what wisdom is this which is given unto him, that even such mighty works are wrought by his hands?

3 Is not this the carpenter, the son of Mary, the brother of James, and Joses, and of Juda, and Simon? and are not his sisters here with us? And they were offended at him.

4 But Jesus, said unto them, A prophet is not without honour, but in his own country, and among his own kin, and in his own house.

5 And he could there do no mighty work, save that he laid his hands upon a few sick folk, and healed them.

6 And he marvelled because of their unbelief. And he went round about the villages, teaching.

New Revised Standard Version

HE left that place and came to his hometown, and his disciples followed him.

2 On the sabbath he began to teach in the synagogue, and many who heard him were astounded. They said, "Where did this man get all this? What is this wisdom that has been given to him? What deeds of power are being done by his hands!

3 Is not this the carpenter, the son of Mary and brother of James and Joses and Judas and Simon, and are not his sisters here with us?" And they took offense at him.

4 Then Jesus said to them, "Prophets are not without honor, except in their hometown, and among their own kin, and in their own house."

5 And he could do no deed of power there, except that he laid his hands on a few sick people and cured them.

6 And he was amazed at their unbelief. Then he went about among the villages teaching.

MAIN THOUGHT: And when the sabbath day was come, he began to teach in the synagogue: and many hearing him were astonished, saying, From whence hath this man these things? and what wisdom is this which is given unto him, that even such mighty works are wrought by his hands? Is not this the carpenter, the son of Mary, the brother of James, and Joses, and of Juda, and Simon? and are not his sisters here with us? And they were offended at him. (Mark 6:2–3, KJV)

LESSON SETTING

Time: circa A.D. 27–30
Place: Nazareth

LESSON OUTLINE

I. **Jesus Travels Home to Nazareth (Mark 6:1)**
II. **Jesus Is Amazing, but He Is Rejected and Questioned (Mark 6:2–3)**
III. **Limited Faith Results in Limited Ministry (Mark 6:4–6)**

UNIFYING PRINCIPLE

Some people amaze us by their displays of unprecedented and unexpected wisdom. What happens when people show such extraordinary wisdom? Mark tells us the people in Jesus' hometown were astounded, as well as offended, by Jesus' wise teachings, and the religious leaders were incensed when Jesus' wisdom challenged their understanding and traditions.

INTRODUCTION

Interesting things can happen in the house of the Lord on the day designated for worshiping, studying Scripture, and fellowshiping with the saints. If have attended church a good portion of your life, it is more than likely (perhaps the norm) that you have experienced some unexpected or unusual occurrences in the house of the Lord. The stories we could tell might make for some great books!

During our previous session, Jesus' wisdom as a twelve-year-old boy astonished everyone in the temple. While they did not fully understand His heavenly mission at the time, they did not mock and reject His wisdom and divine understanding. Quite the opposite happened in Mark 6:1-6, as we will discover during our study today. In the place where one would expect Jesus' message to be received wholeheartedly and enthusiastically, the opposite happened. This lesson reveals that wisdom does not impress everyone. While Jesus' wisdom amazed some, others chose to be offended by His words.

EXPOSITION

I. JESUS TRAVELS HOME TO NAZARETH (MARK 6:1)

Mark 6:1 begins by informing us Jesus "went away from there and came to His hometown." To understand the context for chapter 6 and the importance of "there" in this verse, it is important to read the previous verses. In Mark 5, Jesus and His disciples "went across the lake to the region of the Gerasenes," where He drove demons out of a man (5:1–16). Mark 5:17 explains Jesus' miracles were met with opposition. Some people begged Him to leave their region, while others (such as the man who had been delivered from demon oppression) begged Him to stay. Despite the healed man's pleas, Jesus decided to leave and move on to the Decapolis (5:20), which refers to ten Greek cities spread throughout Syria, Jordan, and Palestine. It was the region south and southeast of the Sea of Galilee.

Soon afterward, Jesus' ministry led Him to cross over to the western side of the Sea of Galilee (5:21), near Tiberias. It was there Jesus healed Jairus' young daughter from her affliction or illness (5:22–43) and the woman who touched the hem of His garment (5:25–34).

So by the time we get to Mark 6:1, Jesus has moved farther west from the Sea of

Galilee, thereby arriving in His hometown of Nazareth, where He spent most of His life prior to launching His public ministry. Jesus did not travel there alone; His disciples followed or accompanied Him. The presence of disciples and followers indicates Jesus had become a trusted and respected (by some) rabbi (or teacher). Perhaps it's reasonable to think that returning home would provide respite from the opposition and the stresses of ministry, but actually the opposite happened here when Jesus arrived.

II. Jesus Is Amazing, but He Is Rejected and Questioned (Mark 6:2–3)

After arriving in Nazareth, Jesus and the Twelve went to the synagogue (the Jewish place of worship) on the Sabbath (which would have been between sunset on Friday and sunset on Saturday) to teach all who were willing to hear (v. 2). Yes, Jesus and the disciples went to church!

That Jesus was in the synagogue and teaching presumes He had received an invitation to teach, because He would have been a visiting rabbi. He accepted the opportunity to speak about His identity as the Messiah and His mission to seek and save the lost exactly as the Old Testament had prophesied. Compare the response of the people in the synagogue in Mark 6:2 with the response in Luke 2:47—many who heard Jesus were astonished and amazed at His words and demeanor.

However, in Nazareth there was a different level or type of astonishment. Remember, these people watched Jesus grow up and interacted with Him during the first thirty years of His life. They had spent their lives getting to know Him as one of the neighborhood kids and son of Mary (and Joseph), not as the Savior of the world. Some were amazed; others doubted and resented Him, asking, "Where did He get all this wisdom and the power to perform such miracles?" (v. 2), as they could not fathom such wisdom emerging from their local community with no opportunities for higher education.

In addition to questioning the source of Jesus' wisdom and miraculous power, the people in the synagogue (which more than likely included other rabbis and certainly the religious leaders) called attention to the job they had known Jesus to have held along with His earthly father.

Joseph was a carpenter. In that age, carpenters were artisans who specialized in building and working with wood, metal, and stone. Mark 6:3 is the only place in the Bible where Jesus is referred to as a carpenter, giving us insight about Jesus we would not know otherwise. The parallel passages do not give Jesus the same title. For example, Matthew's Gospel records, "He's just the carpenter's son," emphasizing His father Joseph's vocation as a carpenter (Matt. 13:55). Luke's Gospel records, "Isn't this Joseph's son?" (Luke 4:22), emphasizing Joseph as Jesus' father rather than the vocation of either.

By calling attention to the fact they had known Jesus as a carpenter, they were actually belittling and discrediting the amazing words and actions they had witnessed in Him. In essence, they were saying He was a common laborer, no different from themselves.

It was hard for the community of Jews in Nazareth to see Jesus' divinity, believe in His preaching, and receive Him as the

Messiah, because the people were focused solely on the external and human qualities they were able to recognize. Rodney Cooper in the *Holman New Testament Commentary on Mark* wrote, "There may be none so quick to judge our fitness and competence as those with whom we grew up" (p. 100).

After describing His vocation, the Nazareth synagogue attendees moved on to attacking His family. He was mentioned as Mary's son (Mark 6:3), and Joseph was left out of the list completely. A factor in omitting Joseph perhaps was because he had passed away by this time. In addition, whenever a Jewish man is identified as his mother's son, it is usually because people were insulting or speaking to or about a person in a derogatory manner. (People gossiped then just as they do now, thinking they see situations as they are yet really not understanding at all. Remember, Mary had become pregnant prior to marrying Joseph, and this miracle was an act of the Holy Spirit and not the flesh.)

Yet another reason they might have been insulting Jesus was because they could have perceived He was abandoning His familial responsibilities to Mary as His mother's oldest son. (Notice that verse 3 lists Jesus' half-brothers and mentions He has sisters—James [author of the book of James], Joseph, Judas [most likely the author of Jude], and Simon). If in fact Joseph had died, the responsibility would have fallen to Jesus to take care of His family. Jesus' focus on itinerant ministry throughout Judea instead of working as a carpenter to provide for the family in Nazareth might have caused the people to take this opportunity to look at Him with jaundiced eyes and speak against Him for neglecting obligations. Of course, the simple underlying fact of the matter is they were jealous.

Notice their reaction to Jesus at the end of Mark 6:3: "They took offense at Him." Indeed, He was captivating. His words pierced the hearts of the listeners and caused them to wonder if He really was the Messiah for whom they had been waiting. Nevertheless, they rejected Him and refused to investigate whether He was more than just a boy from Nazareth, much less accept the truth of His complete identity as the Son and God and Son of Man.

III. Limited Faith Results in Limited Ministry (Mark 6:4–6)

In verse 4, Jesus brought to their attention a well-known proverb of their time: "A prophet is not without honor except in His own town, among His relatives and in His own home." By using this familiar proverb, Jesus identified Himself as the One the Old Testament prophets foretold would be rejected, ignored, mocked, and eventually put to death.

The people's limited faith and their refusal to open their hearts and minds to Jesus' message resulted in limited opportunities to experience and receive His ministry. Jesus knew their hearts, and He was aware that miracles would not move them to listen, believe, repent, and receive from Him. If that were the case, they would have responded to His teaching (see v. 2).

Throughout this unit, we have been studying texts from Gospel passages that demonstrate people's various reactions to Jesus' wisdom, miraculous power, and powerful insights and understanding. Notice in verse 6 that the text speaks of Jesus also being amazed: "He was amazed at their lack of faith." The NRSV translates this verse, "And He marveled because of their unbelief." This is one of two verses in the Bible that describe Jesus as "amazed" or indicate that He "marveled."

Luke 7:9 informs readers Jesus also was amazed by the centurion's faith: "When Jesus heard this, He was amazed at him, and turning to the crowd following him, He said, 'I tell you, I have not found such great faith even in Israel.'"

The end of Mark 6:6 tells us that after His rejection in the house of worship, Jesus left the synagogue and "went from village to village, teaching the people" (NLT).

The Lesson Applied

Jesus was mocked instead of received. He was rejected by those who knew Him best. Thomas Edison, the inventor of the light bulb worked hard to develop a new way to provide light, one that would be much safer than lanterns and kerosene lamps. His invention was deemed "unworthy of the attention of scientific men" and "a fairy tale." Those who ridiculed him more than one hundred years ago never could have known how the world has come to depend on his invention. In fact, many of us probably never have known life without electric light bulbs.

Greatness always is subject to being misunderstood, and the unfortunate reality is that people more often prefer to reject what they do not understand because it's easier than attempting to grasp something that's unfamiliar to them. This is what happened the day Jesus entered the synagogue in Nazareth. Instead of seeking wisdom to discern the truth and what God might be doing through His Son, Jesus, the people closed their hearts and minds and chose to be offended.

In response to this lesson, the question we must grapple with is: Do we behave the same way as the people in the synagogue—hard-hearted, close-minded, and easily offended by what we do not understand—especially when it comes to spiritual truth and how God is at work in people, our communities, the church, and in the world? When we find ourselves easily angered by that which we do not understand, remember the guidance this Scripture passage offers: "Understand this, my dear brothers and sisters: You must all be quick to listen, slow to speak, and slow to get angry" (James 1:19, NLT). Furthermore, by maintaining one's composure, one is able to control the situation more appropriately.

Let's Talk About It

1. **Have you ever experienced rejection or skepticism from those who know you best? How does Jesus' example in Mark 6 encourage His followers to continue fulfilling our God-given purposes despite naysayers and skeptics?**

   People who know us and have grown up with us might be shocked when we change our way of living, behaving, speaking, and relating to others. We all know people who knew us "back in the day" or who were our "ride-or-die" back in the day; but when Christ becomes the priority of our lives, everything changes. From heaven's perspective, change for the glory of God is good.

Jesus' example reminds us that if He had haters among those who should have received Him, then so will we. It should be comforting to see an example in Scripture of our Savior and Lord enduring the same challenges we will face when we are following Him. There is no need to become angry, discouraged, or sidetracked when others do not understand all God is doing in, with, and through us. When the religious leaders and the Jewish people in the synagogue rejected Him, Jesus simply took His message somewhere else. We would be wise to follow His example.

2. **Now that we have studied the text of Mark 6:1–6, we have discovered that not everyone could accept the wisdom with which Jesus spoke. When have you been unable to receive the wisdom of Scripture, or wisdom from a family member or from a more mature brother/sister in Christ? What made it hard to accept what they were trying to say?**

We often are slow to receive wisdom from others when it clashes with our current actions and behaviors. Like the religious leaders and Jewish people in the synagogue, wisdom from heaven convicts us. Often we would prefer to continue in our own understanding and the path we are traveling rather than repent of our actions and seek forgiveness. It is easy to see the mistakes others are making and to point a finger of blame. Jesus points this out in the Sermon on the Mount.

3. **When confronted with something you do not understand, are you more likely to take offense (as did the people of Nazareth), or are you most likely to pause, pray, and seek godly wisdom and understanding? What practical steps can we take to avoid taking offense simply because we lack understanding?**

Becoming offended quickly and easily creates barriers in our hearts and minds, and it is actually a sign of immaturity. Let us not become easily offended as did the people in the synagogue in Nazareth. The Book of James reminds us to be slow to speak and respond, but quick to listen and hear what is being said (1:19). When confronted with new information or concepts we do not understand, it is best for us to purposefully pause. Pausing to check the new information presented to us provides us with an opportunity to let the new information sink in, allows us time to pray for the Holy Spirit to give us discernment and clarity, and gives us a moment to formulate questions that might lead us to deeper understanding.

HOME DAILY DEVOTIONAL READINGS
JULY 20–26, 2020

MONDAY	TUESDAY	WEDNESDAY	THURSDAY	FRIDAY	SATURDAY	SUNDAY
Wisdom, Source of Abundant Life	Jesus Does What the Father Does	Love as I Loved You	Spirit of Truth Dwells in You	Love Binds Believers to God	Spirit of Wisdom Promised to All	Jesus, the Way to the Father
Proverbs 3:13–18	John 5:19–24	John 13:31–35	John 14:15–17	John 14:18–24	John 14:25–31	John 14:1–14

WISDOM: THE WAY, TRUTH, AND LIFE

ADULT TOPIC:
FINDING ONE'S WAY

BACKGROUND SCRIPTURE:
PROVERBS 3:17; 8:32–36; JOHN 14:1–14

JOHN 14:1–14

King James Version

LET not your heart be troubled: ye believe in God, believe also in me.

2 In my Father's house are many mansions: if it were not so, I would have told you. I go to prepare a place for you.

3 And if I go and prepare a place for you, I will come again, and receive you unto myself; that where I am, there ye may be also.

4 And whither I go ye know, and the way ye know.

5 Thomas saith unto him, Lord, we know not whither thou goest; and how can we know the way?

6 Jesus saith unto him, I am the way, the truth, and the life: no man cometh unto the Father, but by me.

7 If ye had known me, ye should have known my Father also: and from henceforth ye know him, and have seen him.

8 Philip saith unto him, Lord, show us the Father, and it sufficeth us.

9 Jesus saith unto him, Have I been so long time with you, and yet hast thou not known me, Philip? he that hath seen me hath seen the Father; and how sayest thou then, Show us the Father?

10 Believest thou not that I am in the Father, and the Father in me? the words that I speak unto you I speak not of myself: but the Father that dwelleth in me, he doeth the works.

11 Believe me that I am in the Father, and the Father in me: or else believe me for the very works' sake.

New Revised Standard Version

"DO not let your hearts be troubled. Believe in God, believe also in me.

2 In my Father's house there are many dwelling places. If it were not so, would I have told you that I go to prepare a place for you?

3 And if I go and prepare a place for you, I will come again and will take you to myself, so that where I am, there you may be also.

4 And you know the way to the place where I am going."

5 Thomas said to him, "Lord, we do not know where you are going. How can we know the way?"

6 Jesus said to him, "I am the way, and the truth, and the life. No one comes to the Father except through me.

7 If you know me, you will know my Father also. From now on you do know him and have seen him."

8 Philip said to him, "Lord, show us the Father, and we will be satisfied."

9 Jesus said to him, "Have I been with you all this time, Philip, and you still do not know me? Whoever has seen me has seen the Father. How can you say, 'Show us the Father'?

10 Do you not believe that I am in the Father and the Father is in me? The words that I say to you I do not speak on my own; but the Father who dwells in me does his works.

11 Believe me that I am in the Father and the Father is in me; but if you do not, then believe me because of the works themselves.

MAIN THOUGHT: Jesus saith unto him, I am the way, the truth, and the life: no man cometh unto the Father, but by me. (John 14:6, KJV)

JOHN 14:1–14

King James Version	*New Revised Standard Version*
12 Verily, verily, I say unto you, He that believeth on me, the works that I do shall he do also; and greater works than these shall he do; because I go unto my Father.	**12 Very truly, I tell you, the one who believes in me will also do the works that I do and, in fact, will do greater works than these, because I am going to the Father.**
13 And whatsoever ye shall ask in my name, that will I do, that the Father may be glorified in the Son.	**13 I will do whatever you ask in my name, so that the Father may be glorified in the Son.**
14 If ye shall ask any thing in my name, I will do it.	**14 If in my name you ask me for anything, I will do it.**

LESSON SETTING

Time: circa A.D. 30–33 during the Passover just before Jesus' death

Place: Jerusalem

LESSON OUTLINE

I. I'm Going Away, but I'm Coming Back (John 14:1–3)

II. Jesus Answers Thomas' Question— I'm the ONLY Way (John 14:4–6)

III. Jesus Answers Philip's Concern— I and My Father Are One (John 14:7–11)

IV. Jesus Calls for Greater Works (John 14:12–14)

UNIFYING PRINCIPLE

Some people say there are many ways to salvation and everyone attains it by following his or her own way. What are we to make of such claims? Just as Proverbs contrasted the way of wisdom with false ways, Jesus proclaimed He is the way, the truth, and the life through whom His disciples would come to know and understand God the Father.

INTRODUCTION

Have you ever checked into a hotel and it seemed as if the staff members were completely unprepared for your arrival? When you arrived, no one was available at the front desk. Once you received your room key, you found out there was no WiFi. When you opened the door to your room, the bed was unmade, and there were dirty linens on the floor in the bathroom. For this reason, you decided to eat a meal in the hotel's restaurant so housekeeping could clean your room, only to discover they were out of one of the items you ordered. More than likely, you have not experienced such an extremely bad stay at a hotel because they would go out of business quickly if guests had these kinds of experiences too often.

In contrast to the previous scenario, nothing is comparable to arriving somewhere and all the preparations have been made for you. It is as if someone had taken the time to pay attention to all the details, which communicates love and concern. Today's passage is John 14:1–14, a familiar text to many. As Jesus prepared His disciples for His death, we will observe Him comforting His disciples by informing them He's preparing a place for them, by answering questions and concerns, and by calling for them to do greater works than He has done.

Exposition

I. I'm Going Away, but I'm Coming Back (John 14:1–3)

In John 13:1–17:26, Jesus began to prepare His disciples for His crucifixion and resurrection. This was a farewell address of sorts, designed to inform them of everything necessary of which to be cognizant in His absence. John 13 informs us this was the time of the Passover Festival (13:1), and Jesus took this opportunity to wash their feet (13:1–20), to predict that Judas will betray Him (13:21–30), to emphasize a new commandment to love one another (13:31–35), and to predict Peter's impending denial of Him (13:36–38).

As we move into John 14, the disciples were noticeably concerned about the implications of everything Jesus was saying to them. Jesus had told them, "My children, I will be with you only a little longer" (13:33, NIV). Addressing one's preparations for death always has been a hard-to-discuss topic. It was no different for Jesus' disciples, who probably did not feel ready to do life and ministry without Him. This is why Jesus began chapter 14 with a command: "Do not let your hearts be troubled." He was giving them information about what was ahead, not to worry them but to prepare them. Being able to recall what He had said while watching it play out just as He said would comfort them and strengthen their faith in the days ahead.

Jesus went on to say in John 14:1, "You believe in God; [so] believe also in me." Recall that Jesus already told them, "I and my Father are one" (10:30, NKJV). The disciples were faithful Jews who already trusted and believed in God. In this verse, Jesus reaffirmed He and His heavenly Father were one; just as they believed and trusted in God, they were to believe and trust in Jesus as well. They could count on everything Jesus said to be true because He had given plenty of evidence to prove Himself the Messiah: turning water into wine, performing miraculous healings, calming stormy seas, feeding thousands from meager provisions, raising Lazarus from the dead, and more.

Jesus continued by describing His Father's house in verse 2. Most of us love thinking about the heavenly mansion in which we will dwell in glory one day. While the KJV tells us the Father's house has "many mansions," other translations render this "many rooms" (NIV), "many dwelling places" (NRSV), and "more than enough room" (NLT). The point Jesus is making here is that there is plenty of space in heaven for all of Christ's followers.

Jesus went on to say He had no reason to mislead them: "If it were not so, I would have told you" (v. 2, KJV). That is, if He says it, then that settles it. Jesus affirmed He would not be leaving them high and dry; He was leaving for a purpose: "I go to prepare a place for you" (v. 2, KJV). Our arrival in heaven will not catch Him by surprise as did the scenario of our introduction. Instead, the preparations are being made; every *i* will be dotted, and every *t* will be crossed.

In verse 3, Jesus assured the disciples He would return for them and gave His reason for coming back—so those who receive Him as Savior may live eternally with Him in heaven. They needed to be confident His imminent death on the cross would not be the end.

II. Jesus Answers Thomas' Question—I'm the ONLY Way (John 14:4–6)

Jesus made an interesting, yet presumptive, statement in verse 4: "You know the way to the place where I am going" (NIV). Perhaps the disciples should have known the way. Recall what Jesus said earlier in John 3:16–17: "For God so loved the world that He gave His only Son, that whoever believes in Him shall not perish but have eternal life." Perhaps this should have been confirmation that intimate knowledge of the one and only Son of God would be the passport to heaven.

However, Thomas (perhaps best known as "Doubting Thomas," who needed additional confirmation that Jesus had risen from the dead) was vulnerable and honest, yet wise enough to make a statement and ask the question the other disciples probably were thinking: "Lord we don't know where You are going. How can we know the way?" Instead of becoming frustrated or offended because he did not completely understand what Jesus was saying, Thomas wisely posed a question that paved the way for Jesus to declare the exclusivity of the Gospel. Jesus declared, "I am the way, the truth, and the life. No one comes to the Father except through Me" (14:6). That is, salvation comes only through faith in Christ alone.

We live in a world where universalism is rampant. Many want to believe there are many paths to God and everyone will make it to heaven someday. Most people want to avoid offending or hurting others' feelings, perhaps because we may fear backlash from social media or simply want to prevent being ostracized for our views. In John 14:6, Jesus boldly and unapologetically affirmed Himself to be the only way to the Father. Consider this: Would our heavenly Father send His only Son to live on earth and die an excruciatingly painful death to pay the penalty for our sins, and then make the path to heaven multiple choice? Absolutely not. Despite the resistance we might face, we must be willing to declare the truth of the Gospel. We cannot compromise our faith or belittle the sacrifice of our Savior. Kenneth Gangel comments in the *Holman New Testament Commentary on John*, "[Jesus] embodies the way to God, the truth about God, and the life in God."

III. Jesus Answers Philip's Concern—Believe I and My Father Are One (John 14:7–11)

In verse 7, Jesus continued reassuring the disciples by emphasizing the link between the heavenly Father and His Son. Certainly we can understand why it might have been difficult for the disciples to understand this relationship. We can compare this to the Trinity and the difficulty many people today have with understanding God existing as Three in One.

Similar to Thomas, who needed concrete clarification of the things Jesus was saying, Philip made a comment that expressed his own desire to understand more deeply: "Lord, show us the Father and that will be enough for us" (v. 7, NIV). The NLT translates the end of this verse, "we will be satisfied." Phillip basically requested physical evidence or some type of revelation from the Father. If he could receive this, then he could believe.

Notice Jesus responded with three poignant questions in verses 9–10, designed to lead Philip to discover the right answer on his own. "Don't you know Me … even after I have been among you such a long time?... How can you say, 'Show us the Father'? Don't you believe that I am in the Father, and that the Father is in Me?" Philip and the disciples needed to realize there is no difference between Father and Son. Both are God; both are the same; the Father is working through the Son and speaking through Him (v. 10).

Notice Jesus' plea in verse 11, "Believe Me," or, "Just believe." Jesus wanted His disciples to trust Him fully whether or not they understood fully. He wanted them to trust that He and the Father are One. If that was too much for their brains to comprehend or for their hearts to trust, then they should believe Jesus and the Father are One based on the evidence—the work they had seen Him do and the miracles they had seen Him perform during the past three years of His public ministry (v. 11).

IV. Jesus Calls for Greater Works (John 14:12-14)

Continuing to strengthen their faith, Jesus said in verse 12, "Verily, verily I say unto you" (KJV), "Very truly I tell you" (NIV), and "I assure you" (HCSB). There is to be no doubt about the words He was preparing to say, though the thought of doing greater works than our Lord probably seemed as incomprehensible to His disciples as they do to us. This may seem impossible, but consider the fact that Jesus' earthly ministry was limited to three and a half years, all within the boundaries of Palestine. Modern inventions and technology, such as cars, airplanes, the Internet, and social media make it possible for us to minister in *greater* ways than Jesus. It is hard to imagine God doing greater works through us, but it is entirely possible when we yield ourselves to God and follow the leading of the Holy Spirit.

Kenneth Gangel said in the *Holman New Testament Commentary on John*, "We find a leadership principle here as well. All parents should be able to say to their children; all pastors should be able to say to their staffs; all leaders should be able to say to their followers: You have the potential to do greater things than I have done. To empower and develop followers whose [ministries] exceeds the impact of their mentors is to follow the model of Jesus."

We end this section of Scripture with one of Jesus' promises that we love to claim: "And I will do whatever You ask in My name, so that the Father may be glorified in the Son. You may ask for anything in My name, and I will do it" (14:13–14). This is not name-it-and-claim-it prosperity doctrine provided in these verses. Jesus was not saying we can ask for whatever we want as long as we stamp "in Jesus' name" on it. In fact, Jesus clearly said the point of asking is to glorify His Father. Thus, this promise applies when our prayer requests align with God's will and bring Him glory. First John 5:14–15 parallels the same message: "This is the confidence we have in approaching God: that if we ask anything according to His will, He hears us. If we know He hears us—whatever we ask—we know that we have what we asked of Him."

The Lesson Applied

John 14 is a beautiful reminder that Jesus is our everything. Not only is He preparing a heavenly home for all of His followers, but He also has paid the ultimate price to ensure we know the way to the Father. Songs such as "When We All Get to Heaven" excite us about what awaits us when we die or when Jesus returns for us. The third verse of the song encourages us, "Let us then be true and faithful, Trusting, serving every day; Just one glimpse of Him in glory will the toils of life repay." Indeed, serving and ministering for the Lord on this side of heaven may present its challenges, but Jesus affirmed in John 14:12 that the Holy Spirit empowers us to do greater works for the Kingdom.

All that we go through here in this world will all be worth it when we hear the Father say, "Well done good and faithful servant" (Matt. 25:23). The best way to end this lesson is with the last verse of "When We All Get to Heaven": "Onward to the prize before us! Soon His beauty we'll behold; Soon the pearly gates will open; We shall tread the streets of gold."

Let's Talk About It

1. **First Peter 3:15 informs us, "But in your hearts revere Christ as Lord. Always be prepared to give an answer to everyone who asks you to give the reason for the hope that you have. But do this with gentleness and respect" (NIV).** When the Holy Spirit provides opportunities for us to share the Gospel, we may be fearful and/or hesitant, or we may be dogmatic and domineering. John 14:1–14 reminds us Jesus is only way to heaven, but 1 Peter 3:15 urges us to be ready to share our faith gently and respectfully. When sharing the Gospel, why is it necessary for us to pray for wisdom regarding what to say and how to say it? Remember that not everyone is fluent in church-speak. Not everyone you encounter grew up in church and knows the lingo. As a representative of Christ, you must make account for that when witnessing to others. Meet people where they are; don't talk over their heads or speak down to them. Be certain of what you know and why you believe as you do, but share that truth with love and respect when talking with others about our Savior and Lord.

2. **Recall Jesus' challenge in John 14: "Believe Me." In response to this lesson, how does the Holy Spirit work with us?**

The Holy Spirit works in us according to our level of faith. The key word in this pericope is *faith*. Our faith must be intentionally deposited in Christ as the Son of God.

Home Daily Devotional Readings
July 27–August 2, 2020

Monday	Tuesday	Wednesday	Thursday	Friday	Saturday	Sunday
Suffering on Behalf of the Church	Saved by God's Mercy	Ask: God Will Supply Your Needs	Rejoice in Your Sufferings	God's Loving Actions Toward Sinners	Grass Withers but God's Word Stands	Wisdom Overcomes Trials and Temptations
Colossians 1:24–29	Titus 3:3–7	Luke 11:9–13	Romans 5:1–5	Romans 5:6–11	Isaiah 40:1–8	James 1:1–11

FAITH AND WISDOM

ADULT TOPIC:
ASK FOR IT

BACKGROUND SCRIPTURE:
JAMES 1:1–11

JAMES 1:1–11

King James Version

JAMES, a servant of God and of the Lord Jesus Christ, to the twelve tribes which are scattered abroad, greeting.

2 My brethren, count it all joy when ye fall into divers temptations;

3 Knowing this, that the trying of your faith worketh patience.

4 But let patience have her perfect work, that ye may be perfect and entire, wanting nothing.

5 If any of you lack wisdom, let him ask of God, that giveth to all men liberally, and upbraideth not; and it shall be given him.

6 But let him ask in faith, nothing wavering. For he that wavereth is like a wave of the sea driven with the wind and tossed.

7 For let not that man think that he shall receive any thing of the Lord.

8 A double minded man is unstable in all his ways.

9 Let the brother of low degree rejoice in that he is exalted:

10 But the rich, in that he is made low: because as the flower of the grass he shall pass away.

11 For the sun is no sooner risen with a burning heat, but it withereth the grass, and the flower thereof falleth, and the grace of the fashion of it perisheth: so also shall the rich man fade away in his ways.

New Revised Standard Version

JAMES, a servant of God and of the Lord Jesus Christ, To the twelve tribes in the Dispersion: Greetings.

2 My brothers and sisters, whenever you face trials of any kind, consider it nothing but joy,

3 because you know that the testing of your faith produces endurance;

4 and let endurance have its full effect, so that you may be mature and complete, lacking in nothing.

5 If any of you is lacking in wisdom, ask God, who gives to all generously and ungrudgingly, and it will be given you.

6 But ask in faith, never doubting, for the one who doubts is like a wave of the sea, driven and tossed by the wind;

7, 8 for the doubter, being double-minded and unstable in every way, must not expect to receive anything from the Lord.

9 Let the believer who is lowly boast in being raised up,

10 and the rich in being brought low, because the rich will disappear like a flower in the field.

11 For the sun rises with its scorching heat and withers the field; its flower falls, and its beauty perishes. It is the same way with the rich; in the midst of a busy life, they will wither away.

MAIN THOUGHT: If any of you lack wisdom, let him ask of God, that giveth to all men liberally, and upbraideth not; and it shall be given him. (James 1:5, KJV)

LESSON SETTING

Time: A.D. 44–62
Place: Jerusalem

LESSON OUTLINE

I. Joy in the Midst of Trials (James 1:1–4)
II. Ask for Wisdom (James 1:5–8)
III. Boast in Spiritual Treasures (James 1:9–11)

UNIFYING PRINCIPLE

People desire to be seen as wise. What is the source of wisdom? James' letter affirms that God gives wisdom generously and ungrudgingly to those who ask in faith.

INTRODUCTION

According to James 1:1, James identified himself as the author of this letter or book. This James is Jesus' younger half-brother, a son of Mary and Joseph (see Mark 6:3). Because his name appears first in the list of children in Mark 3, James is more than likely the oldest of Jesus' half-siblings. Many scholars believe James was not a follower of Jesus during His public ministry (see John 7:1–5). However, James became a believer and follower after seeing the resurrected Christ (1 Cor. 15:7). James more than likely was among the group waiting for the Holy Spirit on the day of Pentecost (Acts 1:14), and Paul identified him as a leader in the early church (Gal. 2:9).

Wisdom has been the connecting thread throughout this quarter's lessons. During the first unit of the quarter, we discovered more about wisdom from the Proverbs. Last month, we studied wisdom through the lens of the Gospels. In our last five lessons, we will study wisdom from the perspective of the book of James, a letter full of practical guidance that still holds true for today's modern Christians. The title for our lesson provides a prerequisite for receiving the wisdom we need in order to live successfully: We must *ask* for wisdom.

EXPOSITION

I. JOY IN THE MIDST OF TRIALS (JAMES 1:1–4)

Back in the day when people hand wrote letters to one another, there were key components every letter needed to have. Usually the letter would begin with a date, a greeting that began with "Dear [Name of Recipient]," the body of the letter, and a closing. In today's text, James was writing a letter that began the way most letters did during his time. James 1:1 includes the sender's name, the letter's recipients, and a short greeting. Notice that James did not identify himself as a brother of Jesus, which would have been his right to do. He did not name-drop or insinuate that being a relative of Jesus afforded him special treatment or recognition. Instead, James humbly identified himself as a devoted servant of "God and the Lord Jesus Christ." James' audience, "the twelve tribes scattered among the nations" (v. 1, NIV), referred to Jewish Christians who likely were driven out of their homeland of Israel because of the persecution Christ followers faced.

After beginning with brief pleasantries, James jumped right into the message he wanted his readers to receive. Remember, his readers probably had experienced religious persecution, and verse 2 describes the perspective they should have of life's challenges. James commanded his readers, "Consider it pure joy, my brothers and sisters, whenever you face trials of many kinds" (NIV). James was not saying

Christians should look for trials or that Christians should act as if they are happy about difficult circumstances. The word *consider* suggests James wanted them to think a certain way about their trials; their feelings were not his priority. Getting into our feelings and viewing our circumstances through emotions can cause us to miss God's agenda when we encounter life's challenges.

Two authors have noted: Joy proves quite different from happiness, so that this verse does not support the idea that a Christian must smile all the time! *Joy* may be defined as "a settled contentment in every situation," or, "deep, steady, and unadulterated thankful trust in God."

Notice James said, "whenever," not "if you face trials." This is because trials are inevitable parts of the Christian experience. That is, Christ followers are not exempt from hard times. James suggested Christians are called to look at trials as opportunities for joy because of their potential for producing something good in us. This calls us to develop consciously positive attitudes toward trials, which are contrary to the normal, typical, human response.

In verse 3, James explains to his readers why it is important for them to have the proper perspective as they face challenging circumstances: "because you know the testing of your faith produces perseverance" (NIV). God allows trials and tests to prove the value and maturity of one's faith, and He intends for trials to produce perseverance and endurance in Christians. Perseverance is the ability to endure through various levels of testing or suffering. Recall from verse 1 that joy results from settled contentment and steady trust in God. The trials and tests only produce perseverance and endurance in Christians when our trust is in God. Otherwise, we fall prey to the habit of complaining and throwing pity parties for ourselves.

Paul echoed a similar perspective regarding our approach to trials in Romans 5:3–4: "Not only so, but we also glory in our sufferings, because we know that suffering produces perseverance; perseverance, character; and character, hope."

Furthermore, Peter said, "In all this you greatly rejoice, though now for a little while you have had to suffer grief in all kinds of trials. These have come so the proven genuineness of your faith—of greater worth than gold, which perishes though refined by fire—may result in praise, glory, and honor when Jesus Christ is revealed" (1 Pet. 1:6–7).

In verse 4, James explains that perseverance and endurance are only part of the end goal. The rest of the goal according to verse 4 is "that you may be perfect and complete, lacking nothing" (NRSV). The word *perfect* does not indicate one is sinless or flawless. Instead, it describes the idea of being mature and fully developed.

Joseph is a biblical example of James 1:2–4. Recall that Joseph's brothers despised him because he was his father's favorite son and because he confessed to having had dreams in which his brothers were bowing down to him (Gen. 37:1–11). His brothers decided to sell him into slavery in Egypt (Gen. 37:12–38). Potiphar's wife betrayed Joseph when he refused to fulfill her wishes (Gen. 39), and Joseph ended up in prison. However, the text informs us in the same chapter, in the midst of all this mess, that "the Lord was with Joseph" (Gen. 39:21). Eventually, God made a way for Joseph to ascend to second-in-command in Egypt (Gen. 41). Because of the famine in Canaan, Joseph's brother came to Egypt to buy food for the family. Through unexpected twists and turns in the narrative, Joseph's brothers eventually find out his identity and begged for him to forgive them.

Notice Joseph's response to his brothers in Genesis 50:19–20: "Don't be afraid of me. Am I God, that I can punish you? You intended to harm me, but God intended it all for good. He brought me to this position so I could save the lives of many" (NLT). Joseph trusted in the Lord and affirmed that God was up to something good, including the period of time when he did not fully understand his circumstances (refer back to Gen. 37). Joseph persevered and remained faithful to God throughout his ordeal and time in Egypt, and his maturity and completeness became evident in the way he comported himself with his estranged brothers. He could have sought revenge as he had the power to do whatever he desired and would have been within his rights. However, he was able to view his circumstances as an opportunity to bless rather than harm those who had sought his harm.

II. Ask for Wisdom (James 1:5–8)

Remember James was writing to an audience of persecuted and scattered Jewish Christians who had myriad difficult feelings about the challenging and perhaps dire circumstances they were facing. Now that he had instructed them regarding how to think differently about their "various trials" (v. 2), he described the resources needed to overcome such trials successfully, along with directions for accessing them.

Verse 4 ends with the idea of believers being mature and "lacking nothing." Verse 5 continues by calling attention to wisdom, a critical attribute Christians must not lack in order to gain or to be able to demonstrate spiritual maturity. James gave them an instruction that seems obvious in verse 5: "If any of you lacks wisdom, you should ask God." While asking God for this gift might seem obvious to us, sometimes those who are experiencing life's challenges will ask for what is needed when necessary, and others times they won't due to the pain and/or confusion they might be experiencing.

When Christians struggle to deal with and/or make sense of difficult life circumstances, we often withdraw from God as well as from the body of Christ, perhaps assuming we can handle or fix things on our own or believing others do not or cannot help us. However, James said this is when we most need to lean into our loving heavenly Father for five reasons (see v. 5).

First, God is giving. We serve a generous God who wants to give us wisdom to view our trials from His perspective. An old song reminds us, "You can't beat God's giving, no matter how you try." Second, God gives generously because His supply is unlimited. Third, God gives to all because He is not a respecter of persons; He has no favorite recipients because He loves us all. Fourth, God gives without finding fault, humiliating us, or blaming us for failures. Finally, God promises to give wisdom to those who ask for it, and He cannot break His promises (v. 5).

Verse 6 provides a condition that must be met in order to receive this blessing from the Lord: faith. "But when you ask, you must believe and not doubt" (NIV). Here *faith* refers to confidence in our awesome God. James was not saying believers never should question God; rather, he was explaining we must have unwavering faith in God's character. We must trust God because of who He is, including when we do not fully understand all He is doing in our lives and in the world around us. When Christians trust God, they will not be "blown and tossed by the wind" (v. 6) of doubt and skepticism; they will not be "double-minded and unstable in all they do" (v. 8). If we stop to think about it, those who doubt often lack the stamina to commit themselves to the Lord. They oscillate between trying to obey the Lord and following their own paths and choices. An inability to endure faithfully, with the aid of prayer, is indicative of a doubter's overall character.

Our prayers for wisdom must not vacillate between faith and doubt. We must persevere in prayer, confident that God will answer our requests according to His will. First John 5:14–15 reminds us of the reason we are able to approach God with confidence: "This is the confidence we have in approaching God: that if we ask anything according to His will, He hears us. If we know He hears us—whatever we ask—we know that we have what we asked of Him."

God equips Christians with wisdom to view circumstances from His perspective, often revealing how life's challenges fit into His plan. His wisdom also assures us God is with us so we will maintain the strength to remain faithful, persevering and enduring in the Lord when life does not make sense. This is reminiscent of what Paul says in 1 Corinthians 15:58: "Therefore, my beloved brethren, be steadfast, unmovable, always abounding in the work of the Lord forasmuch as ye know that your labor is not in vain in the Lord."

III. Boast in Spiritual Treasures (James 1:9–11)

After affirming that God generously gives wisdom to those who ask in faith, James gave examples of trials for two different groups of people—the wealthy and the poor. James began by speaking of "believers in humble circumstances" (v. 9), referring to those who are poor or who might be deemed insignificant based on the world's standards. They can be viewed as poor and living "in humble circumstances" because of their social status or due to the persecution they have faced because of their decision to follow Christ in a world that was hostile to the Gospel.

James wanted the "lowly brother" (v. 9) to remember they "have something to boast about, for God has honored them" (v. 9). James wanted the poor in particular to find delight in their spiritual positions and avoid the temptation to complain about their circumstances.

Conversely, James instructed the materially rich to "boast that God had humbled them" (v. 10). People who have been blessed with material possessions can be tempted to boast in their wealth. However, James said worldly riches will pass away (v. 11), while God's wisdom will last for eternity. Thus, the wealthy can boast that God has humbled them enough to understand this world's treasures are temporary.

Wealth actually can be a challenge or barrier to our peace with God. Possessing wealth without spiritual wisdom eventually results in emptiness. Similar to the poor, the rich should revel in the spiritual privileges the Lord has opened to us all.

The Lesson Applied

Once there was a father with a four-year-old son who did not want anyone to help him. He always would say, "Daddy, I'm a big boy. I can do it." One morning, the father and his son were in the kitchen preparing breakfast. The son wanted cereal, so he opened the refrigerator to get the milk and climbed on a stool to reach a box of cereal. Because the son said, "I can do it, Daddy," his loving father watched as the boy made a huge mess. Pouring the cereal, flakes landed on the table and floor. The father started to say, "Son, let me," but the boy interrupted, "Daddy, I can do it." As the boy started to pour the milk, the jug proved to be too heavy, and he lost control of the jug. Milk spilled everywhere.

Then when the son looked at his father—milk running down his face and all over the floor—he said, "Daddy, I need help." His father did not scold, berate, or tease him with an, "I told you so." He simply cleaned up his son, cleaned up the mess, and prepared a fresh bowl of cereal for the growing boy.

The father was waiting to help his son; the son simply needed to ask.

James reminds us we often are similar to the stubborn four-year-old, but our heavenly Father stands ready to help us through our trials and to provide the wisdom we need when we humble ourselves and ask.

Let's Talk About It

1. **James 1:2 commands us to "count it all joy" when we experience various trials in our lives. Why should we have joy as we suffer afflictions?**

   Our experiences as Christians allow us to suffer for the cause of Christ and for human salvation. Therefore, the Lord's brother, the head of the Jerusalem Church ratifies the glory of suffering for the Lord's cause. We also should have joy because it means others will be saved by His and our sacrifice. The eternal outcome of our sacrifice makes the temporary measure of suffering pale in comparison.

2. **How is James 1:5 relevant to your life today?**

   This verse encourages us to make use of the vast resource we have before us. God is the giver of wisdom. To seek Him is to seek guidance for the living of life. The failure to pursue this sacred wisdom results in unnecessary pitfalls.

Home Daily Devotional Readings
August 3–9, 2020

Monday	Tuesday	Wednesday	Thursday	Friday	Saturday	Sunday
Impartial Relationships with One Another	Praised for Steadfast Faith in Persecution	The Poor Blessed; the Rich Criticized	Suffering for Doing the Right Thing	God's Choice—the Foolish, Weak, Lowly	Treat the Rich and Poor Impartially	The Wise Hear and Do Good
Leviticus 19:13–18	2 Thessalonians 1:3–5, 11–12	Luke 6:20–26	1 Peter 3:13–19	1 Corinthians 1:26–31	James 2:1–7	James 1:19–27

AUGUST 9, 2020

HEARING AND DOING THE WORD

ADULT TOPIC:
"TALK IS CHEAP"

BACKGROUND SCRIPTURE:
JAMES 1:19–27

JAMES 1:19–27

King James Version

WHEREFORE, my beloved brethren, let every man be swift to hear, slow to speak, slow to wrath:
20 For the wrath of man worketh not the righteousness of God.
21 Wherefore lay apart all filthiness and superfluity of naughtiness, and receive with meekness the engrafted word, which is able to save your souls.
22 But be ye doers of the word, and not hearers only, deceiving your own selves.
23 For if any be a hearer of the word, and not a doer, he is like unto a man beholding his natural face in a glass:
24 For he beholdeth himself, and goeth his way, and straightway forgetteth what manner of man he was.
25 But whoso looketh into the perfect law of liberty, and continueth therein, he being not a forgetful hearer, but a doer of the work, this man shall be blessed in his deed.
26 If any man among you seem to be religious, and bridleth not his tongue, but deceiveth his own heart, this man's religion is vain.
27 Pure religion and undefiled before God and the Father is this, To visit the fatherless and widows in their affliction, and to keep himself unspotted from the world.

New Revised Standard Version

YOU must understand this, my beloved: let everyone be quick to listen, slow to speak, slow to anger;
20 for your anger does not produce God's righteousness.
21 Therefore rid yourselves of all sordidness and rank growth of wickedness, and welcome with meekness the implanted word that has the power to save your souls.
22 But be doers of the word, and not merely hearers who deceive themselves.
23 For if any are hearers of the word and not doers, they are like those who look at themselves in a mirror;
24 for they look at themselves and, on going away, immediately forget what they were like.
25 But those who look into the perfect law, the law of liberty, and persevere, being not hearers who forget but doers who act—they will be blessed in their doing.
26 If any think they are religious, and do not bridle their tongues but deceive their hearts, their religion is worthless.
27 Religion that is pure and undefiled before God, the Father, is this: to care for orphans and widows in their distress, and to keep oneself unstained by the world.

MAIN THOUGHT: But be ye doers of the word, and not hearers only, deceiving your own selves. (James 1:22, KJV)

LESSON SETTING

Time: A.D. 44–62
Place: Jerusalem

LESSON OUTLINE

I. **Quick to Listen (James 1:19–21)**
II. **Quick to Do (James 1:22–25)**
III. **Quick to Practice True Religion (James 1:26–27)**

UNIFYING PRINCIPLE

People read and talk about doing good but find it difficult to help the most vulnerable in society. How is righteousness accomplished? According to James, righteousness is achieved by hearing and doing the Word of God.

INTRODUCTION

James is the author of this letter or book and Jesus' younger half-brother, a son of Mary and Joseph (see Mark 6:3). Though he did not believe in Jesus as Messiah at first, following Christ's resurrection, James became a prominent leader among the disciples.

Inspired by the work of Dr. Martin Luther King Jr. and the African American Civil Rights Movement, Caesar Chavez became one of the best-known activists for the rights of Latino Americans. In an attempt to stir his audience to action, Chavez said, "Talk is cheap … it is the way we organize and use our lives every day that tells what we believe in." Chavez's words certainly apply to civil rights, but they apply to every aspect of our lives. Words are important, but our actions tell the real story. In today's lesson, James proved that talking about our faith is not enough; actions are the real proof of our faith.

EXPOSITION

I. QUICK TO LISTEN (JAMES 1:19-21)

James began verse 19 with an endearment, addressing his readers as spiritual family members rather than as a dictator over them. He loved them and felt compelled to ensure they heeded a crucial principal: "Everyone must be quick to listen" (v. 19). Here he was addressing the believers as individuals as well as the universal Church or the body of Christ. The word *listen* is indicative of "giving one's full attention to a speaker, hearing intentionally, and listening for understanding." Often people react quickly to what they hear without taking time to process fully what has been said. In fact, we sometimes are thinking about how we will respond rather than listening while someone is talking to us.

Notice James exhorted Christians to do the opposite because the person who is "quick to listen" also out of necessity must be "slow to speak and slow to become angry" (v. 19). The word *slow* denotes "a sense of hesitation or delay." Fully listening requires a shift in one's focus and attitude of unselfishness, attending to the words and needs of the speaker first. Being "quick to listen" requires Christians to slow down their reactions in order to pay attention rather than focusing on their own wants, needs, feelings, and opinions.

The advice to be ready to listen requires a willingness to hear and act according to what is being said. To be slow to speak demands we remain silent until we have a clear understanding of what the speaker is saying and possess the ability to respond appropriately. This admonishment is a call for restraint so we do not react based on a misunderstanding and serves to mitigate ill will or feelings of bitterness.

James went on to describe why it is necessary to maintain a long fuse: "because human anger does not produce the righteousness that God desires" (v. 20). Notice that Solomon also connected anger with foolishness: "People with understanding control their anger; a hot temper shows great foolishness" (Prov. 14:29). "Control your temper, for anger labels you a fool" (Eccl. 7:9).

God desires Spirit-filled, righteous behavior from His children. The Spirit-filled life is characterized by gentleness and self-control (Gal. 5:23), but a telltale sign that a person is being led by the flesh is his or her "outbursts of anger" (Gal. 5:20). Paul seemed to emphasize the same principle in Ephesians 4:26, where he instructs the Christians in Ephesus to "be angry and do not sin," as anger usually leads us to respond emotionally, irrationally, selfishly, and sinfully.

We live in a world where we are encouraged to express our feelings, whether godly or ungodly, good or bad, peaceful or insensitive. Yet James 1:19 reminds us our words matter. We prove ourselves wise from God's perspective when we take time to listen to God and others, to think, and to prepare our responses carefully.

Not only is human anger divisive, but angry Christians also prevent the unsaved from seeing the light and love of Christ. It is impossible for people in the world to want to ascribe to the Christian lifestyle when they observe angry and quarrelsome behavior among believers who profess to worship and serve God. Acting in anger will not lead Christians to accomplish God's will, so James instructed his readers to "put away" or "get rid of" or "lay aside" (v. 21) their pre-Christian lifestyles, including anger, so as to live humbly by the principles of God's Word (v. 21).

God's Word is said to be implanted in this verse, meaning that similar to a seed, the truth of the Gospel takes root in the hearts of believers. Paul described this process as welcoming the message of God and allowing it to influence and work effectively in our lives (see 1 Thess. 2:13). James explained the prerequisite for welcoming God's Word to influence our lives is to rid our lives of all filth and prevalent evil (v. 21). Obedience to God's Word leads to holy living and develops godly character. James said getting rid of the filth and receiving the implanted Word "can save you" (v. 21), meaning our obedience to God becomes evidence of the internal experience of salvation.

II. Quick to Do (James 1:22-25)

Have you ever heard a parent say to a child that his or her instructions were going in one ear and out the other? This phrase highlights a common struggle of parenting. Children might hear, but they choose not to follow the instructions. James addressed this issue with his brothers and sisters in the faith in verses 22–24. Despite the persecution or "various trials" (1:5) they faced, it is imperative for Christians to live out their faith in fear and trembling, obeying God's instructions. God is not content when His people simply attend church to hear powerful, soul-stirring sermons. He wants us to absorb every message from His Word—whether through a sermon, personal Bible study, a Gospel song on the radio, or any other means He chooses—and adjust our lives in response. Allowing His Word to go in one ear and out the other without transformation is a blight on an otherwise Christian life.

When the "implanted word" has taken root in a believer's heart, the result will be more than idle listening. This is because the implanted Word will impact the believer's actions and result in holy living. Therefore, James continued with the command to "be doers of the Word, not hearers only" (v. 22). In Jewish life, hearing Scripture read was an essential element of the people's religious experience; however, James said hearing is not enough. In the Greek, the command to be doers means "to *keep on becoming doers* of God's Word." James is describing a lifestyle of increasing obedience, submission to God, and maturity that results from fearing the Lord (see Prov. 1:7 and the lesson from June 7). A doer of the Word actively and continually obeys God's instructions as a priority. By insisting on obedience, James was not negating the importance of hearing God's Word, but highlighting the need for acting on it in response to all that we hear.

James said people who simply hear the Word without taking action and applying it to their lives actually are deceiving themselves (v. 22). Such self-deception occurs when we mistakenly think or believe we truly are in alignment but actually are in error. A hearer can nod agreeably and say "Amen" to support any truth that is being said while still failing to act in accordance with what they've heard. Our churches are full of such people. However, God wants us to continue to mature as disciples of Christ through obedient action. Those who hear and learn the message without doing anything are the target audience for Jesus' warning against this error (refer to Matt. 7:21–27).

Note that James was not contradicting himself in verses 19 and 22–25. In verse 19, James praised listening and condemned taking action without taking time to listen. Conversely, he also condemned merely listening without responding with appropriate action in verses 22–25.

In verses 23-25, James provided an example to demonstrate the folly of hearing but not obeying God's Word. Today's mirrors usually are made from glass, but in New Testament times, mirrors were made of polished metals such as copper, bronze, silver, and gold. People used them for the same reasons we use them, to make sure our appearance is satisfactory. Ancient mirrors produced reflections that were dim and warped at best; however, one would have a good idea of how he or she looked. James likens people who simply hear the Word to people who glance in the mirror, walk away, and two minutes later have no idea who they are and how they look (v. 24). The same thing happens spiritually when we notice or hear truth from God's Word only to jump to something else without remembering to apply what we heard or addressing what the mirror revealed needed fixing.

Conversely, the Christian or the doer of the Word who "looks intently into the perfect law that gives freedom" (v. 25, NIV) and perseveres in allowing it to shape his or her actions and direct his or her life will be blessed. Looking intently describes a Christian who listens to the Gospel's message with a desire to learn and grow. The desire to grow results in a Christian persevering in and continuing to do what the Word says (v. 25). In addition, the *active* Christian overcomes the propensity to forget by putting into practice what he or she has heard.

James was not saying that not obeying the Word is a matter of salvation in this verse. (James' explanation of the relationship between faith and works or good deeds will be discussed more fully in next week's lesson). Instead, James clearly suggests a relationship between hearing the Word, obeying the Word, growing spiritually, and experiencing God's blessings. Notice that James' words echo the blessing Jesus pronounced in Luke 11:28: "But even more blessed are all who hear the Word of God and put it into practice."

III. Quick to Practice True Religion (James 1:26–27)

James devoted the last two verses of chapter 1 to defining what it means to practice true religion, to be a doer of God's Word. First, doers of His Word watch what they say and realize their words are indicators of their commitment to the Lord. Second, doers of the Word demonstrate their devotion to God by caring for the vulnerable in society. Finally, doers of the Word refuse to let the world corrupt them.

Verse 26 further explains what it means to be slow to speak (see also v. 19) and begins with a conditional statement: "If anyone among you thinks he is religious." In this verse, the word *religious* describes one's piety, worship, or devotion to God. James was explaining what happens when a person is not a doer of the Word. James indicated that one who is truly religious and devoted to God demonstrates his or her devotion by controlling his or her tongue. People who are hearers only, however, may say or think they are religious, though they are unable to keep a "tight rein on their tongues" (v. 26) or "bridle their tongues."

The image of a rein or bridle is connected to horses, and this metaphor describes putting a bit into the animal's mouth in order to restrain, direct, and/or guide it. James was saying the tongue is destructive when it is unrestrained and uncontrolled (see also James 3). Thus, controlling one's tongue is evidence of a person who is actively and purposely engaged in obeying God's Word. Christians fool themselves and are poor witnesses for Christ in the world when they claim to be religious yet are reckless with their language and use destructive words.

In verse 27, James affirmed that loving ministry and holy living go hand in hand as they prove that practitioners of such activities are performing true religion by acting on the principles in God's Word. "To look after" (NIV), "to visit" (NKJV), "caring for" (NLT) in the original Greek usually appeared in conjunction with visiting the sick and incarcerated, thus suggesting the word *distress* confirms that those who follow Christ are compelled to attend to society's most helpless. *Distress* implies these people are suffering, in pain, and need someone to come to their aid. James essentially asked, "Do you realize that meeting practical needs is not a suggestion or optional but is central, obligatory, and mandatory to true faith?" Social justice is necessary, but it's not sufficient apart from being motivated by God's purposes.

James went on to command his siblings in the faith to be in the world but not of the world as we often hear said in church (v. 27). He exhorted his readers to keep themselves from being polluted by the sinful, fallen world system. We are called to be salt and light to the world that desperately needs our Savior. We cannot blend in with the world and liveGod-honoring, set-apart lives. Christ-followers must be hearers and doers of the Word.

The Lesson Applied

Today's lesson proves that when it comes to our faith, words alone are not enough. It is not enough to intellectually know and believe the truths in God's Word's without taking corresponding action. Indeed, talk is cheap, but action always speaks and reveals the truth of our hearts. In the days ahead, let us commit to being quick to listen, quick to do, and quick to practice true religion.

Let's Talk About It

1. **James 1:19–21 focuses on speech as an area for demonstrating obedience to God's Word, calling for godly speech as a demonstration of one's commitment to the Lord. Reflect on words you said during the past week. Which descriptor best applies to you: quick to hear, slow to speak, slow to anger, a complete hindrance to the righteousness God desires?**

One person's thoughts may inspire another or provide clarity. James focuses on our own individual speech, how it should reflect our religiosity, our relationship with the Lord God. The Scriptures forbid us from ridiculing others and yet praise God with the same tongue. John adds those who would love God must love their brothers and sisters as well. Our words reflect the inner disposition of our hearts.

2. **James emphasized that listening and obeying are two different actions. Which one of these things does James prefer us to focus on?**

James is correct to point out there is no *either/or* as far as this question is concerned. We are called upon to hear the Word of God, and we also are called upon to be doers of the Word that has been proclaimed, taught, or read. In other words, hearing leads to doing. Paul noted in Romans 10 that preachers are called to proclaim the truth of God. Both John the Baptist and Jesus followed the way of Old Testament prophets who came proclaiming, "Thus, saith the Lord." Their proclamations are not to fall on deaf ears, however. The call to hear is also a call to respond to the divine initiative.

Home Daily Devotional Readings
August 9–16, 2020

Monday	Tuesday	Wednesday	Thursday	Friday	Saturday	Sunday
Abraham Blessed for Fearing God	Spies Saved by Rahab's Quick Actions	Forgive Others as God Forgave You	Devoted to Good Works, Avoiding Distractions	Works Guided by Loyalty to God	Receive God's Mercy by Showing Mercy	Faith and Works Must Go Together
Genesis 22:9–19	Joshua 2:1–7	Matthew 18:23–35	Titus 3:1–2, 8–11	Deuteronomy 6:4–9	James 2:8–13	James 2:14–26

FAITH WITHOUT WORKS IS DEAD

ADULT TOPIC:
"JUST DO IT"

BACKGROUND SCRIPTURE:
JAMES 2:14–26

JAMES 2:14–26

King James Version

WHAT doth it profit, my brethren, though a man say he hath faith, and have not works? can faith save him?

15 If a brother or sister be naked, and destitute of daily food,

16 And one of you say unto them, Depart in peace, be ye warmed and filled; notwithstanding ye give them not those things which are needful to the body; what doth it profit?

17 Even so faith, if it hath not works, is dead, being alone.

18 Yea, a man may say, Thou hast faith, and I have works: shew me thy faith without thy works, and I will shew thee my faith by my works.

19 Thou believest that there is one God; thou doest well: the devils also believe, and tremble.

20 But wilt thou know, O vain man, that faith without works is dead?

21 Was not Abraham our father justified by works, when he had offered Isaac his son upon the altar?

22 Seest thou how faith wrought with his works, and by works was faith made perfect?

23 And the scripture was fulfilled which saith, Abraham believed God, and it was imputed unto him for righteousness: and he was called the Friend of God.

24 Ye see then how that by works a man is justified, and not by faith only.

New Revised Standard Version

WHAT good is it, my brothers and sisters, if you say you have faith but do not have works? Can faith save you?

15 If a brother or sister is naked and lacks daily food,

16 and one of you says to them, "Go in peace; keep warm and eat your fill," and yet you do not supply their bodily needs, what is the good of that?

17 So faith by itself, if it has no works, is dead.

18 But someone will say, "You have faith and I have works." Show me your faith apart from your works, and I by my works will show you my faith.

19 You believe that God is one; you do well. Even the demons believe—and shudder.

20 Do you want to be shown, you senseless person, that faith apart from works is barren?

21 Was not our ancestor Abraham justified by works when he offered his son Isaac on the altar?

22 You see that faith was active along with his works, and faith was brought to completion by the works.

23 Thus the scripture was fulfilled that says, "Abraham believed God, and it was reckoned to him as righteousness," and he was called the friend of God.

24 You see that a person is justified by works and not by faith alone.

MAIN THOUGHT: For as the body without the spirit is dead, so faith without works is dead also. (James 2:26, KJV)

King James Version	*New Revised Standard Version*
25 Likewise also was not Rahab the harlot justified by works, when she had received the messengers, and had sent them out another way?	**25 Likewise, was not Rahab the prostitute also justified by works when she welcomed the messengers and sent them out by another road?**
26 For as the body without the spirit is dead, so faith without works is dead also.	**26 For just as the body without the spirit is dead, so faith without works is also dead.**

LESSON SETTING

Time: A.D. 44–62
Place: Jerusalem

LESSON OUTLINE

I. The Relationship Between Faith and Works (James 2:14–20)
II. Examples from Abraham and Rahab (James 2:21–26)

UNIFYING PRINCIPLE

According to James 1:1, James is the author of this book. This James is Jesus' younger half-brother, probably the oldest of Mary and Joseph's children after Jesus, Mary's firstborn. James initially was not a follower of his elder brother, but probably was among the group waiting for the Holy Spirit on the day of Pentecost. Paul identified him as a leader in the early church.

INTRODUCTION

Some people make bold claims about the standards by which they live, but their actions negate those claims. How can we tell when someone is genuine? James said the one who has faith will demonstrate that faith by his or her works, as did Abraham and Rahab.

Almost everyone is familiar with Nike's "Just Do It™" slogan. In 1988, Nike introduced the slogan as part of an advertising campaign designed to increase their business in North America. Using this slogan to fuel their marketing efforts from 1988-1998, Nike grew their business from $877 million to $9.2 billion in worldwide sales. One campaign objective was to target all Americans regardless of age, gender, or physical fitness level, which led to people wearing the Nike brand as a fashion statement and not just for exercise. Nike's fundamental objective was to represent sneakers as a fashion statement to consumers, especially females, teens, and males ages eighteen–forty. To do this, they paid numerous athletes millions of dollars to endorse their products and encourage consumers to purchase Nike products.

In today's lesson, "Just Do It," James is not encouraging readers to buy expensive tennis shoes or other products but encouraging readers to demonstrate their faith by their actions and good works.

EXPOSITION

I. THE RELATIONSHIP BETWEEN FAITH AND WORKS (JAMES 2:14–20)

James was writing to Jewish Christians who had faced persecution because of their faith in Christ. Despite the hardships they experienced, James encouraged his audience to demonstrate the transformation that following Christ had made in their lives, not by their words but by their obedience. In last week's lesson, James explained the necessity of hearing and responding with obedience to the Word (see 1:19–27). In chapter 2, James discussed the sin of favoritism (vv. 1–13) and then illustrated the relationship between faith and works, an extension of his claim in verse 1:22 that Christ-followers must "be doers of the Word, not hearers only."

James posed two poignant, rhetorical questions in verse 14. The goal of these questions, which have obvious negative answers, is to elicit critical thinking about the relationship between faith and good works. The first is, "What good is it ... if you say you have faith but don't show it by your actions?" James spoke gently yet with authority. This first question in verse 14 is designed to cause readers to think about the extent to which they have internalized their faith. Discussing faith as an intellectual exercise is not enough. It is one thing to talk about faith in Christ but something completely different and more powerful to internalize faith and live by the principles Christ taught.

The second question is, "Can that kind of faith save anyone?" Is there power in a faith that is only worth discussing? A faith that is powerless to change a person's life is shallow, and James led his audience to consider whether such faith has power to save. His goal was not to suggest believers can lose salvation by disobedience, but to call for believers to reflect and examine themselves to determine whether their lives exhibit evidence of true faith in Christ.

Continuing the argument that one's faith necessarily must affect his or her actions, James provided an example of how faith should drive one's actions. In verse 15, James cited an example of "a brother or sister," not a stranger. "Brother or sister" could refer to a fellow Christian, a family member, or an acquaintance. James said if such a person doesn't have food or clothing (basic needs), it would be most appropriate for a Christian to help meet these needs. Should they provide well wishes instead of practical help? The obvious answer in this example is no. This is not the way a Christian should treat his or her brothers and sisters in Christ when blessed with the ability to help.

This example proves the absurdity of claiming to follow Christ by using words to substitute for actions. James said faith in Christ that is not accompanied by godly character and good works is dead (v. 17). Jesus warned those who verbally express their commitment to Him without corresponding action (Matt. 7:15–27). John said it this way: "But whoever has this world's goods, and sees his brother in need, and shuts up his heart from him, how does the love of God abide in him? My little children, let us not love in word or in tongue, but indeed and in truth" (1 John 3:17–18, NKJV).

James provided another example in verses 18–19 to demonstrate the absurdity of separating faith from works. This time, James posed what might be the view of an imaginary opponent in disagreement with connection between faith and good works. The counterargument could be, "But someone will say, 'You have faith; I have deeds'" (v. 18, NIV). Such *either/or* arguments are futile. In response to this rhetorical scenario, James insisted in verse

18 that real faith shows itself by actions: "I will show you my faith by my deeds." We must have faith *and* works, because a real commitment to Christ manifests in the kind actions we take toward others. That is, faith produces works, and we cannot have one without the other.

To prove one's intellectual beliefs is not enough, James highlighted Judaism as a monotheistic faith—the belief in the one true and living God—that would have been easy for his Jewish audience to affirm. Their belief in one God (James 2:19) was rooted in the Ten Commandments (Exod. 20:1–6) and the Shema (Deut. 6:4–5). Any devoted Jew would affirm faith in Yahweh. In fact, many people today affirm belief in God. Yet intellectual ascent is not enough to receive salvation, because "even the demons" (James 2:19) profess to believe in one God and shudder at the thought of Him (Matt. 8:29). Intellectual belief is not enough to save one from eternal damnation. Acknowledging God's existence does not equate to meaning a person has repented of sin and made a commitment to follow and obey Jesus Christ as the only means of salvation. Saving faith, the faith to which James refers in these verses, requires knowledge, trust, and obedience.

Remember this lesson is part of a unit about wisdom. We have considered wisdom in Proverbs, the Gospels, and now the book of James. Previously, we have discovered folly as the opposite of wisdom, and in verse 20, James used strong language: "You foolish person." In no uncertain terms, James said the one who still believes faith can be separated from works, including after the evidence he has provided in 2:14–19, is spiritually ignorant. However, the cure for foolish thinking also is provided: a willingness to learn.

II. Examples from Abraham and Rahab (James 2:21–26)

In hopes of teaching those who truly are willing to learn and think differently, James elaborated on two heroes of faith from the Old Testament to provide evidence that faith without good works is useless and ineffective. These examples are listed among the faith heroes in Hebrews 11, and they serve as examples of people who demonstrated their faith through their actions. Again, James used examples of people with whom his Judeo-Christian readers would have been familiar.

The first example was Father Abraham (2:22–24). Referring to Abraham as "our father," James emphasized their common Jewish heritage, initiated when Abraham obediently responded to God's call by faith (Gen. 12:1–9). When God called Abraham, he was seventy-five years old; his wife Sarah was sixty-five. God promised a multitude of blessings: "I will make you into a great nation. I will bless you. I will make your name great, and you will be a blessing" (Gen. 12:2). However there were a couple of problems. Abraham and Sarah had no children. She was barren, and they were beyond childbearing age; yet an heir was needed for God's promises to be fulfilled. Thinking it impossible for him and Sarah to conceive, Abraham asked if one of the slaves born in his household could be his heir. God promised "one who comes from your own body will be your heir" (Gen. 15:3).

Though Abraham and Sarah tried to help God produce an heir (Gen. 16), Ishmael was not the heir of promise. Again, God affirmed Abraham and Sarah would give birth to a son, regardless of how impossible it seemed to them: "The Lord said, 'I will certainly come back to you in about a year's time, and your wife Sarah will have a son.' Now Sarah was listening at the entrance of the tent behind him. Abraham and Sarah were old and getting on in years. Sarah had passed the age of childbearing. So she laughed at herself: 'After I have become shriveled up and my lord [speaking of Abraham] is old, will I have delight?' But the Lord asked Abraham, 'Why did Sarah laugh? Is anything impossible for the Lord? At the appointed time I will come back to you, and in about a year she will have a son'" (Gen. 18:10–14).

At the appointed time, Abraham and Sarah gave birth to Isaac. Abraham was one hundred years old, and Sarah was ninety. Twenty-five years had passed between God's initial promises in Genesis 12 and Isaac's birth in Genesis 20.

Fast forward to Genesis 22, where God asks Abraham: "Take your son … your only son Isaac, whom you love, go to the land of Moriah and offer him there as a burnt offering on one of the mountains I will tell you about" (Gen. 22:2).

We cannot imagine the emotions Abraham and Sarah probably experienced in response to this command. They had waited so long for the miraculous birth of their son, and now God wanted them to sacrifice him?

In one of the greatest acts of faith, the Bible tells us in the next verse that Abraham got up early the next morning, preparing himself and Isaac to do exactly what God commanded. Notice Abraham's words corresponded with his actions: "The boy and I will go over there to worship; then we'll come back to you.' Abraham took the wood for the burnt offering and laid it on his son Isaac ... Isaac said, 'The fire and wood are here, but where is the lamb for the burnt offering?' Abraham answered [in faith], 'God Himself will provide the lamb for the burnt offering, my son'" (Gen. 22:6–8). And that is exactly what God did (Gen. 22:12–14).

James used this example to prove Abraham's faith in God's ability to keep His promise and make Him a great nation was demonstrated by his words and corresponding actions. Describing Abraham's faith, James essentially said his faith and actions were working in tandem (v. 22) with his outward expression making his inner faith complete.

Abraham's saving faith showed up in his complete obedience to God by his willingness to offer Isaac (foreshadowing Christ as our sacrificial Lamb). The faith James commended moves the heart and controls the life. Again, James was exhorting readers that true faith must be alive and vital.

The second example is Rahab (James 2:25). Unlike Abraham, long considered to be the father of the Islamic faith as well as Judaism and Christianity, a man of great prominence who was and is respected by the Jewish people for his faith and character, Rahab was cut from a different cloth. Notice the descriptor that follows her name in James 2:25: "the prostitute." She was not a Jew; however, she is listed among the faith heroes in Hebrews 11. Rahab's story of faithful action is captured in Joshua 2.

To prepare for battle in Jericho, Joshua sent two spies to investigate the land (Josh.

2:2). The king of Jericho was well aware they were coming, and he "sent word to Rahab and said, 'Bring out the men who came to you and entered your house, for they came to investigate the entire land" (Josh. 2:3). However, the text informs us that Rahab had hidden the two spies and intentionally misled the king's men to ensure the spies' safety. If her neighbors or the leaders of Jericho found out about her disloyalty, she could be put to death. Regardless, she willingly risked her life to protect them from their pursuers.

Why would this Gentile prostitute risk so much for the Israelites? Joshua 2:8–13 makes it clear that Rahab had faith in Israel's God. In a beautiful declaration, Rahab said, "I know that the Lord has given you His land … for we have heard" (Josh. 2:9–10). She and the people of Jericho had heard all about what God had done on Israel's behalf, and Rahab believed the God of Israel not only would give the Israelites Jericho, but also would save her family if she, by faith, risked her own safety to help Israel's spies. Rahab's faith in action pleased God and saved her family.

Though Abraham and Rahab were quite different, they share one similarity: a demonstrable faith in God—not by their words, but by their actions. James' argument is that the same faith and action must be present in our lives.

After providing two examples of people who exemplified faith in God by their actions, James' concluding thought is summarized in 2:14–25: "For just as the body without the spirit is dead, so also faith without works is dead" (NIV).

The Lesson Applied

James did not beat around the bush. Christians must provide evidence of their faith through their actions—just do it! Abraham and Rahab proved our faith must be active together with our works. Faith without good works is useless and ineffective, so let's leave this lesson determined to be Christians whose actions align with the faith we profess to have in Almighty God.

Let's Talk About It

1. What does James mean by "faith apart from works is dead?"

What James is doing in verse 20 is reinforcing how faith and works relate to one another and how they are to be carried our in the Christian life. He seeks to establish as a foundation for responding to the divine initiative that faith is not merely verbal assent. Rather, faith is active. It has legs and hands. The presence of faith is observed in what one does and not merely in what one says. Faith and works, or should I say obedience to the Word of God, is essential.

Home Daily Devotional Readings
August 17–23, 2019

Monday	Tuesday	Wednesday	Thursday	Friday	Saturday	Sunday
Unwise Not to Listen to Teachers	Testimony of a Wise Teacher	Slander and Abusive Language Not Allowed	Use Tongue to Speak God's Praise	Believers Anointed with Fire and Tongues	Tongues and Teachers Are God's Gifts	Speech Is for Healing and Refreshment
Proverbs 5:7–14	Isaiah 50:4–11	Colossians 3:1–11	Psalm 119:169–176	Acts 2:1–12	1 Corinthians 12:27–31	James 3:1–12

TAMING THE TONGUE

ADULT TOPIC:
"BITE YOUR TONGUE"

BACKGROUND SCRIPTURE:
JAMES 3:1–12

JAMES 3:1–12

King James Version

MY brethren, be not many masters, knowing that we shall receive the greater condemnation.

2 For in many things we offend all. If any man offend not in word, the same is a perfect man, and able also to bridle the whole body.

3 Behold, we put bits in the horses' mouths, that they may obey us; and we turn about their whole body.

4 Behold also the ships, which though they be so great, and are driven of fierce winds, yet are they turned about with a very small helm, whithersoever the governor listeth.

5 Even so the tongue is a little member, and boasteth great things. Behold, how great a matter a little fire kindleth!

6 And the tongue is a fire, a world of iniquity: so is the tongue among our members, that it defileth the whole body, and setteth on fire the course of nature; and it is set on fire of hell.

7 For every kind of beasts, and of birds, and of serpents, and of things in the sea, is tamed, and hath been tamed of mankind:

8 But the tongue can no man tame; it is an unruly evil, full of deadly poison.

9 Therewith bless we God, even the Father; and therewith curse we men, which are made after the similitude of God.

10 Out of the same mouth proceedeth blessing and cursing. My brethren, these things ought not so to be.

11 Doth a fountain send forth at the same place sweet water and bitter?

New Revised Standard Version

NOT many of you should become teachers, my brothers and sisters, for you know that we who teach will be judged with greater strictness.

2 For all of us make many mistakes. Anyone who makes no mistakes in speaking is perfect, able to keep the whole body in check with a bridle.

3 If we put bits into the mouths of horses to make them obey us, we guide their whole bodies.

4 Or look at ships: though they are so large that it takes strong winds to drive them, yet they are guided by a very small rudder wherever the will of the pilot directs.

5 So also the tongue is a small member, yet it boasts of great exploits. How great a forest is set ablaze by a small fire!

6 And the tongue is a fire. The tongue is placed among our members as a world of iniquity; it stains the whole body, sets on fire the cycle of nature, and is itself set on fire by hell.

7 For every species of beast and bird, of reptile and sea creature, can be tamed and has been tamed by the human species,

8 but no one can tame the tongue—a restless evil, full of deadly poison.

9 With it we bless the Lord and Father, and with it we curse those who are made in the likeness of God.

10 From the same mouth come blessing and cursing. My brothers and sisters, this ought not to be so.

11 Does a spring pour forth from the same opening both fresh and brackish water?

MAIN THOUGHT: Even so the tongue is a little member, and boasteth great things. Behold, how great a matter a little fire kindleth! (James 3:5, KJV)

James 3:1–12

King James Version	*New Revised Standard Version*
12 Can the fig tree, my brethren, bear olive berries? either a vine, figs? so can no fountain both yield salt water and fresh.	**12 Can a fig tree, my brothers and sisters, yield olives, or a grapevine figs? No more can salt water yield fresh.**

LESSON SETTING

Time: A.D. 44–62
Place: Jerusalem

LESSON OUTLINE

I. Not Everyone Should Be a Teacher (James 3:1–2)
II. The Positive Potential of the Tongue (James 3:2–5)
III. The Negative Potential of the Tongue (James 3:5–8)
IV. Two Sides of the Same Tongue (James 3:9–12)

Unifying Principle

The spoken word can be either an affirming or destructive force in our lives. How can affirmation prevail in our interactions? James said that only through discipline can the fruits of godly wisdom be made manifest in our lives.

Introduction

James, Jesus' half-brother and author of this letter, became a believer and follower after seeing the resurrected Christ (1 Cor. 15:7). He more than likely was among the group waiting for the Holy Spirit on the Day of Pentecost (Acts 1:14). Paul identified him as a leader in the early apostolic church (refer to Gal. 2:9).

Today's lesson title, "Bite Your Tongue," is an idiom dating back to the writings of William Shakespeare. If we are biting our tongues, it is impossible to speak clearly. Through the years, this idiom has become a socially acceptable way of saying, "Keep it to yourself! Don't say that!"

In a previous lesson, James emphasized the necessity of Christians controlling their tongues. Recall that he addressed the fact that our godly actions and good works prove the reality of genuine faith (see 2:14–26). Today, we return to the subject of the tongue with verses that shed more light on speaking wisely and elaborate on the tongue's potential, which challenges believers to use wise, God-honoring words.

Exposition

I. Not Everyone Should Be a Teacher (James 3:1–2)

In many church settings, people often want to have the spiritual gifts that receive the most attention. Yet, instead of dwelling on the benefits we might receive from teaching, for example, we must consider the extent to which we actually are gifted and prepared to carry out such work. James began chapter 3 by instructing those who desired to be teachers in the church. James warned that only a small number of people actually should be teachers because "you know that we who teach will be judged with greater strictness" (v. 1, NRSV).

Teachers play important roles in the Church. The calling to teach in the Church is a calling to prepare, study, and communicate the truths in God's Word prayerfully, as well as live accordingly. Without prepared teachers, churches will suffer from false and theologically inaccurate interpretations of Scripture, which will harm the body rather than edify it. No one is perfect, and the calling to teach does not require perfection. However, teachers will be held to a higher level of accountability on the Day of Judgment. So, James encouraged Christians to consider carefully whether they have been called to this ministry.

Notice the word *all*. James assured us the struggle with sin is an experience that is common to all human beings. Only Jesus was able to live in the world without sin. The word *mistakes* may refer to errors in judgment, acting in ways that dishonor God and using the tongue inappropriately.

II. The Positive Potential of the Tongue (James 3:2–5)

In the context of verses 1–2, we know James was affirming that perhaps one of the most challenging things for any Christian is to maintain control of his or her tongue. In verse 2b, James said, "Anyone who makes no mistakes in speaking is perfect, able to keep the whole body in check." James made it clear no one has reached the level of sinless speech. Note that he prefaced that remark by saying all of us make mistakes. The word *perfect* implies completeness or maturity. One's ability to control his or her tongue is one demonstrable way of exercising and displaying one's spiritual maturity.

Verse 2b goes on to introduce the reality that the tongue controls one's entire body. The tongue guiding the body seems to have a double meaning here. Not only was James referring to the tongue guiding one's physical body, but also to teachers' words controlling the church body, again emphasizing the responsibility teachers have to the church's spiritual health.

In verses 3–5, James gave two illustrations regarding the tongue's potential, highlighting how something small can control something large. In the first illustration, James pointed to an example any equestrian would understand. Bits are used to influence horses and give them direction. They are placed in horses' mouths so riders are able to communicate what they want their horses to do. When riders apply pressure to the bit by moving one or both reins, this tells the horse to stop whatever it's doing or which direction to go. When the pressure is released, the horse can resume action and experience relief from the bit's pressure. So, a small bit in a horse's mouth is able to control a 750-pound horse.

In the second illustration, James challenged his readers to consider lessons that can be learned from mariner terminology, which is logical as many of his readers lived and worked in sailing and/or fishing industries. Verse 4 says, "Though they are so large that it takes strong winds to drive them, yet they are guided by a very small rudder wherever the will of the pilot directs." Winds propel boats; but a rudder, which is a small mechanism on the bottom of a boat, steers the boat in the direction the pilot wants it to travel.

In verse 5a, James explained the purpose of both illustrations. Not only do they show how something large can be controlled by something small, but also great results can come from small influences, such as the tongue. An equestrian uses a tiny bit to control a horse, and a navel captain uses a rudder to steer a ship. Likewise, the tongue guides the whole body to it's folly or success depending on how it is used.

III. The Negative Potential of the Tongue (James 3:5–8)

In verses 5–8, James employed a third illustration to illustrate the destructive power of an uncontrolled tongue. Though small, the tongue possesses the ability to destroy a large target. James offered an interesting comment to compel his readers to think critically immediately after he praised the positive impact tongues can have: "How great a forest is set ablaze by a small fire" (v. 5b, NRSV)! Forest fires begin with a small spark, and James used this analogy to emphasize the magnitude of damage a few unwise or unkind words can cause, especially when said in haste or without regard for their impact.

In verse 6, James compared the negative and widespread power of the tongue to a fire. Verse 6 says, "The tongue represents the world of wrongdoing among the parts of our bodies." He said it has the power to produce three negative results. First, it "pollutes the whole body" because it can corrupt and defile one's mind, personality, and actions. The tongue sets the course of one's life on a destructive path and "is set on fire by hell." So, instead of glorifying God, it becomes a tool of the enemy.

In Genesis 1:26, God declared one role of humanity is to rule over the animal kingdom. Despite our ability to domesticate many species, James said one beast we will not tame is the tongue, which is "a restless evil, full of deadly poison" (v. 8).

IV. Two Sides of the Same Tongue (James 3:9–12)

After noting the positive and negative power of the tongue, James closed this section of his letter by describing the contradictory nature of the tongue. First, James affirmed we use our mouths to praise our heavenly Father (v. 9). By this, he was referring to the best that can come from our mouths. Ironically, we use the same tongue to "curse those who are made in the likeness of God" (v. 9). Cursing in the context of this passage refers to using words to verbally abuse others (often in anger), expressing hateful wishes toward others, using profane language, and insulting our fellow human beings who have been made in God's image; therefore, to do so is to curse that which is holy.

Blessings and cursing can come from the same mouth (v. 10), but James exhorted his readers not to give the tongue opportunities for the latter. Instead, taking cues from nature, we consistently must use our tongues to honor God. James provided examples from nature in verses 11–12 to paint a picture of consistency found in nature. Springs consistently produce fresh water. The water is not fresh one day and bitter or salty the next. In addition, fig trees consistently produce figs. There never will come a time when olives will come from fig trees.

Although our tongues may not model consistency, the Holy Spirit desires to do a work of transformation in us. We cannot tame our tongues on our own, but when we yield our mouths to the power of the Holy Spirit, He will use our mouths to speak wise, God-honoring, Spirit-filled words.

The Lesson Applied

Our words matter. We live in a world in which we have opportunities to speak from a variety of platforms. For example, we can say our words aloud, and we can express ourselves through social media. When people say whatever they want, often without considering the consequences or impact on others, our tongues (as James would say) are destructive fires.

Today's lesson makes it clear we can allow the Holy Spirit to control our tongues, or our tongues will control us. When controlled by sinful desires, the tongue can serve as a weapon of mass destruction. However, when a person reveres and fears the Lord (Prov. 1:7), the tongue can be an instrument of love, grace, and blessing. We cannot tame our tongues without yielding to the Holy Spirit, but as we allow Him to do this work in us, He will transform the words that come from our mouths into means of inspiration, healing, and refreshment for others.

Let's Talk About It

1. **Why does James prohibit slanderous speech?**

   The brother of our Lord Jesus prohibits hurtful speech because it does not reflect the presence and power of God in one's life. That is not to say that constructive criticism should not be wisely offered. We all need it to help us mature and make wise decisions. However, James puts the prohibitive brakes on using speech that demeans and destroys a person. He points out the dichotomy between praising and elevating God on the one hand and destroying our fellow persons on the other by using words that belittle and debase them. God made people in His image and likeness. To debase others is the equivalent of debasing Him. Therefore, our speech must be used to edify, never to demand and destroy.

2. **What is the key to controlling the tongue according to James 3:1–12?**

   The key to controlling the tongue is to give it over to the power of the Holy Spirit. Only the Spirit of God can control and eliminate sin in its various forms. However, the key is for us to allow the Spirit of God to sanctify and cleanse us from *all* unrighteousness. We must be receptive to His work and permit the Spirit access to our hearts. When we permit the Spirit to enter into our lives, He transforms, enlightens, and empowers us to doing things God's way. The Spirit of God acts as our guide and convicts us of sinful thoughts, behavior, and speech (see John 14–16). He also leads us through the process of sanctification, cleansing us daily from all sin and evil.

Home Daily Devotional Readings

August 24–30, 2020

Monday	Tuesday	Wednesday	Thursday	Friday	Saturday	Sunday
Wisdom about End Time Signs	Wisdom for Speaking a Prophetic Message	Wisdom in Knowing Hearts Without Blame	Wisdom in Speaking Clearly	Living Gracefully with One Another	Wisdom in the Prayer of Faith	Acting Wisely with Patience and Love
Matthew 24:3–14	Jeremiah 38:1–6	1 Thessalonians 3:6–13	Matthew 5:33–37	1 Peter 4:7–11	James 5:13–20	James 3:13–18; 5:7–12

TWO KINDS OF WISDOM

ADULT TOPIC:
WISE UP!

BACKGROUND SCRIPTURE:
JAMES 3:13–18; 5:7–12

JAMES 3:13–18; 5:7–12

King James Version

WHO is a wise man and endued with knowledge among you? let him shew out of a good conversation his works with meekness of wisdom.

14 But if ye have bitter envying and strife in your hearts, glory not, and lie not against the truth.

15 This wisdom descendeth not from above, but is earthly, sensual, devilish.

16 For where envying and strife is, there is confusion and every evil work.

17 But the wisdom that is from above is first pure, then peaceable, gentle, and easy to be intreated, full of mercy and good fruits, without partiality, and without hypocrisy.

18 And the fruit of righteousness is sown in peace of them that make peace.

• • • 5:7–12 • • •

7 Be patient therefore, brethren, unto the coming of the Lord. Behold, the husbandman waiteth for the precious fruit of the earth, and hath long patience for it, until he receive the early and latter rain.

8 Be ye also patient; stablish your hearts: for the coming of the Lord draweth nigh.

9 Grudge not one against another, brethren, lest ye be condemned: behold, the judge standeth before the door.

10 Take, my brethren, the prophets, who have spoken in the name of the Lord, for an example of suffering affliction, and of patience.

New Revised Standard Version

WHO is wise and understanding among you? Show by your good life that your works are done with gentleness born of wisdom.

14 But if you have bitter envy and selfish ambition in your hearts, do not be boastful and false to the truth.

15 Such wisdom does not come down from above, but is earthly, unspiritual, devilish.

16 For where there is envy and selfish ambition, there will also be disorder and wickedness of every kind.

17 But the wisdom from above is first pure, then peaceable, gentle, willing to yield, full of mercy and good fruits, without a trace of partiality or hypocrisy.

18 And a harvest of righteousness is sown in peace for those who make peace.

• • • 5:7–12 • • •

7 Be patient, therefore, beloved, until the coming of the Lord. The farmer waits for the precious crop from the earth, being patient with it until it receives the early and the late rains.

8 You also must be patient. Strengthen your hearts, for the coming of the Lord is near.

9 Beloved, do not grumble against one another, so that you may not be judged. See, the Judge is standing at the doors!

10 As an example of suffering and patience, beloved, take the prophets who spoke in the name of the Lord.

MAIN THOUGHT: But the wisdom that is from above is first pure, then peaceable, gentle, and easy to be intreated, full of mercy and good fruits, without partiality, and without hypocrisy. (James 3:17, KJV)

James 3:13–18; 5:7–12

King James Version	*New Revised Standard Version*
11 Behold, we count them happy which endure. Ye have heard of the patience of Job, and have seen the end of the Lord; that the Lord is very pitiful, and of tender mercy.	**11 Indeed we call blessed those who showed endurance. You have heard of the endurance of Job, and you have seen the purpose of the Lord, how the Lord is compassionate and merciful.**
12 But above all things, my brethren, swear not, neither by heaven, neither by the earth, neither by any other oath: but let your yea be yea; and your nay, nay; lest ye fall into condemnation.	**12 Above all, my beloved, do not swear, either by heaven or by earth or by any other oath, but let your "Yes" be yes and your "No" be no, so that you may not fall under condemnation.**

LESSON SETTING

Time: A.D. 44–62
Place: Jerusalem

LESSON OUTLINE

I. Two Kinds of Wisdom (James 3:13–17)
II. Waiting Patiently for the Lord (James 5:7–12)

Unifying Principle

Throughout history, many have risked their lives by resisting oppressive regimes, thus saving others' lives. What motivates us to defy evil and bless strangers? James contrasted using wisdom for good and evil.

Introduction

James, Jesus' half-brother, wrote this letter to encourage Christians in practical concerns. Today's lesson will increase our understanding of true wisdom by helping us think maturely about demonstrating heavenly wisdom and waiting on the Lord.

Exposition

I. Two Kinds of Wisdom (James 3:13–17)

The first part of James 3 is devoted to controlling the tongue. Today, we return to the unit theme of wisdom.

James began verse 13 with a rhetorical question to make his readers think critically about themselves. Recall that James began chapter 3 by addressing believers who desired to become teachers, and he emphasized the responsibility and accountability required for teachers (see 3:1–2). James continued to speak directly to those desiring to become teachers while also addressing the total readership. Thus, his words are relevant to all believers.

James rhetorically asked, "Who is wise and understanding among you?" (v. 13a). The word *wise* describes someone who has the ability to make practical decisions that honor God. The word *understanding* describes someone who has gained expert knowledge and can use it effectively. In essence, James was asking readers to examine themselves to discern, "Who actually knows what is right and practices it?"

James provided the appropriate way for one to show wisdom: "Let them show it by their good life, by deeds done in humility that come from wisdom" (v. 13b). James affirmed that good works are evidence of faith. Notice he stressed how good deeds should be done: "in humility" (NIV) or "with gentleness" (NRSV) because the intent is as important as the action itself. He insisted that one's "good life" (NIV), "living an honorable life" (NLT), "good conduct" (NET) is evidence of wisdom.

James expounded on two types of wisdom in verses 14–18. In verses 14–16, he addressed earthly wisdom first by providing two character traits of those who follow earthly wisdom. Such people, James said, "harbor bitter envy and selfish ambition in their hearts." Envy and selfish ambition are rooted in self-centeredness, not in seeking the good of others. James instructed such people to stop bragging and denying the truth. In verse 15, James definitively declared this type of unwise behavior does not come from God above (compare with James 1:17) ; instead, it is "earthly, unspiritual, devilish."

James further described the results of envy and selfish ambition produced by earthly wisdom: "For where there is envy and selfish ambition, there will also be disorder and wickedness of every kind" (v. 16, NRSV). A church cannot function as Christ intended when each believer is looking out for him or herself.

The conjunction *but* in verse 17 indicates James shifted to a different topic, turning his attention to true wisdom. He clearly indicated the source of true wisdom is "from above," that is, from God. Wisdom from above is completely different from the wisdom of the world.

Similar to the way in which Paul listed the fruit of the Spirit in Galatians 5:22–23, James listed characteristics of wisdom from above: pure, peaceable, gentle, willing to yield, full of mercy and good fruits, without a trace of partiality or hypocrisy (v. 17). People with true wisdom are pure, pertaining to moral uprightness and undefiled intentions. Those who are pure live with unwavering devotion to God, including when it is not popular or easy.

People who are living according to God's wisdom are peaceable and encourage peace rather than division among others. Such people demonstrate godly wisdom by being gentle with or considerate of others and by being "willing to yield." Some translations render "willing to yield" as "submissive," "open to reason," and "accommodating."

James continued, emphasizing that wisdom from above is "full of mercy," referring to being compassionate toward others, and full of "good fruits," indicating wisdom produces God-honoring deeds. Finally, James emphasized that heavenly wisdom has no "trace of partiality," meaning without favoritism, or "hypocrisy," referring to sincerity and genuineness.

The final verse in chapter 3 describes the reward of walking in true wisdom. Those who plant seeds of peace will reap "a harvest of righteousness."

II. Waiting Patiently for the Lord (James 5:7–12)

James was writing to Jewish Christians who had faced persecution because of their faith in Christ. Despite their hardships, James encouraged them to "be patient, therefore, beloved, until the coming of the Lord" (v. 7a). He conveyed the idea of genuinely loving his brothers and sisters in Christ and wanting the best for them. He encouraged them to be patient regardless of what they faced. The word *patient* carries the idea of "enduring, bearing burdens, and standing strong in life's battles while trusting God's sovereignty in the process."

To paint a clear picture of what it means to wait patiently, James provided an example that agrarian people would understand. In verse 7b, he spoke of how farmers wait for the seeds they have planted to grow, patiently trusting God to provide "early and late rains" in the fall and spring, respectively. No matter what farmers do, they are powerless to bring the rains; they must wait, trusting God to send rain.

Life's trials can make us impatient, and we often grumble and complain when we feel God is not working fast enough on our behalf. However, being patient requires us to develop stamina in suffering long, especially when God does not change our circumstances according to our schedules. Regardless of how long it takes—including "until the coming of the Lord" (v. 7)—let us commit ourselves to waiting patiently and obediently for the Lord. Having hope that Christ will return encourages contemporary believers just as it encouraged early Christians facing persecution. When He returns, He will deliver us from the cares of this world, reward us for our faithfulness, and provide an eternal home for all who have professed faith in Him.

Meanwhile, James urged his readers not to grumble and complain (v. 9). The word *grumble* connotes the idea of "judging, criticizing, and faultfinding." Perhaps the hardships these people faced made them vulnerable to blaming and overly criticizing one another. James' warning about God's judgment is reminiscent of Jesus' teaching in Luke 6:37: "Do not judge, and you will not be judged; do not condemn, and you will not be condemned. Forgive, and you will be forgiven."

James cited examples from the Old Testament of real people who demonstrated what it means to wait patiently for the Lord. In verse 10, he reminded readers of the patience of the prophets. The prophets often were ridiculed, and their words often were dismissed, though they "spoke in the name of the Lord" (v. 10). Despite this, they wholly devoted themselves to the Lord without grumbling and complaining; they endured suffering; and they persevered despite obstacles. The prophets' ultimate goal was to please and glorify God.

In verse 11, James said, "Indeed we call blessed those who have endured." We all love a good testimony that speaks of what God has done and can do, and we all love the saying that God can turn a test into a testimony. Yet we do not like tests. Given a choice, we would prefer not to suffer at all. In the Greek, "those who have endured" describes faithful men and women of God who have remained faithful to the end. We celebrate such endurance and faithfulness in others, and James called readers then and now to faithfully endure. Again, he highlighted one of the best examples of one we praise for enduring to the end: Job. James seemed to indicate the Lord had a purpose for allowing Job to experience calamity, that Job and all those around him would realize "how the Lord is compassionate and merciful" (v. 11). James was reminding us to watch for God's grace and mercy as we "meet trials of various kinds" (see 1:3).

Recall that in chapter 3, James wrote about using the tongue in ways that honor God. Again in chapter 5, he reminded believers that our words matter, especially related to making commitments. He instructed readers to say what they mean and mean what they say: "Let your 'Yes' be yes and your 'No' be no" (v. 12). Every Christian must make it a priority to live, speak, and act with wisdom and integrity.

The Lesson Applied

As we have walked through the teachings of James, we have learned about wisdom as we persevere through trials, hearing the Word and responding with obedience, demonstrating our faith through good works, using our tongues to honor God, living by the principles of heavenly wisdom, and waiting patiently for the Lord during seasons of difficulty. Regardless of what we face, there is godly wisdom to help us with such matters. James 1:5–6 reminds us the wisdom that's desperately needed and desired is only a prayer away: "Now if any of you lacks wisdom, he should ask God, who gives to all generously and without criticizing. But let him ask with faith without doubting." We triumph in all circumstances by remembering God is with us and by seeking His wisdom in prayer, Bible study, and fellowship with other Christians.

Let's Talk About It

1. What is the true way of wisdom that comes from above in contrast with the wisdom that comes from "below?"

James contrasts the wisdom from above with the wisdom from below as coming from God and Satan, respectively. The wisdom from above leads to good fruits, peace, and a positive outcome for the person who seeks it. On the contrary, those who act on their own initiative and desire do so from a selfish disposition that is unpure, devilish, and evil. Galatians 5:19–21 calls these decisions and actions the works of the flesh. They result in adultery, fornications, uncleanness, hatred, idolatry, wrath, strife, envy, murder, drunkenness, and a host of other less than desirable alternatives. God wants us to be in fellowship with Him, therefore He gives us His Spirit that leads us to produce meekness, love, joy, peace, faith, temperance, and a host of other positive actions that come from having a relationship with Him..

Godly wisdom comes from above for the purpose of helping us develop and cement our relationship with God. It helps us demonstrate our religiosity so we might influence others to seek the Lord also. Wisdom enhances the fellowship between God and humanity.

Home Daily Devotional Readings

August 31–September 6, 2020

Monday	Tuesday	Wednesday	Thursday	Friday	Saturday	Sunday
Rachel, Mother of Joseph and Benjamin	Joseph Checks on Brothers at Dothan	Jacob Convinced that Joseph Is Dead	From Slave to Ruler of Egypt	Jacob Lives with Joseph in Egypt	Caution, Disputes May Lead to Violence	Jealously Divides Families
Genesis 30:22-24; 35:16-20	Genesis 37:12-17	Genesis 37:29-36	Psalm 106:1-6, 16-22	Acts 7:9-15	James 4:1-7	Genesis 37:2-11, 23-24, 28